S

Alan Twigg

STRONG VOICES

Conversations with Fifty Canadian Authors

Harbour Publishing

STRONG VOICES

Harbour Publishing Co. Ltd.
P.O. Box 219
Madeira Park, BC   V0N 2H0

Cover design by Fiona MacGregor
Book design by Alex Baggio,
Creative Graphics, Sechelt, BC

Printed and bound in Canada by Friesen Printers

**Canadian Cataloguing
in Publication Data**

Twigg, Alan, 1952–
    Strong voices

    ISBN 0-920080-96-0

    1. Authors, Canadian (English)—
20th century—Interviews.* 1. Title.
PS8081.T95 1988   C810'.9'0054
C88-091379-7   PR9184.T84 1988

This one's for Martin.

Contents

Acknowledgements

Portions of this book have been previously published in *Quill & Quire, Books in Canada, NeWest Review, Dandelion,* the *Province, Vancouver Free Press, Georgia Straight, BC BookWorld*; or have been aired on the CBC-FM program *Audience*.

Some of the interviews in the present volume were previously published in *For Openers: Conversations with 24 Canadian Writers* (1981). In some cases they have been edited slightly for inclusion in the present volume. These are: Margaret Atwood, bill bissett, Matt Cohen, Marian Engel, Hubert Evans, Sylvia Fraser, John Gray, Robert Harlow, Jack Hodgins, Robert Kroetsch, Margaret Laurence, Norman Levine, Dorothy Livesay, Hugh MacLennan, Ken Mitchell, Alice Munro, Susan Musgrave, Al Purdy, Jane Rule, Michel Tremblay, Peter Trower and Rudy Wiebe. The interviews with Leonard Cohen and Robertson Davies amalgamate their *For Openers* material with recent interviews. The interviews with Edna Alford, Pierre Berton, Sandra Birdsell, George Bowering, Anne Cameron, George Faludy, Brian Fawcett, Timothy Findley, D.M. Fraser, Mavis Gallant, Gary Geddes, Edith Iglauer, W.P. Kinsella, Myrna Kostash, Patrick Lane, Norman Levine, George Melnyk, W.O. Mitchell, Farley Mowat, Andreas Schroeder, Josef Skvorecky, Audrey Thomas, W.D. Valgardson, Guy Vanderhaege, Stephen Vizinczey and Eric Wilson are appearing for the first time in book form.

Assistance from Canada Council Explorations was essential.

My sincere thanks to the fifty people who contributed most to the making of this book. I am indebted to their generosity and I have been enriched bytheir wisdom and humour. In print and in person, they have all changed me.

Foreword

The past decade has given me a remarkable and privileged education. I hope this book succeeds in passing along that education.

These are not, as I presumed when I began to do these interviews in 1978, discussions about literature and writing. They are, I see more clearly now, discussions about examining and enriching life.

The wisdom of bill bissett, Leonard Cohen, George Faludy, Robertson Davies, Margaret Laurence, Jane Rule, Michel Tremblay, George Melnyk, Mavis Gallant, Hugh MacLennan, Farley Mowat, Margaret Atwood, Alice Munro...

In retrospect, I have enjoyed a rare feast of intelligence. Now I'm simply the waiter. You choose the courses that are most to your pleasure.

I wish to make only one point before you begin: If I have learned anything at all, I have learned that there is no one point on the literary spectrum — or, for that matter, on the wide spectrum of human intelligence — that is more viable or "better" than any other.

All these strong voices have something to say. It's only a matter of wanting to hear them speak and listening with an open mind. And an open mind, in turn, can lead one towards an open and compassionate heart.

I'm not there yet. And I may never get there. But I'm less lost than I was ten years ago.

A.T. September 1988.

Edna Alford

EDNA ALFORD was born in Turtleford, Saskatchewan in 1947. She was educated at the University of Saskatchewan and attended writing workshops at the University of Calgary and Fort San, Saskatchewan. In 1982 she was co-winner of the Gerald Lampert Memorial Award for her first short story collection, *A Sleep Full of Dreams* (1981). This book about senior

citizens passing their final days in a nursing home quickly received critical recognition for its power, originality and truthfulness. A second collection of short stories, *The Garden of Eloise Loon* (1986), is more sophisticated and fragmented in its scope and more obviously concerned with literary techniques.

Edna Alford lives near Livelong, Saskatchewan. She was interviewed in 1985.

T: I knew I wanted to talk with you when I read your story "The Children's Bin" in *More Saskatchewan Gold*. What got to me was your description of that little four-year-old girl who is hospitalized with one kidney. It was extremely wrenching writing.

ALFORD: It was a very painful section to write. And in fact the story was originally written without it. I gather this happens to a lot of writers. I had the story in my head but that part wasn't written. Coming to terms with the story involved writing it. I had spent a lot of time at the writing school at Fort San. The set of buildings at Fort San used to be a sanitarium. An institution like that can generate a sadness, a tremendous sadness.

T: Was there some autobiographical element in inserting the four-year-old girl? Because the writing is different in that section. I wondered if you had been institutionalized for a health reason when you were very young.

ALFORD: Yes, when I was close to that age.

T: Now you've published *A Sleep Full of Dreams*, which is about people stuck in institutions.

ALFORD: Yes, but a lot of people share those experiences. Very people get through life without experiencing something which is really painful. Don't you think so?

T: Yes. But not many people end up writing about it unflinchingly.

ALFORD: Well, the important thing about that experience was my separation from the group. I come from a family of five children with many aunts and other relatives. A large extended family. I think my isolation from them did two things. I began to be contemplative during that time. And I also felt a distancing from the people who loved me. That taught me a lot. It was a positive thing and a negative thing. There was a time when I kind of associated that whole exper-

ience with my religious instruction, which was Anglican. . . At one time my definition of God was a matter of distance. The further you were away from heaven, the closer you were to hell. The whole thing was relative . . .

T: Let's go on to something easy. Livelong, Saskatchewan. It sounds like a name for a town that a writer would make up.

ALFORD: It's a very small town. A lot of my family still lives around there and I was born very close to there. Now I live twelve miles north of it, in the bush. We're learning to become self-sufficient. We have no water and things like that. And the roads are terrible. It's difficult to get out sometimes. But it gives me a lot of time alone to work! Learning to come to terms with the bush. The year I moved back to Livelong they took the grain elevators down and the railway ties up. That generated a whole cycle of stories . . .

T: Before that you must have worked in some sort of institution, like Arla in *A Sleep Full of Dreams*.

ALFORD: Yes. More than one, actually. Some experience in Saskatchewan and some experience in Alberta. And I worked in psychiatry in Calgary for a number of years as a group therapist.

T: One of the things I like about *A Sleep Full of Dreams* is that Arla is not always charitable towards the people she's helping. That ambivalence gives the stories a fascinating edge. She's not comfortable with her feelings either way.

ALFORD: And I think that's the case with a lot of people and their attitudes towards the elderly. In North American society there's a death denial, first of all, and a cult of youth. And those two things working together create this barrier to understanding how we feel and why we feel the way we do. Some of the things that Arla felt, which were not acceptable ways of feeling, I was determined to look at.

Canada has the highest rate of institutionalization of the aged of any country in the industrial world. Lots of European people who have read these stories have difficulty relating to the form of this institution. I don't think they have an analogous institution. So it was something I wanted to look at. Because I had people that I cared a lot about who had gone through this. In fact, the writing of those stories almost directly paralleled the decline and death of my grandmother.

T: Is that Hanna Tomena Robbestad, to whom the book is dedicated?

ALFORD: Yes. I had just finished working and I had just married and moved away. I had to leave her. I think in some ways the writing became a way of being with her. It was a kind of haunting. It took me a long time to realize that's what was happening.

T: Since Canada's treatment of elderly women is especially poor, have you felt that your book has had any sociological impact?

ALFORD: I have, yes. In fact, it's on a number of reading lists for schools of social work. And I've had quite a bit of response. The one thing I didn't deal with in this book is abuse within these institutions. Physical abuse. I thought about it. At some time I might address that. But within the context of this book, particularly since my character worked alone, I definitely did not see her in that position as that sort of person. I could have been done indirectly, I suppose.

T: I think this book is going to become increasingly well known over the years. It's one of the first books of fiction that deals directly with the emotional territory of looking after old people . . .

ALFORD: And also what it's like to be one of them . . .

T: Were you very much aware that

you were exploring new territory?

ALFORD: No, I wasn't at the time I wrote. But I agree. There is so little written about people at that stage of life. There are so few characters. It's astonishing how little there is.

T: As more and more people are getting older in our society, there's going to a crisis in the care of the aged.

ALFORD: Yes, yes. The average lifespan is being extended and the baby boom is aging.

My main concern is that when any part of the human race becomes compartmentalized or isolated in institutions, it's a diminishment of the whole. Because I have learned so much from people in that older age group myself, and because it would have been a terrible deprivation for me not to have known those people, I see this compartmentalization as a really negative thing. Something that is not just harmful to old people and eroding their dignity. But something that is a threat to everybody.

T: What you're concerned with is wholeness.

ALFORD: Yes. I see *A Sleep Full of Dreams* as being a book about compartmentalization. It's there in the form. You will go into one room and then into another room and into another room. It was suggested at some points that I might want to write a novel out of the stories. But I was absolutely determined that it be presented in this form. The form to me was integral to this book.

Not only are we into compartmentalization and specialization within society, within the language that is happening. And at the same time various parts of the human psyche are not talking. And so all kinds of strange things are happening. In a story of mine called "Transfer" the character is involved in psychiatry and she speaks in a lot of sociological jargon. This woman spoke like that until I realized what was happening to her. She was running away. These days there are all sorts of strange, contradictory positions held by the same people, even within the same head, within the individual.

T: You've said *The Garden of Eloise Loon* is about the loss of "long distance vision." What's long distance vision?

ALFORD: This comes from a very short piece called "Head" at the start of the second book. A man leaves the prairie and comes to work in BC. But he leaves his head in a stone pile back in the prairie. Prairie people are always talking about how they have all this light, the flatness, so they can see for miles and miles. Well, I read this newspaper article which talked about loss of long distance vision. They've discovered that urban people lose that faster. That triggered the story. This man took his vision for granted. He left it there. He thought it would always be there. He went about his business. Then he gets laid off from his job at the mill and he goes back to find it. And he finds that it's gone.

T: You could have written the story so that he went back and found it again. He could have been resurrected. You could have saved him!

ALFORD: I did. I did. I have a companion piece at the end of the book called "The Lineman." In that story they're taking down the elevators, taking up the tracks, dismantling the whole thing, and he goes back to work for the railway to take up the tracks. A character named Jack Loon, who is really as crazy as a bag of hammers, is the person who does the resurrection.

T: There's a line in your story "The Children's Bin," that jumped out at me. "She will look for resurrection everywhere. She will work with very little light, will wander the earth like the silly ghost of Goethe at his death who cried, 'More light, more light.' " Are you conscious of working with

resurrection as a theme?

ALFORD: Yes. I'm working with the variety of ways in which experiences with resurrection can occur, especially in *The Garden of Eloise Loon*. When I look back through my first collection, I can see I was working with that there as well. But in the second book it's become really dominant. Working with images of light, and loss of light.

Maybe it's natural to be concerned with light on the prairies. Someone spoke to me recently about how the prairie winters must affect prairie writers. With so little light in the winter, we end up having dark messages. Well, I don't believe that. There really is a tremendous amount of light in the winter. Although there is less time for the light, the light is more intense. The reflection of the sun is just blinding, very intense, a lot of the time.

T: Your grandparents were Norwegian. Do you think you have inherited something of a Norwegian temperament?

ALFORD: The murky type! Yes, maybe it's there. But I'm more interested in geographical connections. I'm really interested in the northern vision. The Ontario Art Gallery had a show called "Mystic North" that really impressed me. It confirmed what I believed about the geographical situation actually being more important than the ethnic. Seeing painters from all of these northern countries reflecting similar visions. And using light in similar ways. I was familiar with the light in their landscapes.

I think there are similarities in the northern writers, too. I found that quite early in looking at the great Russian writers. And the Icelandic writers in Canada. Valgardson. Christiana Gunnars. So I feel an affinity with prairie writers for the same reason I feel an affinity with Norwegian writers or Russian writers.

T: In one story you wrote, "He knew that no matter how bad things were now, no matter how boring and stale and tedious his life had been, things could get worse." How do you respond to the charge that you're a depressing writer?

ALFORD: Talking to readers, I sometimes get the reaction that the stories are depressing. But for me, when I'm working with the stories, there are some things that make me very sad about them, and some things that make me very angry, but I don't ever feel it's depressing. In fact, I don't feel that I am a depressing writer. I feel that all human experience is valid.

T: I agree. And if you can write with enough sensitivity about things, the sensitivity translates into caring.

ALFORD: Yes. I hope so. I hope it confers a kind of grace. Also it seems to me that life is really difficult for most people. I have some obligation as a human being to respect that. Living, for a lot of people, is so complex. That complexity should be reflected, especially if it's a really difficult experience such as coping with death. It's entitled to light, to recognition.

T: The basic attitude to death in our society seems to be that we should deny it as long as possible, that way we only have to deal with it suddenly at the end. But then in reality death doesn't often turn out to be sudden.

ALFORD: No, it's usually not very sudden at all.

T: Maybe all this has a lot to do with watching hundreds of deaths on TV shows where people die suddenly.

ALFORD: Yes. The process of dying has become foreign to most of us.

T: In looking at death, have you thought much about your own death?

ALFORD: Not really. I'm more concerned with the separation and the loss. The loss of people that I care about. As Emily Dickinson said, "Parting is all we know of heaven and all we need of hell."

Margaret Atwood

MARGARET ATWOOD was born in Ottawa in 1939. Her unwavering resolve to hold up new mirrors to present-day society, regardless of how unflattering or unsettling the resultant images are, have made her one of Canada's most widely recognized and respected writers. Her varied novels are *The Edible Woman* (1969),

Surfacing (1972), *Lady Oracle* (1976), *Life Before Man* (1979), *Bodily Harm* (1981), *The Handmaid's Tale* (1985), which was short-listed for the Booker Prize, and her semi-autobiographical *Cat's Eye* (1988). Her poetry collections include *The Circle Game* (1966), *The Journals of Susanna Moodie* (1970), *Power Politics* (1973), *Selected Poems* (1976), *Two-Headed Poems* (1979) and *Selected Poems II* (1986). Short story collections are *Dancing Girls* (1978) and *Bluebeard's Egg* (1983). Her major non-fiction work is *Survival: A Thematic Guide to Canadian Literature* (1972).

Margaret Atwood lives in Toronto. She was interviewed in 1979.

T: Did you come from a typical liberal background?

ATWOOD: I came from a very isolated background. This is probably the key to some of my writing. I grew up isolated from society in a kind and non-violent family of scientists. When I hit society I was shocked. I'm probably still in a state of culture shock!

T: And you always will be?

ATWOOD: Probably. Because I was only exposed to a small range of human behaviour, the good side. But the bad side is pretty bad. If you grow up being told, "On Saturdays we burn crosses on people's lawns," then you can't be so easily shocked. You become numb to it. "On Fridays we go down to the corner bar and beat each other up and then we go and kill some Jews or Catholics or blacks or whatever." You can get hardened to that kind of thing. But I've never become hardened. So whatever radicalism I possess comes out of that.

T: What's radical about *Life Before Man* is that it's the first Canadian novel I know of that seriously conveys an awareness that the human race can become extinct. Was that a conscious theme while writing the book?

ATWOOD: Yes. It's why the novel is set in the Royal Ontario Museum. And why Lesje is a paleontologist who studies dinosaurs.

T: And why the characters exhibit predatory behaviour?

ATWOOD: Absolutely. Not just the character of Elizabeth but also how our society encourages people to be that way.

T: Sometimes I wonder if we're heading into an age of examining ourselves for evil.

ATWOOD: Being aware of how awful we can be might be a self-preservation technique. Certainly when you do that it stops you from turning other people into the devil.

You're unlikely to say that everything is the fault of the Germans or any other group you want to use as a scapegoat.

T: Our scapegoat in Canada has always been the United States. In your work you are really concerned with dispelling that pretense that Canadians are somehow morally superior.

ATWOOD: People can be morally superior when they are in a position of relative powerlessness. For instance, if you're a woman being victimized then you can afford moral superiority. But once you have power, you have to take responsibility. Some of your decisions may be harmful to others. I think Canada has been able to afford moral superiority because it's been relatively powerless. I don't think, and I never have thought, that Canada's inherently better. In fact, all you have to do is look at its past record. Scratch the country and it's quite a fascist place. Look at the attitudes to the War Measures Act or the RCMP opening the mail. Canada's not a goody-goody land of idealists. If we got to a position where we needed some witches to burn, I'm sure we'd find some and burn them. That's why I find Canada potentially a somewhat scary place. Underneath, we're not much different from anywhere else.

You look at mankind and you see something like Dante's *The Divine Comedy*. You see the Inferno at one end with everybody pulling out each other's fingernails, as in the Amnesty International bulletins. Or you see the Purgatorio, shaped like a mountain, with people climbing up it or sitting still. Up at the top there's what used to be called Heaven with what used to be called God. Only now we've replaced Heaven with a kind of Utopian vision of what humanity could be if only . . . Fill in the blank. The trouble with real life is once you try to implement

Utopia, you end up with the Inferno. You end up pulling out a lot of fingernails from the people who don't agree with you. That is, as we say, the Human Condition. That was the catch-all phrase when I was in graduate school. Whenever you came to the point at which you didn't know why things were the way they were, you said that was the Human Condition.

T: Do you think it's our swing back to conservatism that's going to solidify some standards of morality again?

ATWOOD: I don't know whether it's a question of standards. It might be more a question of fear. I think a lot of people do things because they're frightened. In times of stress, or what people think of as times of stress and hardship — because of course this country is not in stress and hardship, people are not starving in droves in the street, we're doing a lot of whining that would be pretty much sneered at in other parts of the world — people get frightened. They think they may not be able to get jobs. Or they won't be able to get the kinds of jobs that they might like to have. Whereas in the early sixties, people didn't feel like that.

So now we're retreating back into our rabbit holes. We're pulling in our tentacles so they don't get stepped on. When that happens, you want to form a monogamous relationship with somebody, hoping that it's going to keep you warm and safe.

T: This runs all through your work. The idea that fear is more primordial than love.

ATWOOD: Yes. Because in a society like ours where people are pretty much out there on their own hook, there's no real social support system for them, no small tribe or clan or integrated structure that's going to support an individual in it; so fear is a real motivating factor. And because you don't really know where the danger is coming from, fear takes the form often of a generalized anxiety or paranoia. You don't know who the enemy is. You don't know what direction you'll be attacked from. So everybody ends up constantly swivelling around, looking for the next threat. People are afraid of whatever's out there. And rightly so.

T: And that influences who you love and how you love them.

ATWOOD: Yes. Are you loving someone out of desperation and need or are you loving someone because they're "them," as we say? But now marriage is retrenching itself. People are getting married a lot younger again because in times of economic hardship, people retreat to the domestic burrow. But perhaps these marriages will be formed on more equitable terms. One hopes, with marriage nowadays that people are going into it with different expectations. In 1955, the husband was the breadwinner and the wife would have children; the husband was the boss and the wife kept her mouth shut. I'd like to think that some of that has changed.

T: I think maybe one of the problems now is that people may be getting married without enough expectations.

ATWOOD: Or without any.

T: We're together and if it doesn't work out we can always drift off somewhere else.

ATWOOD: None of this stuff would make much difference if it weren't influencing the lives of children. Society has always said, "You have to preserve marriage for the sake of the children." I've never really bought that one. But on the other hand, when breakups start happening on a large scale, you have to think of the consequences. We may be producing a lot of isolated, self-protective, narcissistic children.

T: What do you say to the argument

that your books only add to the *ennui* of the present? That bleakness begets bleakness?

ATWOOD: That's like saying everybody should write happy books. As far as I can tell, people in a crisis would much rather have that crisis admitted. When a friend of mine was dying, everybody tried to jolly him up. They said, "Oh no, you're not going to die." The fact was he knew he was dying and he wanted to talk about it. I think people in a crisis would rather have somebody say, "This is a crisis, this is real." That's much more comforting than saying here are John and Mary, they live in this bungalow, they have a washing machine and three kids, and they're really happy. What could be less cheerful if you're in a bad situation than being told normal people are happy? A lot of normal people aren't happy.

T: I agree. People always talk about censorship from the government or censorship through economics. But the main form of censorship in our society is really self-censorship.

ATWOOD: Exactly. People will say, "I don't want to hear about it" or "I don't want to read about it." But for me the novel is a social vehicle. it reflects society. Serious writers these days don't write uplifting books because what they see around them is not uplifting. It would be hypocritical to say the world is inspirational. It's not. These days the world is a pretty dismal place. You can blank that out. You can destroy your Amnesty International newsletter without reading it. But that doesn't make that stuff go away. The less you pay attention to it, the more it's going to be there for somebody else.

We think we can go on playing with our toys forever. But if you're not aware of the fact that you may die, you're much less careful about other people. One of the crucial moments in

any life is when you come to that realization.

T: When did you come to that realization for yourself?

ATWOOD: Sometime in my twenties. I had had a romantic, adolescent notion of death earlier but I hadn't really felt that solid moment when you realize your life is not going to go on forever. That people you know aren't going to be here forever. That we're going to die. What was it the Greeks used to say? "Call no man happy until he is dead."

T: Do you think it was essential to you as a writer to come to terms with death?

ATWOOD: It's essential to everyone as a human being.

T: But there's always been this particularly strong awareness in your poetry that life is transient.

ATWOOD: Life is transient. War is hell.

T: Birds fly.

ATWOOD: Right.

T: Do you get sick of hearing critics say your poetry is better than your novels?

ATWOOD: People often have difficulty handling somebody who does more than one thing. That's their problem. It's not a difficulty for me.

T: Do you think it's been an advantage for you because you can carry into prose that poet's instinct to "make it new?"

ATWOOD: I don't know whether my poetry is an advantage to me as a novelist or not. For me poetry is where the language is renewed. If poetry vanished, language would become dead. It would become embalmed! People say, "Well, now that you're writing successful novels I suppose you'll be giving up poetry." As if one wrote in order to be successful. The fact is, I would never give up poetry. Poetry might give me up, but that's another matter. It's true that poetry doesn't make money. But it's the heart of the language. If you think of language as a series of concentric circles, poetry is right in the centre. It's where precision takes place. It's where that use of language takes place that can extend a word yet have it be precise.

T: Often your novels explore a world that people don't want to think about or they don't want to see. Stories that are so modern can frighten people.

ATWOOD: Some people are frightened of my work, that's true. A real kind of heavy shock set in around *Power Politics* in 1971. But then three or four years after they appear, my books aren't shocking any more. Because that's where people have come to.

A lot of writers write about their childhood or what it was like in the small town where they grew up. Things that happened twenty years ago. On the pain level, these books are easier to read than something more immediate. When it's in the past, you know it's over. But the closer something is to you, the more shock value it can have. It could be you. That's why some people find me pretty terrifying. They confuse me with the work.

T: Also people are still wary of any woman with power.

ATWOOD: Yes, but I think more and more, as people get used to the idea that I'm around, some of that fear goes away. I can find there's more openness now to what I'm doing than there was before.

T: Your *Survival* hypothesis has been rather fiercely attacked as "fashionably radical, bourgeois individualism." Do you take any of that Marxist criticism seriously?

ATWOOD: No, I don't have very much time for the kind of purist leftism that defines itself as the only true religion. It's like Plymouth

Brethrenism. They're so puritanical that they don't even go after new members. They're just interested in defining their own purity as opposed to the evil of everybody else. That kind of leftism is useless in this country. It has no sense of its constituency. it doesn't know how to address them. So if they want to call me names that's fine, nobody's listening.

I work on a magazine called *This Magazine*. As far as I'm concerned it's the best of the small left magazines in Canada. One of the members, Rick Salutin, wrote a piece on *Survival* as a Marxist book. He was talking about how it had an awareness of historical development, how it took into account its place as a political instrument in that development and how it made a connection between the economy and the culture.

T: When you have a nation that is only two or three generations removed from the pioneer experience, is it really possible for us to have had anything other than a literature which is predominantly concerned with survival?

ATWOOD: That's one of the things I'm arguing. Although I don't think that's the only determining factor. In Western Canada that pioneer exper- ience may be only two or three genera- tions removed, but in Eastern Canada it's often eight or nine. So it's not the whole story.

T: The whole story is that our colonial status as a nation has spawned a literature of failure.

ATWOOD: No, I said a literature of survival.

T: Either way, being victimized politi- cally has created a nation that is lacking in self-respect.

ATWOOD: Yes, Canada doesn't go for the brass ring.

T: Since you wrote *Survival* have you become any more optimistic about Canada's progression towards

attaining self-respect politically?
ATWOOD: Culturally, you could say Canada's doing okay. Writers have a union now and they're standing up for their rights. We've even got a film industry of sorts. But that's a very small group of people. When you look at the economic situation you can see that things have in fact gotten worse. More of Canada is foreign-owned than when I published that book in 1972. So maybe our burst of culture is only a mushroom that will disappear in three or four years. Our entertainment market may be taken over by bigger interests now that Canada is becoming a more lucrative market. For instance, chain book stores now control over forty percent of the business. If they control sixty percent, they will start dictating what will be published. Publishers will send them their manuscripts first and the chain will say what gets published. They will have a stranglehold on writing, and the market will be even more foreign-dominated and junk-dominated.

This is not optimism or pessimism. It's just looking at things that are there.

Pierre Berton

PIERRE BERTON was born in Dawson City in 1920. He opted for a newspaper career while being educated on the west coast. He became a managing editor of *Maclean's*, associate editor of the *Toronto Star* and a panelist on Canada's longest-running TV program, *Front Page Challenge*. The kingpin of Canadian non-fiction, he is arguably the country's best-

known writer, averaging a book a year for three decades as a popular historian. *The Mysterious North* (1956), *Klondike* (1958) and *The Last Spike* (1971) won Governor General's Awards. Other noteworthy titles are *The National Dream* (1970), *The Invasion of Canada* (1980), *Flames Across the Border* (1981), *Why We Act Like Canadians* (1982), *Vimy* (1986) and a study of prairie settlement, *The Promised Land* (1984). *Starting Out* (1987) chronicles the first twenty-seven years of his life. His most ambitious history is *The Arctic Grail* (1988) about the search for the Northwest Passage and the North Pole. He was chairman of the Writers Union in 1987–88.

Pierre Berton lives in Kleinburg, Ontario. He was interviewed in 1984.

T: Are there any newspapers across the country doing a good job these days?

BERTON: No. I'm really distressed by the state of the press. It's gone flabby and dull. And uninspired and unintelligent. With the possible exception of the *Globe & Mail*. The *Toronto Star*, the greatest newspaper in Canada, is so flabby and so heavy it splinters the doors. And you can go through it in about two minutes. It's all predictable. Their idea of an investigative piece is to count the number of prostitutes on Isabella Street at midnight. That's a big story for them.

T: And *Maclean's?*

BERTON: It's a pretty good magazine but it's not what it was.

T: You once said your magazine work with *Maclean's* in the fifties gave you the best training for writing books...

BERTON: That's absolutely true.

T: What was so special about that environment?

BERTON: The editors. You couldn't get away with a thing in *Maclean's*. You couldn't waffle and you couldn't hide. If you made a statement they'd want to know where you got it from. Editors like Arthur Irwin would write things in the margin like "Evidence." He'd make sure the reader knew. Or he'd write, "Who he?"—that meant tell us a bit about this guy. You'd have to rewrite your piece two or three times. You'd have to do more research. They'd check your grammar, your spelling, the way you wrote. They'd point out if you were copying *Time* magazine. You could never print an article in *Maclean's* that wasn't rewritten.

T: Then you became an editor there yourself.

BERTON: That was the greatest way to learn. Fixing other people's copy.

T: Nowadays we've got journalism schools. Would you advise an aspiring non-fiction writer to take that route?

BERTON: I think it's a waste of time to go to university for four years of undergraduate work in journalism. I think you should take a broad course, as I did, and learn a lot of different things, then finish it off with a year of journalism. The trouble with journalism school is that the best journalists aren't teaching there.

T: Do you look at the personalities of your parents to understand why you became the sort of writer you are?

BERTON: Sure. First of all, journalism runs in the family. My grandfather, Phillip Thompson, was the best known journalist in Eastern Canada during the nineteenth century. And my mother wrote all the time, as an amateur. My father was a frustrated scientist with an enormous curiosity about everything. I get my journalist's background from my mother's side and the curiosity from my father's side.

T: Were you confident at an early age that you would write?

BERTON: No. My parents didn't want me to. My father wanted me to be a scientist. And I wanted to be a chemist. I had a lab in my basement. I initially took two years of chemistry at college. In trig and calculus, I was top of my class. But I wasn't very good in physics. One day I had to ask myself why I wasn't doing very well in physics and not that well in the chem lab. And the answer was that I was spending all my time on the college paper. I thought, "That's what I like to do. So that's what I better do."

My father was upset. My mother said, "I come from a journalistic family. You'll never have a clean shirt." She said chemists made as much as eighty dollars a month, some of them. As a journalist I'd always want for money. But I said I couldn't help it. I switched to UBC from Victoria.

T: To start writing for their paper, the *Ubyssey*.

BERTON: Yes. One thing I had noticed was that every editor of the *Ubyssey* and every major writer on the *Ubyssey* got a job downtown. This was '37. Jobs were scarce. I thought, "That's what I'll do. Never mind the University of BC. I'll just drift through there. I'll work on the *Ubyssey* and learn journalism. I'll get a job at one of the papers as a campus correspondent." That's exactly what happened. I eventually worked downtown for the summer, got taken on, and became city editor at the *News-Herald*. Because I was the only guy who knew how to write headlines. And I'd learned that at the *Ubyssey*. So the *Ubyssey* was certainly important to me. Before coming to Vancouver from Victoria I already knew the names of everybody who worked on that paper. But I didn't know that some of those people would become lifelong friends, and that I would marry one of them.

T: Perhaps your scientific leanings from your father were just strong enough to keep you from going all the way towards becoming a novelist. So you've ended up telling stories, but the stories have to be true.

BERTON: It's interesting. When I did *Klondike*, I thought about how I should do it. I knew if I did it as a novel I could sell it to the movies. It's a natural. But I couldn't bring myself to make anything up. I thought the story was so good. I couldn't not tell the story as a journalist. So what I did was read *The Good Earth* by Pearl Buck. And *Pilgrim's Progress*. I wanted to get a slight feeling of Biblical prose because it's an allegory anyway. *Klondike* isn't the story of the Klondike. It's the story of man's search for himself. I never say this in the book. But you have to have that in your head when you're writing it.

T: Do you think Canada, by its nature, is more of a non-fiction country than a fiction country?

BERTON: Oh, yes. There's no doubt about that. For several reasons. First of all, Canadians have very little show business background. Our background is documentaries, public affairs and satire. You have to remember that it's much cheaper to do public affairs than high bucks entertainment. And this is a small market. Secondly, it's just the nature of the Canadian. I think it goes back to the fact that there's no blood in our history. That is, we're not a revolutionary country. You have to have some tribulation to produce some body of dramatic or fictional culture, I think. You really do. Look at the Irish. Look at the Russians. Look at the British and the Americans. We haven't had a bloodbath. We haven't had a revolution. We're not a revolutionary people. We don't rise up in a wrath and get passionately angry about anything.

T: So we favour an undramatic, non-fictional culture. And Pierre Berton books.

BERTON: Well, my approach has always been anti-romantic. Very few people understand this. People say, "You create heroes." On the contrary, I pull them down! Look at *The Dionne Years* if you want an anti-romantic book. I think most of my work isn't romantic. I think most of my work is epic. I love epics.

T: With this line of reasoning do you think fiction writers in Canada would be well advised to pay more attention to non-fiction and history?

BERTON: Well, look at Timothy Findley. His successful books, which are certainly brilliant pieces of imagination, are also rooted in reality. And he does a lot of research.

T: There's a general assumption that a fiction book is a work of creativity, whereas a non-fiction book is simply a matter of hard work.

BERTON: Yes. And that angers me. It's just as difficult. You can't make anything up!

T: Findley's creativity is obvious and yours isn't.

BERTON: And that's how it should be. If they perceive it, then you haven't done your job. It should all read like peaches and cream. My whole secret is to try and make it read like a novel. First of all, I try and make my books look like a novel. For instance, if I quote a passage from somebody else, and I don't do it often, I don't put it in smaller type indent it. I put in in large type and just put quote marks around it. Because I don't want people to open this book and have it look like a textbook. The textbooks make it very tough for the rest of us who are writing history. History in most people's minds is like a textbook. Well, I want history to look like a novel.

Secondly, you have to do exactly what you would be doing if you were writing a movie. I think all writing really — whether it's films, radio, television, novels, even newspaper stories — is a collection of scenes. So first, what a writer has to do is get the scene right. That is, he's got to get the texture, he's got to get the background. It's like a jigsaw puzzle. If there's something missing, I've got to go out and find it. What was the weather like, for instance? Were there clouds in the sky? Once you get your scene, then you have to know will it be narrative? Will it be dramatic? How do you start? How do you finish?

The third thing is, how do you connect the scenes up? That's the hardest part. This was especially true of the war books. You're dealing with very powerful and intimate stuff. This is where the creation comes in. You can't create a character. You can't give them anything that isn't documented. I discipline myself. I put footnotes at the back. Not just for the academics, but for the readers. I hate a book that doesn't have notes. I want to know where a guy found something out.

T: Margaret Laurence has said that writing a novel is an exercise in failure. Do you feel this with non-fiction, as well?

BERTON: Oh, yes. A year later you look at the book and think, Jesus Christ, I could have done better than that. Most of my books could be rewritten. Some of them I really would like to rewrite. What separates, I think, the amateur from the professional, is that the amateur continues to go on with the same book. The professional says, "Enough! I've learned something. It's flawed. But nothing's perfect. Maybe I'll learn a little more on the next book." But the amateur keeps fiddling with the book until it's worse and worse and worse. There's such a thing as too much rewriting. There's a moment comes when you should leave the bloody book alone. The professional will know when that moment has arrived. He should build on each major book.

T: Do you have an inventory of books in your mind? the ones that particularly nag at you?

BERTON: They all nag at me. Some nag at me more than others. And I know how to fix most of them. The main secret is to hide your research. That's the hardest thing to do. To know your research so well that you can write it without the research showing. It takes a long time to learn the techniques of hiding your research. If you look at *The National Dream*, the research does show in that book. It's a heavy book. And the academics like it, maybe for that reason. But if I were to do *The National Dream* again, it would be a shorter book. I wouldn't be quoting so many documents. I'd be putting more of it into my own words.

T: What else?

BERTON: I would totally rewrite *Hollywood's Canada*. It's a weird book. It's a cult book. There's a class of people that love it. But for me it wasn't a successful book. I loved it as a movie buff. But I would rewrite it differently. I wouldn't take it so seriously — I got angry there. I'd have a lot more fun with it. I'd make it much shorter. I'd put in more pictures.

T: Most individual chapters in *The Settling of the West* could have been expanded into books. That's another thing that's overlooked. The condensation process involved.

BERTON: That's right. I cut the shit out of it. I determined to stop writing long. The problem with that particular book was putting it together in the right order. It has to start in 1896 and end in 1914. It has to move through time. But you're moving back and forth, overlapping, describing a lot of different elements. I wrote the book four times. And parts of it more than that. I think it stands as the easiest reading book I've done. Whereas the two books on the War of 1812 are over two hundred thousand words. I actually cut *Flames Across the Border* by twenty-five thousand words. Jack McClelland wanted three books but I said no, two's plenty. Probably one too many.

T: I was pleased to find some new material about the Doukhobors in *The Settling of the West*.

BERTON: Yes. I get annoyed at the academics. They always say, and it's always untrue, that there's nothing new in my books. The first way to attack that statement is to point out that there's new stuff all through the books. But another way is to point out that what they're saying is that we professional historians and academics know it all. They forget that ninety-nine percent of the people really know nothing. It's elitist. What they're really saying is that history is too good for the masses.

T: A little book of yours I like is *Why We Act Like Canadians*.

BERTON: I was driving to the Canadian Club one day, about to make a speech on the subject, and I thought, "Why am I speaking for nothing to the Canadian Club when I can put this into a book?" So I went home and I knocked it off. I wrote it very pompously at first. Then I realized it had to be informal. I wrote it as a series of letters. That helped the writing. I thought it was a potboiler for me. It was fun. But that book, by God! People rave about it. It sold and it still sells. I just wrote from my own research. Talk about recycling. These were just ideas I had accumulated over the years. The odd thing is, I could have spent more time on that book, made it longer, and it would have been worse. You could have done a 250-page book. Lots of material, lots of evidence. But I didn't have time. McClelland was saying c'mon, c'mon, we need the book. So I knocked it off. And it's probably better for it.

T: The line I like most in *Why We Act Like Canadians* is "Canadians respect institutions, not individuals." It has occurred to me that if a person such as yourself understands and believes that maxim, they might even conclude that in Canada one should make efforts to institutionalize oneself. To do a book every year.

BERTON: Some reviewer referred the other day to "the notorious Berton book factory." As if there's something obscene about turning out too many books. I love that word, notorious. What's notorious about staying at your job? I don't set out to do a book a year. In fact, there are several years when I haven't. And other years when I've done two. It's just what I do, you know.

T: But you must realize you're respected as much as an institution, as you are as an individual.

BERTON: Oh, that's wonderful, that's great. That keeps me going. I have no objections to that. You have to publicize the book so people know it's out. A lot of people buy my books sight unseen. People come down and say, "I buy all your books. I want this one." But if I did a couple of lousy books in a row, they'd stop that.

T: Over the years you've cautioned us to preserve the Canadian character against the domination of the Americans. Is that situation changing at all? For better or for worse?

BERTON: Well, I've changed my mind on this to some extent. I don't think the problem is so much economic domination, which I used to think, as it is cultural domination. And I think we're stronger culturally in everywhere but two fields. When I first came to Toronto, it was a cultural desert. Now, my God, you open a Toronto paper! You've got a smorgasbord of drama and music being offered to you. And about half of it is Canadian. This is true also now in radio. Radio was almost entirely American when it began here.

But there are two areas where we haven't yet come to grips with this problem. Unfortunately they're the two most important areas. The visual areas. Film and television. We've not got a Canadian film movement yet. The fact of the matter is that American and European films are still dominating the culture. And the reason is that nobody at the government level has had the guts to tell Hollywood they've got to leave some of their money in Canada for production. That's all you have to do. It's as simple as that. You just say fifteen percent of your gross box office receipts must remain in Canada to finance Canadian production.

On the television level it's worse than it used to be. This is because of the proliferation of cable and also because the CBC is not being taken seriously at the decision-making level. The CBC is getting squeezed and squeezed and squeezed. It hasn't got the resources to do what it does very well. It can do excellent drama. People watched *The National Dream*. They loved it. You can make high-rated programs that people like. Trouble is they only have the resources to do a little bit.

I think if you're going to have a Canadian identity then it's going to come from the culture, not so much from the economic end. So maybe it doesn't matter quite so much if the Americans own everything.

T: So you're not talking pessimistically.

BERTON: No. I think the country has a much stronger sense of itself than it did when I grew up.

T: Thirty Berton books later!

BERTON: If an idea pops into my head, I write it. The children's novel, *The Secret World of Og*, has sold over a hundred thousand copies. It just popped into my head one day. I've got lots of stuff to publish. I'm not a frustrated writer. I write for my own amusement anyway. I always did. When I was in the army I wrote letters to everybody. I just write. I like writing.

Sandra Birdsell

SANDRA BIRDSELL was born in Morris, Manitoba in 1942. Her first collection of short stories about the Lafreniere sisters and their family, *Night Travellers* (1982), evoked a fictitious Manitoba rural community called Agassiz. A second volume of connected stories, *Ladies of the House* (1984), presented the Lafreniere sisters

as mothers and wives. Both books have been critically acclaimed and have drawn justifiable comparisons to the early work of Alice Munro. They have been re-published as one volume, *Agassiz Stories* (1987). Birdsell is also a scriptwriter, playwright, winner of the Gerald Lampert Award for New Writing and a National Magazine Award for Short Fiction.

Sandra Birdsell lives in Winnipeg. She was interviewed in 1984.

T: The way your stories come together, jumbled and fragmentary, going back in forth in time, it strikes me as being almost hallucinogenic.

BIRDSELL: Well, if you asked me the one thing I like about my work the most, I would say it's an ability to go in and out of the mind almost within the same sentence. That's the way memory works. So I know what you mean about fragmentation. But as a larger picture, they come together. Sometimes I think I'd like to invent a new form of punctuation because of the way I write.

T: Because it's not always clear if it's the author or if it's a character doing the thinking. And you're just trusting what comes.

BIRDSELL: Yes. In fact a lot of times I write with my eyes closed, to get rid of myself and my space, to write out of the character and the character's place.

T: This explains everything. The lady writes with her eyes closed!

BIRDSELL: That's why I had to switch to a typewriter. I couldn't do it by hand. When I'm creating something new, I get really, really tired. It's hard work because I'm trying to dig things up from the unconscious mind. So sometimes I'll have to close my eyes. Other times, if something has stopped, I'll go and lie down for fifteen minutes. The rest of the story will come to me and I'll get up and type it. Or I'll read over a story before I go to bed, if I'm having a problem with it, and I'll dream it and I'll get up and write it.

T: Your stories also remind me of something Michel Tremblay mentioned about his fiction. He says he's writing his tetrology to say "I love you" to his characters.

BIRDSELL: I've said this many times. I really love the people I'm writing about. I grew up with these women. I know what makes them cry, what makes them laugh. I could never be mean to them. And I have this really strong sense of loyalty to my family. You don't badmouth family. I wouldn't want to hurt them.

But at the same time I don't understand people who say they're waiting for their parents to die before they're going to write a novel. I think a writer's got to be able to take chances. You have to go right out there, exposed. You have to be willing to do that. Somebody once said a writer can't have secrets. And it's true. You can't hide behind something. I'm thinking of a lesbian writer who was not admitting to anyone that she was a lesbian. She says until she got rid of that secret, her writing never came alive. It's true. You can't hide.

T: So far, with Mika and her three daughters, you've got four main female characters. How do you keep your storytelling balanced between them all?

BIRDSELL: I think basically I want to discover where each character is. I know right now, for instance, where Lureen is. I know where she is outside of the book. But I'm not sure where Betty or Truda are. I'll explore that for my own curiosity. I'm usually conscious of the fact that I've left this character someplace and this character in another place and so on.

It's kind of neat because you can live these different lives as you write. You can be Lureen, who's more or less muddling her way through life, but who's a gutsy, energetic kind of person just the same. Or you can be artistic and pursuing like Truda. Or you can be Betty's character, the musical one, the one who's always searching for the lost child she gave up for adoption.

T: How long did it take before you developed this approach? and your style?

BIRDSELL: Well, the first year I started writing I wrote thirty short stories and they had absolutely nothing to do with any of these stories now. Some of them were published, maybe three of them, and I hope no one ever reads them. So it was a process over a number of years. I wrote a novel in between. I'd say my style has only come about in the last three years.

What really triggered the whole writing thing was a non-fiction article, "I'll Come On Sunday." I wanted to record what had happened when my father died. In realizing that he was gone, I knew that I had lost so much. I got this urge to start putting things down and that became a daily thing. It started to take shape as fiction, as short stories. I entered that article in a non-fiction contest in the States through the *Writer's Digest*. I won first prize. It was a portable typewriter. When you get a portable typewriter, you've got to do something with it.

But it wasn't until people started calling me a writer that I realized, well, I guess I am. I didn't like that label at first. I felt it put a lot of pressure on me. What was before a very pleasant thing to do suddenly became terribly important.

T: Do you come from a family of storytellers?

BIRDSELL: Well, my dad was a fiddle player. He used to play for barn dances. Music, parties, dancing. He could be quite gregarious. He used to tell stories. And he had a good sense of humour. My mother, on the other hand, was always too busy to tell stories. She has a Mennonite background and fiction doesn't have a very high priority. Fiction to them is like telling lies. We were encouraged to read books that would improve ourselves in some way. If we ever read fiction it was things that had some kind of moral standard or teaching. But I've noticed lately that my mother has begun to tell me stories of her youth, now that she's less busy.

T: Like Mika, was your mother "as serious as a mousetrap?"

BIRDSELL: Well, you know, she had nineteen pregnancies. Eleven children lived. She was very serious. She had to be. She had come over from Russia with her parents in 1926. She had to make do on a shoestring budget and she managed extremely well.

T: It's not always wise to make autobiographical assumptions but I have to ask . . . did your father ever make you stand on brown paper and send the cut-outs to Eaton's to get you new shoes?

BIRDSELL: Yes! We did that! With our hands as well, for mittens. That's exactly how we ordered our shoes.

T: But your characters never seem to feel that they're hard done by.

BIRDSELL: No, because everybody growing up in the town seemed to be in the same situation. There were very few people whose children didn't dress the way we did. I think the hard thing I felt growing up was that our family was so large. There was something that wasn't nice about that. People were always making comments about my mom being pregnant again. We learned to feel very uncomfortable about it. I was always "one of the Bartlettes." I was never me.

T: On top of this, you've said you also felt isolated in your own family.

BIRDSELL: I was the fifth of ten. The sister right next to me died when she was eight. That left a gap between me and the next one. So I couldn't fool around with my older sister, who was four years older than me. The ones next to me in age were twins and they were really together. So I was isolated. It gave me a good viewpoint, I think, to look at the older family and to look at the younger family. Even now I am a solitary person within the family.

T: Do you think being suspended in the middle like that was one of the reasons you did poorly in school?

BIRDSELL: I don't know. My grandfather always said he felt sorry for me because of that lack of attention. He tried to make up for it. Consequently, I was very fond of my grandfather. But I was the bad child. Now when I go home and we tell stories, it's always about the naughty things I did. "Remember when Sandra . . ." I was always in trouble. Now I know why. I was just looking for attention.

In school I was bright enough but I was always acting out, always in detention, always playing hooky or being kicked out. I liked school. The problem was, and still is, I can't stand having a lot of people around me all the time. People think just because I come from a large family that I should love it or be used to it. But I was never used to it. Much of the time I preferred living in my head. As a small child, all my games were imaginary games. Imaginary friends. I used to play with Dale Evans and Roy Rogers all the time. I had wonderful times playing by myself.

T: So you never inherited a "clenched-jaw approach to life"?

BIRDSELL: No. I was too adventurous. And I was so strong-willed that my parents just gave up on me let me grow up my own way. They really did.

T: So you left home at fifteen.

BIRDSELL: Yes. I worked in southern Manitoba as a waitress for a while. Then I went to Winnipeg and worked. Then I came home and tried to go back to school. It didn't work. So then I got married.

T: You had three kids. Like Alice Munro, did you find raising your daughters particularly insightful in terms of reminding you of your own upbringing?

BIRDSELL: Oh, yes. Tremendously. I learned so much. For one thing, it becomes evident as soon as the child gets up on its knees and starts moving around the house that it's its own person. As soon as they get up on their knees and start crawling, they start moving away from you. That's their journey away from you. I think I sensed that.

Now my oldest daughter is married and has a daughter and she says to me, "Mom, where did you get your ideas from? You were a feminist back there in 1958, '59, '60." I think it was just that I was born with this overwhelming sense of what's fair and what isn't. Now when I'm writing about raising children and about male/female relationships, I don't think I'm reacting out of any feminist sense so much as a sense of what's right and what's wrong for each individual; what is fair or unfair.

T: After having children, how important was Robert Kroetsch in terms of your becoming a writer?

BIRDSELL: Very important. Robert Kroetsch was well known in the literary field. The fact that he noticed me and took me aside and counselled me and admonished me for my lackadaisical approach to writing was crucial. Until then I was really just fooling around. I thought it was a neat trick. I could string together sentences. He forced me to think seriously. I can remember leaving his office and crying all the way home because I realized I had to get serious about something for the first time in my life.

That was the turning point for me. There was a lot of pressure on me to go out and get a job. I had to make a decision to do that or write. I knew I couldn't do both. I applied for an arts grant. I really didn't have much going for me but Kroetsch wrote a wonderful recommendation. It resulted in me getting two thousand dollars. It suddenly gave me credibility in my family. It gave me guilt-free time to work. How else do you explain to your family that you're going to spend six hours a day writing something that will probably never make much money? Especially when you need money.

T: What about Rudy Wiebe, who shares your Mennonite background?

BIRDSELL: Yes, Rudy has been very supportive, too. He took one of my first short stories and put in an anthology called *More Stories from Western Canada*. He also wrote such a wonderful letter to me once that I wrote him back and told him he had just poured gasoline on my fire. That letter kept me going for another year. I've been fortunate in that I've had some people like Rudy who have been behind me since the beginning. They've seen through my lack of education and they've accepted my coming to the craft as just a housewife.

T: Whereas some haven't?

BIRDSELL: Well, very often I've met other writers whose first analysis of me is here's this nice little housewife who's writing stories. And in some instances there's even been some cruelty towards me on that level, outright cruelty. What invariably happens is that as I stand up to do a reading the attitudes change. They start circling around and start talking to me as though I had a brain.

This happened to me so much the first five years that I grew to expect it. In terms of my own personal life, I sometimes think part of my problem is not being able to be angry with people. I understand people too clearly. So that even though someone might be hurting me, I can't get angry with them. Or if I get angry, it's for a few minutes and that's it. Because I know why they're saying the things they're saying.

T: In terms of this, "The Bird Dance" strikes me as a very heartfelt story.

BIRDSELL: It's probably the most autobiographical story. It's probably

the closest I'll ever come to writing anything that's autobiographical.

T: Painfully so. "It made me feel as if I'd been doing that bloody Bird Dance for the past twenty years and was still doing it, in search of the perfect shower gift for someone I don't even like."

BIRDSELL: What I wanted to show in "The Bird Dance" is that often you keep doing the same thing over and over and over again, even though you know it's not going anyplace. So breaking off relationships and cutting off people is something you can never do easily. Things aren't solved that quickly.

T: Making generalities, I see *Night Travellers* as being about Mika's generation and the inability to express inner selves. And *Ladies of the House* is about the younger generation which has to renounce the religious life and live for themselves.

BIRDSELL: Yes. Live here and now. When I was growing up I used to listen to all these conversations between my mother and my elderly aunts. They were really a bad influence on her really. They were coming from Russia and they were much older than she was and they were giving her terrible advice. I would listen to them talk about the hereafter, this whole business about living so that it will be okay later on when you die. Yet whenever anybody died there would be so much weeping and wailing. It puzzled me. I'd say, "Look, if the hereafter is so much better than here, how come you're all so upset?"

T: But at least having that Russian Mennonite background gave you some sense of rules and traditions. You could then go ahead and choose to live in or outside the rules.

BIRDSELL: Yes, I agree. There are a lot of young people wandering around today who are almost lost. They don't have a framework to push against that they can look to and make some decisions about, for or against. They listen to one thing and then another. And people have always looked outside of themselves for something larger to worship. All of a sudden we have a whole lot of people who don't seem to have anything.

T: Maybe writing has this purpose for you. Giving you some bearings.

BIRDSELL: Well, I have a strong sense of who I am. Maybe through my writing I'm just coming to terms with it more and more. The writing of these stories, especially the "Spring Cleaning" story, was me trying to come to grips with my past, my religious upbringing, my culture. Trying to meld the past with the present. I also write to make some sense of what happened to people around me, to make some kind of order, and to maybe come to peace with a lot of things. I think a lot of writers are doing this. Trying to find some sort of order out of disorder. To recreate their world.

T: There's a line, 'Always, Bible verses, given in love but becoming brick walls, erected swiftly in her path.'

BIRDSELL: Yes, yes. Used the wrong way, to make a personal point or put pressure on the other person. In a lot of ways people who practice traditional religion to me are extremely narrow. It's an extremely confining and unimaginative and uncreative life. Like you say, they're living totally within that framework or rules. I find that so repugnant because there's no freedom of thought, there's no daring to think or even question those rules. That's my background. *All* my family are fundamental Christians.

But I'm lucky now in that I have got a church where I can go. It's a non-denominational church in Winnipeg. Its base was Presbyterian at one time long ago. People are fairly conservative but they give me that freedom to be who I am, they accept me and they allow me to grow.

T: The old woman in "The Wednesday Circle" speaks of God and says, "We obey because we fear punishment, not because we love."

BIRDSELL: Exactly. Yes. But I want to act out of love, with joy. To be able to be free to do that in love. That's what I'm looking for. That's what I'm looking for.

bill bissett

bill bissett was born in Halifax in 1939. He dropped out of UBC to form blewointmentpress. The author of over fifty poetry titles, bissett was the subject of controversy in parliament in the late 1970s over whether his chanting oratory, phonetic spelling, use of four-letter words and spiritualism were worthy of Canada Council subsidization. Critics often claim bissett's most

important work is his life. He is an accomplished performer of his work and a prolific painter with a very identifiable style. Major titles include *awake in the red desert* (1968), *pomes for yoshi* (1972), *Sailor* (1978), *selected poems: beyond even faithful legends* (1980) and *northern birds in colour* (1981).

bill bissett lives in London, Ontario. He was interviewed in 1978.

T: I've come to collect your life story. So let's start at the beginning.

BISSETT: I was born in Halifax. I started working when I was thirteen or fourteen in record stores. I used to do commercials for one store where I had two characters. I was like a hip young kid and I would push the rock n' roll and then I had this other voice where I would push classical music and stuff. And I worked in a gas station. Crap like that.

T: Was your family middle-class?

BISSETT: If there hadn't been so much sickness in the family it would have been like upper-middle-class. But there were hospital debts continually. My mother was sick for years. Then I was sick for three years when I was ten, eleven and twelve. Two years in the hospital, then another year to get better.

T: What did you have?

BISSETT: I had peritonitis. That's when you have an appendicitis operation and something goes wrong. The doctor leaves a hand in, or a glove. I dunno. The poison spreads through your blood and you can't crap. I couldn't go to the bathroom for two years. They put tubes in you, so you get these scars.

Lately I've been meditating. I worry less, have a more relaxed body system, smoke a little less tobacco, drink a little less coffee. I'm starting to get healthier without going on a head trip. It's just sorta happening. So anyway, hair is starting to grow on my belly. It's covering the scars and it's so far out. Like in Halifax when I'd go swimming they used to yell at me all the time. They wouldn't play with me sometimes because I had too many scars. So I'm getting more confident on beaches!

T: Thanks to some hair on your belly.

BISSETT: Yeah. It took a long time for me to get better. They didn't think I would live. After the twelfth operation it was okay. I missed two grades and just carried on. I couldn't do sports or nothing. I finished high school and went to Dalhousie University for two years.

T: What did you take?

BISSETT: English and philosophy. I was supposed to be a lawyer because my father was one. He was a very idealistic lawyer who would take cases from people who couldn't afford to pay. He was never sick so he was always grumbling about doctor bills. That's where everything went. So no one wanted me to be an artist. I think my mother mightn't have minded but she had gone into spirit by then.

T: Do you ever look back on those years in the hospital and speculate how being aware of life and death at such an early age might have affected you? Most kids growing up these days aren't tuned into that.

BISSETT: Unless you're in Chile or Vietnam. Yeah, that was pretty bizarre all right. Everything was backwards. I used to get presents before each operation. It was tempting to have an operation, just to get a present. I used to think a lot about dying. And movie stars. That's when I got into movies. I used to have movie stars all over my wall. They were my friends. They talked to me. They were closer to me than anything.

T: Were you the eldest son by any chance?

BISSETT: Two daughters and me. Then I wanted to leave Halifax. I used to run away all the time. When I was legal age, I split. I ran away to a circus once. The cops used to always get me back. So I came out west and starved here. Then I got a job with the library downtown and went to UBC. I did two years but I could never finish.

T: When would this be?

BISSETT: Around '64. I'm not sure. Anyway, I remember I was in this Milton course because they thought I had promise as an English student person. But I didn't have that much promise because there was this seating plan and stuff and I would never sit in my right seat. I couldn't deal with this seating plan at all. There was a lot of other crap I couldn't deal with either. I wanted to write and paint.

I remember I had to get this dumb language credit. I was writing this exam for German or something. I didn't like studying that stuff. I'd already bummed out of two other language courses. It was cool but it was weird. So I just put my pen down and walked out of the campus. It was my own little interior drama. I never came back.

T: Did you have many art friends in those days?

BISSETT: No. I hardly knew anybody. I worked at the library and I read. I started meeting other writers and stuff downtown eventually, but I never melted with the university scene.

T: Did you have any books out by then?

BISSETT: No, the first issue of blewointment started in '64, I think. I went directly into that when I left school. In '65, maybe there were three issues. It was a group thing. By '67 we were doing about five books a year. In the seventies it averaged seven books a year.

T: Where did the impetus to start blewointment press come from?

BISSETT: We started it because no one else would print us. Visual writing was just too weird for other magazines. I guess that's the way most presses start. You get a bunch of people who are organically together and no one else will print them. It just grows and grows.

T: Then you got busted?

BISSETT: Yeah, me and this folk singer from Seattle got busted. We were like the second bust in Vancouver. It was really a hot thing. A big deal and crap like that. The social

workers were trying to take our child away. The police were coming all the time and I was getting beaten up. It was really getting bizarre. Crap was flying in every direction. The cops would come to bust the place and they'd tear my paintings apart. They would scream, "Why do you paint like this? This is insane!"

T: Did you get dragged down by all that?

BISSETT: Well, we understood it all and fortunately we had a really great lawyer, Sid Simons. And Warren Tallman, the poetry professor from UBC, was a character witness. But like if our daughter walked down to the neighbourhood pool and took her pants off, which all the other kids did, the police would bring her home. We'd get picked on. But there weren't any hippies yet. They didn't have a word to identify us. They didn't know what we were.

T: Post-beatnik, pre-hippie.

BISSETT: Yeah, they didn't know what destruction we might do. All we were doing was painting and writing and living and smoking a little dope. Stuff like that. Me and Martina. We've gone different places but it's still together.

T: Then you got busted again later in the sixties, is that right?

BISSETT: For possession. It was another big hoopla with a two-year trial. But it was like old times for me. Then things got raging in the seventies when blewointment got a bit more Canada Council support. In 1978 we got a two-thousand dollar increase, so we were printing nine books on sixty-eight hundred dollars.

T: Compared to other publishing houses, that's not much.

BISSETT: We were running seven thousand dollars in debt all the time. But you keep hanging in there and conditions eventually improve. The dope thing isn't so heavy any more. No one is frightened by paintings any more. And concrete poetry doesn't scare people so much now.

T: So you more or less survived that era intact.

BISSETT: Yeah. Warren Tallman put his house up for me on the second trial for bail. Just incredible, really.

T: Do you ever get tired of people asking why you don't capitalize your name?

BISSETT: It's just because there's nothing to emphasize with it.

T: Yeah, I know but—

BISSETT: It's fun when people ask because then I get to talk about spelling and stuff like that.

T: So let's talk about spelling and stuff like that. You're someone who seems to believe there's a power-mongering segment of society "up there" somewhere, so if you spell in a way that's foreign to those people, it keeps the poetry safe. Maybe it's a protective thing. The only people who will read them are people who want to read them.

BISSETT: Yeah, I never thought of that. Wow, far out.

T: They open a book and feel instant irritation. So maybe there's also a political side of you that wants to provoke a reaction, too.

BISSETT: Far out.

T: Also if you spell phonetically like you do, it gives you an affinity with people who aren't literate. Like children.

BISSETT: Like a lot of people don't spell right. Like maybe two-thirds of the world or something. That's really neat. Those are three super reasons right there, aren't they? Of course the other reason is simply to get words closer to the way they really sound.

T: Do you see the pendulum in society swinging back to the right these days?

BISSETT: Yeah, there's a conservative backlash. But that conservative backlash is funny because the

revolution never got off the ground. We're having a backlash without even having had a revolution. It's very Canadian!

T: Would you agree Canada has a tendency to be liberal about artists just so long as we can ignore them?

BISSETT: Unless you're saying something they can use for their benefit, it's a freak-out. That's the trouble with politicians. I think political activity can be tremendous if it can be communal in some way. Like the world is a commune. Politics should be for getting things together. Like providing guaranteed minimum incomes or fixing things so that senior citizens aren't eating cat food. Or cleaning the water. There are legitimate things that our politicians should be concerned about.

T: Is there any difference for you between where your paintings come from and where poetry comes from?

BISSETT: I think they come from the same place. I approach them both the same way, feeling what can come through me rather than directing it. Sometimes when you look at a linear or more traditional poem, it might look like it's been worked. But it's still receiving. Like it's an "always learning" thing. I might direct with notation and polishing in different drafts, making it closer to how it really is, but it's still trying to listen and hear and see how it is. To let the poem or the painting become what it is. Like one time I was painting and the brush started dancing. It was really exciting because the figures came alive.

T: Are you aware of a common theme in your painting? Because I notice a lot of your figures are illuminated with a glow, like a sun radiating from out of the figure's inside.

BISSETT: I'm sort of aware. Like when I came out of surgery after my brain thing I started seeing people with auras.

T: Tell me about that accident. What happened?

BISSETT: I was at this party after this concrete poetry show I'd been in. There was a folding door made to look like a wall, so it would blend in. The door was supposed to have a latch, because if you went through it was twenty feet to the concrete. I was leaning against this door and I fell through. Or at least that's what they tell me because I don't remember. Those brain cells have gone.

It took two years to get better so we took it to court. The insurance company was bucking it. The thing that came up in court was whether the cat had gone down for its milk or not. They unlatched the door to let the cat down for its milk. So there was this testimony as to what time I had fallen through. If I'd fallen through after the cat had already come upstairs, that would prove I couldn't have fallen through. Even though I did. On that basis, the judge threw us out of court. I don't remember any bowl of milk! I never even saw the damn cat!

So they took me to the hospital. My brain was bleeding. People from the party had left me there for a while because it was a party, you know. Then they got it together to take me to the hospital. They left me in emergency. Then this shrink came in. He started yelling at me. He thought I was catatonic. He was taking me to Riverview for shock treatment. But my brain was bleeding, so that would have killed me.

I couldn't move. My hearing would go and then it would come back again. I couldn't say words. It was really weird. This shrink was bundling me up into a stretcher.

Then this neurologist who was an intern came in . She was fantastic. She said, "Stop! That's an inter-cerebral bleed." He said it wasn't, it was catatonia. "He's a screwed-up artist

and we're going to shock him and rehabilitate him."

So they made a deal. They'd take me to the operating room and go into my brain. If it was an inter-cerebral bleed, then I'd go to a neurology ward. If it wasn't, he would get me. She won.

T: How long were you unable to communicate?

BISSETT: About a week. I was paralyzed on my right side for about three weeks. They sponged up the blood in my brain. I was a staff patient. I didn't have a private doctor. They took me back to a ward and they'd use me as a demonstration for classes. They'd bring in these students and say this is a person who has not got long to live. You see I had aphasia, which means the echoes were not meeting in my head. It means you can't function. Then also I had edema, which is something connected with memory loss. Plus a swelling of the brain or something. And I was paralyzed, so I was like a write-off.

T: Could you talk yet?

BISSETT: No. But I got inspired by this neurologist. She was there all the time. There was this light coming from her head. She said my chances were very little but if we really pushed we could make a good try of it. She was the only person there who thought I might live. She wanted me to believe that, too, if nothing else than a joke before dying.

I remember Gerry Gilbert came over one day and they were having this group poetry reading which I was supposed to be part of at the Art Gallery. He wanted to tape me. He said it would be great. My last poetry reading! Some other people there at the time got a little uptight. They thought it was a little morbid. But I couldn't really handle a reading anyway.

Warren Tallman was so far out. He brought me tapes of Allen Ginsberg,

Ezra Pound, Robert Duncan. No one could stay very long but nurses would come in and play the tapes for me. It was to remind me that I was a poet. It was so far out. I couldn't remember who anyone was half the time.

But there was something lucky about it all. The accident happened just after I got out of Oakalla. I'd paid my fine and done my time. But the federal justice department was uptight. They figured I hadn't been punished properly after the two-year trial, a five-hundred-dollar fine, and a little bit of time in Powell River, some in Burnaby, some in the city bucket here and a few weeks in Oakalla. They were appealing. They had to appeal within thirty days of my coming out. They came to the hospital with the papers. The head nurse told them I'd be dead within a week. So that was that.

T: Have you ever tried to get in touch with that neurologist?

BISSETT: I'm going to try and find her again. She was so incredible. She was maybe twenty-five. To all those sixty- to seventy-year-old doctors, she was a toy to them. And I was a dead person. They didn't believe her at all because they'd seen so much. But she just kept believing.

Then I got epileptic and started having seizures.

T: And that really convinced them.

BISSETT: I was a complete write-off! A combination of aphasia, edema, paralysis and epilepsy is about it! But she was fresh. She kept working on me. She started bringing me balls to squeeze even though I couldn't move my hand. She would leave the ball in my hand anyway. She said, you'll get the idea, you'll make the connection. She was sticking pins in me everywhere. She came in with these blackboards and taught me the alphabet all over again. She said, if you live, your right side is never going to work, but

we don't care. She said there's a lot of people worse off than that.

She got me into occupational therapy as soon as she could get me there. There you see people who have parts missing from their bodies, or if they have parts there's no feeling because their spine got blown away. So you don't get self-pity at all.

She started programming me with my left side. The first day in occupational therapy, it took seven people to get me there. They held me up in front of this ping-pong table. Two guys were sending the ball towards me and they were in worse shape than me! I mean, they had lots missing!

T: I'm sorry. I shouldn't laugh.

BISSETT: Well, it is funny. I couldn't laugh but I made gurgling noises. Anyway, two toes twitched one night. My neurologist had this very crackpot theory but she wanted to share it with me. The epilepsy was supposed to mean you're finished, but she figured it might mean there's something that's ticking. So she was getting really excited.

She had me in a sling. She said you're a painter, you're going to keep painting. It doesn't matter what kind of machine we have to make for you to sit in. We can put batteries in you, we can do lots of things.

After the epilepsy, I became spastic. The other people all hung their heads, but she was getting real excited. At least it was movement. Playing ping-pong, I'd miss the ball and fall on the table. It was a riot. She said rest was fatal. She took my sleeping pills away. She'd say if all you can sleep is four hours a night, that's all your body needs. If there's nothing to do at night, you've got balls to squeeze. Or you can prick yourself with pins.

T: Are you completely recovered now?

BISSETT: Pretty well. I remember the first time I ate in public. It was really far out. I was living with a whole bunch of people as an out-patient. My whole right side was spastic. We had a wood stove. I started to cook some food and everything fell into the fire. I started crying. Everyone freaked out.

We lived in this old warehouse and no matter what was going on, I'd always coped. Things used to get pretty raging there. We had this big bolt on the door because we used to get raided and stuff. We'd be smoking outrageous things inside and the cops couldn't get in. So we'd always been crazy there, but they'd never seen me like this before. So I had to go out by myself to this restaurant where everyone used to hang out. I ordered food. It was bacon and eggs, the first thing I'd eaten all day. They brought it and I picked up my knife and fork. That was it. It was all over the floor.

Little by little I got less and less spastic. I had dyladin for about six months. I had barbells and weights. And I had to type. They would check to see how many hours I spent typing. It was terrible. You'd feel like breaking the typewriter.

T: After all this, you started seeing auras.

BISSETT: Yeah. Hers was the first. But they still thought I would just die in my sleep one night. I got freaked out and crawled out the window once. They found me spastically walking along Broadway and brought me back. She calmed me down and got me inspired again.

T: So do you think your art has come out of this experience to a great extent?

BISSETT: Yeah, a lot.

T: Maybe when you have to relearn almost everything at a later age, you really pare things down to essentials.

BISSETT: It's like a fresh start. You get reprogrammed with a new bunch of cells. It's really far out. More people should have it happen.

GEORGE BOWERING was born in BC's Okanagan region in 1935. With the encouragement of UBC's Warren Tallman and visiting American writers, Bowering and his friends founded a mimeographed magazine called *Tish* in 1961. Since then he has become one of the most prolific and respected "post-modernist" writers in Canada, receiving Governor General's Awards

George Bowering

for poetry in 1969 and for fiction in 1980 with *Burning Water*. His most recent novel, *Caprice* (1987) is a comic historical tale set in the Okanagan.

He was interviewed in 1987.

T: You've equated being born in BC with being pure. As if growing up in an undefined region can be an advantage.

BOWERING: Yes. It has always meant a lot to me that even when I lived in a town as a kid, the town didn't have any street names. Or there was a rumour that there were street names but nobody knew what they were, you know. In some plan down at the village office the streets actually had street names but there were no signs on street corners. I think that's important.

T: I've read you were born in Keremeos, in Penticton and in Oliver. Where were you actually born? I've read three conflicting things on this!

BOWERING: It's more than three!

T: So I want to know.

BOWERING: Why?

T: Because I want to be accurate.

BOWERING: How do you know what I tell you is going to be accurate?

T: Fine. I'll write that George Bowering said that he was born in such-in-such.

BOWERING: I was born in Penticton. The building is still there. It's an old folks home now. My parents were living in Peachland at the time. Then we moved to Greenwood, where my Dad was teaching school. We were in Greenwood when they started moving the Japanese-Canadians there. Joy Kogawa is about six months older than me, so we were probably at the same school track meet in Midway.

T: So was Greenwood the place that didn't have any street names?

BOWERING: No. Oliver, BC. We lived in two orchards south of Oliver and then we moved into Oliver. My father was supposed to be teaching math but he was teaching chemistry. He was a science teacher. He knew how to do everything. He knew how everything worked. But he didn't like organic chemistry. He didn't like those inelegant formulas.

T: Your father was obviously a key influence.

BOWERING: My father was a real quiet guy. He had a hardly-ever-smile wit. And he was a super athlete. When I was a kid I was really slow, but I got to know a lot about athletics. He was really smart and he settled for less than he should have got. That was partly because of the Depression. He should have been able to go farther than he did. But on the other hand he never complained about that.

T: This thing about athletics is obviously pretty key . . .

BOWERING: That's why I'm playing ball now at the age of sixty-five, right?

T: Your father used to be the score-keeper and he was really hard on all the hitters.

BOWERING: Me too. When I became a scorekeeper I was hard on hitters. Or they used to say I was. There's a lot of things like that I have inherited from him. Like my intolerance for bad grammar and bad spelling. It's an extension of his. One of things I like about my wife is that she can spell. I keep seeing my father in me all the time.

T: Where's your father now?

BOWERING: He died about ten years ago. Something like that.

T: What did your parents think of their son, the writer?

BOWERING: My father never talked about it. My mother always thought of it as something like a hobby. One morning at three a.m. I told her I would steal her mad money to get a book published. I told myself it was true at the time. But it was my mother who taught me how not to spend money and how not to show your feelings. She was the instructress. She was the one who taught me to be a puritan as a kid. And I really am a puritan.

T: Audrey Thomas says if I do an article on you I should talk to all the women who knew you.

BOWERING: Was she using a euphemism in that verb?

T: No. It wasn't meant as a loaded statement.

BOWERING: The funny thing is I've always found it a hundred times easier to talk to women.

T: It's because you're so compulsively competitive with other men!

BOWERING: One doesn't have to compete with anyone.

T: "Reunion," your short story about your high school reunion, made me wonder if you ever think of moving back to the Okanagan.

BOWERING: Occasionally. Once in a while. That story "Reunion" is one of my most directly transcribed stories. Usually I won't do that at all. But there's a certain power in doing that, like you've stuck your finger in something.

T: The truth has been known to have some power.

BOWERING: Yeah. But don't screw around with it, right? You know the best scene in Hubert Evans' *Mist on the River*? It's where they're fishing and Miriam is catching that fish.

T: They're symbolically wed...

BOWERING: Yes. She's got this fish between her legs and she's grabbing it and he feels a strange sensation! The fish tail is slapping the water! It's a really good scene.

T: I know you don't like mundane narrative lines but this is not a post-modernist interview. Why are you fracturing the narrative here?

BOWERING: That was what you call anecdotal.

T: Well, I'm fond of organized thoughts. I think your father would approve.

BOWERING: Okay.

T: Progression from A to Z. You're back at your high school reunion.

Then suddenly a fish is slapping between somebody's legs.

BOWERING: Well, in every chapter of that novel you can see what Hubert Evans is trying to tell you. And he knows what he's doing. He's trying to tell white people down here in Vancouver about Indians. But then there's this one chapter in that book when it gets loose, when it gets a little bit away from him. Like when you're skiing too fast. That scene has got that quality to it. As a writer you give up a little bit. You say I'm going to let them hear this.

T: And you think your reunion story is the same way?

BOWERING: It's something like that.

T: Another story like that is "Protective Footwear," where you're just speaking the truth about being out with your daughter walking in the woods.

BOWERING: Yes. It's directly out of life. I wrote three more stories this summer, the first stories I've written in eighteen years or so, and one of them is like that. You'll like it. You'll hate the other ones.

T: I don't hate any of your stories. It's just that sometimes it's irritating to feel this clever guy is so confident about whatever is coming into his head that he won't go back and make it any easier for someone to get ahold of...

BOWERING: Yes, but a story shouldn't be easier to read than life is easier to live.

T: Why did you stop writing stories, and why did you start writing them again?

BOWERING: You get older and you haven't got time to write them. The older you get, the less time you have for writing.

T: That's if you're teaching at a university. But you can make a choice.

BOWERING: I used to be able to handle everything. Now I can't handle anything. I hate to think what it's going to be like in another ten years. Maybe I'll never write anything. It used to be I would justify myself to myself by writing every day. For years, every day, something. Now I don't.

T: But this way at least you're not manufacturing writing. "I am a writer. I will write."

BOWERING: What about people who do other things, like make leather belts? They do it all the time.

T: So how many books have you done now? How much have you justified yourself?

BOWERING: I don't know. Do you call a thing that's "really" short a book?

T: Most writers do.

BOWERING: Fewer than bill bissett.

T: I think it must be over forty titles by now.

BOWERING: Fewer than bill bissett and more than Fred Wah.

T: It's over forty, right? So now you can relax, stop, slow down...

T: ...and write something really good!

BOWERING: You think I publish everything?

T: Oh, no.

BOWERING: Jesus, you should see my unpublished novels. No, you should not see them! One, two, three...six unpublished novels. Some of which are unpublished because I don't want to publish them. Two because I couldn't finish them. And one because I was only twenty-two when I wrote it. That was a long one.

T: Do you look back over the books that you've done and see major steps?

BOWERING: Yes. I usually think about that in terms of poetry.

Probably the turnaround book in terms of prose is that one called *Autobiology*. That was a real changeroo. I decided not to write in terms of any prose fiction I had already ingested. And that was the first book I wrote by hand. I wrote the first section of it in a backyard in an Irish section of London, England. Then I didn't write any more till I came home to wherever it was, Montreal, I guess. I wrote the rest of it by hand. I'd never done that with prose before. That's probably the most important book in that regard.

T: The book of yours I really like is *A Short Sad Book*.

BOWERING: Nobody ever writes on that. Everybody's writing articles now on *Burning Water*.

T: I actually go back and re-read *A Short Sad Book* from time to time.

BOWERING: It's an emetic for Canadian literature! It's important. Then I stepped back and did the narrative for *Burning Water*. Then I stepped back even farther and did *Bernice*!

T: *Caprice* is acceptable experimental fiction. When I read it I thought, "Is Bowering having us all on here? Is he saying, 'I'll write something that they like and I'll show them how easy it is to do it? And the laugh will be mine.' "

BOWERING: Yes. Now people will write about *Burning Water* and *Caprice* together. I even let Penguin talk me into putting in quotation marks for people talking. And all the reviews *love* it. They say this is wonderful. He's smartened up and decided to quit that bullshit and write a book. I immediately went out and wrote a weird one just to satisfy myself.

Anne Cameron

ANNE CAMERON was born in Nanaimo, BC in 1938. Her stage adaptation of a documentary poem, *Windigo*, led to the formation of the first native theatre group in Canada. She then began writing award-winning scripts for film and television such as *Ticket to Heaven* and *Dreamspeaker*. Her novelization of *Dreamspeaker* (1979) earned the Gibson Award for

first novels. A second novel, *The Journey* (1982), is a feminist western. *Earth Witch* (1983) is one of the highest-selling books of poetry ever published in Canada. She is best known for *Daughters of Copper Woman* (1981) and *Dzelarhons* (1986), two reworkings of coastal Indian legends passed on to her by Nootka and Coast Salish women. A provocative educator, Cameron is also a riveting public speaker and the author of numerous children's books. *Stubby Amberchuk and the Holy Grail* (1987) is her most recent novel. A collection of short stories, *Women, Kids and Huckleberry Wine*, was published in 1988.

Anne Cameron lives nine miles north of Powell River, BC. She was interviewed in 1982 and 1987.

T: Looking back, how did you evolve into a writer?

CAMERON: Nanaimo was a coal-mining town. Really ugly. Every weekend somebody was beating somebody up, usually under the noses of their kids. The world was crazy. The only place there was any real order was in books. I could read before I started school. I don't know how that happened. Nobody remembers teaching me to read. I just loved it. I was about eleven when I realized that everything I ever loved to read had to be written by somebody. And I was hooked. My dad used to say I didn't need a babysitter. All I needed was a roll of toilet paper and a pencil stub. When I ran out of books to read I'd write my own.

My dad was coal miner, and then the mines closed. People not brought up on Vancouver Island have no idea what it used to be like. You can read about the Deep South and you could be reading about the Island. Or you could read about Wales a hundred years ago. It was insular and ugly. Neither side of my family had ever been anything but hard-working, dirt poor. So when it came to writing my mother said, "Well, that's a nice dream, dear, but you have to be able to feed yourself." Yet at the same time, when I was thirteen or fourteen, even though my mother could not afford it, she found the money to buy me a typewriter. She said, "After all, if you're going to spend so much time scribbling, you might as well learn to type because there's always room in the world for a good typist." But that was not why she gave me that typewriter. It was sort of like, thou shalt not offend the gods. You don't put the dream into words or else they'll take the dream away from you.

T: From that fairly rough environment, how did you acquire the organized mind that makes a book?

Did you consciously teach yourself form?

CAMERON: It was totally unconscious. I have virtually no education that way. I don't have enough credits to go to university. I had the equivalent of about grade ten. Because I did horrible things like refuse to take home economics. I wanted to major in library and they wouldn't let me. But if you listen to storytellers, each story has a beginning and an end. How you get between the two places is like the individualism of the storyteller. If that is form, then I learned it by listening to Welsh coal-mining women telling their stories. And they, in turn, had a different form than North English women telling stories. And their form, in turn, was very different from an Indian's.

I got English stories from my maternal grandparents and Scots stories from my paternal grandparents. I lived with my maternal grandmother for a couple of years. That was really strong, really positive, really beautiful. One side of the family would be talking about the Battle of Bannockburn and the other half is talking about the time they went up and they freed the slaves in the Highlands. Then there were Chinese stories, which are very different, too. I grew up halfway between Chinatown and the Indian reserve.

T: Was starting Tillicum Theatre the first transition you made from doing writing privately to doing things publicly?

CAMERON: Well, I was writing and typing for a newspaper called the *Indian Voice*. I was living on the mainland. There was a centennial playwriting contest. Just sitting around rapping about that, we decided to put together this play based on a bunch of my poetry. That dragged on eternally. At one point we were going to pull our entry out. But then we said, hey, one of the things they're always saying about Indians is that they never finish anything, so we'll leave our play in the competition. Lo and behold, we won. So they took the play out to Matsqui Penitentiary and got the cons doing it, knocked everybody on their backsides with some guerrilla theatre. So I figured, hey, why did we need them? We could have done it right here. So we did. And that was Tillicum Theatre. We used kids from high school who were either dropouts or still in school trying to pass remedial reading. It gave them something to do instead of slinging rocks at cars. As far as I know, none of the kids involved with Tillicum Theatre have been adversely involved with the law.

T: One of the best evenings of theatre I ever saw was in the Matsqui Penitentiary. They did *Threepenny Opera*.

CAMERON: Yes. There's something to be said for finding another way to make your protest. Because I really do believe that most of the people in prisons are political prisoners. That we're conditioned and educated in such a way that there really is no conceivable option of protest. So people adopt what some call criminal lifestyles. Not because they're inherently rotten people. Now society needs ten percent of its population in some kind of conflict with the law or else a multi-billion dollar industry falls down. We set up another world into which these people go. And once they're in prison, it's none of our business what they do to each other or what other people do to them. I believe most prisoners are no more of a threat to me than most members of the RCMP.

T: Is that based on theory or experience?

CAMERON: It started out political. It has become very personal. The RCMP don't like it when somebody says, hey, hang on, you're not

supposed to read my mail. You say it publicly and the next thing you know they're hassling your kids. They pulled my kid over and checked his motorcycle four times on the way home one night. He had long hair and he was my kid. The first time they're doing their duty. The second time it's an accident. But four times in one night?

T: You've written, "Politics is something the women allowed to happen to keep the men occupied during the long dark months of winter, but sometimes, for a woman, it's as if your whole life is ruled by politics of one kind or another until it gets to where you can't even mind your own business." Do you see hope in terms of educating women to vote collectively?

CAMERON: Yes. Vote as a block. Vote for the one who promises the best deal for women. And if they don't deliver, vote them back to hell out again. I would love to see the women band together so that in the next provincial election, they voted out the incumbent. Don't vote for anybody. Vote against the incumbent. Even if it means putting Jerk-off George in. Then you could tell him, hey, look George, count the number of people in this town who are women. That's the majority of the vote that got you in. You toe the line or you'll be out next time. They're killing themselves for the chance to be fools. So get a tame fool and send him in. If you get enough of them in and you tell them what to do, you can change the overall system.

T: It mentions in *Copper Woman* that the book is for women dissatisfied with the learning in "men's universities." But it's really in opposition to much more than that.

CAMERON: It's in opposition to so-called "history." The stories in *Daughters of Copper Woman* are hundreds, if not thousands, of years old and were given to me over a period of about a dozen years by extremely old women on reserves all over the island. The question that gets asked most often about them is, "Is this history or is this fiction?" Nobody ever stops to ask if the crap they push down your throats at school is history or fiction. History as it is taught in the schools is the conquerors' version of what happened. *Daughters of Copper Woman* is very different. That book has more truth for me, as a person who was born on the Island, and certainly for me as a woman, than anything the school system ever came up with.

Once upon a time maybe four percent of the population controlled military and economic power. They took language and made it another kind of power. At first it was only the first-born son who was given the gift of being taught to read and write. That first-born son used his gift to communicate with other first-born sons until he found someone who thought the same way he did, so they could combine their armies and take more power. For years neither the women nor the poor were allowed to read and write.

Since women have only recently started to read and write we have done a remarkable job of catching up. But we have found we have inherited a flawed tool. All the words have been given their meanings by someone else —
by men. When you say this is National Brotherhood Week, it means something wonderful. But if you say it's National Sisterhood Week the president of your bank will laugh. A master is a great thing. But what's a mistress?

It gets very upsetting. We don't know whether to start inventing a new language or try to reclaim the one we've got. Or just go back to bed. The boys control the television, the newspapers, the movies. And the government. Some people call it

democracy. And some people call it oligarchy. But whatever it's disguised under, it's something even older than that. It's a patriarchy.

Daughters of Copper Woman suggests that there was a time on the Island when the boys didn't control everything. You inherited from your mother. When a woman married a man, he moved where she lived with her mother and her aunt and her sister. She didn't have to go out somewhere and get her face punched in with nobody to help her. He moved. And if he didn't behave, he got sent home and the children stayed with her. It was not the man who asked the woman to get married. It was the woman who honoured the man by inviting him to be the father of her child. Then the patriarchs came and brought rape. The Social Credit government, as big a patriarchy as you're going to find, cancelled the funding for Rape Relief because those uppity bitches who run it aren't doing what they want them to do. They want battered women to go to the police for help. But if you had just been raped, beaten, humiliated and pissed upon, would you particularly want help from the police? When the patriarchy has just raped you, they expect you to go to the patriarchy for help. You write the Attorney General to complain and he sends back four pages of complete babblerap.

Politics sucks. The system sucks. Once you realize it sucks, your next step is to try and do something about it.

T: As a writer you can work on your own, outside the system. What happens when you move into positions such as writer-in-residence at SFU?

CAMERON: It's difficult. All of the film instructors at SFU were male. I know of at least four women in film who are professors with incredible qualifications who applied for jobs at

Simon Fraser University. One of them made the short list. None of them got hired. I say that's no accident whatsoever. They all teach film from a feminist perspective. Meanwhile, you get a bunch of teenage boys turned loose with cameras and you get sexist film. One guy wanted to make a film about rape. There's a lot of rape at Simon Fraser, particularly with the women out jogging. He thought it would be interesting to do a comedy. I'm sorry, I didn't laugh. They're all into stereotypes in their film. It's always the woman who gets the pie in the face. Nobody's saying, hey, will you look what you're doing? Take out all the women and put in blacks and call them niggers and see how long it would last.

T: Have you also had problems working with organizations like the National Film Board and the CBC?

CAMERON: Yes. The CBC and I clashed head on on the film I was working on concerning battered wives. I felt there was a commitment that had been given to me from the very beginning that I could write my script from my perspective. That commitment, which I felt was very firm, seemed to hold until about four-fifths of the way through the script. At the last minute I was told *they* say... *They* say? I said who are *they*? I took my name off it because I would not make the changes to my script. There was a hell of an uproar. They wanted to do a whole publicity routine "From the Award-Winning Typewriter of..." They finally brought in a male writer. He made the changes. At the end of the film the woman walks out of Interval House in Toronto with a set of matched luggage. In reality, eighty-seven percent of the women who walk out of Interval House walk out with their stuff in a black garbage bag.

T: People have no difficulty agreeing there is a Newfie culture. Or that Québec has a separate culture. But there are no generally observed definitions of what we have become in British Columbia.

CAMERON: That's because the same thing has happened to BC and our provincial identity and psyche as happened to women. *They* have been defining us. Back in Toronto they make jokes like, "The continent slopes to the west and all the nuts roll to the West Coast." That's a crock. We know the nuts roll as far as the Rocky Mountains. That's why we put those mountains there. Only the crafty ones make it through to this side.

T: You really have a an "us" and "them" sense of the East and West.

CAMERON: Because I lived back there for over a year. It further convinced me that people out here are not really part of their country. My mother grew up here. My father grew up here. I was born here. Anything that I am is because of that. I think many people in BC feel this way. We identify with British Columbia much more than we identify as Canadians.

T: In some societies it's been standard practice to consult the major writers about major social issues. But in BC I'd say most of the people working for BC's newspapers and TV stations don't even know who the leading BC writers are. A writer who tries to interpret BC in any depth ends up feeling like a subversive against the global village culture.

CAMERON: Well, I'm not socially acceptable anyway. But look at Jack Hodgins. I mean, he taught high school in Nanaimo and won the Governor General's Award. And those pizmyers at Malaspina College couldn't even get it together to get the guy to go up there and read his stories. So finally Jack leaves Nanaimo and goes to Carleton University and everybody in Ottawa is kissing his feet but he's dying of homesickness. I used to send him care packages. We sent him a souvenir of Nanaimo Bathtub Day. A picture of Mayor Frank Ney in his pirate's costume.

T: So the universities are not much further ahead than the major media outlets.

CAMERON: Well, when I had three kids under school age and I was living in New Westminster, Simon Fraser University was advertising for mature students. I was just about ready to come out of my gourd. I was bored. I was having an identity crisis all over everybody's life. I thought, well, I can get a babysitter for the kids. I'll go to university. So I applied. Somewhere in all my junk I keep lugging around I still have this letter from Simon Fraser saying I didn't have the academic qualifications even to go as a mature student.

So twenty years later, with no more academic qualifications than I ever had, they had me teaching out there. My kids were rolling in the aisles! Mom's too stupid to go as a student but they'll take her as a teacher. For me, that just says it all. It's like you have to prove that you're mentally competent before you vote but you don't have to prove the same thing before you run for office.

T: So if you were suddenly education minister, how would you change things?

CAMERON: I'd have some classes only for girls. So that the girls don't get overshadowed by the boys vying for the teacher's attention. Because those are things still as a society we don't allow girls to do. I find it really interesting the number of really incredibly bright women who have come out of convent schools. Also I'd want much more sex education. And I would want much more physical stuff for the girls in the first three grades. Balancing. Dance exercises. Softball. Competition can be

good, really good, when you realize that you are the one you're in competition with.

T: What about simply having sexually segregated schools?

CAMERON: No, I think we're strangers enough now.

T: As a British Columbian, what do you think we aspire to in this place? What's your definition of who we are?

CAMERON: I think basically our main aspiration is to be left alone. I think that is what most of us out here want. We've got this belief, a belief that is probably totally illogical, that we are not the ones who raped the forest. And now they're doing it to the ocean with their fish farms. *They* are doing it. And they are companies from somewhere else. And we want *them* to go away, to take their goddamn money with them, and to leave *us* alone with our beaches the way they used to be.

What I find really weird is that people come here, usually first on holiday, and they wander around saying how beautiful it is. How marvellous. Then they go home. Then they retire here. They no more than retire here than they set about agitating for the things they had back home where they admitted it was ugly! During the Lyell Island controversy I wound up stamping my foot and saying that as far as I was concerned if you haven't been born on this goddamn coast for at least two generations you keep your mouth shut. And of course that would include our premier, who only came snuffling in here at age twelve. And I was halfway around the bend and totally illogical and I even hurt some of my friends' feelings but I didn't want to hear opinions from any folks from Saskatchewan who hadn't seen a tree before they retired out here.

We've learned bugger-nothing. The Indians had a lousy immigration policy.

Leonard Cohen

LEONARD COHEN was born in Montreal in 1934. His poetry, novels and songs are known around the world. His books are *Let Us Compare Mythologies* (1956), *The Spice-Box of Earth* (1961), *The Favourite Game* (1963), *Flowers for Hitler* (1964), *Beautiful Losers* (1966), *Parasites of Heaven* (1966), *Selected Poems 1956–1968* (1968), *The Energy of*

Slaves (1972) and *Death of a Lady's Man* (1978) and *Book of Mercy* (1984). His records are *Songs of Leonard Cohen* (1967), *Songs from a Room* (1969), *Songs of Love and Hate* (1971), *Live Songs* (1972), *New Skin for the Old Ceremony* (1973), *The Best of Leonard Cohen* (1975), *Death of a Lady's Man* (1977), *Recent Songs* (1979) and *Various Positions* (1984).

Leonard Cohen lives in Montreal. He was interviewed in 1979, 1984 and 1985.

T: For some reason, people don't like the idea of some guy who lives much of the time on a Greek island and has thousands of women wanting to spend just an hour with him . . .

COHEN: The guy you're describing, I don't like him already.

T: In Stephen Scobie's book on you, there's an A.J.M. Smith quote from 1928 that says Canadian literature will not improve "until we have been thoroughly shocked by the appearance in our midst of a work of art that is both successful and obscene." If that's true, then obviously *Beautiful Losers* makes you deserving of a Governor General's Award.

COHEN: It did become successful and certainly it's obscene in some places. *Beautiful Losers* only sold one thousand copies when it came out. Then the landscape opens up as more people have a certain kind of experience. Not that it's so important that this book becomes clearer. I understand it's only a very small thing in this world.

T: You once said there's nobody in this country who can appreciate your work.

COHEN: I don't know if that's true. Critics have to make a living. For instance, there's an analysis of *Beautiful Losers* in a book called *Savage Fields* by Dennis Lee which is pretty good. It's certainly better than anything I could do. His approach is so comprehensive and brilliant. Only once every couple of years do I get that brilliant.

I'm pretty well writing out of the trench. Trying to get my nose and eyes over the edge of the trench to see who's shooting at me. But Dennis Lee's up there on a watertower looking over the whole landscape.

T: Speaking of critics, what do you think of the theory that your work has arisen out of the fifties? Scobie writes, "Cut off from social contacts and responsibilities, the self turning in on itself becomes perverse and morbid, seeking death."

COHEN: If an argument is put forward forcefully enough, I'll go along with it. In fact, I'm even starting to buy critics' versions of my work.

T: Do you buy the version that you're a black romantic in the tradition of Baudelaire, Genet and Rimbaud?

COHEN: I don't reject these things. If somebody says something to you, it's more like an opportunity to evaluate where they're coming from. Black romantic. I don't even know what that means. It sounds okay. Black, I guess, is solemn, lightless, heavy, desperate.

T: Black romanticism is the negation of self. Like that line at the very end of one of your songs, "I guess you go for nothing, if you really want to go that far."

COHEN: I don't know. I think maybe some writers move in an atmosphere of bewilderment and astonishment. They sit down at a table two hours a day and try to locate themselves. Or justify themselves.

T: Previously you've always avoided aligning yourself with political groups. Could you tell me why you went to Israel "to fight the Arab bullet"?

COHEN: Well, there is a line in the Bible, "You shall not stand idly by your brother's blood." I do feel some communion, some sense of brotherhood with Jews. I do have some old fashioned emotions about those things. I feel a sense of solidarity with their struggle. I also feel it with the Egyptian struggle. That's the trouble. You can embrace both sides of the question.

I didn't feel that good being on Egyptian sand. We shouldn't really have been there but I knew we had to be there. The time I really felt bad about it was when an Israeli soldier came up to me and gave me some Egyptian money. He'd got it off a corpse or a prisoner. It was a souvenir. He put it in my hand and he walked away. I thought it belonged to some guy who was probably going to spend it on a beer that night. I just buried it in the sand.

Neither side is right. We know that right off the top. To press people into military service isn't right. The Israelis have lost the cream of each generation. So have the Egyptians. This is the real human crunch. This is the real human predicament. This universe is only to be tolerated, it's not to be solved. All these things are unclear but amidst this incredible lack of clarity we have to act. That's what the whole tragic vision is about.

T: A lot of people are going to figure the ambivalence that results is a cop-out.

COHEN: Well, with a lot of work that we call poetry—that intense writing—what really emerges are the harmonics. You put different ideas or approaches together and they strike fire in some way. Something emerges from that juxtaposition that has resonance.

T: So you're just trying to tune in on an energy when you write?

COHEN: I consider a lot of my work to be a kind of *reportage*, trying to make a completely accurate description of the interior predicament.

T: So it isn't always rational.

COHEN: It isn't always rational. It doesn't follow the laws of logic. Or even of rhetoric. You have to juxtapose elements to get something that corresponds to an interior condition. All poetry is based on differences. Wherever there's tension, wherever there's life, wherever there's the positive/negative, female/male, yin/yang. That's what creates the universe.

That's the kind of writing I like to do. Where you're writing on an edge, where you're really trying to get it right. I don't mean so it endures and the next generation looks into it, although it would be nice if it happened. I'm interested in only one thing: if it lives.

T: You've written somewhere that you believe in God...

COHEN: Because I've experienced the absolute.

T: And the absolute is zero?

COHEN: It's a zero that is continually manifesting as one, two, three, four, five, six, seven, eight, nine, ten.

T: A totality?

COHEN: It's the fundamental ground or field which is nothing, the still centre or whatever metaphor you use for it. It's neither dead or alive. It is an indescribable energy. That's zero. It's so empty that myriads and myriads of forms rush in to fill it at every second.

T: You've said having sexual intercourse is the greatest peace. Is that zero?

COHEN: The sexual embrace is beyond self. You don't exist as you. Your partner doesn't exist as your partner. That is the place we all come from. Then we come back to life. That zero or emptiness or absolute is when we don't have any questions.

The self we have is just the result of a question. The question is who am I? So we invent a self, a personality. We sustain it, we create rules for it. When you stop asking those questions in those moments of grace, as soon as the question is not asked and the dilemma is dissolved or abandoned, then the true self or absolute self rushes in. That's our real nourishment.

A real religious education makes that experience available to people. The kinds of religious education available today are mostly concerned with a very specific definition of what God is. Just to define God specifically is a great mistake. It's better to have a kind of education that doesn't even mention God, that allows people to experience that absolute or the dissolution of the particular self.

T: In *Beautiful Losers* you wrote, "disarmed and empty, an instrument of grace." Can you make that condition happen?

COHEN: Those conditions arise spontaneously. Often they're the result of writing. I have in a poem, "How sweet to be that wretch, forgotten by himself in the midst of his own testimony." When an experience is embracing or total you don't know who you are. When you jump into a pool of really cold water, when you hit that water there's no you.

T: How often is your writing a dive into cold water?

COHEN: From time to time. There is no explanation for it. It's free from an explanation. It's like explaining the kiss you give your wife. you can explain it from a sociological point of view, from an erotic point of view, from all kinds of points of view . . . but it really doesn't have anything to do with that moment of the embrace. You can speak about it, but it's just a kind of gossip.

When you're writing out of the total embrace of the experience of the emotion of the moment, what comes out of there is really authentic. People ask what does that song, "Suzanne," really mean? The people who lay back and are ravished by the song know exactly what it means.

T: I used to listen to that song all the time. I didn't fathom it at all but you're saying I understood it simply because I enjoyed it instinctively.

COHEN: Yes. If the thing is authentic you tune into it immediately. You embrace it immediately. It includes you. That's what I mean to say. The song also includes you because it's really authentic. Afterwards you can say why it included you,

but that's not so important.

T: Now, about your music. Do you try and write with the melody and lyric coming together at once?

COHEN: Different ways. Usually that's what happens. That's certainly the way "Suzanne" was written and "That's No Way to Say Goodbye" and "Famous Blue Raincoat."

T: Do you recognize the influence or kinship of Bob Dylan?

COHEN: I've always recognized him as a great poet. And certainly we like each other's work. I met him after a concert in Paris last year. We went to a restaurant and spent the afternoon exchanging our new lyrics. He's a friend.

T: You're both Jewish.

COHEN: Well, I know I was certainly touched by synagogue music and liturgy. And the Bible had a mighty influence. I think it's probably true that most Jewish writers are affected by those traditions. But it's not something we've talked about much.

T: Perhaps the US/Canada border has made a significant difference. Extroverted Americans/introverted Canadians. So Dylan is the public speaker and you're a private speaker.

COHEN: It's a nice thought.

T: There's one song of yours, "Sisters of Mercy," that I particularly like. The lyrics are so enigmatic that for years I thought it must be about either nuns or prostitutes. I was surprised to learn how autobiographical the song is . . .

COHEN: I actually wrote that song in Edmonton. There were two young women on the street. I met them in a doorway. There was a snowstorm. They mentioned they had no place to stay. I told them they could stay in my room. There went right to sleep. It was a beautiful night. The North Saskatchewan River was iced over. I just sat there in an armchair, watching them sleeping. I wrote the song in one night.

That's very unusual for me. When they woke up I sang the song for them.

T: Do you carry around an inner story like that for each of your songs?

COHEN: That's an interesting way of putting it. Yes, sometimes I do invoke an inner story, I suppose. Especially when you're singing a song every night on a tour. You go back to that inner story in your own mind and you can use it as a door to get back into the song as you're performing. To make it fresh.

T: Do you have any ideas as to why Europe, and particularly France, has responded so strongly to your work?

COHEN: It's something I've thought about a lot. I used to just say, "It's because they can't understand the words." But it probably has more to do with their musical traditions over there. Also, artists are less brutalized by their record labels in Europe. The American record companies are far more profit-oriented. Somehow my music was dubbed not commercial enough for the States. So they took away the support for touring. And of course that hurts your sales. They don't promote you as much.

T: How many concerts have you played behind the Iron Curtain?

COHEN: I've done four concerts in Poland. There were very good. I think the audiences identified with the polarities expressed in the songs.

T: Maybe if you live in a country with an oppressive government, the expression of the private voice becomes more important, more precious.

COHEN: I think that's it.

T: Conversely, on the bright side, a lack of interest in your work here could indicate North American society is relatively healthy.

COHEN: Yes. My music seems to go over particularly well in places with bad governments. Or new governments. Spain and Portugal. Places like that. And Scandinavia. Whereas in Germany I've declined in popularity. The intellectual establishment there doesn't find me sufficiently left-wing. The audiences are always hospitable everywhere you go because they've made the effort to come out and see you. But you can pick these things up from the reviews.

T: How important is the title of the album *Various Positions*?

COHEN: The critic for *Le Monde* said each song on *Various Positions* is a complete universe. I don't know about that. I just know the title is true. To me, it's simply an accurate description of the work. One of the songs is called "Dance Me to the End of Love," which I also made a video for. It's a kind of Eastern European wedding dance. Another song is "Coming Back to You," which has a country n' western feel. Another song is "Hallelujah." Another is called "The Law." So they're various positions.

T: Do you think your reputation as a "literary" figure restricts your sales in North America?

COHEN: Certainly in some quarters of both establishments—the literary and the musical—my two activities work against me. The president of Columbia Records greeted me as "Our Poet from Canada." in Europe I've never had to justify myself as a singer but certainly in North America the legitimacy of my enterprise is called into question. And similarly, until *Book of Mercy* came out, people in the Canadian book world tended to think I had sold out to the music business.

T: Tell me about *Book of Mercy*. What were the circumstances that generated it?

COHEN: Silence. I was silenced in all areas. I couldn't move. I was up against the wall. It was the only way I could penetrate through my predicament. I could pick up my guitar and sing but I couldn't locate my voice.

T: Then what happened?

COHEN: I began to have the courage to write down my prayers. To apply to the source of mercy. At first I had tried to deal with it by not writing. I felt that writing was a kind of self-conscious activity that might come between me and what I wanted to speak. But I found that was the way that I speak. I found that the act of writing was the proper form for my prayer. It was the only type of sound I could make I didn't bring much to it. I didn't bring concerns about whether there is a God or not. Those are just questions of the mind. The mind has the capacity to question but not to answer.

T: so you didn't decide to write *Book of Mercy*. It decided for you.

COHEN: That's right. Now I find it's the toughest book to talk about. Because it is prayer. One feels a little shy about the whole thing. We're such a hip age. Nobody wants to affirm those realities. It doesn't go with your sunglasses. But I know that the voice in the book is true. And I know that the book is true. It lifted me up to write it.

T: *Book of Mercy* is entirely on a spiritual plane...in a materialistic age. It's thoroughly un-modern.

COHEN: Yes. I think the book will have to be around for a while to find its place. You can't think of it as some book by some guy that you think you already know something about. If the book hangs around for a while, if it has that staying power, then people who need it can use it.

T: The voice of the narrator reminded me somewhat of Kahlil Gibran.

COHEN: Well, that's okay. People love that writer. He's been put down by the intelligentsia. But he speaks to millions of people. And the things he says are true. You get a feeling for a certain ecstasy in the man's life. You get the feeling that he really perceived those things. Yet it's incredible how

people will put him down.

T: That's because many people don't think someone like Kahlil Gibran is sophisticated enough. For many people sophistication in art is a necessity, an ultimate virtue.

COHEN: Sophistication is the current style. We're growing rich. Our cities are getting big. Our kids are going to university. It's appropriate for the times. But the practice of religion, the gathering of people to articulate the burden of their predicament, those things are important, too.

T: In music, because you don't have much of a vocal range, I think many people assume you don't have enough flexibility or sophistication as a musician.

COHEN: I think you're right.

T: But as you put it, "People say I'm a mediocre musician because I might only use three chords. I have merely decided to opt for the greatest simplicity." That statement reminded me of a John Fogerty quote about B.B. King. "B.B. King plays one note better than anybody."

COHEN: I like that. It's like what the young girl said after the old man made love to her. "You older fellows don't have the stamina but at least you get it right the first time."

T: Maybe your lyrics are so abnormally complex that your songs require a sense of musical simplicity for balance. So if your wrote simpler lyrics, you might want to use more complex arrangements.

COHEN: Except I never have a strategy when I write. I don't have any assembly line approach to it. The kind of writer I am, I'm never raking it in on any level. You're always starting from scratch. I don't have a James Bond series going on or anything. I find it all gets harder rather than easier. I have the tools. I know how to use them. But the content becomes more and more difficult. And there is no guarantee that the difficulty of the process will produce excellence. I just try to let the song function for itself in the end. I've merely learned a few tricks along the way.

T: When I turn on the radio these days I find lots of music but a dearth of good songs.

COHEN: You should try listening to country music. George Jones, for instance. He has great songs. If we think the audience can handle it, we do "The Tennessee Waltz" with the band. Those are terrific lyrics. I didn't know the second verse so I wrote one for myself. "She goes dancing through the darkness to the Tennessee Waltz / And I feel like I'm falling apart / The stronger the drink / The deeper the sorrow / Since she left and broke my heart."

T: When you go back and look at the lyrics to those old songs which have lasted like "Tennessee Waltz" and "Goodnight Irene," the lyrics are almost perfect.

COHEN: "Silent night, holy night, all is calm, all is bright."

Matt Cohen

MATT COHEN was born in King-ston, Ontario in 1942 and raised in Ottawa. He is one of Canada's most prolific fiction writers, a rare contra-diction of the axiom that writers should only write about what they know. After early experimental works, *Korsoniloff* (1969) and *Johnny Crackle Sings* (1971), he published a Gothic melodrama, *The Disinherited* (1974),

a futuristic novel about a cross-Canada train journey, *The Colours of War* (1977), a tale of violence on an island, *Wooden Hunters* (1978), a bittersweet romance, *The Sweet Second Summer of Kitty Malone* (1979), a tale of passion in a small town, *Flowers of Darkness* (1981), a historical novel spanning 1391 to 1445, *The Spanish Doctor* (1983) and a cross-continental tale of a female heroine, *Nadine* (1986). He has also published short stories in *Columbus and the Fat Lady* (1972), *Cafe le Dog* (1983) and *Living on Water* (1988).

Matt Cohen lives in Toronto.

T: Most young writers are advised to write about what they know. You've said you only began to write well when you started writing about what you didn't know.

COHEN: Yes. It started with *Johnny Crackle Sings*. I just made it up. I did the same thing with the best stories in *Columbus and the Fat Lady*. The *The Disinherited* was like that, too. There was a period of about six months when I was doing the central parts of all those books. My writing totally changed. I had finally written through all the preconceptions I had about what writing was and just started writing about whatever it was that engaged me most deeply.

T: Of those books, I think probably *The Disinherited* was the real break-through.

COHEN: Yes. The strange thing was that even though it's an extremely straightforward novel compared to my previous writing, I actually wrote it at exactly the same time that I was writing my most bizarre stories.

I also wrote another novel between *Johnny Crackle Sings* and *The Disinherited*; that was a real disaster. It was my attempt to write a linear novel. McClelland & Stewart probably would have published it if I insisted but I was unsure about it, so they offered me an advance for another novel. I made up a plotline for *The Disinherited* and I was thinking it would be a trashy, commercial novel. But I was living on a farm at the time and I guess that experience was getting through to me. It never occurred to me at the time that it would be a good novel.

T: It's a bit like a Gothic soap opera.

COHEN: Sure. There are a lot of soap opera elements. Struggles within a family are soap opera material. I'd show parts of it to people as I was writing and they'd all say it was terrible.

T: That's interesting about being

unable to write a straight, linear novel. On the first page of your very first book there's a mention about how time stretches both ways. Now it seems you're using that lateral sense of time more and more as the stylistic backbone of your novels. Do you intentionally give your stories that elasticity of time?

COHEN: No, I don't. But I'm amazed by what you're saying. It's great to have been so consistent.

T: Don't you agree that you tend to immerse your characters in time just as deeply as plot?

COHEN: It's true that if I feel I have the past and the present—or some idea of the future and the present—co-existing in the same sentence then there's a counterpoint happening which gives the writing an extra energy. I feel at home writing that way, and now I've learned how to create those situations in my novels.

T: Do you conceive of novels in a linear fashion and then jumble the incidents?

COHEN: No, all those replays just happen. Some sort of crossroads is reached which opens up the past. Just as sometimes a sentence might open up for a detail. I never know when it's going to happen.

T: As an example, there's that memorable scene in *The Sweet Second Summer of Kitty Malone* where the boy suddenly recalls being lost in the snow and the wolves kill his dogs. Would that be planned?

COHEN: Not really. When that scene started, I realized there was going to be a flashback. I thought it would be very brief. It was only as I started writing it that the scene developed. It goes on for ten or twelve pages. I probably wrote it in about an hour, which is very exceptional for me. To write that much that fast.

When that happens it feeds one of my theories about my own writing which is that I make it all up unconsciously. Then at the right moment I blurt it out. Then I fix it up. There's a certain amount that seems to form itself beneath my awareness.

T: So you trust your instincts when things come spontaneously like that.

COHEN: Usually what I write very fast turns out to be just fine. One of the weirder things is that I have to revise least when I write very fast. When I write quickly, it comes out structurally developed, and always ties in with what has been written before — it's as if I'd prepared it in a dream the previous night.

T: That flashback scene in the snow reminded me of Robert Harlow's *Scann*. Do you purposely try to be experimental with form when you write?

COHEN: No, I don't really care. I just want each book to be right for itself. Styles change so quickly, and people's labelling changes so quickly, that between the time you start a book and finish a book everyone's idea of what's experimental could totally change. I've read *Scann*. And I liked it a lot. But it's a story within a story and I don't think I could pull that off.

T: Aside from that awareness of the dynamics of time, your books strike me as unique because you're so aware of how the dynamics of sex and violence can appear as two sides of the same coin.

COHEN: Yes, I think passion is violent but I don't think all violence is passionate. Passion cuts across what people intend in their lives. It can be inconvenient or it can be totally destructive.

T: That was especially true in *Wooden Hunters*.

COHEN: Yes, in those characters sex and violence were intermingled. They couldn't distinguish between one and the other. To open one was to open the other.

T: A character in that book says sex is like a drug; you get addicted to it. Is that also true of violence?

COHEN: I suppose it could be.

T: It's like if there's something inside us we can't get out, when we finally learn how to get it out, it becomes pleasurable. So it becomes a habit.

COHEN: Right, I couldn't have said it better myself. I think that's exactly true. Once Laurel Hobson becomes more open in that book, she can't stop.

T: Yet passion is also healthy because it reaffirms people are alive.

COHEN: That's one of the problems of destructiveness. There's a scene in *Colours of War* where Theodore is making love to Lise. He hears a noise at the door so he goes out and sees some soldiers have trapped Felipa in a compartment. That's when he gets in a fight with them for the first time. It's only because he's sexually aroused. Otherwise he wouldn't be able to.

So, yes, in *The Colours of War* and *Wooden Hunters*, sex and violence come from the same source. I don't know whether that's good or bad, why passion affects different people in such different ways.

T: Because Matt Cohen likes one character and he doesn't like the other.

COHEN: Is this the only difference between good and evil? That you like one person and not the other? Maybe it is the only difference. I don't know. I question the morality of my characters but I don't come up with any answers. I'm still naive enough to think there must be some difference but I can't figure it out.

T: Maybe it's because your characters are all so extremist. Somebody once said life is nine-tenths habit. The people in your novels seem to inhabit that other one-tenth a lot.

COHEN: That's true. Of course one writes books about people in their more or less critical moments.

T: In *Kitty Malone* somebody says, "You might be getting old and droopy but at least you still know how to make a fool of yourself." Are you like that, too?

COHEN: Yes, I guess. But I'm finding it harder and harder to be extremist. It takes quite a toll.

T: You're not the only writer named Cohen to come up against that.

COHEN: Yes, but in some people the impulses stay really strong all their lives.

T: Which is basically what *Kitty Malone* is about.

COHEN: Sure. The whole idea that people should grow up is contentious. I'm not part of the human potential movement. The idea is like health food or something. It is important that I keep seeing my life clearly, but I'm not sure I'm a "better" person than I was ten years ago because of it.

T: What came through strongest in *Kitty Malone* for me was the way you showed how everybody's lives are fused together. That "fusion" thing seems much more essential to your characters than say, a sense of intellectual self-awareness.

COHEN: Yes, it's really a comforting book that way. It's about those solid emotional events that flow under things. It was really an enjoyable experience to write because it seemed I was on such sure ground.

T: Did you set out to write a positive book then?

COHEN: I didn't set out to do it, but I realized it was going to be positive once I was writing it. I realized it was going to be sort of a romance. I thought that was great. I couldn't imagine how I'd gotten onto such an affirmative footing.

T: Is it amazing to see the different response you get when you write a positive book?

COHEN: Exactly, yes. That's a very odd feature of the whole thing. People like a positive book better, as if it's a better book! Maybe it is a better book! I don't know. But certainly people responded more warmly when I toured with *Kitty Malone* than ever before. Because it's not a political book.

T: The opening scene in *Kitty Malone*, where Pat Frank takes a candle up to the child's room, struck me as perhaps unconsciously illustrating what the book — and most of your other books — seem to be saying. The less far ahead people can see, the more fragile and unhappy they are.

COHEN: That's interesting. I've never consciously thought that. But as you said that, I couldn't help thinking of Violet Kincaid in that book. She is a relatively calm and happy character precisely because she has this highly developed sense of the future.

T: It's probably why the farm atmosphere of Salem in your novels attracts you. In the country you can live with a sense of being in a continuum more than in a city. You can see further ahead of yourself. It's why Theodore Beame retreats to Salem in *The Colours of War*.

COHEN: Yes, everything is going to crumble around him. That's definitely the place he can cope the best. Because that's where he was brought up. For some people the right thing to do is to leave home and go somewhere else. It's almost inevitable for them. For other people it's almost inevitable to go away and come back. I think I understand those people who come back better than those who go away.

T: The continuum idea is why *Wooden Hunters* is a depressing book. There's no sense of future till the very end.

COHEN: Yes, *Kitty Malone* is more optimistic that way. But a real difference between the two books is the security of the actual ground on which they stand. In *Kitty Malone*, the actual physical presence of the farm is never in question. They can assume the grandfather's house will remain unthreatened. Whereas in *Wooden Hunters* the island is being logged and massacred.

T: Do you think it's a generational continuum people crave?

COHEN: No, I think it's more the physical presence of the landscape. The crucial experience for a lot of my characters is that they try to get too much from other people. When they try to get less, it's better. They have to relate to other people through the landscape, not at the cost of it.

T: I was going to ask you about your religious background in relation to this continuity business.

COHEN: I'm Jewish but I wasn't brought up very religiously.

T: I thought you taught religion.

COHEN: Actually that was in a department of religion, which is very different from a department of theology. I was teaching the sociology of religion. I used to take acid and read the books to get me in the mood for teaching. So it wasn't very conventional.

T: Have you been influenced as a novelist by taking acid?

COHEN: It's undoubtedly true that I have been. I think drugs definitely influence my view of reality. I also changed a lot when I started taking drugs. I wonder if I'm supposed to be saying these things in an interview?

T: If you don't you'll only be censoring something which is probably pretty important. I think it's a pretty fascinating area.

COHEN: Well, I don't know what the value of it has been for me. Like I said before, I don't know what the truth is about my books anyway. But certainly all the ideas for my novels and stories, with the exception of *Kitty Malone*, came during times when was taking drugs. I'd also say that except

for my first novel, most of what I wrote, starting with *Johnny Crackle Sings*, up to and including *The Colours of War* and *Nightflights*, I wrote while taking drugs. I don't know what the significance of that is. Maybe none. I don't know.

T: With me, drugs help you see how there's this gate between your conscious and unconscious. If you take some drugs, the filter can get lowered. What would have come to you unconsciously starts pouring in consciously for a change.

COHEN: Yes, initially I guess drugs helped me become less blocked. But I don't think I had any ideas that I wouldn't have had otherwise. It's just that the hesitation between thinking something and writing it down disappeared.

T: I almost suspect you could write a plausible description of how an elephant feels giving birth.

COHEN: That would be good.

T: But those scenes take me outside the flow of fiction. I have to stop and realize something is being created for me.

COHEN: You're saying there are certain limits within which fiction has to exist. I think exactly the same thing. This is just an instance where my limit is past yours. It's an aesthetic objection on your part.

T: I have another aesthetic objection then. Too many of your phrases pop out at me — like "reminding herself of a neurotic cow" or "suspended like pregnant black marshmallows" or "the brain burning itself out with the sour electric smell of an overheated battery."

COHEN: How do you know brains don't have smells? Maybe people feel that when their brains are burning out.

T: Was there any allegory in *Johnny Crackle Sings* between the life of a rock singer and the life of an aspiring artist?

COHEN: Sure, in a parodying way. The whole idea of the rise and fall of fame applies to everything. What was so much fun about *Johnny Crackle* was that his persona as a rock singer was a total fraud. It was as much comic as tragic that he was rising and falling at all.

T: Are you cynical then about the way some writers rise to the public eye and others don't?

COHEN: I'm never cynical about the way people rise. If writers get good feedback and people read their books, then they probably really deserve it. But I do think there's lots of writers who deserve it equally whose books aren't read.

One of the facts of writing is that it's part of the entertainment business. Some writers may not be happy about that, but that's the way it is. So people come into style and go out of style. They might write a couple of books which are very good and don't do very well; then, with another book which isn't so good, they get what they should have got before.

T: Are you becoming more aware of the entertainment value of literature?

COHEN: No, I've always thought that writing is show business to a certain extent.

T: Show and tell business.

COHEN: Yes. I think people should just write the books they're going to write and be aware that it's hard to guess what's going to happen. Even publishers can't manipulate that.

T: Do you ever feel under a pressure because Matt Cohen is being groomed as the new White Hope for McClelland & Stewart?

COHEN: Not really. People have asked that. I know McClelland has sometimes said things in public about me. But I guess I've been writing for so long now that the idea of myself being unformed seems bizarre, in fact I think I could quit writing quite soon.

That's a real eastern habit, though — to make writers into starlets. That was my first perception of the writing scene. I thought how interesting it was that writers get converted into starlets.

T: Which is really out to lunch.

COHEN: It's completely ridiculous.

Robertson Davies

ROBERTSON DAVIES was born in Thamesville, Ontario in 1913. He was educated at Queen's University and Balliol College, Oxford. From 1938 to 1940 he was a teacher and actor at the Old Vic in London. He returned to Canada and became editor and later publisher of the Peterborough *Examiner*. From 1963 to 1981 he was Master at Toronto's Massey College. A

novelist, playwright, literary critic and essayist, Davies is most widely known for his Deptford trilogy, comprised of *Fifth Business* (1970), *The Manticore* (1972) and *World of Wonders* (1975). The trilogy's three first-person narrators tell intertwined stories that reflect Davies' concern that "the fear and dread and splendour of wonder have been banished." The second novel in another trilogy sequence, *What's Bred in the Bone* (1985), was shortlisted for Britain's prestigious Booker Prize. The other novels in this trilogy are *The Rebel Angels* (1981) and *The Lyre of Orpheus* (1988).

Robertson Davies lives in Toronto. He was interviewed in 1979, 1981 and 1985.

T: Why have humourists fallen from fashion in Canada?

DAVIES: Oh, I think it's because of the extremely sore skin of our times. Humour very often consists of shrewd perceptions about people. It's usually funny at someone's expense. Nowadays if you're funny at anybody's expense they run to the UN and say, "I must have an ombudsman to protect me." You hardly dare have a shrewd perception about anybody. The only people you can abuse are WASPs. They're fair game. But most of the people who want to mock them aren't very good mockers because they don't understand what a WASP is.

T: But humour always makes a comeback.

DAVIES: Of course. It has to find an outlet because it's a basic element of civilized life. But there are always people who mistrust it and dislike it. You find whole periods of history where humour is completely choked off. For instance, if you look at the period from about 1640 to 1660 in British history, you won't find much humourous writing in it. The people down on humour then were the same people who are down on humour now. The Puritans, the people who are terribly touchy about any kind of criticism or evaluation that isn't made exactly on their terms.

T: Are we experiencing a new puritanism in a liberal age?

DAVIES: Oh, yes. It's a very puritanical age. It's not puritanical about some of the usual targets of puritanism like sex, but it's extremely puritanical about human rights. And children. All sorts of things like that.

T: In your essay on Stephen Leacock you say humour is the result of tension in the mind. Are there particular tensions in Canadian society that form the basis of a distinctly national humour?

DAVIES: I think we do have something which more or less approaches a national humour, and it's something that Stephen Leacock evolved with great brilliance. The characteristic of it is a kind of patterned innocence which covers a very great bitterness. never is it so sharply shown as in Leacock's *Sunshine Sketches*. You analyse what he says about the little town and it's a snake-pit. But he says it with such charm! The charm is convincing because it probably seemed charming when it happened.

T: The Canadian public seems to think of you primarily as a man of intellect and education; whereas you think of yourself primarily as a man of feeling and intuition. Doesn't this variance limit people's appreciation of your work?

DAVIES: I think that it does. This business about me being so elaborately educated isn't true. I am very spottily educated. This is both because of the kind of schooling I encountered and because I was not capable of assimilating a fully rounded education as it existed at the time. Now I tend not to think my way through problems but to feel my way through them. I judge them on intuition and values. That's a feeling person rather than a thinking person.

T: If this why you turned away from a career in psychiatry?

DAVIES: Oh, yes, I think so. The extreme tightrope-walking involved in psychiatry would have been too hard for me. As a psychiatrist, you've got to keep your cool all the time. That's very, very hard work.

T: Also psychiatry is a banishment of wonder. It's basically putting explanations on sensations.

DAVIES: Yes. And when you become a professional explainer, you're in great trouble.

T: This would explain why you've developed a fascination with insanity.

It emphasizes the frailty of reason.

DAVIES: Yes. Attempts to explain what is happening in the mind of the insane person are often very wide of the mark.

T: Magnus in *World of Wonders* says he grew up in a world where there was much concern about goodness but little love. Is that a fair description of your environment?

DAVIES: No, my family was more highly temperamental than that statement would suggest.

T: What about your society?

DAVIES: Oh, my society was very cagey about using the word "love." But there was a great concern about goodness or what would win approval.

T: You're probably most out of step with the times when it comes to your opinions on education. I look at Canada and I see a country that has made great progress in terms of developing a fairly high median level of education. Whereas I think you look at Canada and see how our middle-class society has discouraged excellence.

DAVIES: My opinion is very much conditioned by the fact that I teach in a university. I'm perpetually meeting young people who are products of our Canadian system of education. Sometimes I am shocked an alarmed on their behalf by the things they have not been introduced to and which I think they need if they're going to do the kind of study and work that they want.

I feel that in the yearning to make education acceptable and possible to everyone, certain tough things have been omitted. We have gone for breadth of education rather than depth. You can't really have both because there's only a limited amount of time you can spend going to school.

In the old days, when education was somewhat narrower, I think that it was in certain respects more effective. To come down to an example, I think that the modern training in history is not nearly as effective as it used to be. You get people trying to study something like literature who haven't really any notion of the historical background of what they're reading. This is short-changing them. People like myself have to give them a quick course in history before they can get to literature.

But all systems of education are riddled with faults. The plain fact is that we are not enjoying the fruits of a splendidly organized and completed educational setup. We are still in the midst of a great educational experiment which began about a century ago. It was decided everybody ought to be made literate up to a certain standard. We're still trying to find the most effective way of doing it. So no wonder we've got problems. We're in the middle of something, not at the end of it.

T: You also hold the unfashionable view that art is aristocratic, not democratic.

DAVIES: What I mean when I say art is aristocratic is that it is selective. It's not a mass thing. There never is a mass art that lasts very long or explains very much. But I don't mean aristocratic in the sense that it's produced by high-born people for high-born people. I just mean it's produced by special people for people who can understand.

T: Can we assume then that artists are born and not made?

DAVIES: I think that's true. All kinds of people come to see me and want advice on how they can become writers. But if you're a writer, you know it. You can improve what you are and become a better writer. But if you come to me and ask how can I become a writer, there is no answer.

Yet many people have this curious notion about writing. They know perfectly well they can't be a painter but everybody thinks somehow they may be a writer.

T: That's because everybody can write on a certain practical level of efficiency.

DAVIES: Yes. And a lot of technical writing or writing on factual matters may be very good indeed. But when you get over the bridge to what is imaginative and intuitive, then either you can do it or you can't. Nobody can teach you.

T: How far along were you in your writing career before you came to the conclusion that the function of literature is equivalent to the function of dream?

DAVIES: I don't think I ever came to any such conclusion.

T: It's in one of your essays.

DAVIES: Well, all art has some association with dream because it arises from the unconscious. Novels, poetry and plays and so forth are not exceptions to the general rule. So virtually everything that is written seriously, and isn't simply manufactured out of whole cloth, has some relationship to dream.

T: As the emphasis of your career has shifted from humour to drama, then from drama to novels, have these changes corresponded with changes within yourself?

DAVIES: Well, those changes of emphasis are not so great as they might appear on the surface. I think novels contain a great deal of humour and drama. Inevitably themes are broader in later work. So it's more a question of development than total change.

T: But the talents of a playwright and the talents of a novelist are quite separate. Wasn't it difficult making that switch?

DAVIES: No, I don't think it was. it seemed to be more or less inevitable. At the time I was writing plays in Canada, the opportunities for getting them produced were not very great. Productions were often unsatisfactory,

for reasons that were really nobody's fault. It wasn't a time when we had a theatre that could work very well with a new script. The temptation was therefore to write a novel, where you can control the whole atmosphere.

T: I'd like to talk about being a critic. Samuel Marchbanks is a social critic. In order to say many of the things you wanted to say, did you invent him as a character to say them?

DAVIES: Yes. He says things which cannot be said in any other way. Because you don't want to hit things hard, perhaps in a full-dress article, but there are things which nevertheless need to be said on matters that might occupy only a paragraph.

T: After almost ten years, I'm slowly learning that boldness and frankness are not always virtues in criticism.

DAVIES: Well, you're quite right. Criticism is necessary and valuable. But you also have to recognize what being a critic means. A great many years ago I knew a very remarkable psychiatrist, Dr. Robert Gillespie. He was killed in the Air Force during World War Two. I remember him telling me one time that nobody has ever psychoanalytically examined the wellsprings of criticism. Why does somebody want to be a critic? What do they think empowers them to take on that responsibility? And what restrictions do they feel are imposed upon them by what they are doing? Where does criticism come from? And who basically are they criticizing? Nobody's ever done that. And yet I think a critic ought to reflect on those things. The more experience you have of criticism, I think, the more you are inclined to spare the rod. Because you aren't sure quite what you're doing.

T: Besides the Samuel Marchbanks columns, you've also written criticism under your own name.

DAVIES: Oh, yes. At the same time I was at the *Peterborough Examiner*, I was writing book criticism for *Saturday Night*. And I very quickly made a rule for myself that I would not criticize a book that I couldn't praise unless it was so harmful that I thought something had to be said about it. In that way I put aside books that I thought were mediocre. I'm very pleased that I seemed to cover nearly all the good Canadian books that have lasted and praised them warmly. Not always without qualifications but chiefly positive. The kind of criticism that hurts a writer is so often the kind that is given with one hand and taken with the other, until very little is left, until you feel that your work has been treated as a mediocrity. It's neither been scorned as incompetent nor praised as good. Of course critics who want to hold the balance very carefully sometimes end up being disliked.

T: When you bring out a novel, do you read the reviews with any serious interest? Or are they merely amusing?

DAVIES: No, I read them all. I take what they say seriously. But not with absolute literal seriousness. Many, many years ago I read a saying by Thornton Wilder which I thought was very sound. He said, "Be heedful of criticism of your work. But you must not let it touch you too deeply or you will find when you write your next book the critic is writing it for you."

T: *What's Bred in the Bone* is a real page-turner. Do you sense as you're writing a novel how popular it's going to be?

DAVIES: Well, I'm very anxious to maintain interest. I've read too many novels which were admirable in a great many ways except that there were long and boring passages in them.

T: But your books are loaded with all sorts of information and side-trips into arcane matters.

DAVIES: But I think they're related to the plot. For instance, in *What's Bred in the Bone*, there's a great deal about the technique of painting and restoring. It's related to the plot. And I also think people are interested in knowing how it's done. I try to make my side-trips relevant.

T: In that book there's a remark that an artist must achieve a unity of his or her masculine and feminine qualities. He must understand he's a composite of male and female.

DAVIES: That idea has been with me for a very long time. It's a commonplace notion that there's a strong element of masculine in most women and of femininity in most men. If it is too slight in either case the person isn't particularly interesting. You get the exclusively feminine and rather silly woman. Or you get the ugly, stupid man. There must be a compensating element. There's a simple physical connotation to this. When a child is generated it's a genetic matter whether it's masculine or feminine. There are strong evidences of feminine genes in men and masculine genes in women. And it's not surprising that they have some voice in the personality and the intelligence of the person. So inevitably we're a mixture of both. It's a very good thing. I wouldn't wish to be without the feminine element in me. It keeps you from just being a blockhead!

T: Do you ever monitor your behaviour or feelings and think, oh, this is the masculine side of me operating? Or I'm in my feminine mode now?

DAVIES: All the time. Yes.

T: Do you ever read books or see plays and afterwards you think the author must have been lopsided?

DAVIES: Oh, yes, quite frequently. The English novelist Kingsley Amis comes to mind. He writes extremely masculine-toned books. He's very harsh about women. It seems to me that he has perhaps allowed something to influence or hurt him in some sort of way and it's harmful to his very considerable gifts as a writer.

T: Does masculinity, taken to its most extreme possibilities, lead to Nazism? Can politics be explained in these terms?

DAVIES: Yes, I think you're right. Those extreme masculine views can lead to Nazism. But you see Nazism also had a weak, sentimental, silly side to it . . . I'm trying to think of the film in which there is a very striking scene of a Nazi youth singing a song about the beauties of Germany.

T: *Cabaret.*

DAVIES: That's it. That was part of Nazism. And the Fuhrer's supposed love of children. That's the sentimentalism coming out. And this I think is fascinating. It comes out in their art. The art that was produced and approved by the Hitler regime was very sentimental indeed. It was not inventive. It was not explorative. It was not firm in any sort of strong direction. It was just soppy muck.

T: So politics and art can be seen as balancing poles.

DAVIES: I think that they are balancing poles. And you notice this sometimes, too, in Soviet art. It's not so sentimental, perhaps, but it is terribly unadventurous, and stuck in the mud. I'm talking about their painting and sculpture at the moment. I think this is what happens from that excessive, macho spirit which they foster.

T: So how do you characterize Canadian politics? And are we getting art which is the mirror opposite?

DAVIES: Well, in Canada the government only fosters art through the Canada Council. The government won't initiate anything or tell you what to do. The government won't say we want pictures of a strong, masculine prime minister striding across the wheatfields pursued by little children!

T: Maybe that's because our politi-

cians fortunately don't appreciate the power of art.

DAVIES: Well, certainly Canadian politicians are very rarely people of much cultivation. They don't read. They don't reflect. This was one of the reasons why Pierre Trudeau was such an oddball. And also, I think, Lester Pearson. I think it's a pity we didn't get Stanfield as a big figure in Canadian politics because he's a man of great culture. That's a rarity in Canadian politics. It does, in a way, reflect the country. Canada still insists upon playing Little Joe to itself and trying to present that image to its neighbours. But it won't do because something's going on in Canada which is really a revolution. The politicians have never caught onto it. And it's an artistic revolution.

T: Are you talking about a revolution in terms of quality?

DAVIES: A year ago I was at a conference in Vienna about Canadian literature. There were forty European universities represented. All of them had institutes of Canadian studies. And I have just been to Italy and there are twenty universities in Italy with institutes of Canadian studies. The other day I went into a bookshop. The bookseller was making up a great big carton of my books in paperback that he was sending to a university in Hungary. Our stuff is going to Europe and Asia and South America. Canadian studies is particularly big in Brazil.

One of these days Canada is going to wake up and be shaken to its foundations by the realization that it's a country of great reputation and fame and that it's the artists who have made it so. While the politicians sat on their behinds and whined about freight rates and wheat! There now, you see, I'm losing my cool!

T: You once described Canada in Jungian terms, saying we had a "shadow," which was our habit of emotional repression. Does having such a strong shadow help Canadian artists or hinder them?

DAVIES: I think it has helped them. It gives a nation one appearance externally and something very different inside. That has evidenced itself time and time again in our history. And in our literature. For instance, in the work of writers like Margaret Laurence and Hugh MacLennan. It's there with the people who have written seriously about Canadian life.

T: It seems to me that our writers possibly know this country better than the politicians.

DAVIES: That is quite possible. A writer hasn't an awful lot to gain except his own enlightenment when making his acquaintance with the country and its people. A politician is always looking for some kind of advantage, some kind of angle. So their perception is likely to be shallow. The perception of the writer is not. Nobody cares what he thinks, so he's able to look more intently.

Also the politician is always on the spot. There's always somebody pushing a microphone in his face and wanting to know what he thinks. He probably doesn't think anything but he has to say something.

T: Writers are essentially tuned into the psychology of a nation.

DAVIES: Yes, but it's very hard to persuade a country like Canada that it has any psychology. Or that a psychological observation may be a weighty one.

T: I think this comes near the root of why your work is refreshing. You give the reader a sense that self-analysis can be pleasurable as well as painful. Do you yourself ever recall experiencing any memorable moments of personal insight?

DAVIES: Nothing like a flash of lightning. It's more a matter of a thing that happens in the course of a few weeks.

T: Do you think psychology is on its way to becoming our new religion?

DAVIES: Psychology and religion have always been very closely linked. Nowadays people are extremely cautious about committing themselves to any sort of religious statement so they tend to put psychological tags on what might formerly have been considered religious insights. But I don't think that it matters very much. Basically it's the insights that are important, not the tags that go with them.

T: Can you articulate the connection for yourself between a sense of wonder and religious feeling?

DAVIES: A sense of wonder is in itself a religious feeling. But in so many people the sense of wonder gets lost. It gets scarred over. It's as though a tortoise shell has grown over it. People reach a stage where they're never surprised, never delighted. They're never suddenly aware of glorious freedom or splendour in their lives. However hard a life may be, I think for virtually all people this is possible.

This is very unhappy, very unfortunate. The attitude is often self-induced. It is fear. People are afraid to be happy. Puritanical parents used to say, "If you laugh before breakfast, you'll cry before night." This sort of thing has been driven into us so much that we're almost terrified to rejoice. Or to think we're lucky.

How lucky people are! Look out of that window. An absolutely superb autumn day. Both of us are sitting here, neither of us is experiencing any pain. We're not hungry. We're aware. This is happiness. So many people tend to think that happiness must be a kind of glory which is absolutely unrepeatable. But it's an endlessly renewing thing.

Marian Engel

MARIAN ENGEL was born in Toronto in 1933. She was raised in Galt, Hamilton, and Sarnia and later lived in Montreal, Cyprus, the US and London, England. In Canada, "a country that cannot be modern without guilt," she explored deeply felt personal dilemmas in three early novels, *No Clouds of Glory* (1968), *The Honeyman Festival* (1970) and

Monodromos (1973). Her Governor General's Award-winning *Bear* (1976), a dream-like tale of a woman's amorous relationship with a bear, reached into the depths of mythic imagination. A heroine in *The Glassy Sea* (1978) joins a contemplative order of nuns. *Lunatic Villas* (1981) is a comedy about a single parent and her family. In 1973 she served as the first chairman of the Writers Union of Canada.

Marian Engel died in 1985. A collection of short stories, *The Tattooed Woman* (1985) appeared posthumously. She was interviewed in 1978.

T: What do you mean when you say writers are chosen?

ENGEL: When I talk to Margaret Laurence or Peggy Atwood, I find we all went out and bought our little notebooks when we were eight or nine. There are a lot of writers who don't do that, but I expect the majority do. Kids know whether they have a burning ambition or not. They begin to place it. Being chosen is just a Presbyterian way of phrasing it.

T: Where does the will to stick with it come from?

ENGEL: It comes from the background. In our family we were trained as kids never to give up. It's been particularly true of the women. The girls pick out a goal and go straight to it. It can't be a gene. It must be conditioning. Before I wanted to be a writer, I had wanted to be the best whistler in the world.

T: Would you elaborate on your upbringing?

ENGEL: We moved a lot. My father was a First World War pilot who wound up teaching auto mechanics. He was a technical school teacher with a Type B certificate. During the Depression, it was the Type B teachers that they fired. They just let them go. He lost a job in Port Arthur. Then we went to Brantford and that job didn't pan out. Then we went to South Dakota because he was sick, obviously for good reason. He had ulcers. Then we wound up in Galt for five years. Then we went to Hamilton. Then we went to Sarnia when I was about twelve.

T: So you grew up under conditions where you were aware that things were not secure.

ENGEL: Yes. There was always the social insecurity of being new people. And we had relatives and neighbours to keep up with but we had very little money. Those of us who were trying to be middle class on twenty-five hundred a year got very bitter. My God, my mother was a genius with a nickel. And am *I* ever mean!

T: Did you have one of those classic childhoods where you were always lonely?

ENGEL: Yes. My sister was six years older and I didn't have any brothers. Mother was good about that, too. She said go into the back yard, get four sticks and give them names. Writers *are* chosen!

T: Do you think that early isolation is why you have an affinity for islands in your work, both literal and figurative?

ENGEL: I'm easily harassed, so I'm always dreaming of permanent withdrawals. Convents, islands and great thumping houses in the country. Writing a book involves the Big Withdrawal from society, too. Mostly I do it in the winters. When it's over, what happens to me and to several other writers I know is a great plunge back into the world. If I was the only person who lived this way I'd be worried about myself. But I know many writers who do the same thing.

T: Can you write while you teach?

ENGEL: I have a horrible time. It ruins your voices. Rudy Wiebe seems to have no trouble. And he gives a lot to his students, too. But because I've got my kids to look after, I'm juggling all sorts of things and I know I'm not being the big humane spirit people expect a senior writer at a university to be. That small piece of me that I'm handing out every Tuesday, Wednesday and Thursday is all there is, kids.

T: How serious a jolt to your life was having kids?

ENGEL: I was terrified when I had them. I was going to have a quiet baby with spectacles who sat under the table and read. But I had twins. So I wrote my agent and asked what I should do. He wrote back and said the more responsibilities his writers took on, the better writers they became. I grit my teeth and say that. It may not be true, but it's helpful.

T: In *The Glassy Sea*, the nun says when she's being practical, the dreamer in her dies. Is that work/contemplation split a problem for you, too?

ENGEL: Yes, and it was fascinating to write about. Hang it all, I haven't darkened a church door in thirty years. Except for funerals. But it will always continue as a tension for me. I will be a guilty napper, but I will still nap. In fact, I do most of my work in bed these days.

T: So that's a problem with novel writing, too — balancing the craft of writing over a long period of time with the more "creative" part of the job.

ENGEL: It's a terrible problem. I'm not the only writer to have it. You see, a writer's life is essentially contemplative. I know a lot of people who live unreflectively and are happier than I am, but I don't get any pleasure out of living that way. I probably reflect obsessively and narcissistically and excessively. Right now I'm scrambling around working to get some money, then I'm going to sit down on a stump and just think.

T: Do you have to watch your reflective nature doesn't get out of hand when you're writing?

ENGEL: I think so. You have to become another person. if there's been any change in my books it's that I've become more skillful at becoming another person. Then I have to make sure that this other person does not distort my everyday reality. My friends and relations do not, after all, act according to the scenario I have imagined for them.

T: Is that skillfulness the result of craftsmanship? Or is it because you've exorcised all your biographical material?

ENGEL: I can cheerfully say there is almost no autobiographical story left to tell that interests me. Next week, that may be another matter, of course. But now I feel I've got rid of all that material. I can really go ahead.

T: Do you worry about going through the rest of your life being pegged as the woman who wrote *Bear*?

ENGEL: Oh, God. Before it was published I remember I met a friend who's with CBC news and he said, "Are you really going to publish that book about the bear?" I said sure. He said, "If you don't publish that book you'll have about eight lines in the history of Canadian literature; if you do publish it you'll have one." I knew then I had to publish that book — and then a great many more.

T: What made *Bear* convincing to me was the lyricism of the writing. Did that book seem to take you over as you wrote it?

ENGEL: It was a very strange, completely instinctual book. It was based on a lot of research that I had done on Ontario pioneers so it had a firm intellectual base. But the lyricism was just there. I won't say it wrote itself because I can remember doing draft after draft. But some of it wrote itself. I regard it as a piece of luck.

T: You mean luck in the sense that you were the perfect person to write that book? You just happened to plug into it?

ENGEL: Yes. It was a case of all the elements coming together, which they don't always do. I don't think it's the be-all and end-all of book-writing but I think it's a nifty piece of work. People can communicate with *Bear* who wouldn't like my more intellectual books because it's the acting out of a statement. That's what's good about *Bear*. It's acted out rather than preached. I tend to be preachy.

T: And as you said in *Sarah Bastard*, "All intellectual missionaries tend to lechery."

ENGEL: Did I write that? Aren't I clever! That's the happiness of writing. Occasionally you write something good but it doesn't have to be a whole book.

T: So what about your role as an intellectual missionary these days?

ENGEL: My missionary tastes are fast coming to an end!

T: Are you as happy with *The Glassy Sea* as you are with *Bear*?

ENGEL: No. It's got a problem that's inevitable. You can't possibly do as neat a job on forty years as you can on one summer. I haven't learned to deal with forty years skillfully, but it has the defects of its qualities.

T: Was the novel a conscious attempt to write a book different from *Bear*?

ENGEL: My original impulse was to see Toronto with a naive eye. I wanted to bring a stranger to Toronto and see what she would make of it. Eventually she became a nun.

T: The book struck me as an elaboration on your line, "There's a kind of virgin one only becomes with difficulty."

ENGEL: Yes, *The Glassy Sea* is perhaps an elaboration on regaining a kind of innocence. A kindness and an unworldliness.

T: But was that consciously done?

ENGEL: Writing works on many levels. You can't just do it on feelings. I think one of the things I was trying to get rid of when I wrote that book was a certain level of cynicism. Everyone I was seeing for a while, particularly aging media people, had grown so cynical. I thought everything was terribly besmirched. I was trying for myself to clean things up. I don't mean sexually. I don't even mean morally. I mean in the sense of starting to like things again.

There comes a time when you have to give up this sort of facile cynical thinking. It's college-boy smartness. You have to look for the good values in society, too. Or else there's not much reason to belong to a society.

T: Cynicism is certainly not a good quality to try and produce a good book from.

ENGEL: You're right. It belongs to young men of twenty-five, and they're notorious for writing bad books. Salinger is one of the few examples of a young person that age who has written a good book. He took a naive and innocent character who wasn't cynical.

T: You sound like you're enjoying getting older.

ENGEL: I am. I remember when I was Hugh MacLennan's graduate student at McGill, I got into a hideous argument with him because I was furious with him for being so proud of being fifty. But I realize now that I'm forty-five and not fifty, that I'm delighted to have the perspective that I have. I can see why things happened twenty years ago. That's lovely.

Length of time is a great help with writing. My young students try to write about their childhoods but they don't have enough perspective to write well. It's really unfair to a be a nineteen-year-old writer because you have to continue writing but you don't have anything to write about for an awfully long time. Sure, I'd like to be young again, to look better and to have a young body. But you can't have it both ways. Would you like to be twenty again? I'd hate it. You don't know anything.

T: And yet you have that phrase, "If there's someone who is more disliked or hated than an intelligent young woman it's a mature woman who is not at the mercy of the tides of the moon."

ENGEL: Yes, I'm feeling that more and more. Men are really afraid of mature women. They're afraid of them in the same sense that they're afraid of their mothers. They're afraid of being judged. I think that's really sad.

My theory is that the young men in my generation were all Depression kids. If their mothers had to go out and work, they were cleaning women or worked in stores. The boys I went out with, on the whole, came from small families and had the exclusive attention of their mothers when they were very young. They went on wanting the exclusive attention of their wives.

I'm not blaming it all on the men. I'm not a very good housekeeper and I was probably an irritating wife. But sometimes it makes me mad.

T: I think a lot of people your age are somewhat bitter that they were robbed of a great deal by the sexual mores of their youth.

ENGEL: The young have made us very envious. If we could have gone and followed our instincts at nineteen we feel we would have all been a lot happier.

A lot of us have been forced to realize that in this society at this time it seems to be that you can either be loved or accomplish something. That's a terrible choice to make.

T: Have you given up on the institution of marriage?

ENGEL: Not quite! You never can tell. Being an unwilling cook and not of an age to breed, it's unlikely I will marry again. And I've become kind of a bitchy and unreasonable person and too touchy, so I'm probably untouchable. But I still feel it's unfair that any kind of affectionate relationships should be ruled out just because I'm a writer. There are many men I know who have the ability to write books and keep their relationships.

T: In your books there are repeated references to sexual relations being a battlefield. Has sexual warfare become any more humane nowadays?

ENGEL: I hope so. I hope so. It's really hard to tell. I hope the younger ones are making out better than our gang. Still, I always warn the younger women writers — don't use your

married name and watch your relationships.

T: How do you mean, "watch your relationships"?

ENGEL: Be really aware of the fact that writing may change the balance of your life, and you may have to make a decision.

T: I can think of a lot of male writers, too, who were miserably unhappy being married. Like Tolstoy finally running away from home in his eighties.

ENGEL: Maybe the kind of people who turn out to be writers are not the kind of people who are easy to live with or choose easy lives.

T: You don't eschew the "woman writer" label. Do you think feminist-oriented fiction has had its day?

ENGEL: I think it will have reached its zenith very soon. I think people are getting tired of it.

T: That was my reaction to the end of *The Glassy Sea.* It was like I'd heard that whole story before.

ENGEL: I wondered whether parts of that were a sell-out to the women's movement, but I don't think so. The penultimate chapters in my books are always paranoid fantasies. It's happened in every book I've written.

T: Marguerite in *The Glassy Sea* feels there must be some point to her life. Are you sure now that the point of your life is to write?

ENGEL: Yes, I think it is. I can remember when writing was an ambition that could easily be said to be burning. It's no longer that way because I'm there. I'm very lucky. However, if writing ever deserts me, I shall have no life at all.

T: So your motto for the "citizens of euphoria" in *Sarah Bastard's Notebook* still holds true for you today. . . "Only One Basket for Eggs"?

ENGEL: Yes, I'm still a one basket person. I can't help it. But I think all the eggs are different colours. . .

Hubert Evans

HUBERT EVANS was born in Vankleek Hill, Ontario in 1892 and raised in Galt, Ontario. He worked as a reporter before enlisting in 1915. He married in 1920 and built his permanent seaside home at Roberts Creek, BC. His first novel, *The New Front Line* (1927) is about a pioneering World War One veteran in BC. He and his wife also lived in northern BC

Indian villages, resulting in his acclaimed second novel, *Mist on the River* (1954). His *O Time in Your Flight* (1979), written in his late eighties despite near blindness, recounts a year in the life of an Ontario boy in 1899. Revered by Margaret Laurence as "The Elder of our Tribe," the Quaker outdoorsman also published two hundred short stories, sixty serials, twelve plays, three juvenile novels, three books of poetry and one biography.

Hubert Evans died in 1986, after seven decades of professional writing. He was interviewed in 1982 and 1983.

T: Tell me about how you came to write *O Time in Your Flight*.

EVANS: The second time I went to the hospital to get my heart pacer batteries renewed, they opened me up and found something else was wrong. I was in bed for weeks. I thought by golly, time's a-wastin', I better get some of the family history down. So my son-in-law brought me one of those dictaphones from his office. I was awake a lot at nights so I just started in stream-of-consciousness. I could taste the food and smell the smells. Some nights I'd talk two chapters.

Those days I could still see to do a little hunt n'peck typing so in the daytime I typed it out pretty well just as I said everything. It ran to sixty-five thousand words. I had a copy made for the children and then I sent a copy to the Ontario Public Archives. But in the back of my old freelancer's mind, I must have figured I might be able to use this. I told them I wanted it kept under wraps until 1980.

Then four or five years ago I couldn't go out and saw wood or go fishing any more on account of my heart. I was sort of at loose ends so I did ninety pages of the book. But the viewpoint I had wasn't any good. It was too subjective and modern.

You see, I'm an oldtimer. After sixty years I still see a story as a play. The characters are on an imaginary stage and I'm a member of the audience. I just try to get them to show themselves. This can be very limiting. On the other hand, I think it narrows down the focus.

T: So you needed a more objective approach to get you going.

EVANS: Right. So I decided to see the whole world through the yes of a nine-year-old that was me. Anything the boy couldn't comprehend at the time, I just left out. I tried to do as little interpreting as possible. It was like the title. I don't explain where that phrase *O Time in Your Flight* comes from because I never knew it was from a poem when I was a boy. it was just something my mother said.

This has been one of the main tenets of my writing all along: It's far better to have a reader miss a point than hit him over the head with it. If you get the reader concluding, "I know what that character is up to," then you've got participation. The reader becomes part of the story when he's seeing around corners.

T: I imagine writing novels for young people would have helped you learn that approach pretty quickly.

EVANS: Yes, it's been very helpful. I've often though that.

T: And it would also force you to simplify your language.

EVANS: Exactly. Now if I was running one of those creative writing courses in a university, I would have an exercise where people tell stories in Basic English. English has taken on far too many words. There are too many tools.

I know an old chap who retired near here who used to be a big time businessman. One day he decided he was going to take up carpentry. So he goes out and buys several hundred dollars worth of electric tools. But this is a guy who can't even sharpen a hand saw or a chisel! Both my grandfather and father were excellent carpenters even though they had very few tools. They knew how to sharpen them! By golly, they knew how to use them and when not to use them.

It's the same with language. We've got all these words, all these tools. Think of one of the Lake poets writing on the death of a child, then think of Issa, the Japanese poet in the 1500s. Issa on the death of his child uses only twelve words. Whenever I recite it, it still moves me:

> Dew evaporates
> All our world is dew
> So dear, so fleeting

T: Reviews as far back as the 1920s mention your "spare, lean and vigorous style." Did you have to learn to write that way?

EVANS: I'm a two-time high school dropout. The second time I left school I went to work for a newspaper called the *Galt Reporter*. My boss there had been the editor of a prestigious paper called the *Chicago Inter-Ocean*. When I arrived he said two things to me. Learn to use a typewriter within two weeks or you're out. And as far as possible, use words that the boy who sells your paper can understand. Then you'll be writing good English. That's always stuck.

T: Would you say your approach to writing is very much like your approach to life?

EVANS: Yes, I suppose that's true. I knew my wife ever since we were thirteen and we both always had the same idea. To travel light. To not have any encumbrances. To own only what you can carry on your back. For instance, we said we would never own land. Then her home broke up back east and we got sent this piano. Then we had kids. We had to have a roof over our heads so I built this house.

T: How did you become a Quaker?

EVANS: It's a long, long story. My wife was a graduate of the University of Toronto. One of the books she got me reading was Carlyle's *Sartor Resartus*. That book really became my Bible. "Always the black spot in our sunshine. This is the shadow of ourselves."

You see, I went through two years and three months in the trenches in World War One. I tell you, I got pretty damned cynical. I had got to a stage where I would say how the hell does anybody know what beauty is? I remember saying this to myself. I remember thinking a tree may be as ugly as the hair on my arm.

In *Sartor Resartus* his protagonist reaches this point and says he's not going to put up with it. He decides the world is not a "charnel house filled with spectres." From that day on, his attitude changes. Well, in those days there was a thing in Philadelphia called the Wider Quaker Fellowship. My wife and I asked to join because we were universalists.

The Quakers have no creed. They have no minister. It's an attitude. If you believe in life and growth, you can be a Quaker.

T: Did you always want to be a writer?

EVANS: I always thought about it. After I came out of the army I went up north for a year and started writing. In those days, if you could put a short story together, you could sell it. But you couldn't make a living just by writing for Canada. So I wrote pulp stories. The most popular kind back then were war stories by American guys who'd never even been there. I couldn't write about violence so I wrote outdoor stories. Animal stories.

T: What made you start writing for kids?

EVANS: My wife said she'd rather have me digging ditches than writing pulp. Mind you, I've never written anything that I'm ashamed of, but I've written a lot of things that really didn't need to be written. She suggested I write for teenagers because you can still change a person's viewpoint up to the time they're twenty.

T: How old were you then?

EVANS: I was thirty or so. The first thing I did was a syndicated column about factual things I'd seen with animals. The Judson Press in Philadelphia wrote me and asked me to do a book about it. I wrote about sixty-five of these columns in six weeks. The book sold quite well.

T: Was making a living as a writer in the 1920s easier than today?

EVANS: Much easier. If you could tell a story, the market was there.

Today I don't know how people can make a living with fiction. TV has changed everything so much.

T: Did you get much notoriety in those days?

EVANS: Well, listen. When I was doing those outdoor nature stories, I was living in a very fine house in North Vancouver. This was the late twenties. A piece ran in every daily paper across Canada saying Hubert Evans lives in a one-room shack far away from civilization! The truth was I'd never had it so good! I was really in the money.

T: But you've lived through long periods of being virtually unknown.

EVANS: Yes, yes, yes! Of course these days if a writer wants to make headlines he practically has to perform some unnatural act with a farm animal.

T: Perhaps if you hadn't separated yourself geographically...

EVANS: No, I'd had it up to here with cities. This is what I wanted. I wrote to various postmasters along the coast looking for a sheltered cove, a sandy beach, good anchorage and a creek. I came to Roberts Creek and bought this half-acre of waterfrontage for a thousand dollars cash.

T: If you hadn't always written for money, do you think you would have produced more than three adult novels?

EVANS: Maybe I would have. But I haven't got that intense perception and psychological imagination that say a Margaret Laurence or a Graham Greene has.

T: What made you write your novel about the Indians of northern BC, *Mist on the River*?

EVANS: Well, I had quite a number of chums in the army who were Indians. But it was really my wife's Quaker concern over Indians that took us north in the first place. She had this book by an American called *Indians are People Too*. This is what I wanted

to do with *Mist on the River*. Just show them as people. Basically I was just being a reporter.

I could have written about the injustices Indians faced. You know, like *The Ecstasy of Rita Joe*. I've seen all that. I know all that. But I had commercial-fished and trapped and built dugout canoes with these people. I could roll a cigarette and sit on my heels and talk with them. I was one of them. I wanted to show how they were really just like us.

T: Donald Cameron has described that book as "a good man's compassionate regard for another's pain."

EVANS: Bertrand Russell said, "If we want a better world, the remedy is so simple that I hesitate to state it for fear of the derisive smiles of the wise cynics. The remedy is Christian love or compassion." D.H. Lawrence kept on this, too. What the world needs is compassion.

One of my problems as a writer is that I've never been able to write about middle-class, Kerrisdale–West Vancouver people. My head tells me they've got their tragedies and disappointments and dramas like everyone else, but this is one of my blind spots. I'm sorry to say I can't get inside their heads the way I do with older people or down-and-out people or children.

T: Maybe it's because those people will never allow you any communal feelings with them.

EVANS: It's true, I think we do all need to feel ourselves part of a larger family. Living with the Indians for eight years in the Skeena country taught that to my wife and me. The Indians have still got this. But most of us have really lost it.

Of course there are lots of Indians I don't take to, just like there are lots of white people I don't take to. But there's a quotation by Albert — how do you pronounce it? Is it Camus? Is that the right way? He said there is no question here of sentimentality. He said, "It is true that I am different by tradition from an African or a Mohammedan. But it is also true that if I degrade them or despise them, I demean myself."

T: That hearkens back to that Camus quote above your writing desk.

EVANS: I can repeat that one by heart. "An artist may make a success or failure of his work. He may make a success or failure of his life. But if he can tell himself that finally, as a result of his long effort, he has eased or decreased the various forms of bondage weighing upon Man, then in a sense, he is justified and can forgive himself."

George Faludy

GEORGE FALUDY was born in Budapest, Hungary in 1910. In 1936 he was sentenced to eight years in prison for anti-Nazi activities but was able to emigrate to Paris in 1940. He lived in Morocco and enlisted in the US Army in 1942. He returned to Hungary in 1946 as literary editor of the *Voice of the People* but was soon accused of being an American spy. He

was jailed six months in Secret Police Headquarters in Budapest, then survived three years of hard labour at the Recsk Prison, later described in his memoir, *My Happy Days in Hell* (1962). In 1956 he left Hungary after the October Revolution and settled in London. In 1967 he emigrated to Canada. Nine years later he became a Canadian citizen. He is Hungary's leading writer in exile. His other books available in English are *Learn This Poem of Mine by Heart* (1983) and *Selected Poems 1933–1980* (1985).

George Faludy lives in Toronto. He was interviewed in 1985.

T: In one of your poems you've written, "My aunt cut her neck with a razor blade. The rest died in the war in gas chambers. My sister floats upon the icy Danube." Now that you're out of Hungary, are you often visited by your past in your dreams?

FALUDY: Yes. It is beautiful what you say. Because I wrote a poem about this. It is a consecutive dream. It comes very often. The dream is this. I go home to Hungary too early. It is still a Nazi government or a communist government. They catch me visiting my father's house. I run away and I am jumping from balconies. From the fifteenth floor down to the river and so on. Finally they catch me and they torture me. They insist I get up. I have a heavy machine gun before me . . . Then I wake up and I am on the Adriatic Sea or the Mediterranean or the Hudson River or Lake Ontario or the Pacific Ocean. And I feel an incredible happiness that I am out!

I am a Hungarian patriot still and will die as such. But I am happy that I am out. I am happy that I am out because I am not a masochist.

T: Is that why you could call your book about being in the concentration camp, *My Happy Days in Hell*?

FALUDY: Yes. Suffering is not a virtue. That I knew in Recsk. But for a poet it can be excellent. You learn things which you did not know before. In the punishment cell where I was, for instance, it was a dark cell, no light. But it had a wooden door on the forest. The ray of the winter sun was moving on the wall. There was just a little hole in the roof, very small, like a pinhead. The light, like a star, like a planet in the planetarium, moved on the wall from morning til evening. Of a radiance I never saw in my life. It was winter, it was zero degrees maximum, if not less. But when I was standing in the light beam I felt in the South Sea.

And friends came to me immediately when I arrived in Recsk and said, "Oh, how wonderful that you are here. We had no possiblilty during the war to go to university." It was good. We learned very much.

T: You taught them during the evenings?

FALUDY: We made anthologies in the prison where we had no books. But not only me. Many others. We had a man who could whistle *Don Giovanni*, for instance. The whole. And people would sit around him, people who had never heard *Don Giovanni*. Others told *War and Peace* for two weeks in the evenings.

T: You wrote that those who said to themselves, "I'm going to live, I'm going to survive, and that's all that matters," were the ones who usually died. Whereas the ones who kept their spirits alive, the ones who whistled *Don Giovanni* and recited poetry, were usually the ones who lived.

FALUDY: Yes. That is true. That is very important, I think. Because, you know, the body is better than I thought. When you are in a camp under those conditions, which are unbearable with the normal skin, your skin gets harder. You withdraw three or four millimetres under your skin. When you are working, cutting trees, and it is raining for two months, a creek is going down your back, but you feel it is another man's back. When you have a toothache, since you know there is no help, it hurts less.

T: I just finished reading *My Happy Days in Hell* last night. I was particularly struck by the time you took straws from a broom and wrote a poem in blood on toilet paper, "For Posterity."

FALUDY: Yes. I remember back in 1948 a friend of mine in Hungary, a newspaperman, met me in a bookshop. That was a good bookshop because it was in a house which had two doors on two streets. We met there and he said unexpectedly, "George, we have decided and arranged it excellently well that we go this evening to Austria to the British zone." I say no. He says, "If you stay they will hang you." I say, "Let's hope they won't. First I want to live and write about them, how they are." I said, "I stay. I want to see how they are at their worst."

Much later when I came out in Stockholm my friend was there. I had a press conference. He suddenly told this story. I had forgotten. When he told it I thought he was lying. Lying to elevate me. Then suddenly it occurred to me it was like this. I wanted to describe them. The West had not the slightest idea. Not the slightest idea. Solzenitzhen helped thirty years later a lot. But only Orwell had described it. Orwell, who never was in Russia. Orwell, who never was in a communist prison. He's marvellous.

T: So you felt, as a writer, it was your duty to experience reality, no matter how bad it was.

FALUDY: Well, one wants two things. To describe oneself, life, or emotions, or passions. That is one thing. And my century. That is the second thing. The second thing is, in a certain way, obligatory.

The world has two sides. The good things and the bad things. With the atomic bomb and the population explosion and the pollution, finally the balance went out of it. Therefore I consider it is my duty to write about those things. Because it never was so hopeless. It used to be barbarians came and killed every second man. But only every second. My father never was afraid that the race would die. This is the first time since mankind has existed that we face it. Auden knew this and wrote about it. But others are leaving it out. I don't understand. Most poets describe only themselves. When you take any English anthology

now, it might be a very interesting age, but they don't write about it. I don't get it. What is it? What holds people back?

T: I think it's because we're losing our sense of history. If you don't have a sense of history, you don't have a balancing sense of the future. Everything is geared to today.

FALUDY: Yes. This changes everything. Our world has stood since thousands of years, unfriendly but secure. Now suddenly it has become more pleasant, with running water etc., but it can blow up. This changes our psychology totally. Many things. Ethics and morals and so on. All are under the influence. We are like soldiers on leave for three days. We know we have to go back to the front lines and can die in five minutes after our arrival. It changes our lives totally.

T: If your father was a scientist, how did you become a poet?

FALUDY: We fought. He wanted that I become a chemical engineer. In this time the pressure of parents was like in China now. Enormous. So I went to university, first to Vienna. He maintained, when I wrote poems, that in Hungary they have twenty thousand poets and none of them can live from poetry. All chemical engineers have a good job. Finally the end was very bad. He came up to Vienna to visit his colleague who was my chemistry professor. My father asked his friend how he was pleased with me. He said that he doesn't know me.

T: There's a line in one of your poems about how you vowed to be a fine man and a poet. I get the feeling you always thought the two were somehow the same.

FALUDY: Yes. Must go together. In this sense an oppressed country is much better. You can be a good poet here and do not need to be an honest man. The striving to be an honest man is far stronger in an oppressed country.

Which says something good about the human mind. Remember Hungary was occupied by the Turks for 150 years. The next four hundred years by the Austrians. Imagine that Canada was occupied by Lenin since 1917 until you get him out? In Hungary when somebody writes a good poem against a wicked man, it has an impact it wouldn't have here. It is felt. It is in some way our duty to do it. I know during the Second World War in concentration camps my poems against the Germans were very popular. Many people, thousands, knew them by heart. It was a comfort to them in a bad situation. Here when they asked me to write a poem against Nixon at the last election when they elected him, I refused. Here it is not that situation. Nobody is put in concentration camps.

T: Where you grew up the poet and the dictator were clearly on opposite sides. It was very clear what the poet must say. What does the poet do in this place? In Canada? If you were a young man today?

FALUDY: If I was young I would probably organize groups which would, in the night when nobody was there, blow up factories which pollute. I would organize bands, terror groups, for the good. And never let them blow up children and so on. I would go and threaten people who are managers of factories that pollute. The managers are very cowardly people. It is very funny that I never heard in prisons a single factory manager or bank manager who resisted. Not one. Farmers, factory workers, aristocrats, intellectuals, priests, whatever. They were all in the Hungarian Resistance and the French Resistance. But never a manager.

So I believe if I were young I could help a lot for this. Organization. How to organize a general strike. When the Russians came in after the Hungarian Revolution with tanks and murder, I was delegated from the Hungarian Association of Writers to the General Workers Council, which was the basic organ of the revolution. There was only one way. General strike. It was an enormously complex thing. It lasted three weeks. I remember we deliberated sometimes twelve, sometimes fifteen hours, how to make it that bread for the people is there but bread for the police isn't. So that the Russians' barracks has no electricity and the hospital has.

T: How do you compare the Occupation of Hungary by the Germans with the Occupation of Hungary by the Soviets?

FALUDY: It is a big question. First of all, the difference between a leading Nazi and a leading Communist is that a Nazi can save someone. That is how I got out of Hungary. This was in late '38 after the Munich Agreement. I was called to see the Undersecretary of Justice. A semi-fascist. My deadly enemy, I thought. But he says, "George, I remember you from a lecture you gave. What do you drink?" He shows me the warrant for my arrest. It was for a poem I'd written against Hitler. I was charged with inciting peasant revolt and so on. Slandering a friendly nation. All in all I would get fourteen years. I should be arrested immediately. He says, "It is no sense to spend fourteen years here in prison. It is insane. So where do you want to go?" I said to Paris. He says, "No hurry, my son, no hurry. This remains here in my drawer until I get from you a postcard with the Paris Opera House on it." That cannot happen in a communist country because he doesn't dare.

T: So the expression of individual will is more important to one captor than another.

FALUDY: Yes. In Russia, I'm very sorry. There are many Russians I like very much but in general the truth is that there is some responsibility for the very fact that Russia was a totalitarian state, a horrible and sadistic state where freedom is unknown. Even today taxi drivers in Moscow drive around with the picture of Stalin before them. Stalin, who murdered twenty million people. Germany they murdered, I don't know, four or five million people. They have now one of the best governments in the world. They force the people to remember. But in Russia they murdered between fifteen and twenty million people and nobody, nobody, was ever prosecuted for those crimes. Nobody.

It seems the world is divided. There is one half where we have been striving for twenty-five hundred years for some measure of individual freedom. Democracy. For free expression. To speak as we like in a park or a public street. And then you have another part of the world where tyranny is the forum of life. Where they are used to it. The one goes from San Francisco to Poland. And the other half goes from Poland across Asia. It is not a political thing. It is a human thing.

T: Is this the differentiation you make somewhere in your work between the "sadistic East" and the "masochistic West"?

FALUDY: Yes. Yes. Yes. They have no shame, the sadistic East. The Greeks in the fifth century invented lyric poetry with names. That means not anonymous lyrics. They invented free opinion. Look at Aristophanes who placed the tyrant Cleon in his play and was not afraid to satirize him. On the other side is China and Russia and so on, where the dictator is recognized as a great man even if he murders. They were not always free in Europe. But there has always been a desire for this liberty. In China you don't find it. When Andre Malraux went to China and spoke to his old friend, Chou En

Lai — this is in Malraux' memoir — he said you made this revolution because you wanted liberty. Chou En Lai says we have in Chinese no word for freedom. There's no word, no expression for it. I read this. This is not my invention.

T: When you came to the Hungarian border in 1946, did the border guard really say, "Americans, Nazis, it's all the same"?

FALUDY: Yes, that was their view.

T: After you were arrested there, you wrote a poem about being told you would die in the morning. Can you recall those circumstances?

FALUDY: Yes. At the headquarters of the secret police, you got a different secret policeman every two weeks. If you sign everything he needs on the first day, you can talk with him for thirteen days about anything. One gives me poems to read. He says that his nephew wrote them. What do I say about them? I take them with me. It was a big bunch of them. I was very happy. You had three planks and never anything under your head. Now I had a pillow for two days.

The next time I go up to him I see that he is so nervous. It's as if he would be my prisoner and I would be the secret police. I knew why. He asked me how did I like the poems? So I said, "Well, your nephew is writing rather decadent poems." I said he should tell his nephew to discontinue writing those counter-revolutionary poems which have no poetic value. He got pale. He asked the guard to take me away. Then it came. The order that I would be executed.

There was a sulfuric acid tub at the end of the corridor. Occasionally you heard people being taken down the hall, but not pushed. They seemed to be lifeless. Beaten up so that they were unconcious. They opened a door, then you heard a horrible cry. But just one and nothing more. And after six, seven seconds — I counted — you could smell a sulfuric acid smell. If somebody confessed and they were of no other use, they beat him half to death and threw him in the sulfuric acid. He died in a few seconds. It is a horrible death. You are carbonizing.

T: Didn't it occur to you, when you got this man's poetry, to say that it was good?

FALUDY: No. Because it had no sense to court them. They had no power. They were zeros. There is no heritage of things like this in Canada, I believe. Which is a good thing.

T: Do you ever sit in this room now, with your birds, and feel amazement that you have survived?

FALUDY: Yes. Very often. It was twenty-four times, I think, that I had the chance to die. So in this sense I am very lucky.

T: After all this your friends convinced you to come to Canada, telling you there was a job teaching here, even though there was no job. How long did it take before you knew you were glad to be here?

FALUDY: Quite soon. I liked something which takes everyone immediately, and that is the libraries. Here you can get everything. I have seen people standing in a five-hundred-yard queue to get into the Bibliotheque Nationale in Paris, standing for six or eight hours just to get in once. After this, Canada. Its kindness. Its open arms. Canada is incredible. You see this anthology? How long could I live in France, two hundred years? Before I get in a series of modern French poets. It is out of the question. Impossible in any other country. Including even the United States.

Here is different. Imagine I have a lecture in Marseilles. I don't have money to go. So I go to the French ministry of culture and ask them for the money for the train fare. When they hear this, the undersecretary would take the telephone and ask the police to come with a straitjacket. Because I'm insane! Even in the United States if I am invited to lecture in San Francisco, I would get fifty dollars for the lecture. The ticket from Washington says six hundred dollars. So I cannot do it. This is the only country in the world where I can phone Ottawa and say I need two tickets to Vancouver for a lecture. And they don't even ask what is the subject of the lecture.

I like to live in countries which you can leave. Without anybody asking. I felt this the first time when I was crossing the bridge at Niagara Falls to enter the US. We didn't stop at Canadian customs. We only waved to the Canadians. I said, "That's good." That you can leave.

T: What about drawbacks?

FALUDY: The only trouble is that where you have this freedom you don't feel poetry so much anymore. Here I would stand up and say something and everybody would listen politely. In Hungary everybody would listen and follow the poem until the police arrest me. Even now in Hungary, which has eight million inhabitants, a quite unknown poet will be published in fifteen thousand copies.

Poetry, freedom. It is like air. You know you must have it only when it is taken away from you.

Brian Fawcett

BRIAN FAWCETT was born in Prince George, BC in 1944. In 1965 he came to Vancouver to attend Simon Fraser University. He founded a small magazine called *NMFG* (No Money From Government) and published seven books of poetry. His first collection of short stories, *My Career with the Leafs and Other Stories* (1982) mined his memories of boyhood in

Prince George. *Capital Tales* (1984) explored violence and a range of storytelling techniques. *The Secret Journal of Alexander Mackenzie and Other Stories* (1985) reports in fiction the exploitation of BC's hinterlands and identifies the "global village" invasion in psychological and economic terms. *Cambodia: A Book For People Who Find Television Too Slow* (1986) contains one inclusive essay and thirteen wide-ranging stories that reveal the importance of history and memory in the face of increasing global violence and mass communications systems.

Brian Fawcett lives in Vancouver. He was interviewed in 1985.

T: Reading your stories it occurred to me I could put together a book of interviews that uses the premise that I'm an undercover government agent, filing reports, with mug shots of each writer. As if good writers are necessarily enemies of the state.

FAWCETT: Good idea. I think it's appropriate.

T: Perhaps all good fiction writers are in some sort of undefined Resistance.

FAWCETT: Yes. And it's a very peculiar Resistance, isn't it? It's interesting you bring that metaphor up because the first real world topic I became fascinated by as an adolescent was the Spanish Civil War. I always regarded those big battles in World War Two as somebody else's war. I preferred armies like the Spanish Loyalist Army, which was undermanned and being attacked by forces that were much more powerful.

This may have something to do with what got documented in *The Secret Journal*. I see the area that I grew up in around Prince George as being in essentially the same historical position as the Spanish Loyalist Army. The people who lived and live there who ought to be in charge, aren't. And they're losing. They're being defeated every day.

T: In a nutshell, if you had to identify the enemy for you as a Resistance writer, is it the global village?

FAWCETT: Yes.

T: Have you read Marshall Macluhan?

FAWCETT: Oh, yes. Where I really began to understand how far it had gone was when I went to Cassiar, BC, an asbestos mining town of about twenty-five hundred people up near the Yukon border. It's been there for about twenty-five years. It's a settled and peculiarly urban community, all in trailers. They have a satellite dish hooked into Atlanta, Georgia.

When I went up to Cassiar I saw what was going on and I decided I would play the role of the Martian anthropologist. It's one of the devices I use quite a lot, pretending I've just landed from Mars. I started by going to the local supermarket to see what the hell was going on. It had all the latest tapes and posters of Michael Jackson and Boy George. All sorts of international, Los Angeles, global village paraphernalia. I wanted to buy a Cassiar souvenir. The one thing they had was a T-shirt saying WHERE THE HELL IS CASSIAR, BC?. The T-shirts are made someplace else with the words WHERE THE HELL IS already on them. Then they stick in the place name. I've seen the same T-shirts in other small towns. It's like these people have a built-in contempt for where they are.

T: Why were you in Cassiar?

FAWCETT: I went up there to do a reading, ironically, for National Book Festival. At the public library I found they had three thousand hardback American novels. And not one Canadian book. Nothing. Then I went to the school library to read. It took the kids forty minutes to realize I wasn't Michael Jackson and that I was okay even though I was from BC. Because they'd been watching television from Atlanta for the last four years, they didn't understand what I was or what I was supposed to be. I noticed there weren't many books in the school library but the librarian said I was missing the point. "Come and see our video library."

The video library was larger than the book library. I said, "Can you show me any materials on Cassiar?" I wanted to see what they taught their students about the place they lived in. The librarian looked at me like I really had just landed from Mars!

T: And how did your reading go?

FAWCETT: It was during the NHL play-offs and there was a game that night. None of the locals came. But all these miners came from isolated mines that didn't have satellite dishes. They'd heard a real writer was coming. They put on this big spread with twenty-five bottles of wine and what they thought was a fancy Vancouver-style cheese platter. There were maybe forty people there and it was one of the smartest audiences I've ever read for. Then, at the break, they drank all twenty-five bottles of wine in fifteen minutes. Not one person touched the cheese. I had fun that night. I *liked* these people. I sold about fifty books. It wasn't because I was particularly brilliant. I think it was because I was real. I had a material body. There was a party afterwards. When we got there a big Newfoundland dog bowled me over and started licking my face. The Newfie ended up getting the cheese platter, actually.

T: Do you worry that your Martian anthropologist ends up editorializing too much in your stories?

FAWCETT: Waving my hands in the reader's face is a long-time weakness. I get pressure from both sides about this. People wanting me to go straight, and other who recognize why I'm doing it. There's a conventional expectation that eventually real writers have to write a novel and of course if I write a novel I can't be waving my hands in the reader's face constantly. But I don't want to write a novel. Because I don't want to allow my readers into the fantasy of fiction. Then they lose the world, which is full of authors of one sort or another, hiding behind the sets and manipulating people. It's time literature stopped doing that.

T: Michel Tremblay says the same thing about his plays. You always have to remind the audience that in fact they're sitting in chairs.

FAWCETT: And that's partly why I don't want to write a novel. If you look at where the novel comes from, it's was

meant to be read to semi-literate people in the nineteenth century. When there was nothing else to do. It was written to stretch out the story. Well, we have more efficient forms of entertainment now. Also, when I started writing stories seriously in 1981, I'd spent fifteen years as a poet. I had no narrative skills. I acquired them quite fast but the truth is I don't think I have the skills to write a conventional novel.

T: You'd done at least seven books of poetry. Then you switched to exclusively writing fiction. What happened?

FAWCETT: I bought a computer! And just before that, I'd written the title story to *My Career with the Leafs*. That story came directly from a dream I had. It was one of those dreams that told me something about my personality and about the power of invention. I sensed I'd stumbled onto a goldmine.

T: What about the part of that story where you're being interviewed by Howie Meeker between periods and you confess to him you're really a poet?

FAWCETT: That came later. That was a conscious invention. But the walking into Maple Leaf Gardens and not being able to skate, and not hiding it at all, that was dreamed. That dream didn't make myself me out to be a superstar. I wrote the first draft and I thought, holy shit, I've told the truth here in a very peculiar way. The reason it works is because it follows the logic of dream. A part of me said, hey, I can make up stuff! Until that point I didn't think I could or should. I didn't think I was allowed to. So I discovered something about writing. I also discovered I really enjoyed it.

T: But why did you allow yourself to trust the Maple Leaf dream enough to bother writing it down?

FAWCETT: Because I was tired of the horrible seriousness of poetry.

T: Stan Persky is another writer who made a decision to stop writing poetry.

Because he questioned his effect on the world.

FAWCETT: Yes. There's absolutely no audience for poetry. We live in a country that has created an amateur poetry. It's amateur in that it makes no attempt to come to terms with its readership. As a result it has destroyed its audience. For me, though, there was also a purely personal dimension. I was thirty-eight or thirty-nine and I'd spent fifteen years in the laboratory of poetry storing up experiences to write about, and sometimes creating them so I'd have something to be sad about. I was exhausted. I realized I couldn't do this forever. I also realized I was becoming suspicious about why I was doing it — for the self-drama of howling at a bad world. And I realized the character that my poetry presented was not really very much like me. I came off as the most serious poet in human history.

T: Well, I think you'd have a few competitors...

FAWCETT: Well, the point was, or is, that the way I see the world and the way I am as a social being is not terribly serious. I'm a joker. Somehow I just couldn't be that way with poetry. The stories suddenly gave me a more true range of expression. To exercise my sense of humour. To exercise my sense of absurdity. To exercise my love of facts.

T: You were teaching in prisons around that time.

FAWCETT: That's another important factor. I was trying to communicate out what civilization was to people who had no idea that they were living in a civilization with meaningful traditions and values. I regard civilization as those procedures by which we avoid violence. I was trying to find some way to communicate civilization to these guys who really just wanted to talk about their feelings. I felt vulnerable because I

realized I had spent fifteen years myself trying to talk about my own feelings — in a slightly more sophisticated way perhaps but nonetheless it was the same... I would get up at 5:30 in the morning, drive to Agassiz, teach a four-hour class, teach a three-hour class in the afternoon, drive back to Vancouver, walk in the door, turn on the computer and start working for three or four hours. It was an insane schedule.

T: It's interesting because so many of your stories are so clearly intellectual responses to violence.

FAWCETT: Yes. A lot of them do begin with the fact of violence. I try to discover where the violence came from and where it leads to. I grew up in a very violent environment and I think I understand violence instinctually. I spent most of my youth avoiding punches thrown at my head.

T: One story, "A Brief Romance," examines violence and infers there's a sexual element to a fistfight. What's the story behind that story?

FAWCETT: God knows how many fights I'd seen up there but that one stuck in my head. It struck me as a paradigm of a whole range of activity. I mean, of repressed homosexuality and authority. As far as I'm concerned homosexuality is just fine. But repressed homosexuality is a big problem. Because what it leads to is authoritarian behaviour. And to violence.

T: So backtracking a bit. *My Career with the Leafs* was basically going back to your past, scratching the surface, finding gold back there.

FAWCETT: Right.

T: And the second book, *Capital Tales*, seems like an in-between book, one where you're feeling your oats, figuring out what you can do.

FAWCETT: Yes. *Capital Tales* is really an investigation of fiction. I was figuring out how to sort out the categories of fiction. Some of the stories succeed and some of them don't. I'm really fond of that book because of that. I have a sentimental attachment to it.

T: And then you seem to be hitting your stride in *The Secret Journal of Alexander Mackenzie*. You know more what you're saying and why you want to say it.

FAWCETT: Yes, I wanted it to be a psycho-economic history of the northern interior of BC. There was a history of Prince George done in 1944 and the last history of northern BC was written back in the twenties or something. So in a certain sense my book is a psycho-economic history from 1793 to 1987. It's tracing the consequences of Mackenzie's vision as the first white explorer.

T: So Alexander Mackenzie triggered all this?

FAWCETT: No. The book has a very peculiar genesis. I went up with my father to Northern Alberta where he grew up. We were trying to find a number of sites like the coal mine he had worked in in 1929. That sort of thing. We had an incredible winning streak. Everything we looked for, we found. We found the site of the sawmill he had worked at in 1923. My father had left home to work at age fourteen. We were also looking for this place called Fawcett, Alberta. It turned out the name had nothing to do with our family but watching my father's face as he found all these places, well, I think that started the book. He had both a hunger for meaningful history and a contempt for it.

T: Your father eventually became a businessman in Prince George?

FAWCETT: Yes. I grew up in a solid Social Credit background. I grew up in the back of an ice cream plant, actually ice cream and soft drinks. The incident in my book about the dairy owner being forced out of business by a larger corporation is pretty closely based on some events around 1964–65. Not to mention names, but a well-known dairy corporation came into Prince George and told my father they were going to bury him if he didn't sell to them. My father did, because his view of it was that progress is progress.

T: Whereas your view is that often progress isn't.

FAWCETT: We've lived through the period of the most astonishing wealth in human history, and probably the most astonishing levels of material wealth the human race is ever going to experience, and what have we done with it? Not very much.

Most people are leading lives of comfortable misery. Yes, they've got their television sets. Yes, they've got the amenities of the global village. But the quality of life hasn't got that much better. I do not see this as a happy culture. And rather than be bitter or cynical about it, I'm angry. Mostly at the misuse of wealth.

We can't just run around ripping off our resources. We're running out of timber, you know. And we can't say let's save everything either. Logging is a necessary activity. That's how we make money in this province. So how do we renew that resource? How we live in this province for the next two hundred years?

There, I'm getting angry.

T: Most people might not be comfortable with these issues being reflected in fiction . . .

FAWCETT: Right. My response to that criticism is Christ, if all you want out of literature is that nice, brief, warm feeling, why don't you just go and pee the bed? First-rate literature comes from first-rate content. In other words, take the most difficult, most important thing you can find — which is rarely going to be the way you feel about the sun and the moon and the stars — and take a grab at it. That's what I tried to do with *Secret Journal*.

T: Are you writing from any particular ideological base these days?

FAWCETT: Not really. It seems to me that ideology will simply generate problems and confrontations in a binary fashion. I'm trying to look at problems and work out problems as a situationalist. I'm a social democrat, politically. I believe in social democracy. But more because it's inevitable than because I think it might guarantee social justice. We're stuck with it as the only humane alternative open to us. As opposed to continuing along with the capitalist jamboree. The capitalist jamboree is simply going to get us all killed. Or else separate us all so far from each other that we'll never get back to community.

When it comes right down to it, I guess, once again, what I'm basically trying to do is avoid violence.

Timothy Findley

TIMOTHY FINDLEY was born in Toronto in 1930. His first career as an actor caused him to travel widely and to write for the theatre and television. His work is consistently haunted by images of civilization gone mad. *The Last of the Crazy People* (1967) and *The Butterfly Plague* (1969) led to his Governor General's Award–winning *The Wars* (1977), a brilliant depiction

of a sensitive nineteen-year-old Canadian officer in World War One. An audacious political spy novel about fascism and elitism in World War Two, *Famous Last Words* (1981), was followed by an even more audacious rewriting of the Noah's ark myth, *Not Wanted on the Voyage* (1984), Findley's most "difficult" novel, in which deeply felt environmental concerns are matched by the darkness of his imagination. *The Telling of Lies* (1986), is a sublime mystery set in Maine that exposes the extent to which people with power lie insidiously through politics and media.

Timothy Findley lives on a farm in Cannington, Ontario. He was interviewed in 1984.

T: There's something about your work that resists analysis. You're an explorer and not an explainer. To try and enforce analytical ideas on your explorations seems to be not in keeping with the spirit of what you do.

FINDLEY: That's dead right. I'm not an explainer. I am very much an explorer. I don't make the map before I go. I'm not sitting down saying, "This time I'm going to do this." It's all a question of recognition on my part. Trusting the inner thing, whether it's instinct or whatever it is you're trusting. I have to trust what I'm hearing or seeing, or what is there, and believe that in putting it down it is going to take the book further into the jungle. Or out the other side. Or however you want to express exploring.

Sometimes I find I'm writing scenes and I have no idea where they're going. Absolutely no idea. Why am I doing this? A good example in *Not Wanted on the Voyage* is the scene where Noah asks his son to bring Mrs. Noyes on deck to talk to her. She comes up and what happens is she gives him the recipe for a quiche. All of which sounds dumb, really dumb. But in fact it turned out to be a key scene. It has been a great joy to me to discover that's what I've got to do, what I would call being obedient to the instinct to go and open that door, having no idea what is beyond. You've got to trust that it will pay off.

T: Was there a point in your career where you suddenly gained the freedom to trust in that way? Where you lost the sense of an invisible editor standing over your shoulder?

FINDLEY: No, the editor has always been there. The editor is still there. The editor is still a very fearful person saying, "Don't. Don't do this. Don't go in there." But I think what happens is you suddenly realize that in having done the thing that you were fearful of doing, or the thing that you thought

might be meaningless, it reaches other people. When the whole journey is over and it's paying off for them you decide, "Yes. Go more often in that direction. Be less afraid." I think maybe that happened after *The Wars*.

T: To come all that way is a voyage in itself.

FINDLEY: Indeed. And a very long one!

T: Margaret Laurence, in her introduction to *Can You See Me Yet?*, wrote that no true artist should be didactic. One place you didn't refrain from didacticism was in your introduction to the story, "Sometime Later, Not Now."

FINDLEY: Yes. "We are the children of such-and-such an age..."

T: "...We grew up protected from subtlety. We were quiet and with good reason. We knew the big things. Life and Death. But none of the small things. The best we knew was how to be still and quiet. Which meant that we learned excessively not to know ourselves."

I gather that's something quite personal.

FINDLEY: Oh, it is. It's a very personal story. And not for me one of the better ones. I was telling too much precisely as it was, instead of letting it be digested and coming out as fiction. But under some circumstances that would be a very interesting thing to say of the children of the period. Because it was like that. It was that terrible, terrible period of McCarthyism. Everybody felt it. Anybody making noises was... Well, the thing about fiction is that you must learn not to say that. But to show it. I didn't trust that enough. I wanted so much to have people understand the real tragedy that had gone on in that character's life.

T: Those first four stories in *Dinner along the Amazon* are all about loss. About inexplicable loss. For instance, the boy in "War" throws rocks at his father, feeling somehow betrayed because his father is going off to war. Did you lose your father to the war? And did you feel that way?

FINDLEY: Oh, very much in the same way. Absolutely. I say this kindly. I don't mean this meanly. I'm not seeking revenge on my father when I say this. Because towards the end of his life we had a wonderful relationship — how I hate that word — but at that time when I was kid I really did hate him. I'll never forget the day he learned he was going overseas. This was very late in 1943. He was home on leave. In Canada you got leave every eight weeks or so. And the thing that I always got to do was polish the buttons. When he got the phone call saying to go overseas with the next shipment of troops, he jumped up and down on the bed like a child.

I can still feel what it was like in that room, sitting there, with him doing this. It was in the morning. He was sleeping in. I was seeing this grown-up doing this extraordinary thing and thinking, in whatever way a child would think, "You son-of-a-bitch. You can't wait to get away from us." I'm not sure if that was his feeling at all. But it seemed like, "Hallelujah, I don't ever have to see you again. I'm going away to die." Or, "I'm escaping. I'm going on this great thing without you." It was awful. Oh, it was awful!

T: Do you think you transferred some of that tension to *Not Wanted on the Voyage*? Where the anti-life forces are controlled by the father? And the pro-life forces are the realm of the mother?

FINDLEY: I know what you're saying, but no. I think what happens when you're first writing is that you deal with the feelings that are most there. Those get eaten up, or digested. Then you're exploring deeper. The figures in the fiction become larger and extend further into the real world. So I'm thinking more of President Reagan and the Ayotollah Khoemeini when I'm writing Noah. Not my father.

T: In *Not Wanted on the Voyage* there's a line, "cruelty was fear and nothing more." I took that as a reiteration of something you said in *Dinner along the Amazon*, "That was the basis of it, fear, partly distrust and a sort of mythical distrust of the women because of menstruation." Do you feel that much of the violence — the violence which we have to learn to detest in order to keep the species on the planet — is basically coming from those sexual tensions?

FINDLEY: Absolutely. Absolutely.

T: How much?

FINDLEY: Not all. But a lot of it does. You see the manifestations of sexual fears every day. When a large group of men is confronted by the image of a woman walking through a bar, for instance. They all immediately have to do something very male. They all have to pay attention. They're forced to pay attention to her. And they must make sure that each of the other men knows that they're paying attention. I find that very disturbing and also somewhat sad.

I think there are repulsive things about men in groups but there are also wonderfully touching and amazing things about men in groups that women will never know. Men and women have so many walls between them. I was going to say we're pulling down all the wrong walls, but the fact is — *all* the walls are wrong. All the walls have got to go. The problem is we're concentrating on walls already down, forgetting there are walls still up there that no one is dealing with. One of walls still up there is the inability of some men — and a lot of women — to see men as truly sympathetic in terms of their terrible loneliness. Women have loneliness but it's not the same kind. And there are these dreadful assumptions that some people make that it's just terrific to be a man. We're missing that, too. Because it isn't. So to try and put all this into the context of your question . . .

T: It's a gigantic question.

FINDLEY: Sure. Is sex the problem? Yes, it is. It is the problem but it expresses itself in funny angular ways that people are not dealing with yet. These things go on being problems because we think, "Okay, if we make everybody equal, that's the end of it." Bullshit. To be male is still to be male. And to be female is still to be female. When men and women have reached the stage where they understand their equality lies in their human-ness — when the man can say, "We are all human. But I'm not like you. I'm male," it will be different. Maybe we have to get rid of the word *manhood*. It's done a lot of damage to both men and women. I don't know why, but I always associate the word manhood with killing.

But, about being male: it's like a wonderful confrontation between a white woman and a black woman on a television program. The white woman, with *dreadful* condescension, says to the black woman, "But my dear, I understand, and I've always understood, that you're just like me." And the black woman says, "But honey, you don't understand. I'm not like you at all. I'm *black*!"

T: Did you have any pre-formed ideas about treating sexuality on the ark before you went on the *Voyage*?

FINDLEY: No. At the same time I knew that sex and the sexes were an immensely important part of the story.

T: I can see a logical leap from *The Wars* and *Famous Last Words* to *Not Wanted on the Voyage*. You're extrapolating some of the same conflicts

onto a more universal, timeless scale.

FINDLEY: But only you know that. I don't. I agree with you now, after it's over. But I didn't know that while I was doing it. I didn't have the assurance of knowing, yes, B does follow A. I only knew I'm writing *this*. There were moments when I thought, "I won't write this book for anybody else. I'll finish it and I'll keep it because no one else is going to want this book. It's so crazy." I would think that and mean that.

At the same time the floor had been established from which reality said I wouldn't get away with that, you've got to publish this book. Share this experience and these people. So I had that kind of insecurity all the way through. The faeries, for instance. You can imagine the problem of struggling with how you control the subject of the faeries. "How do you keep this from being laughable?" There's such a fine line between the acceptable and the grotesque.

T: And controlling the violence, too.

FINDLEY: Yes, that's right. Sometimes you find yourself saying, "Oh, God, here we go again. Another horror is about to unfold under your pen." But some writer, I can't remember who, once said something to the effect that all writers really only have one or two things to say. You play with variations on a theme. And that made me feel better.

T: So to write well, you accept your compulsions?

FINDLEY: Yes. Exactly. Period.

T: You once said, "I'm a very violent person myself inside. I'm sure I'm more violent in my heart and mind than half the people I criticize for being overtly violent. And that makes me hyper-sensitive to what violence is about."

FINDLEY: Yes.

T: So have you reached a point in your private life where you cease to worry that you have these thoughts in your mind? for the sake of being productive as an artist?

FINDLEY: Yes. I think that seesaw battle is settled now. Settled on the side of accepting.

T: That's an unusual path to health.

FINDLEY: Yes. If I could only give this in a very succinct way...

T: Give it in an un-succinct way.

FINDLEY: This thing about where do things go if you don't deal with them. They go down. And they don't go away. They just go down and become more and more trouble. There is a fear that I have in the darker moments of thinking about these things that letting them become the stuff of all your thought can't be healthy. This is the trouble with being a writer. Your mind works like that. I sometimes find myself thinking, "What happens if I lose control of it? If I lose control of all that fury?" At the end of writing *Not Wanted on the Voyage* I felt rage. It's the only word I can use to describe the feeling. So is there some dreadful kind of "other thing" one would do other than pick up the pen? At its worst, this is the kind of fear that you can have.

How do I say this? Other people sat in their living rooms and watched the TV news recently and saw hundreds of caribou drowning in a river up north somewhere. It was so ghastly. But what was *more* ghastly was the image of people standing in front of the cameras calmly saying, "*We* didn't have anything to do with this massacre; these silly beasts didn't know what they were doing walking into the water." At its worst, at such moments, I really want every machine gun in the world. And that's what I mean about the violence being terribly, terribly real in me. Pray God one wouldn't do anything. But the *thought* is there.

The pages don't stop it. So how do you stop it? There. That's the thing I wish I could be more succinct about.

T: I happened to read *Not Wanted on the Voyage* directly after reading Farley Mowat's book *Sea of Slaughter*.

FINDLEY: Oh, Christ. I can't bear to read it. I don't mean I'm so sensitive, don't touch me, I'll fall over. I just mean that in my mind I've already seen all that and I can't bear to look at it again. But I admire him immensely for writing it.

To be clearer still about this, I have to point out how many people there are who write — ostensibly about "the truth" — in terms of what's going on in the war against the environment and against whatever else is alive in this world — how many of these people are either fudging the truth through lack of professional research — or simply lying through their teeth. Mowat deals with this fact in his work.

T: This business of ignorance and culpability is huge. We like to say, "Oh, they knew all about the holocaust, those Germans." And yet we also say, "Oh, we didn't know anything about Oppenheimer making the bomb."

FINDLEY: Yes, and we didn't know. And so it is possible — yes — that *some* Germans really didn't know about the Holocaust. On the other hand, the Bomb was an underground thing: a secret. The Holocaust could be *seen*. I think to become aware of how dire things can happen, you have to allow a certain amount of paranoia. For instance, during the Holocaust, if only more people had said, "Where are all *my* friends and neighbours?" it might have helped. Good God in heaven, when large numbers of people begin to disappear, isn't there something wrong if you don't become alarmed? Did you hear about the botulisms that were being purchased by a government agency in Ontario? Someone has been buying these horrific poisonous organisms on the sly. Some government people have been arrested. They've been purchasing them somewhere in the States where they create these things in order to conduct scientific research. It can only mean they are doing illegal explorations of mutations of these poisons. *Why? Why? Why could it be? How?* How can these people have access to these things? What does it mean? Why are they fooling around with mutations in botulisms — which is how you poison people and animals with food? Why are they playing around with this at all? Why is there a place they can go and buy these things? Is it better to sit back and say, "Well, that's an interesting story. And when they catch these guys we'll find out what it's about. And we will believe what they tell us"? Or is it better to say, "Something's crazy here." And stop it from continuing. Well, fortunately it looks as if they have been apprehended and stopped in the botulism case.

T: If you follow up on your instincts and say, "What are you doing about those botulisms?" or if you go outside and scream, "They're killing the caribou" you can easily become like one of your crazed characters, a character who has to do something Quixotic and saint-like and awful in order to alert the rest of us about authority and denying our instincts.

FINDLEY: Exactly. And I don't want to be that person. But I know what you're saying. Turning off the instincts. Silencing them is what most people manage to do. That's what they prefer to do.

T: I once saw a photo of you that was taken alongside your pond. You were wearing gum boots. Like Dr. Doolittle. That's the image I had of the author of *Not Wanted on the Voyage* as I read it.

FINDLEY: I'm afraid I can't quite talk to the animals — yet. But they can certainly talk to me. And they do!

That environment where I live feeds me every single day. Whenever I stop writing I go out into that world very much on purpose to be nourished. In fact, if you analyze the terrain in *Not Wanted on the Voyage*, it's Canadian. Noah's hill is in Southern Ontario. When you walk down our hill to the wood, it's that very same walk. So far there has been no recognition that as a place, that landscape is not an exotic biblical landscape, or an African landscape. It is a place with split rail fences and stone walls.

T: And Noah's ark was a Canadian barn. . .

FINDLEY: Oh, yes. The barn we have is quite an extraordinary barn. We've painted it blue. Everybody now loves that barn in the district. They all use it as a landmark because it's on a corner. "Turn left at the blue barn." It has immense haylofts. It has the traditional cathedral-type shape with slatted light coming in, in winter and summer. Down underneath is where the animals are. There are two hundred cattle, a lot of pigs and horses. There used to be sheep. As well as infinite numbers of mice and rats and cats and raccoons.

It became my ark. It really did. I spent a whole night there just so I could listen in the dark. It's wonderful to go in the dark with all those creatures. To be in their darkness. Which we never allow. Being us, being humans, we inevitably light the lamp or follow a flashlight. But the animals — they just stand there — or lie there in the dark. And therefore everything that happens in the darkness is something we should go back and experience and explore. Darkness puts us us in touch with certain "things" in us that otherwise will remain unknown and therefore untapped. For instance, I've never been afraid of the dark unless I think there are people there. Nature's darkness doesn't frighten me.

T: Of all the animals, it was your blind cat, Mottyl, that was most in touch with "things."

FINDLEY: Absolutely. Mottyl, the cat, was really our own cat Mottle, named because of her mottled colouring. She was a calico cat. I wanted a name that would sound biblical but at the same time wouldn't be too cut off from the present. Mottyl is important in the book because Mottyl had the last real glimpses of the "real" world. Any human eye would have embroidered what was in memory, because that's the human capacity, whereas the cat saw exactly what was. But what was there was nonetheless something different from the human memory.

T: Faeries and demons and unicorns.

FINDLEY: Yes, they used to be in our minds...

T: But scientific realism has killed them.

FINDLEY: And also the possibility that we might ever think like that again. It seems to me that by removing ourselves from nature we're losing our imaginations. The creative way of looking at things instead of the passive or destructive way. The other day I was looking out the window and noticed how the cows walking towards the pond suddenly appeared to be Oriental. I wrote something to Graeme Gibson about the cattle being Japanese and how wonderful that was. Just the very dainty way they walked. I was standing at the kitchen sink and the view from the window became a kind of ancient Japanese print.

Just look out the window at nature. Stop killing that. It's all we have.

For me, I love Mrs. Noyes praying to the river. Why not? Pray to everything that is. If God is really everywhere — as some people claim — then why not pray to God through rivers, trees and animals? God isn't somewhere out of sight. At least not my god. And not the god of Mrs. Noyes. That god exists in everything that breathes. The trouble is we're beating everything that breathes to death.

D.M. Fraser

D.M. FRASER was born in New Glasgow, Nova Scotia in 1946. He was raised in Glace Bay, Nova Scotia and came to Vancouver in 1967. He left university to develop an astonishingly original prose style and to publish his first book of critically acclaimed short stories, *Class Warfare* (1974), with Pulp Press, a loose literary and left-wing collective. A gentle habitue

of east-side Vancouver bars, Fraser transcribed the soft-core apocalypse in writing binges that culminated in his brilliant second collection, *The Voice of Emma Sachs* (1983). He died in 1985 in Vancouver. A posthumous third book, *D.M. Fraser The Collected Works: Volume I Prelude* (1988) has been followed by a biographical memoir by Stephen Osborne, *Ithaca: Remembering D.M. Fraser* (1987).

D.M. (Donald Murray) Fraser resides in literary heaven alongside Malcolm Lowry, singing in the highest choirs. He was interviewed in 1983.

T: What were the circumstances surrounding the publication of your first book, *Class Warfare*?

FRASER: That was '74. Pulp Press had been in business two years. I knew the original guys at UBC. Steve Osborne was in graduate school when I was. He was working for a company with a typesetting machine. He did one book all by himself. At some point he said to me, well, it's about time we did one of yours.

T: Did you ever finish your English degree?

FRASER: No. I decided writing and working at Pulp Press was a lot more interesting than working with academics. I made a conscious choice to do the things I like doing. Writing is one of the things I like doing. So *Class Warfare* changed a lot of things for me.

T: Becoming a writer.

FRASER: Yes. When I was growing up in a small town in Nova Scotia, the notion that one could be a real, live writer was totally absurd. Being a writer was always something that other people did. It was a nice thing to fantasize about, or it was a nice hobby, but it was an inconceivable occupation. I was supposed to be a university professor.

T: What was your family background?

FRASER: Perfectly ordinary.

T: Meaning?

FRASER: My father was a Presbyterian minister. My mother was an English teacher. I'm a Nova Scotian Scot Presbyterian on both sides by ancestry, but not by conviction. Our household was fairly paradoxically conservative and progressive at once. I could read anything I wanted. Marx and Freud were available to me at an early age. There was no genteel censorship going on when it came to ideas. It was an intelligent household. We'd go for Sunday drives and get poetry recited. English Romantic poetry.

T: Maybe one day you can do a takeoff on Flaubert's *Sentimental Education*.

FRASER: That's interesting you should mention that. I've been working on and off on an essay of sorts describing my peculiar influences. It's called *A Literary Education*. Flaubert's book inspired it. Mine was an extremely sentimental education. It turned me into the kind of mushball I am now. Blame it all on that!

T: Were you "the small boy with the big ears and the precocious vocabulary"?

FRASER: I was indeed precisely that creature.

T: When did you start realizing you didn't want to be respectable and orthodox like a good Nova Scotian Scot?

FRASER: About the age of ten. But I kept playing the game for an awful long time. I still do. When I go back there to visit. But it's getting a little harder to bring off now. In fact, it's so extremely hard to pull off that I don't think anyone expects it anymore. but I go through the motions.

T: This is Glace Bay we're talking about.

FRASER: Yes, Glace Bay. The best four years of my life were spent there. We moved to Glace Bay when I was about thirteen. I went to high school there. I love the place. I go back there every year. I belong to the Nova Scotia Writer's Union. I regard myself as a Nova Scotian in exile.

T: That's also where Hugh MacLennan was born.

FRASER: Yes. His house is gone now and they've turned the beautiful property into a Kentucky Ernie's or something.

T: Why couldn't you be a respectable professor and live an orthodox life?

FRASER: Because I get too much

pleasure out of the alternatives.

T: Is that why you came to Vancouver? For the alternatives?

FRASER: I was a coward. This was the farthest away I could get and still stay in Canada. When I was twenty I had an offer to go to UCLA but the thought of moving to Los Angeles scared me. I had one of those scholarships you could take anywhere and do anything with. I picked Vancouver because it was far away and because I also had a romantic thing about the mountains. My father had been out here and told me stories. I grew up with a postcard image of the last frontier.

T: There's freedom here to be an individual certainly. It's not formalized.

FRASER: Yes. Toronto has no appeal. New York was too close to home. To a large extent, my expectations of Vancouver were met. It did turn out to be a place where you could create your own identity and do your own thing, as we used to say. You could experiment. It was just that point in the sixties when being weird was no longer an isolated and lonely activity. That's why I've always had nostalgia for that period.

T: Would you agree you're on the fringe of society looking in?

FRASER: Well, it depends entirely on the kind of society I happen to be looking in on.

T: But you once told me you hate going into the west side of the city.

FRASER: I just don't share the concerns of those people. If they have any. I feel like a trespasser. It's not really a matter of being intimidated, it's a matter of having to be on one's guard. It's that world that I can't intuit. In what I think of as my own turf, I can get inside people's minds with a great deal more ease. In a world where I don't understand what they want, why they want it, what they

enjoy, I have anxiety.

T: Is this where the story "Dumbo Nelson" comes in? "When I get off the bus at Merridale Yard, I find it impossible not to picture convicts at their enforced recreation there, exercising, listlessly tossing a volleyball around because they have to"?

FRASER: The actual False Creek place that I went to for that story was one of the low income units that they have for their token indigents. I wasn't there for more than an hour. And I walked home through the development. I began to fantasize about who lived in the tonier apartments. I just invented it. Then I realized I had invented a character of whom I had no intuitive understanding or sympathy for. I began to feel guilty about that. Whey shouldn't I be able to understand? I'd like to work in this area some more. Sometimes I think that story has the desire to become a novel.

T: How do you think bourgeois readers would respond to "The purpose of all art is irrelevance"? Would they realize that can be construed as an attack on their values?

FRASER: A lot of them would understand that from making a show of patronizing and responding to art. Art which is absolutely guaranteed not to disturb their sleep. It's clever and entertaining and harmless in a way that I suppose Valium is harmless. It calms their nerves. They all do things that they probably don't like very much to make the money that allows them to live as they do. I don't begrudge them. But I like art to be extremely unnerving and moving. Some of my stories are funny but I want them to hurt a bit, too. I want you to be moved. But then I'm the sort of person who will go to a comedy movie and cry.

T: But you never manipulate your reader with crises, like, say, the way a pop movie does.

FRASER: No, it's done in the form of a telegram. That is, ideally what I want is for people to fill in all the things that aren't in there for themselves. This is the code, these are the clues, you write the story in your head. You use whatever materials you have from your experience. Interpret it, expand it, change it. If I put it all in there, I'm loading the dice. But I don't sit there calculating effects. There's very little premeditation in what I write.

T: So you're writing in a purely expressive state.

FRASER: But I do polish and revise afterwards. Let's just say it's a relief to have only the typewriter to talk to. It doesn't talk back. I'm not very good at communicating with people. And conversation doesn't give you the opportunity to revise, or to pace around for an hour. You can't have three voices going on at once when you've only got one mouth.

T: Your second collection of stories, *The Voice of Emma Sachs*, is described as a "suite of stories." Was that your idea?

FRASER: Yes. It's a musical catalogue. I wanted to see it in a musical sense. As a concert.

T: Does that explain why you put the title story last?

FRASER: Yes. Behind which hangs a tale. Co-op Radio was holding one of their fund-raising marathons. They asked me to read a story live. I'm really nervous reading. But for some fool reason I agreed to do this. Then I forgot about it. The day of the marathon someone phoned me to remind me I was due to go on live that night. I didn't have anything that I wanted to read. I didn't want to repeat anything. So straight off the top of my head I wrote *Emma Sachs*. I wrote it in the beer parlour on scraps of paper and a pocket diary and anything else I could find. Stumbled down to the studio. I was five minutes late. They had just about given up on me. Got there. Read it. Made half of it up as I went along. I had scraps of manuscript. Then one night when I was totally broke I was in the Niagara. I was sitting at a table with people who were far, far from being broke. This got my dander up a bit. I said, look, if you aren't going to buy me any beer, I'll just have to sing for my supper, won't I? I read it again. I had it in my pocket.

T: When we met before, you said to me, "I haven't written a sober word in twenty years."

FRASER: It's not necessarily a quote I want to send home to mother.

T: But is it true?

FRASER: Probably. I enjoy drinking. The stories come into my head when I'm relaxed enough. Alcohol is the relaxant.

T: Alcohol is supposed to be a depressant.

FRASER: Not to me. Lack of alcohol is a greater depressant.

T: So alcohol is more of a blessing than a curse.

FRASER: Yes. As long as it doesn't incapacitate me to the point where I can't see the typewriter keys or read the words. But I very seldom get to that point. People tend to exaggerate drastically the amount I drink. I resent that. I'm not Bukowski. It gets in the way. Whenever anything about my personal life becomes an impediment to what the words say, then I get annoyed. I don't care what anyone thinks of me personally but I do care what people think of my writing. If that stuff sets up a smokescreen then I may as well not write. Read what the book says. Don't worry about what I do in my spare time. When I die I'll let you know

T: Now there's a quote for posterity.

FRASER: Meanwhile, why publish a book if people are just going to use it as a lever to get a bit of moralism out of it? When I look around this room, probably half the people in this bar drink more heavily than I do and screw up more drastically than I do. And who pays the slightest bit of attention to them? But I publish a book and the picture of a dilapidated lifestyle becomes a barrier to reading the book. That's not what I want.

T: Do you see differences between *Class Warfare* and *Emma Sachs*?

FRASER: Well, I hope the newer book is less self-conscious. I would also like to think it's more accessible. One does tend to change a bit. Off the record, there might be a reason for that. In between *Class Warfare* and *Emma Sachs* a lot of other aspects of my life changed. I got to know any number of people outside the literary world. At Pulp I was defensive sometimes. Life has changed to the point where it's not necessary to be defensive anymore. I've made friends with people in areas that I never would have dreamed of getting near ten years ago. And finding myself at home there.

T: when you were writing your "Manners" column for the *Georgia Straight*, I understand you always wrote your columns at the last minute to meet the deadlines.

FRASER: That's how I write. I improvise. The stories in my books are mostly improvisations. Often I meet someone and it sets off a chain reaction. Or else they're triggered by the recollection of a meeting. A lot of the events themselves never happened. A lot of the characters never existed in this world. I don't know how it happens. That's partly what makes life interesting. One part of me can be sitting there thinking "this is material" but the stories always turn out different than I expect.

T: Do you ever plan a story?

FRASER: I have done but I find it inhibiting. I have a novel that I've been working on, and off, for years, and it's so structured that it plugs me in. I have to do it. But there isn't the spontaneity and the enjoyment of the freedom to improvise. With *Emma Sachs* I had an advantage. I typeset most of the book myself. I could make last minute changes. I could improvise on my improvisations. Most of my colleagues didn't get to see the manuscript until after it was published. I could have got away with murder in that book. And maybe I did.

T: Do you try to write every day?

FRASER: I don't have the discipline. When I get excited about something I'll write. I'll write every day and all night until it's done. But weeks go by when I don't put a word on paper except maybe a letter home. I wish I had the powers of concentration to get up in the morning at seven o'clock and write until eleven the way Updike or somebody like that does. Wouldn't that be lovely? But I like to be surprised. My non-method does surprise me. Once *Interface* solicited a story and I thought, oh, I can't be bothered. I hadn't been writing anything for a couple of months. I was very depressed about the possibility of never doing anything again. All of a sudden the first sentence came into my mind one afternoon. The story was "The Jardine Exhibition." It wrote itself in about two days.

T: One of your narrators says he has a predilection to sit up all night, drinking rotgut rum, listening to the *St. John Passion* and masturbating . . .

FRASER: I can't stand rum. But I do like the *St. John Passion*.

T: From these stories it seems you have almost evolved a doctrine of inaction and observation. You're not an activist. You're radically passive.

FRASER: Well, I'm not going out and bombing things. But I take action when I sit at the typewriter. That's about the only action that I know of that I'm any good at.

T: Let us all be sedentary and unharmful and "God save us from anybody who wants to improve us."

FRASER: It would be a start.

T: Does that amount to a personal philosophy?

FRASER: Well, I guess I just want my bad character to be left in peace and I will happily leave anybody else's bad character in the same kind of peace. I wrote the story "Estchatology" after an evening of being talked to for hours by new converts to EST. They were very nice people, terribly sincere and terribly devoted to their cause. All my problems, or what they imagined to be my problems, were going to vanish if I joined the movement. And I thought, I kind of like my problems, such as they are. They're pretty minor in the reckoning of the world. This world in which people are dying and starving and living in utter squalor. Anything that goes on in my life is pretty small potatoes.

T: There's an interesting tension in "Estchatology" between humour and resentment.

FRASER: Well, I wrote it to poke a bit of fun at those people and also to exercise my sense of being intruded upon. I like people for what they are if I like them at all. And I certainly don't want anybody to subscribe to some idealized version of themselves that they have or I might have. So if there's a moral in that story, that's roughly what it is. It's weird how the story came about. It was Labour Day

weekend. It was the Pulp Three-Day Novel Contest. I was going to write one. I started to write one and then I went down to the bar. Then I realized I couldn't do a three-day novel to save my life. But I went home and wrote anyway. The story "Estchatology" just came out.

T: There's a mixture of extreme tolerance and extreme critical-mindedness in your books which I think is very unusual

FRASER: The trouble is, it's a schizophrenia of a kind...

T: Exactly. That's the friction, the rubbing of opposites, that creates the work.

FRASER: I can't be intolerant of what I love but what I love doesn't necessarily conform to my ideas. My ideas are the intellectual part that got trained to observe and judge. That was what the education was for. That part of me is still very much extant. But it has nothing to do with what I respond to as a person. It has nothing to do with what I will enjoy and from whom and why. It could be a constant battle except I don't regard it as a battle; I regard it as a constant sort of play, a tension... This self-analysis makes me nervous... But the society in which I grew up was repressive psychologically. I was taught to keep my feelings to myself. To be reserved and reticent. Boy, that training took. There are periods when you can overcome it and there are periods when it closes in and you think, my god, I'm giving too much away here. But writing, that's what it's for. You have to give it away.

Sylvia Fraser

SYLVIA FRASER was born and raised in Hamilton. Extensive experience as a journalist followed her graduation from the University of Western Ontario. Her first four novels sought to explore and expurgate conditioned attitudes about her sex. *Pandora* (1972), *The Candy Factory* (1975), *A Casual Affair* (1978) and *The Emperor's Virgin* (1980), a histor-

ical romance set in Roman times, were followed by an ambitious novel about Nazi Germany from the perspective of German characters, *Berlin Solstice* (1984). A personal memoir about incest, *My Father's House* (1987) has finally brought her hard-won acclaim, wisdom, and satisfaction.

Sylvia Fraser lives in Toronto. She was interviewed in 1978.

T: Do you ever regard yourself as a "woman novelist"?

FRASER: Well, there was a time when it was considered an insult to be labelled a woman novelist, but now I almost would consider it flattering, because I think women today are miles ahead of men in terms of emotional health and awareness. Essentially, it's the result of the women's movement. Women have done a lot of intro-specting and it shows in themselves and in their relationships. By comparison, I think men are nowhere . . . I'm sorry.

T: Do you think *A Casual Affair* could have been written by a man?

FRASER: That's an unanswerable question. Nobody else would write my books. A book is as individual as a fingerprint.

T: But do you think there is a woman's perspective as opposed to a man's perspective?

FRASER: A culturally determined one, certainly. However, as a novelist, I have no self-consciousness about writing from the point of view of a male character — or someone who is rich, or poor, or young, or old, or of a different race — because one thing I learned as a journalist, from listening and listening and listening to other people, is that the patterns of humanness under these important differences are much more powerful. It isn't necessary to identify with a character to understand them, or to have compassion for them.

T: Why do you think men are less healthy than women?

FRASER: In my generation, which came of age in the fifties, the ideal for North American males was that of the super-achiever. That pattern was broken, to a certain extent, in the sixties and seventies. Now that jobs are scarce, men of the new generation are becoming conservative again, but I don't think that women are quite ready yet to give up the freedom they got a whiff of.

T: I agree that the sociological climate of any country is basically determined by the economic situation. Like in the sixties everybody could afford to hitchhike across Europe reading Herman Hesse novels. But I can't agree that men are necessarily more conservative than women. The males I know are actively fighting against that. Do you think there might be a difference between east and west?

FRASER: Well, Toronto is certainly very achievement-oriented. Men that I know who are, say, ten years older than I, which means they are into their fifties, are coming to the end of their achieving lives, and they are finding either that they made it and so what, or that they haven't made it and they're never going to. They go through what is popularly called the male menopause, but the ironic thing is that I know almost no women who have a menopause any more — or let's say that it's never mentioned; it's just a physical thing that's dealt with privately, with a few pills or something. But the number of men I know who are suffering from confusion and depression is staggering. I believe it has to do with having been conned. The best men of my generation were conned into the achievement thing and now they're reaping the limita-tions of that, whereas the women I know who went for careers — and I am one of them — were not so single-minded about it. They did not trade off their personal lives for success.

So responses to emotional problems are different. When women are blocked on the level of feelings, they go for detail — they make endless lists of things to do, and make complicated little things with their hands. When men are blocked, they go for structure, which is what our government and business bureaucracies are all about.

T: Do you think it's easier to have a liberated marriage these days?

FRASER: Yes, but it's always difficult for two equal people to try to live together. The most encouraging pattern I see emerging has to do with couples recognizing cycles — it's your turn and then it's my turn. A man runs with a career and making money for a while, then maybe he's tired of that and wants to have a sabbatical, or maybe even change jobs. Then the woman has a chance to be aggressive about her career. Humans have both a feminine and a masculine side and it's dangerous to permanently repress either the one or the other. That's the old sexual stereotype, when he was the breadwinner and she the breadbaker. However, as a cautionary note, I should also say that I think it unwise for couples who marry today to expect, as an article of faith, that they will remain married to each other all their lives. That may happen, and it's wonderful when it does, but I not longer think it should be an expectation or a requirement — then it just becomes another piece of baggage.

T: Has your life been affected by feminism?

FRASER: Dramatically, in that it changed the world in which I live, though all my major "feminist" decisions had been made before that word was a popular part of everyday lingo. You see, I came of age in the Doris Day era of togetherness, when everyone was supposed to want 3.4 children and a two-car garage. Though I did get married, I never wanted children. I didn't want suburbia. I wanted to travel and to have a career, though I didn't know what that career would be. By the time most of our friends had two children and were thinking of taking out a second mortgage the men began to get restless and worried and they became jealous of what they thought to be my footloose, carefree life. They would get drunk at parties and they would come lurching over at me and they would tell me that I was selfish, that I was depriving my husband, even that I was a female castrator. The feminist movement changed all that. The best of those men became more sensitive to what women like myself were about, and the others at least learned to shut up about it. So you see, the feminist movement took the pressure off of me. Ironically, it made it possible for me to be more feminine, less aggressive, because nobody was attacking me any more, and I could relax. So, I've always supported the feminist movement though I'm not politically active. It doesn't suit the life and work of a writer to have too strong a political bias.

T: Do you think extra-marital affairs are, more often than not, to use your own phrase, "venturing into emotional quicksand"? Obviously each individual case is different, but can you generalize?

FRASER: I accept the idea of many kinds of lifestyles, both inside and outside of marriage. It depends what a couple's marriage contract is. People who married out of the forties and fifties were supposed to be mating for life and promising fidelity. That's not necessarily true now. As for myself, I would like to see the locks come off sex. I would like to see a time when people regard sex as a need, in the same terms that they regard eating. To extend the food metaphor — just imagine that if, when you married, you promised that you would eat only with the person you married for the rest of your life, and that it would be disloyal and immoral to eat with someone else. Therefore, whether your mate is hungry or not, that person must eat with you or you can't eat. Follow that through and think of the tyranny of making somebody eat with you even if he isn't hungry. If he doesn't eat with you, you must go hungry. If he eats with you when he doesn't want to, so you can eat, he may find that sickening. Also, he's committed to eating the same kinds of food you eat. Resentment builds up on both sides. The sexual prohibitions have forced us into extremely unnatural and convoluted positions.

All this has to be unlearned for a healthy society. Understand, I am in no way discarding commitment— that's a different matter. Also, sexual fidelity may be a preference throughout a marriage or for a period of time, but I can't see it as a requirement or an expectation. Mind you, it's very difficult for people to change their lives in midstream. What I'm talking about is the future. In the meantime people have to do what they have to do, and of all solutions I think "cheating," and especially the double standard, is the least successful, but I guess that's the only way masses of people today can hold their lives together.

T: That whole thing of possessing one another is pretty deeply ingrained in all of us. It seems to me those changes you talk about are a pretty long way down the line for the majority of people.

FRASER: I'm more hopeful. It was impossible to predict the sixties from the fifties. Analysts usually relate that change to the invention of the Pill. Maybe there's another invention down the road that will free us from our sexual juggernaut. I'm in awe of how fast change does happen these days.

T: Yes, I often think of what it must be like for someone who is eighty years old to be alive today, to come from horse-and-buggy days to this.

FRASER: Well, that's one reason why I write the kind of books I do. The main thrust of all my work is an attempt to make the unconscious

conscious—that's the revolution we're all involved in today, I think. Why the self-help business has become a large industry. We're in a period of transition, and people are confused.

T: What is the transition—from where to where?

FRASER: One of the major differences between a human and an ape is the human's ability to absorb information. Just think of how much a child has to absorb before the age of five just to cope on a minimum level—how to walk, talk, eat, use the toilet, manners, etc. So much of this learning is absorbed unconsciously, and this unconscious programming was vital for human survival. All that worked very well as long as adults were bringing up children to lead the same kind of lives that they led. For example, a blacksmith who brings up his son to be a blacksmith—to live in the same town, to marry a girl just like his mom, etc. As long as lives were static from generation to generation, the programming you received from your parents was of prime value.

What's happening now is that we're all out of sync. We're being programmed unconsciously by our parents to live lives that no longer exist by the time we are ready to lead them. And since our parents were out of sync too, the problem compounds and will continue to compound as the pace of social change accelerates, unless we learn to de-program ourselves. That's what underlies many of the new therapies—most of them coming out of the States. It's a remarkable revolution, and one absolutely necessary if people wish to make life choices based on real possibilities instead of following blind habit in the name of moral values.

T: If the United States is a remarkable nation because it's at the forefront of "deprogramming" itself, why is it on a per capita basis, there are far more leading female writers in Canada than in the States?

FRASER: Yes, I'm quite interested in that. The energy of the women's movement in the States went into non-fiction and a powerful polemic. The important names in the States are non-fiction writers — Betty Friedan, Kate Millet, and so on. The female fiction writers are only just now catching up. In Canada, the energy of the women's movement has gone into a flowering of fiction writing.

T: But why?

FRASER: Well, I can only speculate. I suppose it's a difference in national character. The United States is a great pragmatic nation. It's a how-to nation. Americans are always taking surveys, compiling statistics, taking polls. They're always measuring things in the interest of some sort of factual truth. In my opinion, it's a nation that overvalues fact. Fiction tends to be regarded on the one hand as unreal, therefore escapist and trivial, or as being elitist — a snob exercise of the intelligentsia. Now I happen to regard fiction, at its best, as greater truth — which is the European and, to some extent, the Canadian view. So it's a difference in national preference and national psyche.

T: Is that difference reflected in the publishing industry in general then?

FRASER: It has been. What is happening now in Canadian publishing is that we are being hit ten or twenty years late by the paperback revolution. That means mass marketing and therefore a reverence for mass tastes. In the States ninety percent of the people who sit down to write books are attempting to write commercial books. In Canada, till recently, the overwhelming number of authors were attempting to write seriously. This marks no particular national virtue but simply reflected the fact that there was no mass market

available to Canadians, therefore there was no temptation. Now in the States publishing is essentially a branch of the entertainment business. Books written to entertain do not challenge the status quo. They amuse, they reassure, they ingratiate. They provide an escape from life. Serious books focus on life. They probe, they examine. Therefore anyone who reads them runs the risk of being provoked or disturbed as well as enriched. When a book is judged, by publisher and public, only for its entertainment value, then the serious writer is heavily penalized.

T: Who do you see as your audience?

FRASER: When writing, I don't think about the audience — or let us say that in the past I never have, though the pressure is certainly on now to do so. I mean, I always hope to find an audience, and I don't deliberately set out to alienate people, but in writing I have a very strong idea of what I want to say and I'm willing to do my best to make that as accessible and as popular as I can through the use of craft, but there is a point beyond which I can't divert or dilute what I'm saying and still say the same thing.

My books are full of what I consider hard and challenging truths. Therefore my audience is whomever is willing to take the time and the effort to be a creative reader. To be a creative reader is to participate in the reading of a book with head and heart and all your sensitivities, instead of just letting the words sort of slide through your mind to fill up time, or to collect some facts.

T: To go back to the title of your last book — do you think there is such a thing as a "casual affair"?

FRASER: I think affairs — and I'm talking here about secret affairs — are usually destructive. To begin with, they are usually secret because someone is cheating on someone else, so right there they are surrounded by guilt, lies, hypocrisy. But even within the relationship, there are severe limitations. To a secret affair, you can smuggle in only a part of yourself. Now, it may be that both persons bring the best part of his or herself, in which case the relationship may be idyllic. But how long can that go on; and how often does that happen?

Take the characters in *A Casual Affair*. She's in a state of hysteria most of the time, she's obsessed. Whatever maturity she has, whatever skills as an adult, whatever friends she has are unavailable to her, because she is isolated in the secret relationship. He is a man of considerable professional accomplishment, and a set of traditional values, but these are not what he brings to the relationship. What he brings are his terror of intimacy and his need to play with fire while still being able to control the blaze. Now this can happen in a relationship that is not clandestine, but the real world and ordinary events and the support of friends provides some perspective. In a secret relationship that is not going well, the two people are in free fall. Under such circumstances, in our society, it is usually the woman who is most vulnerable because the man, by tradition, is the aggressor and has control of the action. If he has an active professional life and is married, then he will be virtually unreachable for large chunks of time. She is pushed into the position of distorting her life to wait for the call. If she is normally independent this will be doubly demoralizing.

T: So she says to him about his previous mistresses, "I'll bet there was an oversupply of nurses, secretaries and stewardesses. All women in the service professions who couldn't threaten your position."

FRASER: Yes. A man who is emotionally insecure will usually choose someone he can easily control or victimize. The potential for exploitation, one way or another, is naked. It's the pits.

Mavis Gallant

MAVIS GALLANT was born in Montreal in 1922. In 1950 she left her work as a newspaper reporter in Canada to write fiction in Paris. Since 1951, many of her stories have appeared in the *New Yorker*. Her story collections include *The Other Paris* (1956), *My Heart is Broken* (1959), *The Pegnitz Junction* (1973), *The End*

of the World and Other Stories (1973), *From the Fifteenth District* (1979), a Governor General's Award-winning selection of Canada-related material, *Home Truths* (1981) and *In Transit* (1988). Her two short novels are *Green Water, Green Sky* (1959) and *A Fairly Good Time* (1970). Her non-fiction works include *The Affair of Gabrielle Russier* (1971), about a French schoolteacher's affair with an adolescent student, and a new study of the Dreyfus case and its impact on French society. She was made an Officer of the Order of Canada in 1981.

Mavis Gallant lives in Paris. She was interviewed in 1981.

T: When you left Montreal when you were twenty-eight, did that strike you at the time as being a major turning point in your life?

GALLANT: Oh, I knew. Of course I knew it was.

T: So there was a firm resolve attached to it?

GALLANT: Yes, but not from anything exterior. I think those things come from within one. I wasn't fleeing a war or a depression or enemies or hostilities. I had what was known then as a good job for a girl. I was a feature writer on the *Montreal Standard*, a newspaper that no longer exists. I was well paid for the time. I knew it was an enormous risk. But I gave myself two years. To see if I could live on my writing. I knew I didn't want to be a Sunday writer. "I saved myself from slavery." I haven't had a boss.

T: Thirty years ago it would have been difficult to come back to Canada and live as an independent-minded woman...

GALLANT: Yes. I was divorced. I think I might have married again, because the social pressure on a woman alone was enormous. Mind you, if you listen to the women now, I don't think they're having a much easier time of it. I don't know if they've painted themselves into a corner or what happened.

T: I get the sense the majority are still conventional but at least there is more freedom to be different.

GALLANT: I think people are less disapproving but they still wonder. I think it's the American influence. The Freudian question always comes through. "Why is so-and-so doing this?" Why is he not otherwise directed? People talk in that sort of jargon. Do you?

T: I do.

GALLANT: Are you aware of it?

T: Very much so.

GALLANT: Sometimes it sounds comic to me. I heard someone saying, "I'm a night person. And it's at night that I have my space." I didn't know what was being said. I remember another time someone said, "weather-wise." Of course that doesn't sound funny to you but it sounds comic to me. I'm not making fun of it, believe me. But if I have any gap, it's that.

The other gap is that my approach to people is perhaps not as direct as yours. That comes from living in France. On the plane between Halifax and somewhere there was a very tall man sitting next to me. I'm rather short. I couldn't get my coat up in the bin. I said, "The bins are very high, aren't they?" And he said, "Yeah." And I said, "It's easy for someone tall. But if I want to put my coat up, I have to stand on the seat." He said, "'Yeah, I guess you do." Finally I said, "Would you mind awfully putting it up?" And he said, "Why didn't you say so?" He was sincere. He just thought I was making conversation. He said why didn't you ask and I would have done it right away! But I would be unable to ask directly. I have to learn to. In France I would say the bins are very high up and then someone would guess.

In Winnipeg or Toronto a man spoke to me in the elevator. He said something about the weather outside but it was as if he knew me. I agreed it was great to see a day like this and I said, quite innocently, "Have we met?" He was thunderstruck!

T: Did you find his elevator conversation refreshing or off-putting?

GALLANT: Not off-putting. I'm the one who must be off-putting. But I don't mean to be. Obviously if I stay in Canada long enough, I'll adjust.

Canadians are really quite polite. And they're very patient. That's the first thing that strikes you when you come from a nervous country like France or a particularly nervous city, let's say, like Paris. They stand in line here. When there's a sign in a cafe saying "Please wait to be seated," I assure you people there wouldn't pay the slightest attention to that. They'd just march in and sit down and then argue. I have a tendency to do that. When the people I'm with are Canadians they want to wait but I say, look, there are a lot of empty tables. It's the patience and the calmness. And that slowness of speech. You probably aren't aware of it. People speak much more slowly here. If you listen to the CBC, you notice it.

T: Maybe they're just asleep.

GALLANT: No, I think it's a different tempo, a different rhythm. Nobody's pushing. The only frenzy you hear is on commercial radio. Disc jockeys. It seems like an epileptic frenzy that has nothing to do with life. It has nothing to do with Canada. It's an imported thing. Don't you think?

T: Sure. It's American. I often wonder whether we're more British or more American.

GALLANT: Oh, if you went to Britain you'd quickly find out you're not British. I can assure you. The only real culture shock I ever had in my life was when I first went to England. I had an English father. He was born in England. I'd been brought up on English books. I had English literature very much on the brain. I'd had the English landscape described to me in probably the most nostalgic and unreal terms. And yet that was my greatest culture shock. There was always a slight condescension. Even the questions like what part of Canada do you come from were completely meaningless. They didn't even know where Canada is on the map.

T: One of the things that I was impressed with and I enjoyed in your stories is that sense that the reason people are unloved is merely because they don't fit in.

GALLANT: It's not a conscious thought.

T: You went to all those different schools. Perhaps that's where it comes from?

GALLANT: The reason that thing about the schools comes up all the time is that when I was asked for jacket copy for my first book, which was 1956, a long time ago, I didn't know what to say. I had nothing in particular to say. So I thought, well, where have I been to school? I didn't even know the names. I'd been to seventeen schools. So I wrote that down. It gets copied from book to book. You'll find many writers were subjected to being moved around.

T: Certainly a lot of writers seem to need the experience of going away.

GALLANT: The shock of change. I think it's a good idea even if people are going to go on writing about the part of Canada they live in.

T: There's an A.J. Liebling quote, "The only way to write is well and how you do it is your own business." Do you feel sympathy for that?

GALLANT: Yes. I don't talk much about my work. Until about ten years ago some of my friends in Paris weren't aware of my career as a writer. Often other people will ask me if I live in a writers' community in Paris? No. Writers don't meet to talk about their work. That's a very mistaken idea. Maybe they do more of that here. The whole writing thing seems to be much different here. Do you have the feeling that writers see more of each other in Canada?

T: Yes. The reason is, I think, that a hundred years ago this was all bush, so writing is not an acceptable profession to follow. There is usually an insecurity about being a writer that perhaps you wouldn't get in an older culture. So perhaps the writers here have developed a fellowship out of that.

GALLANT: You mean the old Calvinism again? I can't believe that still goes on. I think they probably have to prove to their parents that they can make money at it. You haven't done it but I'm constantly asked about money in Canada. What do you earn? Can you live on it? Money is an obsession here. I've wondered if people wouldn't walk over their own mothers for a lower interest rate. What was the advance on your last book? Do you own or rent the place you live in?

Well, I'm a born renter. I don't own anything. I never will. Most of the writers I know live in little rented apartments. But in Canada I suspect the writer has to prove to the worried parents, who remember the Depression, that it's all right to do what they're doing. That accounts, I should think, for the immense funding that goes on here.

T: Did you ever question writing as a viable profession? or go through a painful apprenticeship?

GALLANT: I never had that for one second. My goal was to get free and write. The only thing I don't know is why I waited so long. I never sent a story anywhere until I was twenty-seven years old. I don't know why. I had piles of stories. Then suddenly I decided this was it. Twenty-seven, I think, is a watershed age. I've noticed that. Many people make decisions suddenly at twenty-seven. I think they see thirty coming along. Maybe people say it's now or never.

T: "Thank You for the Lovely Tea" was written when you were eighteen, right?

GALLANT: But I typed it when I was thirty. Or about thirty. I found it in a notebook. It was very long and I condensed it. I don't think it's a very good story. The style is slightly affected. That's what the writers I was reading at eighteen were like. I was reading a great many British novelists.

If a young girl were to bring me that story I would tell her to go on writing. But I would hope she would read something else for a change.

T: I try to refrain from asking people whether they write with typewriters or with pens and so on . . . but a friend was over to the house and we were talking about your stories. He thought you probably plan your stories well in advance. I argued the opposite.

GALLANT: I begin in pencil. It's usually a visual image in a situation. Sometimes the first image isn't even in the story at the end. I start it in longhand. Then for the next few days there are bits of the story that come. It's almost as if the story already existed and I was getting scraps of it. I don't sit down and think, now this man is going to do this. It just comes. And I don't know where from. I don't mean I'm a mystic. I don't mean it comes from the planet Venus or anything.

You get an accumulation of things. Written on buses. I'm not joking. Even on match covers. Once I had a story written on a metro ticket. A little bit of dialogue. Then I type it. Then I make all the corrections. The form then is very clear. Once it's typed there's no doubt that that's the beginning and that's the end of it and the story does this. Then I correct in pencil again and it's all around the edges. Then I type it all again to get it clean. Then I think it's no good.

T: And so you put it away.

GALLANT: Yes. I put it away. I've never written anything that from the moment it was more or less clean I didn't think was revolting.

T: What about later? Do you have more affection for some stories and not others?

GALLANT: It's not affection. I don't re-read my work. I had to re-read the stories in *Home Truths* to write the introduction. When I finished reading them I didn't think anything was as good as I wanted it to be. Writing that introduction gave me the only writer's block I've ever had in my life. After thirty years of writing.

T: Did you select the stories for the book?

GALLANT: I had suggested "The Ice Wagon," "Virus X," and "Bonaventure." Those three. I had a bibliography that had been published in *Canadian Fiction Magazine*. I picked out all those that had Canadian backgrounds, Canadian characters, Canadian anything. I sent them all in a list, marking those that were uncollected. All the manuscripts were at the University of Toronto. I think they sent two people and they sat reading and they made a list. Which I approved of. I would never interfere anyway.

T: Don't you feel the presentation, the packaging, and that sort of thing is also part of your book itself?

GALLANT: Yes, but it's got nothing to do with me. I never interfere. I've had that rule from the beginning. I never, never, never interfere. I'm not a publisher. The idea for the book was Doug Gibson's, the publisher's. He wrote to me. I was a bit worried about this arbitrary putting together of stories only because they were Canadian. Then I remembered I had written a book of German short stories that had German backgrounds called *The Pegnitz Junction* and that had been all right. The title was also his. I did ask if it would irritate Canadian readers. Because it sounds a bit peremptory. You know, "home truths." But apparently not. If it has, nobody has mentioned it. And God knows, they mention everything else.

T: Because the "home truths" are undeniable. Not in a broad sense. But it's like when you're telling me that incident on the airplane with the coat. That's a home truth. The reader recognizes those situations.

GALLANT: But it has to be plausible. Even if a thing happened, if it's completely eccentric, there's no point in writing about it. If it isn't plausible, it doesn't matter. It's no good saying I assure you it happened.

T: Do you think that's particular to the short story form?

GALLANT: I think you've put your finger on it. Absolutely.

T: I think that's what I liked about "In the Tunnel." The situation seems almost comic or gross and yet it was entirely plausible.

GALLANT: That's barely caricature, believe me. I was at a dinner party of Brits in exile in the south of France. The man across from me leaned over with those light eyes. He'd been in the colonies. He leaned across and said, "Don't you think there are people so rotten that they have to be killed?" I remember thinking, rotten for what kind of world? Suppose I was an African, brought up with completely different legends, gods, realities, and that man with his very light eyes said this. The story began out of that.

T: Was it much different for you writing your Linnet Muir stories? Because they're in the first person?

GALLANT: It was a lost Montreal. It was a reconstruction in my mind of a kind of city. They're not completely autobiographical. But it would be hypocritical to say I invented everything. After all, I was a young girl who did come back to Montreal, who had no money. Who did work for a newspaper. Who did want to write. I tell you what else is true. That quote, "If it hadn't been for the goddammed war, there wouldn't be any goddammed women here!"

At the time I was very, very left wing. I was always collecting money for strikers. I wasn't sure whether it was moral to work for the newspaper. I pondered and I agonized. It was either that or a dreary office job. But if the rest was true in terms of factual, I'd have twenty lawsuits on my hands.

T: Do you get letters from readers over here?

GALLANT: Yes. Canadians write to put you right about things. They say you said this and I can assure you it's not true. Then it always ends, "If I'm wrong, correct me." I also get letters from people because I've used their names. One man wrote from Harvard saying I'd used his name. It was a common English name. I'd taken it out of the *Times Literary Supplement*. You know, you look for names. After some correspondence, I said, I got it out of the *TLS*. He wrote back and said I wrote that article. I had to write back and say, well, I can't use Smith and Jones, Smith and Jones.

I keep lists of names. I take names out of the phone books when I'm travelling. Names are very tricky. In "The Ice Wagon" there's the name Trudeau. When I wrote that, I just wanted a Montreal family name. I had never heard of Pierre Eliot Trudeau.

When I read that story a couple of weeks ago at the University of Toronto, I had to change it during the reading. I knew "Trudeau" would be a distraction.

T: I think you've got a pretty good name.

GALLANT: Well, I married into Gallant! My maiden name was Young. But I tell young women, especially if they want to go professional, to keep the name they were born with.

T: Do you always answer the letters you get?

GALLANT: Always. The only letters I haven't answered are letters of ridiculous abuse. I haven't had many. Once a woman wrote to me from California saying she had been writing for movies for years but she'd never had a novel published. She said if you could get the crap that you write published, you must have slept with everybody on the east coast. Etc., etc. So I wrote back. "Mavis Gallant has died and we are getting together a testimonial album of people who were inspired by her and who loved her. May we include you?"

Gary Geddes

GARY GEDDES was born in Vancouver in 1940. He was raised for four years in Saskatchewan but grew up primarily in Vancouver's Commercial Drive area. He became a lay preacher for the Baptist church and a singer in one of Vancouver's first rock combos. He received his PhD in English from the University of Toronto and has edited important college anthologies

such as *Twentieth Century Poetry and Poetics* (1969) and *Skookum Wawa* (1975), a breakthrough volume for BC literature. Described as Canada's best political poet by critic George Woodcock, some of his major poetry titles are *Letter of the Master of Horse* (1973), *War Measures and Other Poems* (1976), *The Acid Test* (1981), *The Terracotta Army* (1984) and *Changes of State* (1986). Geddes has led a literary delegation to China, founded a subscription-based publishing company and he teaches at Concordia University.

Gary Geddes lives in Dunvegan, Ontario.

T: *War Measures & Other Poems* is an odd book to come from a westcoaster. Where do the politics and the interest in French Canada come from?

GEDDES: You can't grow up in BC without becoming political. Either you get on the bandwagon and try to milk the land, or become a socialist — there seems to be no easy middle ground out here. I guess my fundamentalist background left me with an overactive conscience too, like all those other Baptists who ended up in the CCF.

As for Chartier, the mad bomber, he was a westerner too. He knew about marginality. He was French-Canadian and an Albertan. I found in his death a symbol for something tragic and deadly in our culture. He had no means of redressing the injustices he felt. He thought politicians were crooks. Many of them are. What good was his vote? He decided to take a stick of dynamite into the House of Commons. Was he going to throw it from the gallery? We don't know. The newspapers laughed at him, as a not-so-beautiful loser, as another Canadian failure, as a fool. One paper denied that his act was Canadian. We don't act separately here, it said; we are violent in groups only. Therefore, Chartier's act is meaningless, essentially American.

T: Your Chartier is not an assassin.

GEDDES: No, he seems cut out for something else. Whether he changed his mind when he got there, seeing all the school children in the gallery, watching the minister of consumer affairs picking his nose and reading the *Globe* or remembering another alternative, that of the Buddhist monks in Vietnam, who gave up their own lives in protest to the American presence — whatever it was, Chartier ended up taking his own life. Who's to say he didn't intend that all along, and who's to say it was not the most powerful gesture possible? Some of our contemporary terrorists should remember that.

T: That was a long answer. It's also a long poem. How do you keep a poem that long from collapsing in the middle, or turning to sludge?

GEDDES: Maybe you don't. I tried something different. I used the form of diary jottings, to keep the sections short and lyrical, highly charged and with the kind of intensity of image of a stopped frame in a film. Kroetsch called those sections narrative remnants, a phrase that makes sense to me. The reader is kept alert by both the intensity of the image, hopefully, and the energy and attention required to stitch together those non-linear, but still interconnected, narrative remnants.

For the long poem, you need many different strategies, but it's the most exciting form in my view, and the one that separates the sheep from the goats. I leave it up to you to decide which is which.

T: How did you come to spend time on Vancouver's Commercial Drive and what part did that landscape play in your life?

GEDDES: When the family returned from Saskatchewan, we lived briefly with my father in Rivers Inlet, where he was gillnetting. That landscape continues to haunt me in quite a different way, for its excess, its exotic qualities, the vibrant colours, the scale of trees and mountain and ocean. Commercial Drive was bleak in comparison, a poor decompression tank for immigrants and white trash waiting for a break to get them into the suburbs. I don't know how much of that I noticed as a kid. I was too busy making a living and trying to survive on the street.

T: Was it all that negative?

GEDDES: That experience was not pleasant, but it wasn't totally negative either. It's the stuff legends and stories are made of. I sometimes wear my poor years as a sort of proletarian badge—fried bologna and baking powder biscuits, hustling coal sacks and hubcaps, living in a drab flat over a store at the corner of Fourth and Commercial—but it was also rather magical, since that's where I began to learn about sex, where I started to earn money from working for a hunchback jeweler, where I bought my first second-hand bike that gave me the freedom of the city.

T: So the poverty is a fiction?

GEDDES: No, but it's convenient legend to use sometimes in polite, pretentious company. We were poor. The family received food baskets at Christmas and clothes from friends at the church. My father had drinking problems and health problems, so there was not always sufficient money available. My mother worked in Toot's Cafe at the corner of Broadway and Commercial for fifty cents an hour and tips, at a time when she should have been at home looking after my younger brother, who was sick.

Still, the Drive had the best view in the city, if you looked north. I'll always miss the mountains I could see almost any day of the week. And the trams and streetcars.

T: The place seems to be central in a number of ways in your life, if only in name.

GEDDES: Yes, it's my St. Urbain Street. My father drove cab like Duddy's father. I learned to hustle on the Drive, working at various jobs, coming quickly to the opinion that only work would get me out of there. Ironically, many of my writer friends are now moving to the Drive; it's the only place I could possibly afford to live if I returned to Vancouver.

I know what you're getting at though. The many different hats I wear as a teacher, editor, writer,

publisher and general propagandist for culture in Canada may have some roots in the Drive. Not in the commercial sense, but certainly in terms of drive. A.Y. Jackson once said that the only way an artist can survive in Canada is to become an institution. That's my impression too. Especially for poets. Who wants to pay for a poem, or a book of poems? So I teach, I do a few odd jobs that are useful and that bring in money to support my family and my almost secret vice of poetry.

T: But you've had some success, and some support too.

GEDDES: Yes, I'd say I've been very lucky. The kid on the Drive would never have believed all this. Still, I was a romantic and had great hopes for myself. I wanted to be a preacher and save the world, from what I'm not sure. Now I think I'd like to save it from people like me.

T: Poetry as a substitute religion?

GEDDES: Yes, fakirs and fakers. Jimmy Bakker and Mahatma Gandhi. I think of writing as a way of getting in touch with my deepest feelings. I don't lay these feelings out on the page like dripping laundry. I wring them out and cut them up into very different forms, to make something new with words that will take others deeply into themselves, not into my life and its problems.

T: You take refuge from yourself in masks.

GEDDES: Which one am I wearing now?

T: The concerned, earnest poet-as-Baptist mask.

GEDDES: Obvious I should throw that one away, it's too transparent. The mask helps me to find a voice. I seem to be able to get into the heads of my characters by using the first person more easily than I could talking about them in the third person.

T: Is that part of the legacy of the coast?

GEDDES: More the legacy of being human, being insecure. Our culture in Canada, perhaps even more so in BC, has always been anti-intellectual, afraid of the mind and afraid of the imagination, resources cherished in many other countries. I had to work hard to overcome the sense that I should be seen and not heard, that my accent was odd and my thought processes were unattractive. We all live with that as Canadians.

Beyond that, however, I have my own need to remain private. A writer gives himself away with every word he writes, I realize that. But I find it difficult, and not entirely valuable, to write about my own daily life. That life sifts into everything, of course, and colours the most seemingly objective material, even something as exotic and non-native as *Letter of the Master of Horse* and *The Terracotta Army*.

T: What is it that is personal in those works?

GEDDES: Frye once said that every poet has one or two structures of feeling that are absolutely central to him and his work, and that these structures are often consciously or unconsciously announced in the title-poems of the author's books. I'd say that I am preoccupied with injured figures, figures caught in the machinery of society or politics or religion. There's something common between the narrator of *Horse*, Chartier, the potter in Xian and Sandra Lee Scheuer, who was killed at Kent State University. Perhaps a good shrink could tell you why I write about these individuals. I might even venture a guess or two myself, but not today.

T: Yeats said "everything that is personal soon rots."

GEDDES: Yes, but he was also writing out of his own deepest needs and desires as he said that. It doesn't really matter what material you begin with. What matters is what you do with that material. Or, what it does with you?

T: What do you mean?

GEDDES: I'm not sure, but it sounds right. Material that is personal becomes objectified in the process of creation; material that is objective becomes strangely personalized, receives its stamp of style, of character. So, too, the author changes in the process.

T: No man steps twice...

GEDDES: That's it, yes. The processes are quite mysterious. The Russian Jewish poet Mandelstam talked about writing his own death — or his wife described the process as it worked in his poems. The poet creates and falls into his own myth.

T: Art as self-fulfilling prophecy, then.

GEDDES: Recently there was a film on television about the life and death of Claude Jutra, a Québec filmmaker of great importance, and a gifted actor and director. He committed suicide not long after he discovered he had Alzheimer's disease. He drowned himself. In one of his early films there is a scene in which the central character walks off the end of a pier and drowns, the concluding moment of the film. There are signs in the other works as well.

Pat Lowther's poems are full of signs that we might say prefigured her own death by violence.

I don't want to fall into this way of thinking about writing, or about art. The author's death is the least important detail. The work is what matters, regardless of the path taken or the price paid.

T: You were talking about material being personal.

GEDDES: Personality is a masquerade. What lies underneath is bedrock, unchanging, eternal, if anything is eternal. That is what art aims to discover. Al Purdy's domestic poems are romances. David McFadden's delightful first-person comedies are fabulous fictions created by a psyche that is quite startling, quite severe.

T: And behind Geddes's poems about injured figures?

GEDDES: Perhaps a degree of violence that desperately needs capping. Is it an accident that this interview is taking place on Main Street in an East Indian restaurant that used to be called, not in jest, the Razor Blade Cafe?

T: Excuse me while I move to the next table.

GEDDES: Do you know the Indian concept of "deep-name"?

T: No.

GEDDES: It's the name by which God would really know you. Not as Alan Twigg, but a real name, such as He-Who-Would-Shoot-From-The-Hip-Before-Falling-Off-His-Horse. That sort of thing. In analysis once I described the experience of having my father come from Saskatchewan, after my mother's death, to take me to live with him and his second wife. I was sitting on the piano bench. I'd had only twelve piano lessons. I'd learned to play a few pieces. When my father arrived at the house, he was sitting behind me on the couch and I was playing the piano. As I recounted this story for the psychologist, I burst into tears. Deep sobs. It suddenly became clear to me that I had been playing for my life. I had to get that piece right or my father would not love me, would

not take me with him. Of course, that was not accurate at all, but that was how I had perceived it at the time and, perhaps, how I have perceived it unconsciously all these years. There I was on my island piano stool. And that is my deep-name: He-Who-Sings-For-His-Own-Life.

T: And of course poetry can be said to be a form of singing too. Just like making music on the piano.

GEDDES: I sang all the time as a kid. Certain songs on the radio used to make me weep. I never knew why, just assumed I was a sentimental slob. Recently, I learned that my mother had sung all those songs to me as a child, even while I was in the womb. The feelings of loss clung to the notes and lyrics. I used to sing in my potato patch in Saskatchewan, and in the outhouse. Poems must have been a continuation of that urge to sing.

T: For self approval, or the approval of others?

GEDDES: Both, obviously. At a certain point, however, the singing serves other functions than self-validation. You start to sing of the tribe, to keep the record, to bear witness. Most poems come to me as a gift. The coincidence of elements that allows me to write a poem has little to do with me. I have to keep alert and keep my language self in good shape, like a volunteer fireman. I have to be there at the right time, ready to work. I believe language is a collective and communal treasure. My job is to try to write another poem, not take credit for what is done.

John Gray

JOHN GRAY was born in Ottawa in 1946 and raised in Truro, Nova Scotia. After stints as a rock 'n' roll keyboardist, he came to Vancouver to study theatre, to co-found Tamahnous Theatre and to later collaborate with Toronto's innovative Theatre Passe Muraille. His musicals include *18 Wheels, Rock and Roll, Health* and his Governor General's Award–winning

Billy Bishop Goes To War (1981), which opened unsuccessfully on Broadway in 1980 after the original production played to packed houses across Canada. Gray has also written children's theatre and is a gifted critic.

John Gray lives in Vancouver. He was interviewed in 1979.

T: *Billy Bishop Goes to War* is one of Canada's longest-touring plays. Has its success surprised you?

GRAY: Yes, it has. Originally our attitude was if the Canadians and Americans like it, that's great. If the Canadians like it and the Americans don't like it, that's okay. If the Canadians don't like it and the Americans don't like it, that's a drag. If the Canadians don't like it and the Americans do like it, we're in deep trouble. We had no idea it would go so far.

T: It looks as if success has come rather easily.

GRAY: I know. I've only written two damn shows. Now I'm starting to worry that I'm going to have to start thinking of myself as a writer. When you do that, there's always a danger you'll start thinking that you have to write, whether you have anything to say or not. I think that's an awful thing.

T: So if a stranger walked up to you and asked your profession—

GRAY: I'd say I work in the theatre.

T: But without having written *18 Wheels* and *Billy Bishop*, you couldn't pay your bills.

GRAY: I know. But admitting you're a writer is kinda like quitting smoking. The worst thing you can do is start proclaiming you're quitting smoking. You'll fail for sure. Hemingway once said don't put your mouth on anything that looks like it might happen, it'll turn to dust every time. In a way, I guess that has something to do with how I write. The worst stuff I do is always written when I have a good idea what it's about. I do much better if I concentrate on the characters and let the play emerge by itself. Then on the third draft I finally start to observe what it's about.

T: It seems *Billy Bishop* is only half about Billy Bishop's life. The other half is about how our generation is linked to Canada's military past. Was that intentional?

GRAY: Yes. Those World Wars explain so much about ourselves, about our attitudes as Canadians. The innocence Canada took into that first war was just appalling. When the figures started coming back—twenty-five thousand men lost at the Somme, for example—people weren't too keen on going, right? That's when conscription started. Then all the French-Canadian resentment against English Canada got started. Then the whole cynicism about government started. All that stuff affects us today.

I think the heaviest years of life are around nineteen to twenty-five. Those are really long, big years. They form you. We didn't fight in a war at that age; some of our parents did. They went through an experience that we don't have a clue about. So there's a monstrous gap between generations.

T: What awareness of war did you get growing up in the fifties?

GRAY: I always knew that my father and his best friend had enlisted together. My father got involved in radar and his best friend became a spitfire pilot. This guy's name was John West. When he was shot down during the Battle of Britain, that's when my father vowed he would name his first-born son after his dead friend.

I was always aware of that. I always wondered who this guy was that I was named after. I wondered about this heavy experience my father must have gone through to do that. Now he's an insurance executive. A middle-class person with bourgeois values and fundamentalist religious beliefs.

T: A Canadian.

GRAY: Right. So what happened to him to make him do this almost poetic gesture?

T: This is why you wrote *Billy Bishop* then. To answer that question.

GRAY: Yes. And that's why I'm

content to perform *Billy Bishop* for a long time. Because it's about me. I don't know if I can tell you exactly how it's about me...but somehow it is. It's my relationship to the events in *Billy Bishop*. You can't really say the play is really telling you that much about Billy Bishop himself. I don't know what he was like. I really don't. And *18 Wheels* doesn't really tell you much about truckers either. So what is *Billy Bishop* about anyway?

T: It's about your perceptions of Billy Bishop's relationship to war.

GRAY: Definitely. It's not really about war at all. It uses war to show that old countries use young countries. Old people use young people to fight their wars. In the process of this, youth is lost. Youth is lost in the sense of a country and also for individuals. Britain lost a whole generation. *Billy Bishop* is about youth and old age.

T: And it refuses to preach about war, right?

GRAY: Right.

T: Many people would regard that as a failing.

GRAY: Yes, I get a lot of that. A certain number of people go to the show with a checklist of things they want said. When they don't get to check off things they came to hear, they feel the show has failed them. They don't appreciate that not preaching allows us to talk to old people, too. Old people are thrilled to see that people of the next generation can recognize that they weren't stupid idiots for going along and fighting. It was so much more complicated than that. *Billy Bishop* recognizes that their experiences had validity, irrespective of whether the war was good or bad.

To say that the play is encouraging war is incomprehensible to me.

T: If Billy Bishop embodies the experiences of a generation then the audience can come and pass judgment by itself.

GRAY: Right. I wanted to give people some conception of what war is like. We have a particular kind of arrogance that comes from the sixties which makes people say not only are wars bad, but people who fought them are stupid. That's unfair. In the First World War those guys were encouraged to fight by their elders. They were victims. Not only did those guys not know what they were fighting for, they didn't even know where they were! Ever! There was no landscape. It was all blown up. There were no trees or hills, nothing. They were simply someplace in France. It was like the moon. You spent three years there until you get wounded or killed. The alienation must have been phenomenal! Surviving in this little vacuum was probably their only real concern. The larger issues of war on an international scale had nothing to do with them.

T: Do you think that's why you audience at Royal Military College even liked the show? Because you didn't overlay history onto Billy Bishop's shoulders?

GRAY: That's partly it. The other reason is simply that those people aren't stupid. You generally think of army guys as being like football players. It really knocked me out to hear the military commandant give this analysis of our show in terms of Canada's history. My jaw was open. It was very perceptive and interesting stuff. To start thinking all those right-wing guys are stupid is naive and destructive to one's own thinking.

T: In the sixties, our generation was so busy formulating some alternate stance of our own that we didn't even try to appreciate what we were defining ourselves against.

GRAY: Yes, that's why *Billy Bishop* would have been a bomb in the sixties. It would have been a turkey. People would have called it reactionary.

T: How much of your conception of what theatre should be has been formed by associating with Theatre Passe Muraille?

GRAY: Quite a bit. I used to be quite the little elitist. I went to university for seven years. Nothing will hone an elitist like seven years in a university. So I tended to do shows for formalistic reasons. Content really wasn't that important. New theatre forms and staging were just as important to me as what a play said.

Then I saw Passe Muraille do *1837* in Listowel, Ontario. It was very revolutionary, that first Passe Muraille show. All these farmers were yelling and standing up and applauding. And these guys were prosperous right-wing types. It just blew my mind to see how people can relate to content. It made the stuff I was doing seem trivial. Like playing little games. It made me rethink the whole thing.

T: Now there's almost a movement growing out of *1837*. Shows like *Paper Wheat* and *The Farm Show*.

GRAY: Yeah. In those shows, the event of having a particular audience becomes just as important as what's happening on the stage. It's now like there's a little glass cube around the stage and everybody sits there and admires the work of art on display.

T: What specific things did you learn from Passe Muraille?

GRAY: How powerful a monologue can be.

T: Any negative things?

GRAY: Well, I also learned the limitations of having actors play tables and chairs and cows and horses. I've pretty well had it up to here with that stuff. I also reacted against Passe Muraille's tendency to go into a farming community and tell farmers how great they are. I've talked to lots of farmers. They're not dummies. You don't have to flatter them. It's also a bit much when actors go into a community and start telling people what they're like.

T: Yes, it's getting very trendy now for a bunch of middle-class kids to graduate from some university theatre program and suddenly become relevant. So they do some didactic piece on nuclear power.

GRAY: And who's going to come? You just consolidate people's prejudices. I don't think theatre is the place of weighty matters like that mainly because you see a play once. You can reread a novel by Kafka. You can analyze it at your leisure. But theatre's different. Look at Shakespeare, for example. His characters are wonderful and they mouth human issues very articulately and poetically, but Shakespeare doesn't attempt to change the world.

T: You're saying the function of theatre is to reflect life, not comment on it.

GRAY: I guess so. Accuracy over opinion. The best reaction you get out of theatre is recognition. Maybe with a novel it's different. But in theatre I know I'm never going to be a person who writes of weighty matters. By that I mean I'm not going to write anything just to give the world my opinions.

T: Did you always want to be a playwright?

GRAY: Not at all. I was very, very bored in school. I was so bad they kept testing me for deafness. I was right down there with the special class types. As a result I was a loner most of the time. That's why I was always known for being musical. It helped excuse me for being such a lousy student. I got most of my acceptance from people out of music, out of playing. When I finally joined a rock n' roll band it was great. I had a Hammond organ. It wasn't like playing the organ; it was like driving a car.

T: Unfortunately most of us have a totally commercialized preconception of what a popular song should sound like.

GRAY: And that's a great shame. There's a whole tradition of songwriting where the songs are more complex. Kurt Weill, for example, is my favorite songwriter. And Sondheim is good, too. His songs fit into a show.

T: Your songs definitely aren't written to be covered some day by Frank Sinatra. It seems you're trying hard to fit them into the flow of a play, too.

GRAY: Sure. It's very American to write a scene around a song. I tend to write the other way round. When I get to a point in the script where something needs to be said that a character can't really say, I can say it in a song.

T: One eastern Canadian critic thought your singing detracted from *Billy Bishop*. For me it was very important that your authenticity on stage could act as a foil to Eric Peterson's exuberance. He plays eighteen characters at once, so it adds a sense of balance if you play yourself.

GRAY: I know. I'm glad you said that. It's the emotions that people go though that are important. If a great singer sang with Eric, he'd have to do things stylistically different than what the scenes require. It would become schizophrenic. God knows I'd never try and become a singer and have people love me for the quality of my voice. But I sing the songs in *Billy Bishop* because I can sing them in the context as well as anybody can. Again you get people coming to the show with a checklist, for Chrissake. When somebody sings a song, they've already decided what it's supposed to sound like. Well, Jesus Christ, how am I supposed to deal with that?

T: Do you have songwriting ambitions that go beyond the theatre?

GRAY: I used to. I had a brief romance with United Artists. I did a few demos and United Artists wanted to make a single out of one. But it was just ludicrous. I mean, there's nothing quite like being rejected by some fifty-year-old bozo with a Beatle hairdo and a medallion on his chest.

It's such a sleazy industry. You get offered a deal that says you sing with us and we get all your songs forever and ever. And if you're really lucky, they'll make a lot of money. It's a very humiliating setup. I just didn't want to be part of it. In Canada it's a branch plant system so you're constantly up against people who can say no but not yes. You're constantly being humiliated just because of the other person's powerlessness. And that person won't admit his powerlessness. There's nothing in it for those labels to promote Canadian artists. Why should they? They've got lots of American artists they can promote up here anyway.

T: What's your new play about?

GRAY: My rock n' roll band.

T: Another totally male world.

GRAY: I know. I don't have any women in my shows at all. I don't know why. I guess I don't really know much about them. I can't get into a woman's head. I only have male visions of women. It's weird.

T: People will invariably compare any new play against the success of *Billy Bishop*.

GRAY: I know. I'm quite reconciled to a turkey. There will be a turkey on the horizon. Then they'll say, well, he wrote two good shows and that was it.

T: People will want nothing less than a follow-up to *Billy Bishop*, using the same format with Eric Peterson.

GRAY: We already thought of that. We'll call the sequel *Billy Bishop Goes to Seed*. Eric and I will sit on stage and drink for two hours.

Robert Harlow

ROBERT HARLOW was born in Prince Rupert, BC in 1923 and raised in Prince George, BC. After working for CBC he headed Canada's first accredited Creative Writing Department at UBC for ten years. *Royal Murdoch* (1962), *A Gift of Echoes* (1965) and more recently *The Saxophone Winter* (1988) explore and psychologically map his native central

BC, as does his technically complex and dream-like *Scann* (1972) centred on a small-town newspaper editor. *Making Arrangements* (1978) is a comic novel about horse racing, *Paul Nolan* (1983) is an urban novel about male frustrations and *Felice* is based on a trip Harlow made to Poland.

Robert Harlow lives and teaches in Vancouver. He was interviewed in 1978.

T: From your books, it sounds like you've had your share of rubbing shoulders with what we euphemistically call the real world.

HARLOW: Well, my father was a railroader who came out west from Maine in 1909. I grew up in Prince George when it was still a small town of two thousand people. I did the usual things there like drive a truck, work in mills, and some timber cruising. When the war came, I was fifteen. I graduated from high school at seventeen and joined the Air Force. I was a bomber pilot for '43, '44 and '45. Then I went to UBC. I'd never even been to Vancouver, except to join up, but I had this ambition to go to university because very few people from my hometown ever did. I got my BA and then took Earle Birney's creative writing workshop in 1946.

T: That was the first creative writing workshop ever taught in Canada.

HARLOW: Yes, that's right. All sorts of people from that class went on to do interesting things, but I think I'm the only writer.

T: What kind of influence was Earle Birney?

HARLOW: Earle was a marvellous role model, a pretty fantastic guy, because I got to see how much energy you had to expend on writing. After I studied some more at Paul Engle's workshop in Iowa, and got married, I was working at the CBC as a producer. Earle phoned me up from UBC one day and asked if I'd be a sessional lecturer for eight months. I went downstairs and saw the boss, who told me I couldn't have leave. So I quit. Then they decided to let me go as sort of a sabbatical. When Earle got fed up with UBC and left, I was approached and asked if I would stay on as head of the newly established Creative Writing Department. I contemplated that decision for, oh . . . about twelve seconds.

T: How much had you written by then?

HARLOW: I'd written a book for my thesis at Iowa. Then I wrote parts of another two novels in the fifties. Then I published *Royal Murdoch* and *Gift of Echoes*. Later on, in 1970–71, I went on a leave of absence and wrote the bulk of *Scann* in about eight or nine actual writing months. I did it with my long-suffering family in Majorca. People think of it as a very formidable book now but I never thought of it that way as I was writing it.

T: Now with *Making Arrangements*, you've written an entirely different book.

HARLOW: I guess I believe an author should be able to write a full spectrum, not write himself over and over. Hemingway, for instance, fell into that trap a bit. He was a great writer but he did write himself over and over again. Most really good writers simply get better and better at the trade and can do a great number of things. People always say "Dickensian" as if he only wrote one kind of book. That's not true at all. His scope was fantastic. The same with Faulkner. The difference between *Sartoris* and *Light in August* is light years.

T: You once wrote, "Many authors are lost to poverty, journalism, hack writing and too much time on their hands." Why do you feel journalism is bad for writers?

HARLOW: When I said journalism, I meant the whole media thing. Journalism is just too close to real writing. It saps your energies. You have to save that energy for yourself it you're a writer. Hemingway was not a journalist when he wrote his first book. For *The Sun Also Rises* he quit work and starved and sponged off women or friends or whatever he could do. You have to be wily every day of your life.

When I was doing what amounted to journalism for the CBC, I didn't really write. There were nine years when I kidded myself I was doing it. Now I save my best brains for when I write in the mornings from six until nine or ten. Then I go out to the university and use my second best brains for teaching. My third best brains are for the evening.

T: Do you ever look at a lot of excellent journalists and see frustrated writers?

HARLOW: Sure. Years ago a friend quit his job with the *Vancouver Sun* and left his family to write the Great Canadian Novel. It didn't happen. Guys dream of that all the time. I don't know how many paragraphs he had at the end of the year but it wasn't very many. Everybody says, "I'm going to go out and write," like they're going to go out and have a baby. You have to do three or four pages a day. It's a craft. It's hard work that does it. You need a lifetime of experience.

You paid me a great compliment when you said *Making Arrangements* seemed to have spontaneous humour. I don't know how many pages of stuff I tore up because I was allowing myself to get into it. That's what technique is all about in writing. To get the author the hell out of his own work so it can be its own spontaneous self.

T: Many people argue that a university can't teach the craft of writing, that all writers have to be self-educated.

HARLOW: There have always been creative schools in various forms. Like in Moscow or St. Petersburg or Vienna at the turn of the century when people sat around and shared their ideas. That's all we do. I share my experience with young people. Now universities have finally recognized the value of that kind of learning environment and they're sponsoring it.

T: With creative writing, is there ever a danger that the "creative" gets stressed over the "writing"? Or do you not separate the two?

HARLOW: That's a very good question. The answer is I think there's something magic about creativity but I don't go around being "creative." That's why I refuse to discuss content in my classes. We only discuss technical arrangements that are needed to fulfill the intent of the author. For instance, last year a student had a story where a woman shoves a gun up her vagina and blows herself up. The class thought the guy who wrote the story was a male chauvinist of the worst order. So I let the discussion go along those lines and it didn't take them long to discover it was fruitless to discuss content. They had to discuss how that could work in his story. That's what happens in a workshop. It's very practical.

T: So you teach writing and not creativity.

HARLOW: Yes. When new instructors come on staff, often you'll find them holding dramatic calisthenics. But that only lasts for a few weeks. Pretty soon they realize the kids want to learn *how* to write. The only way they can do that is by teaching themselves, by writing. In a way, the person who teaches in a creative writing workshop is simply the best writer in that group. If you get one really good writer, that's a good workshop, and everyone in it is suddenly trying to write their asses off to get as good as he or she is.

T: I'd have to say that all the writers I've met of any consequence all have abnormally strong egos or drives.

HARLOW: I like to translate that word ego into drive, too. People with drive stick out. The trick is to learn how to translate that drive into the energy that goes into writing.

T: Do you ever get people who write

extremely well but are too passive about their talent?

HARLOW: Sure. And they don't last long. Sometimes it's not so much passivity as lack of confidence that gets to people. Some of them can't stand any criticism at all. I had a girl turn up the other day and she'd never had her work criticized by senior students before. She came in what looked like a uniform, and with a beret on. The way she wore her clothes, they were like battle dress.

T: What happens to the ones who can't cut it?

HARLOW: The ones who get in and don't make it? I never fail them. I tell them I've made a mistake. It was my fault. I was the one who let them in. We select people by looking at their writing. We ask for a hundred pages if you're a grad student, fifty pages if you're a senior student, twenty-five pages if you come out of high school. You can pretty well tell from that. If I make a mistake, they go away and try another way of learning to write or they read for the rest of their lives. But they'll never call an artist down. They'll never say Canada Council shouldn't give a writer a buck or two to finish a book. They appreciate the work involved.

T: You wrote, "By the time the writer has shown he has talent and has begun to develop, the experience he will need as the basis of his work has mostly been gathered." I would disagree with that.

HARLOW: I think the basic experiences we have are all done by the time we're seventeen or eighteen. The way we're going to treat life and deal with experience form then on is pretty much in place.

T: You're just talking about personality.

HARLOW: The tools for handling life. Even though I know it's pop psychology to say it, you're all in place by age five. People do change when they go through puberty. The edges come off. And getting married and having children are certainly heavy experiences. But they don't usually change you fundamentally. Once the personality framework is there, you just get richer and richer as you get older. According to myth, finally you get to be wise.

T: So you believe if you're going to be a writer, it's from what happened to you in the first twenty years?

HARLOW: I think so.

T: When did you know you had to be a writer?

HARLOW: When I was nine I decided to be a travel writer. I had the gift of gab and I was always good on paper so I thought writing would be easy. But I never really started writing until quite late, when I was twenty-two or so. I'm an anomaly in that respect, but the war intervened.

T: In my teens I made a close correlation between creative energy and sexual energy. Did you think that way, too?

HARLOW: When I first was in university, the sexual tension and hysteria was incredible. We spun like dervishes for four solid years. The good girl/bad girl theory was all there. Now, with the pill, young people are more mature. The energy that might have gone into hysteria can now go into creativity. So yes, I do believe the human animal's first analogies will be sexual. However, I don't think there's any one-to-one relationship between sexuality and creativity.

T: Do you differentiate between therapy writing and someone who's writing from strength?

HARLOW: Sure. Solzenitzhen writes from controlled experience and Sylvia Plath was a therapy writer. Everybody goes through a period in their life when they're like Plath, male or female. But with therapy writing I think the author's usually in the book too much, and the result is neurotic autobiography.

T: Do you see any trend nowadays away from that subjectivism of the sixties?

HARLOW: You know what we're doing now? Fantasy. Science fiction. In the last week I've had three science fiction stories turned in. This is typical. We did it in the fifties, and it was done in the thirties when times were bad, too. In times of great change, people suddenly don't understand the world and turn to fantasy as a way of handling things. Speculative fiction has always been some kind of bottom line. Shakespeare did his *Tempest* after a long life of writing. Tolkien did his *Lord of the Rings*.

T: It's all very well to know how to write. But do you also teach your students how to read?

HARLOW: Very few people ask that question. But yes, it's absolutely essential to writing to learn to read for technique. God bless English studies. It's analysis. Writing is synthesis. The twain do not often meet. In high-class criticism, which everybody hopes they write, I'm sure they do meet. Authors have to learn for themselves both synthesis and analysis. If I'm standing in line at the supermarket, I find myself picking up a nurse romance to see how and what the author is doing.

T: What should aspiring writers read?

HARLOW: Most people say to read anything that comes to hand, and I suppose that's half the answer. The other half is the hard part. All the time you're reading you should be finding out how it's done. And you don't usually start being curious about technical things until after you've begun to be serious about writing. So, one of the things I do with my students is to try to encourage them to be serious about both writing and reading

all the time — see if I can't get them to teach themselves to read as authors, rather than just as readers, and that leads them immediately to seeing how things are done. Then they apply that to their own writing.

Eventually a snowball effect occurs and larger and larger questions rise up for them to answer for themselves — What *is* a novel, for instance? Or, what *can* it be? Read Dickens and you know that he invented a lot of things that it can be — those things that Sterne didn't invent in *Tristram Shandy*. Read Grass and he will show you how to turn Dickens' novel upside down and inside out and make *The Tin Drum*. Read Faulkner and you will see a half dozen other approaches. And then there are the great novella writers — Grass again, Mann, Unamuno, Moravia, Henry James, Robbe-Grillet. Mann does *The Magic Mountain* and *Death in Venice* — a ten-pound novel and a beautiful novella. James does *The Ambassadors* and *Daisy Miller* or *Turn of the Screw*. Grass does *The Tin Drum* and *Cat and Mouse*. Those aren't just long and short books. There's a technical tactic involved. Sooner or later writers reading as authors will begin to build on that tactic and will discover and use the novella for their own purposes — in the way, perhaps, Marian Engel did it when she wrote *Bear*, or Laurence when she wrote *A Jest of God*, or Solzenitzhen when he wanted to do *A Day in the Life of Ivan Denisovich*.

The novella is the basic prose form. It deals with the *energy* generated by individual moments of consciousness — or time, if you will. Once upon a time. The novel has "the times," society, added to those energised moments, and that changed it into an entirely different genre. The short story stops a moment of time so that it can happen for us lyrically, poetically. The best short stories are always poems. And, of course, there are those other parts of writing that are common to all genres that we run into all the time when we read — point of view, for instance, which is a subject vast enough to take up your time for most of your writing life. All the concerns of composition like narrative line, tone of voice, making scenes, the whole lot. There's always enough content, seldom enough technique.

T: That list of books you recited was pretty international, especially for a literary nationalist.

HARLOW: Right. Nowadays I'm becoming pretty chauvinist. The reason is because we have some pretty good technicians among us here in Canada. Robert Kroetsch, for instance. And have you read Betty Lambert's *Crossings*? It's a fine novel. You could write a treatise on its technical aspects. The same could be said for Reshard Gool's book, *The Nemesis Casket*. An absolute gem.

I think the greatest thing that ever happened to literature in this country was the 1967 Centennial. The federal government had to give some money to literature because they gave it to everybody else. Now we've got a lot of excellent writers in this country. The problem now is to get the public aware of what is being produced.

Jack Hodgins

JACK HODGINS was born in the Comox Valley on Vancouver Island in 1938. His primarily comic fictions reflect rather than portray mostly non-urban characters, in the short stories of *Spit Delaney's Island* (1976) and *The Barclay Family Theatre* (1981). His Vancouver Island-based novels are *The Invention of the World* (1977), the Governor General's

Award-winning *The Resurrection of Joseph Bourne* (1979) and *The Honorary Patron* (1987). His frequently enthusiastic/innocent style has also produced the juvenile novel, *Left Behind at Squabble Bay* (1988).

Jack Hodgins lives in Victoria where he teaches at the university. He was interviewed in 1978.

T: Where do you think you got the ambition to be a writer?

HODGINS: I don't know because I can't remember not having it. I loved books from the beginning. There weren't that many around the house and certainly very few around the school. The few books I had, I'm sure I read a dozen times before my childhood was over. The library, for most of my schooling, was just one shelf across the back of the classroom. But there was always something magical about books. The feel, the touch and the smell. I wanted to be one of the people who filled up those books, who did whatever the magic thing was.

So right from the beginning it wasn't just the writing, it was the book that was important to me too. I guess in some sense I would feel that you could sit and write all your life and if it never turns into a book then it isn't real. When I was ten I remember I wrote a murder mystery that was four pages long! I asked my babysitter to type it up, which she did, and then I folded the pages over and sewed them up the back and put a cover on it.

T: Is there anything significant about your family background?

HODGINS: My mother was one of six, my dad was one of thirteen. So every second person in the community was a relative. If he wasn't a relative, he was a friend. So that kind of an extended family is just part of the way I see the world. It's not something I've deliberately gone out of my way to create, except to some extent in *Joseph Bourne*. I knew everybody in my community. I went to school with the kids of everybody.

T: A lot of people have become writers precisely because they didn't grow up in that kind of social atmosphere.

HODGINS: Well, there was still the loneliness of knowing that what was important to me was something that had no relationship with the lives of the people around me. And if they only knew, they would think I was a real freak. Which I was! That created a problem in that I obviously didn't fit into the adult patterns I saw around me. I think in my childhood I equated this problem to a rural/city question. I felt I probably didn't belong in a rural situation. Maybe all city people were like me. But when I got to university in Vancouver I discovered that wasn't true. You carry your own home around with you. This tuned up my defence mechanisms and then in turn my abilities to know what other people felt like.

T: In one of your novels there's a remark that the city of Nanaimo has gone from a frontier mentality to a Disneyland mentality. Has it ever occurred to you that you may be fortunate as a writer to be able to see your society change so drastically?

HODGINS: Yes. I think someone on the CBC radio once mentioned, in a derogatory fashion, that the BC Ferries brought Vancouver Island out of an essential hillbilly culture into the twentieth century. Well, that "hillbilly" culture was my whole life up until my twenties. I've gone from a childhood in a farmhouse without telephone or electricity to being gobbled up by the city of Nanaimo, which is bursting at the seams, creating subdivisions all around us.

T: Also there was a story of yours in *Saturday Night* once about a boy whose mother wanted him to become a concert violinist and his father wanted him to be a logger. Do you think it's an advantage for a writer to be a composite of two opposite parents?

HODGINS: Yes, no question about it. If nothing else it gave me a good start at being able to see things from a different point of view. I'm not writing about myself as many do. I write about the people I see out there. If I'm able to do it at all, I think it's because I've developed a lifetime habit of being super-sensitive to the way other people feel, almost to knowing what's going on inside them. It may have begun as a child as a defence mechanism, as a timid kid trying to figure out where the dangers were in the world, trying to know what people were thinking before they ever got around to acting.

T: Have you studied people's speech consciously?

HODGINS: Yes. And that's still very conscious with me. I think this is the result of having had to go through a very painful experience of quote, "finding my own voice." In my twenties all my writing was very imitative. I fell in love with the writing of William Faulkner and a few other American writers. Everything I wrote had to sound like them. Then when it did sound like them, it wasn't any good either. Towards the end of my twenties I decided I had to either find my own voice, whatever that was, or else give up writing altogether.

Well, the thing that happened was that I didn't find my own voice at all. But I started listening to the voices of people who live on Vancouver Island. I think that was much more important than listening to my own voice. I started to notice that no two people talk the same. Not only are voices different, but people have different speech patterns, different favourite expressions and different rhythms of speech. Once I figured it out, I thought that is probably the most powerful device I can use for making my characters seem alive.

Often if I've got a character set up and I know him very well, all I have to do is listen to him talk. I will worry less about the content of his answer to somebody's question than about the rhythm of his speech. Often, I suspect, what we say is controlled more by the patterns we're comfortable with than what we really think.

T: Most writers go through a period of finding their own self before they can go on to be writers. Was that a problem for you?

HODGINS: I don't know. I've never consciously looked to understand myself. I think I was at least thirty before a consciousness of myself got to any crisis point.

T: How do you mean?

HODGINS: I reached a point where I had to put up or shut up. Either produce or quit fooling yourself. You see there was a whole pile of people, whose names I now forget, who became overnight sensations when I was about nineteen.

And I sort of took it for granted that if you didn't become a published novelist in your early twenties at the latest, it's like the old-fashioned girl who's an old maid if she's not married by twenty-two or something.

All right, I know that's a misconception. But remember, I had nobody to advise me. All I had to go by was the people who got the attention. All those overnight sensations! No doubt, all over the world there were people like me gnashing their teeth saying why do *I* have to wait? Thank goodness I did! I shudder to think what if somebody had published one of my earlier novels. And I suspect that at least one of them is publishable, though not very good at all. If somebody had given me the encouragement of publishing it, I think it would have been very bad. I might have thought, well, I guess I've got it made.

Now I think, if I've learned anything about writing, it's the result of the terrible frustrations of not getting anywhere for so long. I *had* to learn. Because nothing was happening by itself. I had to really work like a dog to make it happen.

T: It sounds like the toughest part of

being a writer is surviving the apprenticeship.

HODGINS: During all those years there was that nagging suspicion that this was all a fantasy, all a dream. I had no reason to believe that I would ever have any kind of success whatsoever. I had no reason to believe I'd ever be published at all. I didn't know any other writers as a kid. I didn't know anyone else who wanted to write until I was well into adulthood. I didn't even know anyone else from my own generation who loved reading. So if I wrote, I wrote behind closed doors. I even read behind closed doors. This was just not acceptable behaviour for a growing boy in a rural community.

T: Most Canadian writers have had the same feeling. We're probably basically still a very young country with a pioneer mentality.

HODGINS: And we're suspicious of the written word, aren't we? That apprenticeship as a writer can be so painful that it seems to me if writers can do nothing else for aspiring writers, they should tell this fact about their own lives.

T: Would you agree the Protestant work ethic influences the reading of literature in Canada?

HODGINS: No question about it. I often get the impression reading much of the fiction written in this country that nobody in Canada ever laughs. Nobody ever makes fun of themselves, nobody ever takes life at all lightly. And yet I look at the real people around me and it seems that almost everybody I know laughs quite often every day. So if there are examples of humour in my work, it's not usually a deliberate attempt to be funny. It's simply a reflection of the way I see people, people who seem to spend a lot of their time laughing, often at themselves. Humour is a perfectly realistic part of life. But you don't get all that much comedy in serious Canadian fiction.

T: Along with that humour, I think the reader also gets a feeling from your work that the person creating everything is enjoying himself. And some of that pleasure rubs off.

HODGINS: That's good. And you're quite right, I am enjoying myself. This may be a case, ironically, of a weakness becoming a strength. I'm very, very impatient with my own work. I'm very easily bored. So I demand that almost every page entertain me. I can only hope that it will entertain the readers about one-tenth as much.

Sometimes I just fly by the seat of my pants. That is, I want to turn the page to find out what happens next. I don't always know. I'm never happy if my writing seems simply beautiful or practical. It can do everything I want a scene to do, to serve the purposes of a novel or short story, but I still throw it away if it doesn't somehow get me so excited that my heart is pounding.

T: That would explain much of the audaciousness of your work.

HODGINS: Yes. But also I abandoned those safe little novels I was writing simply because it was obvious I wasn't getting anywhere by writing safe little novels. Some part of me said, all right, if I'm not going to get anywhere writing safe little things I might as well go way out and risk everything and either fall flat on my face or else maybe at last I might get a foot in the door.

T: And so you can risk having a title like *The Invention of the World*.

HODGINS: Sure. I thought, well, I've already taken all the risks writing this novel so why not go one step further? The interpretation of that title I find most people getting immediately is that the author is the inventor of a world inside a novel. But the one all important image throughout the novel is the image of the counterfeit, so I also wanted a title to point to the hints that are dropped about the invented as opposed to the created world. To me, the word invention is a negative word. I wanted it to be noticeable that I did not call it creation of the world.

I think at one point I was aware of six or seven ways that people could read the novel. For instance, it can also be seen as an historical exploration of why people move to Vancouver Island. It's possible to see the history of Vancouver Island as the history of failed colonies. So I chose *The Invention of the World* because it implies that the different levels of the novel are allegorical and that the primary concern is the search for the return to the "created" world.

T: How do you see *The Resurrection of Joseph Bourne* as being different from your previous books?

HODGINS: Well, some of the challenges I set for myself were to write a continuous narrative rather than a fragmented one. And to create a concert of voices. Using a whole small town as my protagonist, I can float from person to person for reactions to certain events. Plus, I had the advantage of using a location I hadn't used before and a number of people who were quite different from the people I had used before.

T: One thing I noticed in *Spit Delaney's Island* is how people you write about resemble the people Ken Mitchell writes about on the prairies. Except where he examines deviancy as a survival technique, you're looking into how people use their so-called normality to protect themselves.

HODGINS: It's something I'm conscious of doing from story to story. That's a useful, profitable way of examining a person — putting him into a situation where his values are challenged and see how he reacts.

T: But you seem to be fascinated by normalcy, which in a way, is abnormal.

HODGINS: This isn't something I've thought of ahead of time but maybe there's something about this that may be important. To me, everybody is the main character in his own life story. Anyone who goes out of his way to be eccentric or to be overwhelmingly noticeable is attempting, whether he knows it or not, to be the main character in somebody else's life. And that's something I will not tolerate. I cannot stand the thought that there can be people in this world who are not even the main people in their own life story. All people are equally valid. So if that creates a tendency for liking normalcy, I suppose that is an explanation.

T: You yourself don't seem to have one trait that stands out among the rest. Sitting there on the chesterfield, you appear to be eminently normal.

HODGINS: That's terrible thing to say!

T: Maybe that translates into real strength. Are you normal?

HODGINS: Well, the important thing about what you're saying is that I'm not living a role. In fact, as soon as a role is defined, I begin to resist it. I think, in my writing, the people in my stories are so important that I cannot afford to overshadow them by being a person. I can't wear kilts and get drunk in public and insult the Queen. First of all, it wouldn't be natural. But also, I couldn't risk losing my ability to meet people unhampered by an awareness that I was some eccentric person hovering over them.

T: This creates a public relations problem. Good-natured former high school teachers aren't supposed to write great works of fiction.

HODGINS: But I think the greatest novelists in the world today are people like John Fowles and John Gardner. If you learn anything about their lives at all, they are decent people. The person who cares about creating a public image is so busy thinking about "Am I living up to it?" that he's going to be less sensitive to other people.

T: Would you agree then that the most striking aspect of your work is that it appears so unegocentric?

HODGINS: Yes. I write out of curiosity, out of the mystery of these people who are around me. Inevitably I uncover more mystery than I ever solve. Whenever I try a character who is quite close to the kind of person I may be myself, I find myself losing interest in the story. I don't know what this tells you about me! I don't even want to think about what it might tell you about me!

T: Do you think too much can be made of the fact that Jack Hodgins is writing about Vancouver Island?

HODGINS: Yes, it's dangerous to talk that way. Of course it's important to me that I get Vancouver Island right, but if I was only interested in writing about Vancouver Island I'd write a geography book or a history book. I'm interested in writing about human beings. I just happen to be writing about people who are close to me geographically. I try not to think too much about what makes people different here. In making too much of the uniqueness of a people in a region, there's a danger that a writer could write stuff which is nothing but regional. It's important for me to find the things that people in New York or London or South Africa can also recognize. To a small degree, that's starting to happen. People will write to me from far, far away to say your characters sound like my neighbours. That's what I want to hear.

T: Do you think too many Canadian writers place an inflated value on their own individualism?

HODGINS: That's a dangerous question.

T: But it's an important question.

HODGINS: Yes, it is. I know there is a school of fiction writing which believes very strongly that the only window left open on the world now is through yourself. That, I think, is perfectly legitimate for a person who sincerely believes it. But it doesn't happen to fit into the way I see the world.

T: Which is closer to Rudy Wiebe's approach to writing than say, Marian Engel's.

HODGINS: Yes. I think if all of us lived a hundred and fifty years ago, the Rudy Wiebes and Robert Kroetschs and Jack Hodginses would be writing the epic novels and the first-person novelists would be writing lyric poetry. Now we're living in a time when all the borders have been crossed. Some poets can be writing epic poems and some novelists can be writing lyric novels. It doesn't really matter. Basically I think it's a question of finding where your instincts lie. Probably you write the sort of thing that you enjoy reading yourself.

For myself, I often think of fiction as high class gossip. Really, what you're doing is saying listen, I've got a story I want to tell you about the guys who live down the road. This is what they did and isn't that something.

That's partly why I like reading Rudy Wiebe and Robert Kroetsch, and also South Americans like Vargas Llosa and Marquez, and John Nichols, the American. They have this sense of community. Everybody's in on the story. It's not exclusively the story of one person. The whole world is alive and teeming with life. There's a sense in the novel itself that the novel is a complete world. When you open the first page, you're entering a new world. When you close the last page, you're no longer in it.

Edith Iglauer

EDITH IGLAUER was born in Cleveland, Ohio. She married Philip Hamburger and raised two sons in New York. A frequent contributor to the *New Yorker*, she has nonetheless written a great deal about Canada. Her first book, *The New People: The Eskimo's Journey Into Our Time* (1966, reprinted and updated as *Inuit Journey* in 1979) chronicled the growth

of native cooperatives in the eastern Arctic. She profiled Pierre Trudeau in 1969 and internationally known architect Arthur Erickson in 1979. *Denison's Ice Road* (1975) is about the building of a 325-mile winter road to the Arctic Circle. Divorced in 1966, she came to Vancouver in 1973. She married John Heywood Daly, a commercial salmon troller, and moved to Garden Bay on the BC coast. John Daly died in 1978. After writing *Seven Stones: A Portrait of Arthur Erickson, Architect* (1981), she began recording her memories of her late husband and his salmon troller the *MoreKelp*. The result is *Fishing with John* (1988), a memoir.

Edith Iglauer divides her time between Garden Bay, BC and New York. She was interviewed in 1988.

T: In 1945, at the end of World War II, you were in Yugoslavia as a correspondent for the Cleveland *News*. Was that the beginning of your career?

IGLAUER: Well, I didn't know how to manoeuvre myself around professionally until I made that trip. It gave me some confidence in myself. I had articles published. I was paid ten dollars an article. When I got home the editor, Nat Howard, gave me a bonus of a hundred dollars. That pretty well paid for all my expenses. I was technically a captain in the US Army and we ate in army messes.

T: Why did you go?

IGLAUER: My husband Philip Hamburger went over for the *New Yorker* as their war correspondent in the Mediterranean theatre. He was there at the death of Mussolini and did a terrific story on it. Hanging upside down and everything. I was trying to join him, so I got myself accredited to the *News*, which was my hometown paper. I was able to sell the idea to Nat because I planned to go to Yugoslavia and Cleveland has a big Slavic population.

I was the only woman on the Army transport plane. The soldiers were darling to me. They carried my luggage; they really took care of me. I was just a kid still. I landed in Casablanca because I didn't know where I was going. That's where the plane went, and then I had to get myself to Italy, where Phil was. I remember going to Italy, flying over the Bay of Naples. The door blew out of the plane. All of sudden there was this tremendous rush of air. Everybody fell on the legs of the man sitting with his back at the open doorway, holding him down. I can remember sitting there, watching this door sailing over the Bay of Naples, like a great bird.

T: Once you've survived in a bizarre, post-war situation, you can reasonably expect to manage in Northern Québec or Great Slave Lake.

IGLAUER: That's right. The damage, the destruction. Everything was still in ruins. There wasn't enough food. I remember the manager of the hotel in Belgrade came up and had coffee with us every morning because I had brought some powdered coffee with me. From that experience overseas I learned that I'm good at parlaying myself. For instance, in Casablanca I just sat where the planes came in and waited for a space. When I'm on a story I just follow along and let it take me wherever it will.

T: You go passively into situations. But you can also use passivity to manipulate people, to help get information.

IGLAUER: Well, I have found that if you are patient while you're doing a story, the other person is apt to say what you want to hear. If my work is good, it's because I want to hear what's truly going on. It's much better for me to sit there and let things happen. I was trained by the *New Yorker* not to have the writer as the most important person in the story. I learned a lot from A.J. Liebling. He was one of the great writers of the *New Yorker*. Actually, he was notorious for just sitting out his subject. Eventually his subject would break down and begin to babble. If you sit there long enough, amazing things come out.

T: How was Pierre Trudeau to interview?

IGLAUER: He was terrible about giving me one-to-one time.

T: Was that conscious on his part? To show you where the power lay?

IGLAUER: Yes. Very much so. I don't know if any *New Yorker* profile has ever been done where the subject gave so little time personally as he gave me. I had to report around him, get almost all my information from other people. Then when he did see me on a one-to-one basis, it was at lunch at his house. He had a deliberate habit of speaking so fast I couldn't keep up. I had to take notes under the table, but he would never have said the things he said to me with a tape recorder on.

T: Has your estimation of Trudeau changed since 1968?

IGLAUER: I was horrified with the War Measures Act. I'm sorry to say there must have been something wrong with my reporting because it caught me by surprise. Other than that, by comparison with what's happened since, I still think he's the best prime minister we've had. The present one, Mulroney, is not going to ever get a prize for what's going on inside his head.

T: You're on the *New Yorker* staff. Does that mean you have to submit a certain number of articles every year?

IGLAUER: No. I sign a contract every year giving them first reading of my work and I am always, it seems, working on something for the *New Yorker*.

T: How many people are on that "staff"?

IGLAUER: I have no idea. Nobody I know knows.

T: Your old friend Hubert Evans used to joke that any writing in the *New Yorker* was just filler between the ads.

IGLAUER: But he was very, very encouraging to me. One of the reasons I had to finish this book, *Fishing with John*, is that Hubert leaned in the doorway of his house one night as I was leaving and quoted the Scripture to me. He said it was my sacred duty to finish this book. He was always telling me about the fin on the salmon that had become useless. If you didn't use your talents, they will become useless. I was so sorry he didn't live to see me finish this book.

The last time I saw him, which was just before he died, he suddenly turned over in bed and told me what a

wonderful writer he thought I was and that I had to finish the book about John. He went on for about twenty minutes. And this was from a man who was having trouble talking. It was very, very moving.

T: Did you learn anything about writing from Hubert?

IGLAUER: How could you not learn from a man who couldn't see and who wrote a whole book at the age of eighty-seven? I think his last book *O Time In Your Flight* is really a classic, on a par with W.O. Mitchell's *Who Has Seen the Wind*. It's a beautiful piece of work, no matter what his age was when he wrote it. It's almost perfect for what it is. And I think it's criminal that it wasn't given the Governor General's Award. Hubert had a tremendous influence on me. How the devil could I not learn about courage and determination from him? And also about the ability to adjust as you get older. Now I don't dare say to myself, "Well, I'm getting too old to do this or that."

T: Because you remember.

IGLAUER: Because I remember. It was Hubert, more than any other single person, who put me back together after John died. Those Tuesday evening discussion groups at Hubert's saved my life. There was nothing that I wanted to do after John died except die myself. But those Tuesdays at Hubert's were like an electric light; things suddenly began to come alive again, like lights that started to flicker.

He also introduced me to a very close friend of his named Maxie Southwell. I remember the day he put on his coat and got out his white walking stick. He was very old by then. I don't think he'd been out of his house for quite a while. We walked across the dunes to Maxie's house, two or three doors down the beach, and she was waiting. We all had tea together. Maxie served bread and butter and jam. I remember laughing and thinking, "My God, I'm enjoying myself." Maxie, who died before Hubert, although she was a good ten years younger, was very nurturing. With her, I could do no wrong. And to her I was absolutely beautiful.

T: They were like a mother and father.

IGLAUER: Yes. Over the years I never went through Roberts Creek on my way home without staying the night at Maxie's. Of course Hubert was not so thoroughly approving. He was very Calvinist. For instance, he thought I wasted time, and that I was much too social. After John died, in the beginning, I couldn't even sleep. It was like an engine running that would never stop. It was simply terrible. But the minute I got down to Hubert's I would fall asleep. It used to enrage him. He would stop all discussion and say, "Edith! You're sleeping again!" I couldn't help it. I was at peace down there.

T: Did he have a spiritual influence?

IGLAUER: About three weeks after John died, the first time I was going up the coast to be alone in my house, I stopped and saw Hubert. I was crying and Hubert said, "You're expecting too much, too soon. You have to wait a while for John to come back. Don't be in so much of a hurry. He's got lots to do." This was a wonderful thought. To think that this man was going to come back into my spirit or whatever it was that Hubert definitely believed.

Hubert always believed that his wife was still there in the next room. I really held on to that idea. Waiting for it to happen. It probably would have happened without Hubert, but it wouldn't have happened so gracefully. Even now I can't talk about Hubert Evans without wanting to cry. He was so wonderful to me.

T: Does *Fishing with John* commu-

nicate what you want it to communicate?

IGLAUER: I can't tell. I wouldn't be surprised if it only sold twelve copies. Or maybe it will sell a lot. I have no judgement on it. I just had to write it. And when I wrote it I had no judgement on it. It was Bill Shawn of the New Yorker who kept encouraging me. He says it's the best thing I've ever written. I don't know whether it is or not. I'm astonished that everybody likes it so much. It's made several people weep, which has surprised me.

T: Because it's a love story.

IGLAUER: I can't tell. When I started this I was just going to do a piece on fishing for Bill Shawn. Then John died. That transformed the whole thing. What I wanted to do was keep John alive and to have other people know this simply wonderful man. I was so afraid he might recede. There's no question it was a form of survival for me. Bill said, "Just write it as it comes and I'll take what I need."

One of the reasons it took so long to write is that I had an awful time describing that fishing gear on the troller. I had three fishermen reading it the whole time for accuracy. They read it three times each. When the book was ready to be published I got uneasy and I asked Reg Payne to read it too. He used to be the head of the UFUAW. All of them seemed to be fascinated. They made factual corrections but they didn't have a word of complaint.

T: You were with John Daly for only four and a half years...

IGLAUER: But my whole life changed as a result. It's the quality, not the quantity of the time spent that counts. I've had to learn to accept that. It's hard to believe I've lived more years without him than I lived with him.

T: Now, when things happen to you, do you sometimes see events through

John Daly's eyes?

IGLAUER: Oh, all the time. All the time.

T: How did you meet him?

IGLAUER: A good friend in Washington asked me to look him up. I called and he shouted into the phone, "I'm terribly busy. I can't do anything about you. I'm cooking for a dozen people." He slammed the phone down. I thought he was very rude. Then a week later he called me. He arrived talking a blue streak, apologizing that he was wearing his fishing pants. In the middle of the evening he asked if I ever married again whether I wanted a big wedding or to just go off to a justice of the peace. He never stopped talking until two-thirty in the morning.

T: Was there a part of you that was expecting or needing that love affair with John Daly later in life? Or did it come to you as a surprise that it could exist?

IGLAUER: We were both very lonely. You don't admit your loneliness when nothing's happening that's going to make it less so. But when you meet somebody that has all the qualities that you love, and they need you and you need them, well . . . I think most relationships occur out of proximity and need.

T: Excuse me for saying this — but it sounds like your life started with this relationship. You were obviously missing something before.

IGLAUER: I don't mean it to. I had a fascinating first marriage, and Phil and his wife Anna are among my best friends. I see them a lot when I am in New York. My life is definitely divided into two sectors. Living in the United States. And living in Canada. Basically I never really liked New York. It's not a city that excites me the way it does other people. I don't find it the beginning or the end of anything. New York always frightened

me. I always wanted to live in the country.

Growing up in Ohio we had a place in the country, which I still own with my sister, thirty miles outside of Cleveland, where we went every single weekend. Sometimes my father would pick me up when he left work on Friday nights and we would go horseback riding out there. It was marvellous to ride at sunset. In the early years of having this cabin we didn't have any running water, just a pump. As very little girls, we had to wash our dishes in a stream. When I went to the Canadian north, I went right back to my childhood. Plodding along after my father in the snow, having cold feet and cold hands, and not complaining. That's where my adjustment to being outdoors comes from. It's no adjustment for me to go to the Arctic and not have a regular toilet.

T: So you're not running after sophistication.

IGLAUER: No. I'm not a sophisticated person. I never really wanted to be. Life here suits me better.

T: Does this mean Vancouver is the Cleveland of Canada?

IGLAUER: No! John used to always refer to Vancouver as being in Lower Funland. And Victoria was always Crumpet Town. Vancouver is not as advanced culturally here as Cleveland by any means. Cleveland has one of the great art museums of the United States and it also has the best symphony in the United States. The public support for the symphony orchestra here is apparently nil. And I don't see any great collections coming into the Vancouver Art Gallery. I mean, when you get through with Emily Carr and Jack Shadbolt, what have you got? Not too much.

T: You've had two good experiences with marriage. That's two more than a lot of people have.

IGLAUER: Yes. I try to look at it that way. I had a psychiatrist say to me you must feel cheated because you had so little time with John. I said I could choose to think of it that way but I choose to think that I was the luckiest woman on earth to have him at all and to have years which were as happy as that. John said it was idyllic. And it was. Here were two people who loved each and completely trusted each other. It can be just as passionate and just as loving when you're older. And in some ways it can be better because you know what counts and what doesn't. And there's a lot of laughter about things you couldn't laugh about before. And of course all our children were grown so we just had each other. It was totally wonderful.

T: How did John die?

IGLAUER: He dropped dead while we were dancing.

T: Where was this?

IGLAUER: We were at an Indian reservation in The Pas, Manitoba. We were on our way to Thompson, Manitoba to see his son Sean, who is a mining geologist. His other son, Dick, was with us. We were going to have a reunion. But John had always wanted to go to the Trappers Festival. So we went there on the way. We were dancing and the room was full of smoke. I knew he had trouble breathing in stuffy places. He'd had a terrific heart attack before I met him,

in 1962. I said to him, "I think we should leave now. There's not enough oxygen in here." He said, "Let's have one more dance. I'm doing just what I want to do, just where I want to be, with the person I want to dance with, and I'm completely happy."

Then when the music stopped he suddenly turned to me and said he couldn't breathe. He started for the door. By the time I got outside he was lying in the snow with his arms out. I started to laugh because I thought he was playing a game with me. As children we used to play a game called Angel Wings. For just a second, I thought that's what he was doing. Then I realized what had had happened.

My younger son asked me later what I thought about when John died. I remember so clearly what I thought. I saw my life stretching out in desolation. It was just desolate land. In a sense that's how it is inside. But I realized you can't mourn like that forever so I tried to do something positive and turn it around. So I'm happy in way, sure I am. But I miss him terribly.

T: That's a powerful idea. To die dancing.

IGLAUER: He was such a joyful man. If he had to die, that's the way he would have chosen. I think everyone who knew him at all well agreed on that.

W.P. Kinsella

W.P. KINSELLA was born in Edmonton, Alberta in 1935. He passed his first ten years as an only child on a remote homestead near Darwell, Alberta. His bestselling collections of stories about Indians from Alberta's Hobbema reserve are *Dance Me Outside* (1977), *Scars* (1978), *Born Indian* (1981), *The Moccasin Telegraph* (1983) and *The Fencepost Chronicles*

(1986), for which he earned the Stephen Leacock Medal for humour. His equally popular baseball fictions are two novels, the Houghton Mifflin Prize-winning *Shoeless Joe* (1982) and *The Iowa Baseball Confederacy* (1986), and a short story collection, *The Thrill of the Grass* (1984). Other collections include *The Alligator Report* (1985), *Red Wolf, Red Wolf* (1987) and shorter works published in limited editions by Vancouver antiquarian bookseller William Hoffer.

W.P. (William Patrick) Kinsella lives in White Rock, BC. He was interviewed in 1985 and 1986.

T: Who were Rags and Sigs?

KINSELLA: Where did I ever mention that? Rags and Sigs were my imaginary friends when I was around four or five. They were my first fictional characters. I was an only child. I was raised out in the backwoods of Alberta. There weren't any neighbours who had children. So I had all kinds of make-believe playmates. Rags and Sigs were the two that I talked about.

T: Did your parents approve?

KINSELLA: I suppose they had to. I didn't have anybody else to play with! "Go out and play with Rags and Sigs!" It was better than talking to the hogs.

T: And the *Star Weekly* was your big literary influence?

KINSELLA: That's true. The *Star Weekly* was the only thing we got. It came every Saturday. I used to devour it. The fiction particularly. I had learned to read by the time I was five. Sometimes I could read it all and sometimes it was too complicated. I remember "Hugh B. Cave" was one of my favourite writers. And I remember a serial called "Wild Lilac." That was my only contact with the outside world, the *Star Weekly*.

T: Do you re-use the terrain around Lac Ste. Anne where you grew up for your Hobbema stories?

KINSELLA: No, I've never been on the reserve at Lac Ste. Anne. At least not to my knowledge. We were ten miles from it. It might have been ten thousand. We didn't have anything but a horse and buggy for getting around. The home place was very isolated. Forty years this August it's been vacant and nobody's got in there yet to burn it down.

I've never been to Hobbema either. I don't want to go. Because everything I write is fiction. I don't want to be confused by fact.

T: Why did your family move to Edmonton when you were ten?

KINSELLA: Ostensibly so I could go to school. I had taken the first five years by correspondence but my mom didn't feel qualified to teach me anymore. But also I think my parents were sick to death of the farm. They had only gone to the farm because of the Depression.

T: Did you have an adverse reaction to the formal school system?

KINSELLA: I suppose so. I don't suffer fools. And I don't take orders. As immodest as it may sound, it has to do with intelligence. That's why I've always been a lousy employee. I have always worked for people who were only about half as smart as I was. So you automatically become suspect. Stupid people have an innate fear of anyone smarter than they are.

T: What about baseball? Did your dad take you out to the ballpark in Edmonton?

KINSELLA: It was a school friend who introduced me to the Big Four League. I went a few times with him. Mostly I used to go on my own. It was a five-cent bus ride from the East End down to the flats where the baseball park was. My dad talked a lot of baseball. He had played in the minor leagues. He used to drag the *St. Louis Sporting News* home once in a while and it was he who told me first about Shoeless Joe Jackson. But I think he only went out to a couple of Sunday afternoon games with me.

T: Have you still got a copy of your first story? The one about a murder in a ballpark?

KINSELLA: That vanished somewhere when I moved from Victoria to Iowa. I would love to have it. That story was written in grade seven. My mom, I think, still has some of my early efforts. She always threatens to drag them out. I was writing all through high school. I always knew that's what I wanted to do.

T: When were you first published in any form?

KINSELLA: I was about eighteen or nineteen. I'd gone to work for the provincial government. I used to get my work done by ten in the morning so I could write the rest of the day. I should have stayed there. I went into private industry after that and I had to work a great deal harder. I wasn't able to do any writing for several years. From '56 to '63, I think it was. My kids were little and I was struggling like hell to keep food on the table. I did some writing in Edmonton in the mid sixties, but it was mostly journalism.

T: Did you ever get deeply discouraged?

KINSELLA: I was too busy to get discouraged. I hated everything I was doing. Then in '67 I left Edmonton.

T: You opened up a pizza parlour in Victoria without ever having cooked a pizza. That strikes me as something Frank Fencepost might have done.

KINSELLA: Frank has a lot of chutzpah and I guess I did too, at the time. But I did know the economics of the business and that's by far the most important part. I had a friend in Edmonton who owned several pizza places. I sat down with him and saw how I could make a living doing it. So I set it up. There was only one other pizza place in Victoria at the time and I'm a real good financial manager. We were successful from the day we opened the doors. But it's funny you should mention that. I have a story half done at the moment about exactly that. It's the first time I've ever written about the restaurant business.

T: What was the first Silas Ermineskin story?

KINSELLA: "Illianna Comes Home," the first story in *Dance Me Outside*. That was written three or four years before any of the others. It sat around for a couple of years until I took it to Bill Valgardson's class at the University of Victoria. He said, "You've got something here." Over the next summer I got a couple more ideas so I wrote "Panache," "Horse Collars," "Dance Me Outside," "Caraway," "Linda Star" and a couple of others. I gave them to Billy that fall. He said they were great. That was the start of it all.

T: Because those stories are written in sly pidgin English, the reader hardly notices the amount of crime and violence in them. Do you think those stories could be told without that style?

KINSELLA: I don't think so. But that style is deceptive. I don't actually do that much with the diction. It just appears that I do. And of course Silas is getting more literate as a narrator all the time. The sentences are getting longer and the language is getting clearer.

T: I took an inventory of the subject matter in *Dance Me Outside*. There's murder, prostitution, child prostitution, racial discrimination, gambling, a lost baby, rape, suicide, drug dealing...

KINSELLA: That goes back to Valgardson's Law. "Short stories are not about events but the people that events happen to." The murders happen offstage. The guy is castrated offstage in "Dance Me Outside." the suicide-murder takes place offstage in "Caraway." Those events are peripheral. You have to have conflict of some kind. But it's the people that those events happen to that the stories are about.

T: Do you agree that your stories would be ideal for a television series?

KINSELLA: Yes. It's absolutely inconceivable that these stories have not been bought for television. There are ninety-some stories ready-made. I write visually. And I write very visually intentionally. But the people in television are at least ten years behind the times, probably closer to twenty.

Nothing can be done for a couple of years now because Norman Jewison has the characters tied for a movie deal or for TV.

T: Do you still run into people who assume you are a native Indian?

KINSELLA: Occasionally. Last fall a woman came up from the Lummi Indian Reserve just across the border. She taught at the college and wanted me to come and read. She was flabbergasted when she discovered I wasn't Indian. And also very angry. It used to happen more often. When *Dance Me Outside* came out I had all kinds of people phoning around Wetaskawin and Hobbema trying to find out where I lived.

T: Do you generally know the ending of your stories before you begin?

KINSELLA: Well, the ideal way for me to write a story is to get a good opening and then somewhere before I've written three or four pages I want to know the ending. And I want to write it. If you've got a good opening and a good closing there's not much more you need. Any journeyman can fill in the middle. It's just a matter of whether it's eight or ten or twenty pages. But sometimes I do start with an ending. The "Black Wampum" story in *Scars*, for instance.

T: You mention the tradition of *deus ex machina* in "The Mother's Dance." How often do you directly incorporate Greek traditions? How important is that to you?

KINSELLA: I'm doing much less of that now. I'm not writing anything for the academics to grab hold of.

T: So initially you thought you should appeal to them?

KINSELLA: Oh, sure. Originally I wanted to get a teaching position. I was writing to impress the critics and the snottier little magazines. There's a lot more conscious symbolism in my first books. Now I'm fortunate I don't have to do that anymore. But I still throw in symbols. Or I'll retell a Greek legend somewhere. I still like to make their little wooden hearts beat faster.

T: Why do you have such a hostile attitude towards academics?

KINSELLA: It's so fraudulent. This business of taking a book and applying incredible psychological and sociological and symbolic meanings to it. It's a game. An elaborate mind game. It has no validity at all that I can see.

T: Okay, for instance, let's say I was setting out to examine the role of the Indian in Canadian literature...

KINSELLA: You'd have to get off this academic hoopla to do it. I read something in a reputable journal not long ago about Hiebert, this guy who wrote *Sarah Binks*. Now if there is anything that is fun reading and harmless, it's *Sarah Binks*. But this guy was saying how Hiebert hated the Indians because of some statements he made in Sarah Binks's poems. It's insane!

T: But you can find stupidity everywhere. There are stupid garage mechanics. It doesn't necessarily follow that all garage mechanics are useless.

KINSELLA: Every once in a while there is some good critical work done, but it's very few and far between. Most of the effort is totally wasted. Again, when I see the stuff that's written on my work, it's incredible. It's such pretentious shit. They see things that not only I had no intention of writing in the work, but nobody in their right mind would see.

T: For an atheist you have numerous religious concepts repeated in your work. Redemption, faith, resurrection and even reincarnation.

KINSELLA: Oh, sure. Just because you don't believe in something doesn't mean you don't write about it. I don't believe in the Bible but I read it occasionally and I use biblical references. I have retold biblical stories. We're so inundated with Christian mythology that if you're going to write quality work I think it will probably be an integral part of it. Critics could legitimately write about the religious symbolism in *Shoeless Joe*. In fact it is taught in religious studies courses in the US.

T: When the Houghton Mifflin editor called and asked you to expand your Shoeless Joe short story into a novel, did you have any qualms about your ability to do it?

KINSELLA: I knew I could write that length. I'd written one unsuccessful novel before. I wrote to him and said I had never written anything successful longer than twenty-five pages. If I was going to do this I wanted to have a good editor working with me. I assumed that would be the last I would hear from him. Most editors don't really want to work with people. They want the finished product on their desk. But Larry Kessenich was right out of editor's school. He was hot to trot and ambitious. He said he'd be happy to work with me.

T: How did you evolve such a strange plot?

KINSELLA: I always knew I was going to write something about J.D. Salinger. And I knew I was going to write something about Moonlight Graham. And also something about Eddie Sissoms. I thought, well, alright, what if I do all this together? I went and reread all of Salinger. I dug up unpublished stories and found a story with Ray Kinsella in it. I thought, this is the entrance to my Salinger material. He's used my character in a story. I'll use his.

T: Was it hard bringing everything together?

KINSELLA: *Shoeless Joe* was the easiest thing I have ever written. It was just like a baby. It took nine months. And it was virtually not revised at all. About five or six pages were cut, that was all.

T: Have there been any Indians who have played pro ball?

KINSELLA: Allie Reynolds. Chief Bender. Daryl Evans is half Indian...

T: I ask because it seems an obvious idea for a story. Frank Fencepost signs with the Cleveland Indians.

KINSELLA: I've written a story about the Montana Magic. That was a hockey team that the Hobbema Indians actually bought. Afterwards apparently they found out the team was deeply in debt. I took the idea and made the Montana Magic into a baseball team. Frank and Silas end up managing it. And I've written a hockey story recently that I've been doing at readings. Mad Etta ends up playing goal for the Hobbema Wagonburners.

T: If you were commissioner of baseball, what changes would you make?

KINSELLA: I would institute the designated hitter rule in the National League. I would also make them put in grass in the outdoor stadiums like Kansas City. And I loathe mascots. I also object to them playing music. I would absolutely ban music from the ballpark. They should play ten seconds of "America the Beautiful" and that's it. None of this anthem shit. And I'd make sure whoever has the concession for food at Dodger Stadium was awarded the concessions for all the ballparks.

T: Do Americans have different reactions to your work than Canadians?

KINSELLA: Americans are much more effusive. If they like something they say, "Bigawd, this is good. Let's tell people about it." Canadians, if they like something, say, "Well, I like this. There must be something wrong with it."

T: Certainly there's more of a tradition in American society that anything is possible. There's probably a greater freedom to be imaginative.

KINSELLA: Whereas in Canada we have this goddamned English tradition. And there is no one less imaginative than the English. Our Canadian literature is still dominated by a lot of asshole Englishmen who have the nerve to try and tell us what our literature is about. John Metcalf, of course, is the main offender. The very idea that this man, who has no background in our literature whatsoever, should try to tell us what Canadian literature should be about just makes me absolutely furious. There are ten or fifteen of his ilk floating around.

T: You've married an American and you've described Canada as "a nation of docile and gutless people beset by an accountant mentality." Why don't you move to the US?

KINSELLA: That statement was made specifically in connection to our acceptance of metric conversion. However, I would say that if it wasn't for medical insurance I would likely live in the States. It's a much more exciting place to be. Even the politicians aren't quite so stupid. All politicians are stupid and corrupt but ours are not even corrupt. Bureaucracy is so much worse here than it is in the US.

T: When you say you knocked your head against Canadian literature for twenty-five years, does that mean Canadian literature was at fault for not accepting you?

KINSELLA: No. I think I got published about the time I was ready to be published. That statement just means I didn't have the opportunity to pursue my writing. There's a story I frequently tell about my high-school counselor in grade twelve. I had taken these stupid aptitude test which are easily rigged, of course, so that I was able to rig the test so that I showed a ninety-eight percent in the writing column and zero mechanical aptitude.

Which is pretty close to the truth anyway. His advice to me was that I should get a degree in accounting or engineering and then write for a hobby. That still makes me furious to this day. You tend to take that kind of advice semi-seriously. I actually wasted ten or fifteen years of my life. So there's a special place in hell for him.

T: When you were in a position to advise young writers as a teacher, what did you try to pass on to them besides Valgardson's Law?

KINSELLA: I always say to students that writing consists of ability, imagination, passion and stamina. Ability, of course, is the ability to write complete sentences in clear, standard English. That usually eliminates seventy to eighty percent of the people who want to write right there. Imagination is having stories to tell, not autobiography. We have a number of writers who do nothing but write autobiography.

T: Norman Levine?

KINSELLA: I can't tolerate his stuff. There is no story, no imagination involved. That is what fiction writing is all about. Imagination. Imagination is my stock in trade. I have to keep coming up with new things. That's my occupation. We are storytellers. Fiction exists to entertain and for no other reason. If you want to write something preachy or autobiographical, you should write non-fiction.

T: Do you sense a prejudice from some quarters that your work is too enjoyable, too entertaining?

KINSELLA: Oh yes. Of course. These snotty academics are not going to give any credit to anything they can understand that doesn't have twelve-letter words in it and isn't dull. But the stuff they praise, in the main, is poor. Every once in a while they will take a liking to a good writer, like Alice Munro, but it doesn't happen often enough.

T: Let me make a snotty academic observation... I think one very important reason your stories are so popular is the connecting thread of loyalty to the genuineness of his own people from Silas. It makes even the sad and tragic stories inspiring.

KINSELLA: I've described that as being an attempt to inject some humanity into situations which are inherently lacking in humanity. To give an academic answer to an academic question. I use all the tricks of the trade to make Silas an endearing character because he has to be in order to carry the weight of all the stories.

T: I'd go so far as to say you're not writing about Indians and whites. You're writing about hose who are willing to be true to their hearts and those in the majority who can't or won't be true.

KINSELLA: I write about people who just happen to be Indians. It's the oppressed and the oppressor that I write about. The way that oppressed people survive is by making fun of the people who oppress them. That is essentially what my Indian stories are all about. Silas and his friends understand the absurdity of the world around them. They survive by making fun of the bureaucrats and the do-gooders and the churches and all these idiots who have absolutely no idea what is going on in the world but who are in positions of power. Nine out of ten people in positions of power are hopelessly incompetent. It's that one person out of ten that keeps the country running. Silas sees the absurdity of all this. And that's what I have always done. I know the mentality of the oppressed minority. As a writer I am certainly an oppressed minority.

T: Really? Don't you think that is rather a privileged minority to be in? To live the life of a writer?

KINSELLA: For whom? The twelve of us in this country who make a good living from our writing?

T: So you're looking at being oppressed in strictly economic terms.

KINSELLA: Are there any other?

T: But you and Silas are certainly not one and the same person.

KINSELLA: No, Silas is not nearly as bitter as I am. He's not nearly as angry either. Consequently he keeps it fun. Whereas I would like to be out there with a machine gun.

Myrna Kostash

MYRNA KOSTASH was born in
Edmonton, Alberta in 1944. A second-
generation Ukrainian-Canadian, she
received an MA in Russian literature
from the University of Toronto in
1968. In the early 1970s she worked as
a freelance writer in Eastern Canada
before returning to Alberta to write
her "rewritten" history of Ukrainians
in Western Canada, *All of Baba's*

Children (1977). Her second book,
*Long Way From Home: The Story of
the Sixties Generation in Canada*
(1980) was followed by her well-
received feminist study, *No Kidding:
Inside the World of Teenage Girls*
(1987).

Myrna Kostash lives in an Edmonton
housing co-op called Hromada, a
Ukrainian word meaning community.
She was interviewed in 1984.

T: The immigrant experience shouldn't be news. But I found a book like *All of Baba's Children* was news to me.

KOSTASH: Exactly. And the same with suffragism. And is the New Left going to be news? These days I'm really anxious about my own history.

T: Already the counter-culture is being excused as some sort of joke. It's amazing, this process of how history gets buried.

KOSTASH: I know what you mean. You can begin to understand why people hated *Long Way from Home*. It might be the task of the generation after me to write that book. I have so many axes to grind around it. It may take another generation altogether to really look at it and situate it in history.

T: Would you have written a different book about the so-called sixties in the 1980s? As opposed to the 1970s?

KOSTASH: Yes. Knowing what I know now in terms of the way its ostensible audience reacted, I would have written much less ambitiously. I would have probably written a more likable book. I wouldn't have tried to take on the whole thing. I wouldn't make any large claims to understand where the Canadian New Left fits in with the American New Left, for example. How the culture was co-opted. And Red Power. And Separatism. And the invasion of Czechoslovakia. The nature of the cultural revolution in China. Ay-ayay!

I'm very jealous of my colleagues in the United States or England or France, where the subject of the sixties is taken extremely seriously historically. What happened in the sixties in France is still debated.

T: By chance I came across a quote today by John Fowles saying, "People are growing up culture-less." It seems to me that essentially what you're doing by writing books is trying to go against that trend.

KOSTASH: But I also take a position. I have a position on all this material and it becomes clear in the books. The whole point in taking on these big chunks of history is that I have something to say about them, and I have deeply rooted feelings about them, and I have a memory. All that comes into play when I deal with material. I'm not indifferent to it.

T: Has it ever occurred to you that by writing big books about big things you're giving yourself to failure? Defining the experiences of Ukrainian-Canadians. Defining the sixties generation in Canada.

KOSTASH: I never intend to, believe me. I never find out until it's too late. What I seem to have the knack of is picking topics that people haven't really looked at in any breadth. So I discover in the course of my investigations and research that little has been said. My application to the Canada Council for my first book said I was going to the Ukrainian-Canadian town of Two Hills and look at three generations of a family, and by looking at these three generations, getting the story of Ukrainian-Canadians. When I set out to do a book about the sixties, the proposal was to do a book that would be an account from a composite character after interviewing lots of people. I discovered from my research in both cases that there weren't any authoritative accounts of what happened.

T: For those kinds of books, if you speak through your heart, people won't accept your scholarly overview. You can't be in both camps at once.

KOSTASH: That's right. At least that's what happened with the second book. The first one didn't generate the same hostility.

T: Well, every one of your readers already knows something about the sixties first hand, everybody was associated with it in some way, and here you come along setting out to define their experiences and what happened. How dare you?

KOSTASH: Whereas the squabbles that *All of Baba's Children* engendered didn't affect anyone outside the Ukrainian community. Even though within the Ukrainian community I became persona non grata among some people.

T: You were the invasive interviewer from Toronto when you went to Two Hills to research *All of Baba's Children*. Is that why you ended up buying a farm there? To prove either to them or yourself that you belonged?

KOSTASH: Well, it's a funny story. I went to Two Hills because I knew that none of my relatives had ever lived there. But I was such an easterner by that point that I had forgotten the fact that my parents had taught in the school twelve miles down the road in the thirties and early forties. Or that my uncle had been a superintendent of schools for the district. So as soon as I arrived and introduced myself...

T: A Kostash!

KOSTASH: Exactly. "Whose Kostash are you?" "Bill and Mary." "Oh, well come in." It was exactly not the way I had planned to operate. It got me an entree, but when the book came out a lot of people felt violated. "We asked you into our homes, we trusted you, we knew your family, and look what you did to us." As one woman said to me in the grocery store, "You printed all the dirt." I told about the poverty during the Depression.

T: And some of them felt ashamed about their struggles? As opposed to pride in surviving them?

KOSTASH: Yes. Those are accounts of their humiliation. Of their backwardness and deprivation.

T: So did you buy your place in Two Hills with your head or your heart?

KOSTASH: I bought it because I had spent four months in Two Hills and for some reason, I still don't know why, I felt at home. It was a deeply satisfying experience. I couldn't afford a house in the city. So I bought this farm and I named it after the village where the Kostashchuks came from and banged up this sign on it and there it is. And I will not be driven off. Doing that book changed my life. I never went back to Toronto. Had I stayed in Toronto I would have become just another hack. But it took me years to get Toronto out of my system all the same. Always the thought that you're missing something.

T: Do you talk to other writers about the craft of writing non-fiction?

KOSTASH: No. It's very difficult for non-fiction writers to do that because there isn't a critical literature around it. Fiction writers get together and they have a whole tradition of English Lit Crit. Nobody ever talks about non-fiction in those ways. We talk about what we're writing about and how we do the research.

T: Non-fiction. The word itself makes it sound like a secondary activity.

KOSTASH: Yes. And I've found a lot of non-fiction writers have this secret ambition, or not-so-secret ambition, to write a novel. It's a way for them to establish their credentials as a serious writer, and that just infuriates me. Whereas somebody like Dorothy Parker once said, "I don't write 'non' anything." That's more how I feel. And yet we're stuck with that term. What is this thing I write?

I do not imagine worlds. I have a political commitment to non-fiction. I have a political commitment to the real world. The whole point of being a writer is to find out what's going on "out there." There are points when the "out there" and the inside overlap, but basically I have an intense curiosity about what is going on out there. I have never been attracted to fiction. I have never once, not even in a fantasy life, wanted to be a fiction writer.

However, having said that, I'm also at the point where I want to start fooling around more with non-fiction, experimenting within the documentary reality. There are moments when I play around with form in my books already, where I'll have a journalistic account of what happened, then I'll let loose. There's often a part where Myrna lets loose. Like enough of this objective journalism, I'm going to have my say.

T: Now you have a new book about teenage women in Canada. That seems to fit with your other two books. Ukrainian-Canadians. The counter-culture. Young women. They're all people at odds with the dominant culture.

KOSTASH: I didn't realize that! How interesting. Somebody else pointed out that in terms of generations the first book was about my parents' generation, the second was about my generation, and now I'm looking at the generation after me. That also fits.

T: And when you wrote about the singer Rita McNeil you said, "She bridged the chasm between rhetoric and the sensation of sisterhood."

KOSTASH: I said that?

T: Don't worry. It wasn't a bad sentence!

Doing this new book you're doing that, too. Bridging the gap between the rhetoric of feminism and the sensation of feminism.

KOSTASH: Actually you could say that about the other two books. Bridging the gap between the rhetoric of the Left and what the experience of it was. And in the first book, the rhetoric of multi-culturalism and the feeling of being ethnic. Okay, I buy that. It would fit. As a feminist I also want to know whether we're in fact

reproducing ourselves. As a childless woman I want to learn something about the generation of daughters I didn't have.

T: When you meet these young women, do you find yourself dispensing motherly advice?

KOSTASH: Oh! I find myself saying things like, "You didn't know there was a clitoris?" When the occasion warrants, I step in and give them the benefit of what I know. There are basically two areas where this comes up. One is sexuality. The other is money. Jobs, income. I've had to tell each one of my interviewees about the wage gap. They didn't know.

T: Have you asked yourself what sort of life you might be leading if you were the age of your subjects? If you were, say, twenty-one now?

KOSTASH: Well, I'm looking at a slightly younger group, fifteen to nineteen. But I've asked myself that a lot actually. And I'm very glad that I'm not twenty in the eighties.

T: So do you run across young women who seem to be mirrors of what you were?

KOSTASH: Oh, yes. They're there. There are young women who are passionate feminists or who are very much involved in the peace movement. I wouldn't want to be them. That's the difference.

T: Why?

KOSTASH: Because they feel that they are on their own. They don't feel cushioned by any kind of social movements. The women's movement has become very diffuse. There isn't one place you can go to be in the women's movement anymore. They feel like they're cranks in a way. To take these positions in the sixties was to part of an international movement. It was fantastic. It was repeated in the music and so on. Among really conscious women they understand what happened and they've heard about it or they've made a point of finding out. And they feel guilty. I had two women in Toronto tell me, "There you were. You've done all the revolutionary work. And you really expected us to carry on. And we've completely dropped it. We just feel so bad."

T: You once wrote, "I remember like snapshots those wounded, hopeful mid-sixties female faces that have closed over now into masks for women who are disciplining children and reading *Ms* magazine." Do you ever worry that all the energy of the women's movement has been dissipated?

KOSTASH: No. I don't know why I said that. People make claims that the women's movement was the only revolutionary movement that came out of the sixties. And a case can be made for that. And I think it's by no means over. One of the important things to realize is that it's part of a wave, that there's a fundamental impulse in our culture towards women's liberation. We have to ride out each wave. Each time something new happens we get further ahead. So even though people feel depressed that they can't bring out the multitudes for International Women's Day, or that funds to rape crisis centres are being cut, I do not lose hope that basically the wave of feminism is there. Basically we're on a roll. It cannot be rolled back. Something basic has been accomplished. It may not be people in the eighties who carry it on, but it will come again.

The liberation of women is inevitable. I don't despair at all. When I talk to these young women a lot of them say, of course, that they're not feminists. They say they're not feminists because feminism means that you hate men and you don't like your doors opened for you and they do. Then they go on to talk about their lives in such a way that you realize the basic assumptions about feminism have filtered down to their lives in terms of their everyday consciousness. The jobs they want to have. The money they expect to make. They arrangement they expect to have in their family life. It may be argued that they may have all these anticipations and expectations and visions but their real life will be different. Once those two things conflict with each other, then the struggle begins. Then you get conscious feminists.

T: One more thing I want to talk about is female anger . . .

KOSTASH: Aha.

T: The fact that you're willing to express it. I think it's very important.

KOSTASH: We're all expressing it. Why is it interesting? Every woman who writes is expressing it.

T: I don't think that's true.

KOSTASH: Well, my conscious self began with this. I remember I wrote a very long essay when I was fifteen in my diary about why I was angry about being female. It ran the gamut of grievances from having to menstruate and not being able to ask boys on dates to women being confined to menial tasks and housewifery and being exploited as prostitutes and mistresses. That was 1960. I had no idea where this came from. That was before Betty Friedan. I never thought about it this way before but I guess I would situate my anger right with the beginnings of my conscious life.

T: You're fueled by it. And you're adversarial against the major culture.

KOSTASH: Whether it's Anglo or male or right-wing. Yes. Maybe that's why I write non-fiction. Maybe you're not allowed to be dogmatic in fiction. In fiction you always have to deal with ambiguities and people's contradictions and their psychic biographies. I'm not interested in that. I'm interested in the places where people are black and white. Where people come into struggle. Where people are oppressed. I have very little patience with ambiguity. That's probably another clue to being a non-fiction writer.

But perhaps anger is just part of the territory. As soon as you become engaged with the real world you have no choice but to be totally enraged and infuriated by what's going on. The reason that I get so enraged about the situation of women is that I have certain ideas about male power and the patriarchy. But I will agree with you to this point that I had those feelings before I had those ideas.

Like these women I've been inter-viewing, these girls. You say to them, "Are you happy? Do you like being female?" They always say yes. Then you start asking pointed, directed questions and you find that there are moments in their lives which are absolutely infuriating. They hate it, they absolutely hate it. Each comes to terms with it in her own way. I came to terms with it because there was a women's movement which was alive and kicking at the time, right? If there hadn't been a women's movement I'm not sure what would have happened to that rage. I really credit the women's movement for giving me a place to write.

Robert Kroetsch

ROBERT KROETSCH was born in Heisler, Alberta in 1927. His novels exhibit his conscious resolve to mythologize the past of Western Canada and have often involved male quests. After *But We Are Exiles* (1965) and *The Words of My Roaring* (1966), he published his Governor General's Awarding-winning *The Studhorse Man* (1969), about the quixotic

Hazard LePage, who wanders Alberta in search of a mare worthy of his prize stallion. Other major books include *Gone Indian* (1973), *Badlands* (1975), his attempt to take the tall tale to extremes in *What the Crow Said* (1979) and *Alibi* (1984). He has turned increasingly to poetry and non-fiction with books such as *Seed Catalogue* (1977), *The Crow Journals* (1980) and *Excerpts from the Real World* (1986).

Robert Kroetsch lives and teaches in Winnipeg. He was interviewed in 1979.

T: Would you agree that your novels are chiefly concerned with probing how sexuality has influenced the sociology of the Canadian west?

KROETSCH: I can only begin to answer that by saying there's a great deal which is repressed in our society. Look at the vicious need for order that makes us all rush out at five o'clock to have a drink. People used to drink on ceremonial occasions. Now we drink automatically at five o'clock because the pressure we've been under all day is intolerable. We live in a very repressive society. It has to be repressive to make people work eight hours a day. Sexuality is too illogical for society so it's repressed. But the impulse towards sexual "disorder" is inherent in almost all of us.

T: Is this why marriage in your fiction is always depicted as a repression of sexuality, not an opportunity for embracing it?

KROETSCH: I must admit my novels reflect a terrible skepticism about the state of marriage. Perhaps based on personal experience.

T: On personal experience and Sigmund Freud?

KROETSCH: Yes, I do admit it. I do acknowledge that. I liked his statement somewhere that work and love are the two things we have in this world. Putting the two together is very difficult because only occasionally are they the same thing.

Often for a writer, work and love can come together. I'm someone who believes very consciously that the writing energy comes out of a confrontation with the Muse and the Muse takes the form of immortal woman. Often one almost hates a dependence on that. But I really depend on the relationship with a woman for that writing energy.

T: A feminist might label your work as male sexual propaganda because in examining the male desire for

freedom, you've painted an extremely unflattering picture of the role women played in the settling of Canada. Women carry the dreaded civilization instinct. They thwart the Prometheanism of the male.

KROETSCH: That's too naive a statement. When I look at the male world that I grew up in, I think I mock it now a great deal. I think Western Canadian males are into this macho posture which is grotesque. They're acting in a way which doesn't fit any societal need any more. Have you ever been in a beer parlour in Yellowknife? Those men are still hooked on the notion of a quest. They have to ride out and win the favour of a woman. And the way you ride out in this society is so grotesque that it's comic.

T: But except for *Badlands*, it seems only your male characters are "riding out." Don't women have quests, too?

KROETSCH: I don't say women can't. Margaret Laurence with *The Diviners* has written one of the greatest quest stories of our time. It's also a quest which happens to take her through a series of males.

T: That allegorized world of women at home in their Yellowknife kitchens while their men get plastered in the bar is a fair stereotype, I agree. Do you think that men and women cannot exist in harmony?

KROETSCH: No, I don't think that at all. What I think is that our roots are very much in small towns and rural communities. Now we are an urban people. This creates problems we have to solve. We have come into our glorious urban centres with a way of thinking that dates back a generation. You come to Edmonton or Winnipeg and you find the men are still sitting around in huge beer parlours, talking about women in that naive way men will talk about women. At one time this division between men and women might have been a very functional distinction. Now it's harmful. The women who want to participate like men are forced into a kind of isolation.

T: So our problem is really how to become an urban people.

KROETSCH: Yes, that's really what is fascinating about Canada right now. How in hell do we go about inventing these brand new cities? Calgary, Edmonton and Vancouver are surely the three most interesting cities in Canada. Every one of them is full of people trying to define a new version of urban. At the core of that new version there's going to have to be a new definition of the male/female relationship. I'm not writing about breaking the land any more. I'm writing about urban people remembering that rural experience. How we remember it conditions how we act!

Sinclair Ross already wrote about the terrible nature of a 1930s prairie town in *As For Me and My House*. Why should I try to duplicate that novel? I'm writing about people living in this rich society where there's an incredible sense of money, yet people don't know how to spend the stuff. They were taught to grub and save. Now they've got all this wealth and freedom and they don't know what to buy or do. So they buy more beer. My friends won't even buy good liquor for me! That's what I'm writing about!

T: Using a backdrop of rural origins to discuss urban problems.

KROETSCH: Exactly. *What the Crow Said* is not the description of a real community on the Alberta/Saskatchewan border. It's a real community in our imaginations. Where nature and woman can possibly come together. Where an Indian reserve is at one end of town and a Hutterite colony at the other. The book is full of balances and halves which we have to put together. That's what intrigues me now. I'm intrigued by the idea of bringing back together not only male and female, but also the self, with that total relationship with the world. Unfortunately, the men are still more interested in doing the impossible, like building their tower of ice to heaven.

T: A phallic tower of ice.

KROETSCH: Absolutely. And they can't get it high enough to satisfy themselves.

T: Are you at all optimistic about the chances of resolving these warring relationships between men and women?

KROETSCH: That's a serious question. And I don't know. There are days when I feel a little despair and I understand some of the women's lib philosophy that says to hell with men. I don't know if there are mass answers any more. Maybe that's one of the things we have to learn is to do away with the notion of a generalized answer.

That's why fiction is so important. That's why poetry is so important. The inherited system is breaking down. The intrusion into our society of leisure and money has broken down inherited role definitions. We have to work out new relationships. And art can point the way.

T: Let's bury the past and concentrate on the future?

KROETSCH: Yes, I'm against nostalgia. I remember what it was like on the farm. I picked roots and drove a tractor fourteen hours a day. I know how hard these jobs are to do. mind you, I had a relatively easy life, don't let me fool you. But I did do those jobs. I know that our memory is not of Europe or high culture. Our memory is of work. Just look at all the good writers on the West Coast who are using logging as a kind of metaphor for getting at an understanding of what they are.

T: I'd be interested to hear your opinion of Leslie Fiedler's "Huck Finn" theory. He has said men came to North America to flee European civilization and form a homosexual bond with a native male.

KROETSCH: I don't think it explains much in Canadian literature. And it's very glib about American literature. What I find much more intriguing is the power of women in Canadian writing. I would say our culture has a much larger percentage of good women writers than American culture. I don't know why. Maybe it's because Old Queen Victoria was back there as a role model...

T: Or else because feminism came to the fore at the same time that Canadian nationalism did.

KROETSCH: That could be part of it. But Nellie McClung and Catherine Parr Traill were back there long before that. Whatever it was, it's certainly healthy. I like the fact that a woman can now say I'm horny tonight. Or today. Or this morning. That's a great breakthrough in our society.

T: They're breaking out of their role definitions but they don't always find new ones to replace them.

KROETSCH: The same as men. In order to go west, a man had to define himself as an orphan, as an outlaw, as a cowboy. With those definitions, how can you marry a woman? How can you enter the house again? You have to lose that self-definition. That's the problem for the male. He must break his self-inflicted definition of maleness.

T: That would explain why so many of your characters are fatherless.

KROETSCH: Exactly.

T: Your novels are so riddled with significance that I can see the very conscious level of creation turning off a great many potential readers. Does that concern you?

KROETSCH: Yes, it does. Because I think intellectual play is an important part of human pleasure. Why are we, in this culture, so afraid of intellectual pleasure? In a country which has produced such interesting political movements as NDP and Social Credit, why are we afraid to be caught thinking? For instance, right now I just thought of your pun "riddled." When something is riddled it's full of holes or else it's full of meanings. That was a great remark you made. And to me that's fun. That's often what poetry is to me. Intellectual play.

T: So you would never temper down the intellectual input into a novel to make it more accessible?

KROETSCH: No, I wouldn't. I think if I have failed somehow it's not because I'm too intellectual; it's because I haven't given my books enough emotional weight. I realize there's the darker side and sentimental side to life which I could play up more. I'm beginning to acknowledge these things.

T: The disadvantage of being so obsessed with meaning and therefore also imposing form is that it's hard for your readers to gain an impression that your characters are ever responsible for their own actions. There's always an awareness that you manipulate the strings. That's probably why *The Studhorse Man* has been your best received novel, because Hazard Lepage takes over the book from the author.

KROETSCH: Since *The Studhorse Man* I've been much more interested in literature as an intellectual activity, as play. I say to my reader, watch me do this, this is impossible. Then I do it. And of course there's a danger in doing that too much.

T: Do you ever ask yourself how a kid from Heisler, Alberta, developed the mind it took to write your novels?

KROETSCH: The question has intrigued me because it certainly wasn't a literary background. I grew up on a farm. But there was a great deal of talk in that environment.

People were talking about each other, and in that sense inventing each other. Uncles were into politics and loved to make speeches; old aunts were repositories of family history. So I grew up hearing a great deal of talk.

T: What sort of reading material were you exposed to?

KROETSCH: Well, the hired men often had very interesting books up in their rooms! I'd find their old pulp magazines and Zane Grey stories. And there were travelling libraries which came to the schools. This great big box of books would arrive and I remember the delight of plundering through the boxes, which contained everything from best-sellers to the classics.

But I lived an incredibly free life on a huge farm. You had the run of the place. And you lived in your imagination.

T: What about those biblical overtones in your books. Were you religious?

KROETSCH: Well, I wasn't terribly into the Bible actually. My parents were Catholic but I was an agnostic at a very early age. I don't know why that was. I remember thinking they were putting me on with that stuff.

On the other hand I do like the kind of cosmology that religion offers. The Bible is a total story of the universe. I think that's where some of my interest in what I would call cosmology comes from. Those great yarns.

T: The obvious biblical influence that springs to mind is that litany of hockey players' names in *The Studhorse Man*. It's like a genealogy. Mahovolich began Beliveau begat Howe . . .

KROETSCH: The catalogue of names is a great old poetic device. The radio announcers we heard were great at inventing hockey games. We only found out later that the hockey game wasn't at all the way Foster Hewitt described it. He was a fiction maker.

T: Was W. O. Mitchell an influence, too?

KROETSCH: I think he was the first Canadian writer to influence me. He gave me the realization that you could write about the prairies. All the literature I had read was about people somewhere else. Then suddenly I read his *Jake and the Kid* stories and *Who Has Seen the Wind?* The education system had insisted that all writers were dead. I think I was in grade twelve before a teacher told me there were living writers as well as Shelley and Keats and Byron.

T: Were you old enough for the Depression to affect your upbringing?

KROETSCH: Yes, I was very much aware of Social Credit coming into power in 1935 when I was eight years old. The radio was the principal device Aberhart had struck on. He was a genius at using it. I remember the men especially listening to the radio, desperately hoping for an answer. And I remember my dad was a Liberal — I don't know if one should confess this nowadays anywhere west of Toronto! But he was sort of the last Liberal in the Battle River country. I remember the really vehement arguments that went on. I suppose I even had a sense of fright as a child to hear men arguing so vehemently.

T: That would account for *The Words of My Roaring*. Were you always aware of this friction between east and west or did that come later?

KROETSCH: Well, I was in a very ambiguous position in that my father had come from Ontario as a homesteader. He had dreamed as a kid of going out west and being a farmer. In a sense he became a fulfilled person. But he had left Ontario when he was seventeen, so I grew up hearing about this Edenic world called Ontario. That contradicted my sense of politics because we always heard about these capitalists who were manipulating us from back there. I think I still have that very ambiguous sense of good and evil about the east.

T: You've written that the American and British experiences are concealed within the Canadian experience in the same way that Latin words often conceal Greek roots. Do you think the prairies are resolving that conflict ahead of the rest of the country?

KROETSCH: I don't know. Certainly the prairies do have one answer which came out of the Depression. The thirties wiped us all out. Right down to zero. So we started to invent a new concept of self and a new concept of society. Now I'm intrigued to watch that developing in the prairies.

T: You share with Rudy Wiebe a feeling that the natural construction of sentences needs to be altered to jar the reader's equilibrium from time to time. Is it possible, since we're so bombarded by the imitative realism of television, that realism in literature might eventually become counter-productive to art?

KROETSCH: Yes, it has become counter-productive. I find the concept of realism incredibly boring. We can talk for an hour because our culture has sentence patterns and we fill in the slots with words. But I think there's a danger in not learning new models of sentences. Rudy and I fight about the notion of what realism is and we tamper with grammar in different ways, but I think both of us want to dislocate perception.

T: To construct your novels into intellectual mazes, do you have to map everything out beforehand so you don't get lost?

KROETSCH: No, you have to leave room for discovery as you go. One of the pleasures of reading is surprise. To get surprises happening, often you have to be surprising yourself. That's part of what I'm writing about anyway. Metamorphosis. How things get transformed.

T: Do you have to be turned on to write?

KROETSCH: No, I can write every day when I'm really working. Waiting to be turned on could just be an excuse not to write. However, you do have to understand when not to write. Because I believe the body writes the book, not just the mind. How your whole body feels it important. When you wake up in the morning refreshed with that incredible burst of energy, just out of a dream state, you're rediscovering the world. You're being reborn. It's not just intellect that writes the book.

T: Would you ever wake up in the morning and say, "My being is not feeling well today. If I sit down and write today, I will not write well"?

KROETSCH: Yes, I would. We call that a hangover.

Patrick Lane

PATRICK LANE was born in Nelson, BC in 1939. He grew up in the Okanagan region of the BC interior, primarily in Vernon. He came to Vancouver and co-founded a small press, Very Stone House, with bill bissett and Seymour Mayne. He then drifted extensively throughout South America and North America. He won the Governor General's Award for

poetry in 1979 for *Poems New and Selected* and published his *Selected Poems* in 1987, for which he received the 1988 Canadian Authors Association poetry award.

Patrick Lane lives in Saskatoon. He was interviewed in 1988.

T: How much do you see yourself as a product of BC?

LANE: Quite a lot. I grew up in British Columbia in the post-war years. This was before the industrialization of the late fifties when this province was transformed by Macmillan Bloedel and Weyerhaeuser and other large companies. Before that, the little towns where I grew up were tiny communities, self-contained universes all of their own. There was no television. The global village hadn't happened yet. We were a quasi-industrialized collection of serfs and masters.

If somebody got injured or hurt, that was just too bad. There was no compensation to speak of. The IWA had organized only a few of the bigger mills. In fact, I hated unions when I was a kid. I thought unions were a sign of weakness. The real working class wouldn't belong to a union. I think if I remain true to anything I remain true to that world I came out of, and to the people I knew intimately. In that pure intuitive sense you understand the class you come out of.

T: Were you aware of your particular "class" at the time?

LANE: Oh, totally. Totally. Completely class-conscious. I hated the rich. And I was envious. I wanted that for myself. I used to go with a knife up to the neighborhood in Vernon where the rich people lived. I'd go down the blocks and the alleys and I'd slash the tires of the all the rich kids' bikes. I did that one September, every night. The Phantom Bike Tire Slasher. I was enraged and I hated these rich kids. They had everything. There was a profound hatred and I desperately wanted to be there in their world of privilege.

T: Was there any shame in being a tire slasher?

LANE: Oh, no. There was elation, triumph. A feeling of complete omnipotence. Of power. The lonely tire-slasher. I felt no guilt or social responsibility. I felt they deserved what they were getting.

By the time I was getting out of high school in the late fifties my father did move into the middle class. He got a good job and a brand new car every year. Suddenly the world changed. I had nice clothes. We had a big house. But then I left school and I plunged right back down into the working class again. There was no way to transfer that middle class onto me. I got married and I went to work in the sawmills. And it was horrifying. Living in "picker" shacks with the wife and kids. I became a first aid man. I was a first aid man for years because it paid fifteen cents more an hour. Instead of making $1.50 an hour I made a $1.65. That meant I could buy one case of beer a month. I'd pretend to get whacko drunk on that one case of beer, then I'd wait twenty-nine days until I could do it again.

T: You once said that you "wrote yourself out of poverty."

LANE: When I say I wrote myself out of poverty I mean I found an excuse not to have to live the way I was living anymore. Writing, for me, became a way of life. A lifestyle. I delighted in the activity. It allowed me to leave my marriage. That particular wife went off and married a millionaire. I didn't have to pay alimony. I disappeared off the face of the earth for five years. I left Vancouver. I went on the road. I bummed around South America, New York, Toronto, San Francisco, New Orleans.

In a sense I wrote myself out of the poverty that's created in dependencies in relationships. And I wrote myself into the poverty of being completely isolated and alone, which I much preferred.

T: Looking back, can you see why you became a writer?

LANE: I was a bizarre child paranoid wandering through the world with a malevolent view of how the social system worked. My brother and I would read all these books, from Socrates on. I remember reading Nietzsche when I was fifteen years old. And Thomas Mann. We made long lists. There was an intellectual system here and we wanted to figure it out. My brother and I read these things and then we'd compare notes. It wasn't for personal enlightenment. We just wanted to know how the enemy thought.

While we were doing B&Es, I was also leading this other imaginary, intellectual life, or aesthetic life. I always saw that as a way of escaping. I wasn't going to go to the penitentiary. I decided that when I was six years old. Those people my brothers and I hung out with, they're either all dead or in jail. There's not one of them "out." I know five guys right now who are still doing time. The others are dead from heroin or suicide or murder.

So writing became a way out of that. And there was also a desire to create a testament. I remember reading the testament of Francois Villon when I was about thirteen. I remember thinking, "Pat Lane will write a great testament."

T: Your older brother, Red, also became a writer. And so did another brother, John.

LANE: Yes, I don't know too many situations in literary history where three brothers all became writers.

T: T: Were you competitive?

LANE: Oh, it was really brutal, but I was a tough competitor. I had to be. When I was really a little kid, my older brother, Dick, grabbed me and held me down and spat in my face and I said, "You can do this all day, if you want. But when you let me up, I'll kill you." He got scared and let me up. I went and got a two-by-four and waited for him at the corner of the house. When he came around the corner of the house I hit with the two-by-four on the back of the head and he never held me down again. To me that was very simple and straightforward: this is how we're going to operate, older brother, you and I. So he left me alone.

T: So you hit him with the two-by-four not emotionally, but totally rationally.

LANE: It was a completely rational act.

T: It's that unusual cold-mindedness that people respond to when you're describing violence in your poetry.

LANE: They're expecting compassion and sentiment and involvement of feeling, and that is there in the poems but they don't always recognize it. I'm saying, "Look, there's this guy sitting at the bar and he's driving pins into his hand with a beer glass and everybody's sitting there watching him do it. This is what he does. This is his thing in life: to put pins in his hands." This man will sticks pins in his arm forever in this poem. There's no relief from that knowledge.

For me that was crucial to most of my poetry for fifteen years. To elicit response. And to record with an absolute, cold, clear eye. It evolved into a kind of Patrick Lane poem. Violence and a situational anecdote: life is hell. I got really good at that. I could have gone on writing a Pat Lane poem forever. But there was no growth.

T: Your later poems are more philisophical, more concerned with history and asking questions. Do you look back at your work and see the highlights where you changed?

LANE: Well, there's a poem I wrote while I was in South America called "Unborn Things" in which I said compassion is only the beginning of suffering. I think the poem personfied a moment of change in my life. I began to explore the idea of compassion and the kinds of responsibilities a writer has towards the characters he creates. That's the period where I really learned how to write. Prior to that I was just another one of the hundreds and hundreds of people who were throwing words down on a page.

Then in the late seventies my writing changed again. At the end of all those books I had nothing left. It was like I was a musician looking around to make a new piece of music. A new symphony. God, what'll I do? I explored for four or five years. Now I'm working on a group of short stories. And I'm working on a long sequences of poems which are very different. And I'm living reasonably quietly and happily, which is what I think most of us try to do.

T: I'd say the poems from your "middle period" are the most effective. The newer work has more references to other poets. I don't have the energy to figure out what it all means because I don't really care enough.

LANE: Perhaps I've become more obscure. I don't know. I don't even think that I'm writing for an audience any more. I don't expect the great mass of humanity to pick up my book and get excited about it. Did the mass audience get excited about Dylan Thomas or Robert Lowell or Irving Layton? If I write at all, I'm writing for those people who really are interested in the kind of density that poetry can offer.

T: So does poetry necessarily evolve into an elitist pursuit?

LANE: What elite? What poets do you know that belong to an elite? Some novelists might belong, but not the poets. Nobody supports themselves as a poet. And frankly, I don't blame people if they don't read poetry. It

takes a lot of work to read poetry well and people have enough going on in their lives. A good writer needs readers who have as much time as the writer does.

T: So do you qualify as a good reader?

LANE: I hope so. I find myself going back now to texts that I've always delighted in. Writers that I've always loved. I go back to Alden Nowlan and John Newlove. Or Kenneth Rexroth. Or Cavafy. Or some of the Chinese anthologies. It's like listening to old friends. It's like listening to music.

T: Now that you're living in Saskatchewan you've gone from living in the interior of BC to living in the interior of Canada.

LANE: That's right. One of the reasons I moved to the prairie is that the people of Saskatchewan are very similar to the people I remember from the interior of BC. They have a sense of community and solidarity and identity. The Saskatchewan Writers Guild has a membership of fifteen hundred writers. Everybody cooperates. There's none of the back-biting and viciousness and ambition that I used to see in Vancouver. Back in the old days, all the poets would gather at the Cecil Hotel. People would literally walk out bereft and crying because they weren't included in the latest clique or claque or whatever. It was just awful. The terrible cruelties that occurred.

T: Out of that has sprung what George Bowering calls the Poetry Wars.

LANE: That's right. The writers around George don't read my writing at all. Never did. And the writers that I know don't read George. He writes for the world of post-modernism and deconstructionism. The new intellectual wave in poetry. More power to them. But it's a small dance step on the side. I do think that Bowering's

Kerrisdale Elegies is an absolutely wonderful book, the best thing George has written since, god, 1968. But our relationship has much more to do with his relationship with my brother than with our writing.

T: There were three of you connected to the Okanagan and each other. Red Lane, Pat Lane and George Bowering. With your brother in the middle.

LANE: And his history of my brother is so different from my history of my brother. We obviously knew totally different men. Now the writers connected with George remember my brother with great fondness. Dorothy Livesay thought he personified the great working class in a purely romantic way. It was just silly. He just came from the interior like I did. I remember him coming home from Vancouver and telling me what he thought of these guys. Frankly, he was mostly envious of them, and very frustrated. I don't think they liked his writing much at all. They mostly liked him because he was wild and crazy and he did bizarre things.

My brother was a walk on the wild side for a lot of those middle-class kids whose daddies were schoolteachers. He'd take them on journeys. They'd break into houses and buildings. He showed them the criminal element. Wild parties, gangsters with guns, prostitutes. They thought this was great. And the thing was, it wasn't great at all. It was awful.

T: In terms of the Poetry Wars, "The Weight" stands out as a statement from you.

LANE: It's an indictment of Western Canadian literature and the kind of people who have written about our history. I don't believe a lot of writers have loved their country in the way they should have. They've avoided confronting the kinds of honesties that were necessary. Without all the intellectual claptrap and game-playing.

The French philisophical systems and post-modernism and all this nonsense. Instead of real people with real problems. Hundreds and thousands and millions of people are suffering in absolute shit and these people are sitting in their little ivory boxes, dealing with people purely theoretically. They live and write in a middle-class vacuum where only mind matters.

T: Are there any writers who are confronting "your" realities?

LANE: The women. Unquestionably the women. From the cold objectivism of Atwood to someone like Lorna Crozier or Edna Alford or Alice Munro, I think women's writing in Canada has confronted the real social issues of our era. Very rarely do the men deal with how people relate to each other and how community is made and maintained. The best new young poets seem to be women.

T: So has living with a female writer helped you as a writer? Learning by osmosis?

LANE: Through Lorna I've confronted aspects of feminism and I've managed to meet a great number of remarkable writers, most of whom are women.

T: Have you become a good critic of yourself as a writer?

LANE: I hope so. I hope I don't suffer too many delusions about my work. I've seen too many writers who suffer delusions. I swore when I was younger that I wouldn't be like that. To have everybody sit back and say, "Well, it's okay. Pat Lane, he's an old guy. . . the early stuff was really good. Now be nice to him. What the hell, he's eighty. . ." I would cut my throat rather than have that.

T: That's why *Selected Poems* is such a thin book.

LANE: I'd like it to be even thinner. I think there's about ten or twelve poems in there that are really good.

You can't touch them. You can't take a word out or put a word in. The making of a beautiful thing. It's an act of great privilege. It's a great high for me.

T: There's a line in one of your poems that mentions "a terrible patience."

LANE: Yes. That's nice. That's very true. That's what it is. There's a terrible patience in writing. Just as there's a terrible patience in most human relationships. I used to worry. But I don't attack myself about it anymore. I'm willing to wait.

I've realized, for one thing, that so much of writing is physical. You have to get your body geared up for it. It's like setting yourself up for the Olympics, right? You've got five years to get your body tuned perfectly. Maybe you'll win a medal. Maybe you'll even get to cry. But it's really for the enlightening moment of the performance that you do it. If you're a skier you mostly like the feeling of going down the hill. It's perfect and you think, "Goddamn. Five years to get here." For me, poetry's the same thing.

T: Except at the Olympics there are millions of people watching the event. Whereas when a poet is going down the hill of his craft . . .

LANE: Yes, I see what you mean. There's a couple of thousand in Canada that follow it. And my country funds it. But that's the measure of an enlightened country. To invest in that kind of dreaming. You've got to invest in excellence otherwise you'll always remain colonial, a people who work for others, a people who dream another people's dreams. You've got to invest in R & D.

T: Poetry as Research and Development.

LANE: That's what it's always been about. That's how we measure civilization. The great plays and poetry of Greece were found on bits and pieces of parchments or a few discarded shards of goddamn goatskin. Our society will be measured the same way. Except much of the measurement is going to come from video and from film and from a variety of other testaments. I operate in an outmoded form. Poetry is less important to our mass culture now. But diplomats occasionally realize how important it is internationally. When Canada needs to ship out a cultural icon they sometimes ship out a poet. It's important. It's one of the ways cultures communicate with each other.

T: Have you thought about what you could do, at age fifty, if you weren't a poet?

LANE: If I wasn't a poet, I'd be back in the mills, or building houses, or in the mines. It's what I was raised to do.

Margaret Laurence

MARGARET LAURENCE was born in Neepawa, Manitoba in 1926. Educated in Winnipeg where she later worked as a labour reporter, she married in 1947 and lived in Vancouver and Africa before a formal separation from her husband in 1962. She then took her two children to London, England to pursue a full-time career as a writer. Twice recipient of the

Governor General's Award, she wrote fourteen books, the best known of which are her "Manawaka" fictions, *The Stone Angel* (1964), **A Jest of God** (1966), **The Fire-Dwellers** (1969), and **The Diviners** (1974). **A Bird in the House** (1970) allowed Laurence to come to terms with the dark childhood shadows of death and a domineering grandfather in a collection of autobiographical short stories.

Margaret Laurence lived in Lakefield, Ontario until her death in 1987. She was interviewed in 1979.

T: What's really struck me in the course of interviewing authors is the extent to which the state of mind of an artist is usually inextricably tied to the state of his or her society. You must recognize this in your own work.

LAURENCE: Oh, certainly. The thing is, whether I recognize it or not, it's bound to be there. For instance, I don't write a novel with the idea of commenting on society. Or I never set out and say, "Well, now it's Canadian-novel-writing time." I think of all my characters in my Canadian books a great deal more as human individuals than I do as Canadians. I simply have a character in mind, or a group of characters, and I want to deal with their dilemmas. I want to communicate with them.

What happens is the dilemma of one particular woman often turns out to be the dilemma of a lot of women. When *The Fire-Dwellers* was published, a lot of women wrote to me and said how did you know this was how I felt? I didn't know. I wrote that book by trying to connect with one human individual.

T: And that can have far-reaching effects. Yet there are some people who would argue that such fiction is apolitical.

LAURENCE: Yes, I think very many people would define political writing as something which is strictly in the political realm of governments and social issues. But I think what is political in most serious novels is something quite different. For instance, in *The Stone Angel* old age is itself a political dilemma. Death. We're not supposed to think about it. But it's there. It's going to happen to all of us.

If you are writing out of what you know, inevitably what you know is your society around you. So if a writer is aware of social injustice, which I think I very deeply am, then that will be there, too. For instance, people sometimes ask me whether I'm consciously writing feminist novels. No, I am not. Even though I myself feel I am a feminist, I won't write in any didactic or polemical way about it. My protagonists are women and I simply try to portray their dilemmas as truthfully as I can. I'm not doing it for any other reason than because I am interested in a character as a human individual.

T: And that's how literature can be useful.

LAURENCE: Yes. I remember very clearly thinking before I started *The Stone Angel*, "Who will be interested in the life of an old woman of ninety?" Then I thought *I* am interested. Of course it turned out I wasn't alone. The fact that Hagar struggles so hard to maintain some human dignity throughout the period of her dying has meant a great deal to a lot of people. In fact, to my great surprise, I discovered that novel is actually being used in a number of geriatrics courses and nursing courses for the aged. That pleases me enormously.

T: So increasing awareness is itself a political act.

LAURENCE: Yes, I think so. Otherwise I would not be writing novels.

T: Do you think writers actually create change or is their role simply to reflect it?

LAURENCE: This is the question of the chicken and the egg. I don't know. The writer's consciousness if formed by the society, then the writing in turn helps to do something to affect the society. It's a two-way street. For instance, the feeling we got in the sixties that we were a culture that mattered to ourselves and the world has helped our writers, but our writers also helped in forming those feelings.

T: You once wrote, "What I care about is trying to express something that, in fact, everybody knows but doesn't say." Do you think Canadians might be especially dishonest with themselves?

LAURENCE: No. When I said that, I didn't mean people who were being hypocritical. I was referring to people who experience lots of feelings in their lives but they are in some way inchoate. They aren't verbal people. This is part of what writers do. They speak for people who cannot speak for themselves.

T: I asked that question because the pioneer experience and the influence of Victorianism have tended to make Canadians keep their emotions under wraps. That sort of repression could encourage double standards.

LAURENCE: I agree. But, as I hope it comes out in my books, I don't think this country's puritan background has been all bad for us. With Hagar and the generation of my maternal grand- father, whom I've written about in *A Bird in the House*, they created a very repressive atmosphere. Hagar really damaged her children. Yet at the same time that generation imbued us with an ability to survive. Besides, I don't think the puritan work ethic is all that wrong!

T: But there's a National Film Board profile of you which indicates your childhood was pretty bleak.

LAURENCE: Well, even though my grandfather was a very authoritarian man, I myself had the great advantage of growing up in a house where my stepmother, who was my aunt, and my other aunts, were extremely strong and liberated women. I never had the feeling that as a woman I couldn't choose the profession that I wanted to choose. Two of my aunts were nurses, my stepmother had been a high school teacher of English and my mother had been a pianist.

Also, my stepmother was an extremely enlightened woman for her day. For example, when I was young,

she never tried to censor my reading. I can remember when *Gone with the Wind* came out, there were many mothers of daughters who would not permit their little prairie flowers to read this wicked book. But I could always read anything. Mind you, I admit there was not that much hard core porn in the Neepawa Public Library!

T: Do you think the pendulum has swung too far the other way these days?

LAURENCE: Well, a lot of the porn magazines I find *vile*. I detest them. But it's not because they deal with sex. It's because they deal with sex in an exploitive and very largely cruel way.

In terms of novels, I don't believe in writing sex scenes for the sake of bringing in a lot of sex. But if you are to wipe out sex entirely, that's wiping out one whole area of life. I think if you're writing truthfully about a character, you've got to deal to some extent with that side of their lives. As much as the novel demands and no more.

T: You've said that many people misread literature. Can you explain what you mean?

LAURENCE: Misreading comes in when people are unable to see what's going on in a novel because they focus on the wrong things. I'm thinking of people who want to have my books banned, particularly *The Diviners*. A lot of those people not only admit to the fact that they have not read the book, they are proud they have never read it. Their eyes are blind to every- thing except the few sexual passages and some of the so-called swear words. That's a sad and tragic way of reading a book. That kind of reader doesn't want to read. To put it in its broadest sense, the motives are not of love but of hate.

T: Or of fear.

LAURENCE: That's right. One thing the book banners commented on with *The Diviners* was that I dealt with the quote "seamier side of life." Well, the seamier side of life exists. Also they complained that I showed native people in the worst possible light. I was simply incensed and enraged by that reaction! I was trying to show the Tonnerre family as real complex human individuals who had suffered at the hands of society. We are culpable. To say that I was showing them in an unfavourable light, as though I was a racist, is ridiculous. Perhaps the book banners wanted "Hiawatha." But that's not how real life is.

People say to me, well, if it's banned by the school boards then all the kids are going to read it. But I'd just as soon they didn't read it under that particular aegis.

T: We heard a lot of predictions about the possible demise of the novel as well as the possible demise of the church during the sixties, when man was busy landing on the moon. Do you think there's a connection?

LAURENCE: I don't really know. People have been saying the novel is dead for a long, long time. As far as I'm concerned, it's still extremely alive. It simply finds new forms. And God, though very often proclaimed dead, is also very much alive in my opinion.

T: I think if there is a connection between religion and art, it's that they both emphasize that man is not wholly a rational being, that the truth about ourselves must also be "divined."

LAURENCE: I accept that connection. Certainly a very great deal of all serious art is in some way religious, even if the writers and painters don't admit it. This is so with literature because, like faith, it frequently points to the mystery at the heart of things, the mystery and wonder at the core of every human individual. That sense of mystery and wonder comes out of a great deal of

writing, as it does with religious faith. Many writers, including myself, who even though they were not thinking in any specific religious terms, have experienced something while writing which I think of as a kind of grace. This came very naturally to ancient and tribal people. They described it as possession by the gods. Nowadays when people say they have written something that surprises them, in my terms there's a sense of grace happening there.

T: In a good book maybe some of that grace gets passed along to the reader.

LAURENCE: One hopes so. I certainly feel very fortunate to have worked as a writer most of my life because I do feel I have been given a certain amount of grace. Whether deservedly or not, we don't know. But I feel extremely fortunate to have spoken to three generations; the generation before me, my own generation and the next one. People say to me sometimes do you expect your books will be around for 150 years? I don't know and I don't care. I feel I've been lucky in being able to speak to a number of people in those three generations.

T: Do you get many letters from readers?

LAURENCE: I've been very fortunate. People write to me quite often. By far the larger proportion of these letters has been extremely warm and positive. I get a few poison-pen ones, but not that many, thank goodness. And of course I get letters from people who say that I'm sure that you will be tired of hearing this but your book *The Diviners* meant a great deal to me for such-and-such a reason. Well, I would rather hear that than a good review. It means people who are not involved in the world of books professionally are taking the trouble to say your work has spoken to them. That means a great, great deal to me.

That's what literature is all about.

T: Robertson Davies claims Canada still expects nothing from its writers.

LAURENCE: Well, I can only speak personally on that. One difficulty I've had in the last few years is that Canadians almost expect too much. Writers are extremely vulnerable people. It really frightens me when people say to me what are you working on now? When's your next novel coming out? They mean it in the best possible way. But I sometimes think gosh, can I really do anything more? I'm grappling with trying to write something right now. But it really scares me.

T: Do you sometimes wish you could turn off all the tape recorders like this one and retreat from having a public role?

LAURENCE: I do feel like that sometimes. There are moments when I would like to rent a nice cabin in the arctic somewhere. On the other hand, I do feel very responsible for doing what I can to help writers who are younger than myself in whatever ways I can.

T: Was there someone in particular who helped you out when you were young?

LAURENCE: Yes. The writer who really went out of her way to help me was Ethel Wilson. I got to know her during the five years we lived in Vancouver, before my first novel was published. She had read a couple of my short stories in *Prism* so she wrote to the magazine expressing her enjoyment of the stories. Then she wrote to me personally. During the years in Vancouver I was absolutely starved for the company of other writers. Ethel Wilson provided that. The sense that somebody did understand. There's no question that I would have gone on writing, but she provided me with an enormous amount of encouragement. I owe her a

great, great deal. There's no way that I can ever repay her personally. The only thing I can do is pass it on.

T: You've lived in Vancouver, England, Africa and now Ontario. Yet the heart of your work still appears to be the prairies. Do you still consider yourself a prairie writer?

LAURENCE: Yes, I still consider myself a prairie writer. That's where I spent the first twenty-two years of my life and I still have a strong sense of place about the prairies. Literature has to be set somewhere. This is one of the great strengths of our writing. Whether it's Jack Hodgins on Vancouver Island or Harold Horwood in Newfoundland, our writers have a strong sense of place. Even if you're writing out of an urban situation, like Morley Callaghan, you can still write with a tremendous sense of the earth, of the place. We're fortunate that the whole nature of Canada is that we're a conglomerate of regions because this has given an added dimension to our writing.

T: When do you feel Canadian literature began to come of age?

LAURENCE: It began to come of age around the Second World War. The generation of writers before me — like Hugh MacLennan, Ernest Buckler, Sinclair Ross and Morley Callaghan — were the first people not to base their stories on British or American models. They wrote out of the sight of their own eyes.

T: So you see yourself as part of a second generation.

LAURENCE: Yes, I do. A second generation of non-colonial Canadian writers. Now there's a whole new generation of Canadian writers who can almost take this "valuing" of ourselves for granted. I like to keep reminding them that we owe a lot to that generation of writers before me. They worked in terrific isolation. A book wasn't considered any good if it didn't get a seal of approval in London or New York.

All this has changed a great deal during the sixties and seventies. A lot more people are interested in the literature of this country. But in those days we never valued what we had as a nation. For instance, when I was in high school we never read one Canadian book. Then at university I studied the contemporary novel, but all the writers were American. This was when Hugh MacLennan and Gabrielle Roy were writing some of their finest work.

I don't suggest that we should wipe Shakespeare and Thomas Hardy out of our schools. Anybody who is writing in the English language, after all, is in some way an heir to Wordsworth and Milton and Shakespeare anyway. But Canadian writers are taking the language and making it our own. This connects with young people. They want to see what they are and where they came from. Their geographical place. Their people. I have gone to literally dozens of high schools in Canada. The kids are incredibly keen to find out more about Canadian literature. It's because they recognize it as theirs. With a book like *The Stone Angel* they say well, that's just like my grandmother. It's truly their culture.

T: Could there be a link between the extent of a country's nationalism and the quality of its literature?

LAURENCE: Not necessarily. I think a writer can be a good writer and have no conscious feelings about nationalism at all. But here we should stop and define what we mean by nationalism. It can take different forms. Nationalism can be that imperialist feeling Britain had at one time or it can be the nationalism of Nazism, of wanting to conquer the world. A jackboot forever stamping in the face. The way I feel about Canadian nationalism is quite different. We don't have

any territorial ambitions. We simply want to possess and own our own country.

T: A few writers, such as Mordecai Richler, have been reluctant to accept that label *Canadian*. Do you think one writer can be more Canadian than another?

LAURENCE: Of course Mordecai Richler is a Canadian writer. It isn't anything that you choose. I don't have to proclaim I'm a Canadian writer any more than I have to proclaim that my eyes are brown. It's just part of me.

T: Is being a Canadian writer still restrictive financially?

LAURENCE: Kid, being a writer of any kind is restrictive financially!

T: Is that the main reason the Writers' Union of Canada was formed?

LAURENCE: It was formed in order to try and get some better conditions. For example, to help our members get better contracts with their publishers. To try to get some sort of miniscule compensation for library use of our books. To lobby the government for better laws regarding the importation of foreign editions. We like to think of ourselves as a practical working union. We are, however, extremely different from a trade union in that the Writers' Union doesn't have the power to strike.

But there's another reason that isn't economic. When the Writers' Union was first formed in 1973, I was the first interim chairman. In the only address that I made, I said that I thought of the writers of this country as being members of a kind of tribe. Even thought the Writers' Union has got much larger and we sometimes argue heatedly at our general meetings, there is still that tremendous sense of belonging to a community. And we all need that sense of community.

T: Have you ever asked yourself why someone might prefer to read your books in particular?

LAURENCE: They find something

in them that relates to their own lives or has relevance to their own place of belonging. It's the same reason they might read anyone's books, I guess.

T: Except few books express such an encouraging belief in the power of the human will, of changing oneself.

LAURENCE: Yes, there is that. There is this feeling in all my books not of optimism — because you'd have to be a fool to be optimistic in this world — but of hope.

T: And I think people also appreciate being able to get so close to your characters. When that happens, literature can offer people a safe form of intimacy. Perhaps it almost teaches us how to love.

LAURENCE: Well, I hope that a sense of love does come across. If it does, it's because what I feel most of all when I'm writing my books is that each individual human being has great value. Each person is unique and irreplaceable. They matter. Of course, that is a very Western world outlook. But it's profoundly my own.

Dennis Lee

DENNIS LEE was born in Toronto in 1939. In addition to being one of Canada's most respected editors, Lee is revered in day-care centres and nurseries throughout the land as the author of *Alligator Pie* (1974), *Nicholas Knock* (1974), *Garbage Delight* (1977), *The Ordinary Bath* (1979) and *Jelly Bean* (1983). His important books of adult poetry are *Civil Elegies and*

Other Poems (1972) and *The Gods* (1979). His major work of criticism is *Savage Fields* (1977).

Dennis Lee lives in Toronto. He was interviewed in 1979.

T: Most poets designate themselves as poets, then feel obliged to go about creating poems. Why are you so extremely unprolific? And why do you dislike defining yourself as a poet?

LEE: I don't know, exactly. My sense of language is different from most other poets', but I have trouble discussing it coherently. It's true, if I had to spend my life being a "Poet," I wouldn't. And in twenty years I've produced less than thirty poems that seem to be worth keeping between the covers of a book, even though I work non-stop. But this is neither poverty of the imagination nor some special fastidious virtue. It's just the way it works. My first drafts are so godawful, I need an incredibly strong pull from whatever is trying to get written before I can write anything at all.

T: What about your objectives? Do you always know what you're trying to do when you write a poem?

LEE: I write to find out what the poem wants to do.

T: How do you connect that approach to your feeling that you're writing outside the mainstream of Canadian poetry?

LEE: Well, back east there's a tradition of the well-made poem, of people trying all their lives to add three more poems to the mythical anthology of great verse in the English language. And in the west there's a sense of people trying to work from the quick of words, from the process of moment-to-moment being.

This is going to sound quixotic or just like some nifty thing to say, but I mean it literally. When I get together with an empty piece of paper, the main message I get as far as poetry by Dennis Lee is concerned is: Don't Bother. I have lots of private experiences and opinions, of course, but why clutter up the airwaves with more of that stuff? If that's all there is, better the paper stays empty. So I start from square one, which is silence. Often enough I just stay there.

This is very different from a poet who walks down the street, sees a child hit by a car driven by a drunken driver, and feels compelled to go home and write about it, or who falls in love and needs to tell what it's like. That's great, of course. That's being a Poet. But I'm the kind of writer who is always mooching around in an empty space that words may or may not decide to enter, waiting on them tongue-tied.

T: So you're not trying to be socially useful? Or to have some cathartic, therapeutic experience by writing?

LEE: That's right, I'm not. At least not while I'm writing, which is what counts. When people ask, "Do you write for yourself or your readers?" both alternatives are wrong. The only target, the magnet, the one thing that exists for me is the thing that is trying to get itself into words, and isn't there yet.

What happens when "it" is finally born there on the page is a different matter. Then the writer can be concerned for the reader, or self-centred, or whatever. But that's after the event.

T: "The event" being that something which gets a hold of you and says, "Write me."

LEE: Right. I hate to sound so mystical about it. It must sound like a pile of crap. But how I've managed to make even twenty-five or thirty poem-like objects in the last decade is almost beyond me. I often wait so long for something to vouchsafe itself that I can't help asking what am I doing it for, mooching around like that? And then when it does come, you go from famine to feast. There are so many dimensions and overlaps and tonalities to even the simplest thing. You get overwhelmed by the multiplicity of what-is. That's when craft is necessary, just to keep up with it through the scores of drafts.

T: Writing your kind of poem could be likened to editing what-is. Maybe the qualities that make you a good editor have made you a poet?

LEE: That's a good connection to make. And as an editor, I also start by being purely reactive.

T: What's the tie-in between this purely responsive stance and your contention in *The Gods* that artists have been doing "unclean work" and "murdering the real"?

LEE: That's a complicated question. First of all, the notion of artists being murderers of the real has to be seen in a particular historical context. We have to look at the writing of the last two hundred years.

Before that, dimensions of meaning were experienced as residing in the day-to-day world. "What-is" was sacramental, it mediated meaning. But with the advent of the "objective world" of Descartes, of a universe composed of value-free facts, the "feelings" and "meanings" and "values" were severed from the objective world and exiled to the domain of the private subject. The cosmos was no longer taken to be intrinsically meaningful.

By 1800, say, the crisis of living in a de-valued real world had come to be felt *as* a crisis. All the great Romantics had to wrestle with it. Since then, the artist's progressive attempts to resolve it have led mainly through symbolism, and then through various metamorphoses of symbolism: mundane reality must be a symbol of a higher level of meaning.

Symbolism was undercut by post-symbolism where all you can do is celebrate the activity of tracing meanings — or making them up. You no longer believe there is a higher level at which you'll find meaning; that's the old, prescientific idealism. But you go on celebrating the absurd courageous existential activity of *creating* meaning in art, not believing in the meanings themselves. Like Mallarme and later Yeats and Rilke and Joyce.

T: If I understand you correctly, you're saying artists celebrated the idea of creating meanings or values as a compensation for having lost touch with them.

LEE: Exactly. As a compensation for having lost belief in a meaningful cosmos *and* in a higher realm of value. For instance, Joyce set up the sequence of the chapters in *Ulysses* to mime the sequence of books in *The Odyssey*; not because he believed the latter really embodied a literal scheme of meaning, but because all he could affirm was the hope that the patterns of art will somehow make sense of life. He gives us a value-free aesthetic pattern. Well, whoopee! It's an aesthete's solution, a formalist solution, which glorifies the value-imputing imagination of the artist, but at the expense of confirming the devaluation of the real world even further. And in fact it ends up devaluing the "value-imputing imagination" too; there's no longer any credible content to the values it's supposed to be creating. Pound gets all kinds of brownie points for re-activating old myths in *The Cantos*. But nobody takes them seriously, except as demonstrations of what a formalist virtuoso he was. We don't *believe* in them as "values."

T: So you're saying each time this process is repeated, the substance of "value" keeps retreating from us further.

LEE: Yes. Each time the great heroic artists extend what their predecessors did to try and resolve the crisis, they have to relocate the "value" in still more involuted, rarefied, improbable quarters. In the process they de-value the day-to-day reality further and further. They "murder the real" instead of resuscitating it.

T: How do you see today's artists continuing along this route?

LEE: By now, all a lot of the best artists can do is simply rev up our nerve-ends, substitute sensation for meaning altogether. Moment-to-moment art gives you the kind of kicks that eating stimulants or jacking off or killing people can. Nothing *means*: but at least there's always one more *frisson* of raw sensation that can be cranked out. This is decadence, it seems to me: primitive brutalism accompanying high sophistication.

T: Can you give me an example?

LEE: Well, James Dickey's stuff is a good example. Technically his poetry is strong, it's beautifully written. But humanly it's horrendous. The cutting edge of his modernity is this impulse to jolt your nerve-ends one crunch further, one more time, with each new line. And he's good, he's one of the best; he can actually do it. Same with Ted Hughes. Look at the combination of magnificent word-sense and super-gothic blitzkrieg of the nerve-ends in *Crow* or *Gaudete*. This is not some two-bit kid of twenty having wet dreams and power trips on the page; this is one of the best poets of the last few decades, following the deep instincts of his maturity. What a terrible era. These are our authentic necessities now, and they stink.

T: How do you justify your own work as being any different?

LEE: Well, the only step ahead I could find in *The Gods* was to try and identify our condition, to enact it consciously and then name it.

T: But you also write very directly about physical sensation in the love poems. I could say, aren't you asking your "carnal OM on a rumpled bed" to carry a great burden of meaning?

LEE: That's true, but it kind of misses the point. The love poems in the first part of the book actively *enact* the process of becoming idolatrous. They start with the innocent high spirits of falling in love, and end up with the man confessing that he's turned the woman's body into one more idol, because there's so little else that feels real. The poems explore that process, with their eyes open, and they discover this limitation on how far we can make one intense experience the locus of all meaning and value. So I don't think you can tax the poems with just being unwitting symptoms of the problem.

T: Does this mean you think revealing these problems in *The Gods* transcends them?

LEE: I wish it did, but I don't think it's that simple. But at least the book blows the whistle on that kind of idolatry as an unconscious pattern of behaviour. Implicitly and explicitly it questions the whole project of modernity. And it questions being a poet within the stream of modernity, which is what I balk at in particular.

Do we really want to continue this psychic slaughter of what-is from generation to generation? Shouldn't we ask ourselves if it's not self-perpetuating? If it isn't self-defeating? And if the line of heroic advance that always seems to beckon us out of the morass isn't in fact the straight line further into it?

T: So you're anti-romantic?

LEE: Oh, totally. And part of being a romantic is that you always have to find some new taboo to rebel against; the *frisson* makes you feel real for one more go-round. But my love-making poems are not "shocking" or "fearlessly outspoken." In those terms they have nothing to offer, they're dull. I'm not trying to go any further down that road. I'm not cruising for new taboos to infringe. I'm looking to stop the whole knee-jerk performance. Romantic revolt is a great yawn by now. Taboo is dead, we killed it.

T: If romanticism didn't exist, or

modernity generally, could you have written this book?

LEE: No, I'm a creature of my era like anyone else; I write from inside time, my own time. However my temporal arena is not just the 1960s and seventies. My work has a long-haul vista, for better or worse. Some of it must seem dull or bizarre to a person who reacts as though the world began in 1960 because I'm taking my particular moment as the last few centuries.

T: Are you still influenced by whatever religious instruction you received as a child?

LEE: I'm sure I am. In fact, I would like to know more about the particular tradition I was born into. There are things I rejected that I respect a lot more now.

T: What tradition was that?

LEE: The suburban United Church.

T: I was hoping for something a little more exotic!

LEE: No, no, that's the whole point about it. In terms of blah, there can't be many blah-er religious traditions than that. Only Unitarianism gone to seed might be more blah. That polite, philistine, spineless, *nice* suburban Protestant Christianity was what I grew up in. I was shaped by the experience of lacking a concrete sense of the sacramental.

T: That could be the whole function of watered-down Christianity. Perhaps it's not supposed to give you what you need at all; it's an icon, it's function is to perfectly reflect your state of hunger.

LEE: That's the best justification for the suburban United Church I've ever heard. But actually, it's the older Methodist/Presbyterian tradition I've started to respect now. I mean the rectitude, the honesty and the sense that you live an unadorned life. The sense that you work hard at something solid and don't try to impress people with insubstantial glitter. Those are

fairly limited virtues, I know. But if you live in a city like Toronto now, where you're so inundated by trash-with-flash that you practically need hip-waders, that old Wasp integrity, stultifying though it was, starts to look pretty valuable.

T: Then what made you rebel against it?

LEE: In my middle and later teens I wanted something much purer and more intense, and as it happened I soaked myself in the Christian mystics; I read them haphazardly, and daydreamed about being one myself. But then some time by the age of twenty-five I recognized, not very willingly, that my ordinary growing up was being delayed by trying to live in that fantasy, my fantasy. So I relinquished it and rebelled against the Wasp tradition in more conventional ways.

T: What kind of religious instruction or sense of the world do you try to imbue your children with?

LEE: I don't know how to handle that. My youngest child's iconography is very much shaped by American mass culture, super-heroes and so on. He picks it up by osmosis, like all his friends. What do you do to counteract that, in ways that won't just make it seem forbidden and glamorous?

T: Have you examined your motives for writing *Alligator Pie* and *Garbage Delight*? Maybe that's where some answers lie.

LEE: Well, one point of germination for my kids' writing was the impulse to play...I should stop and say I mean play as a direct, shapely release of energy for its own sake...Growing up in a post-puritan society, I'd learned to repress certain kinds of feeling pretty effectively: joy, anger, reverence, delight. So you could say my kids' poetry goes back and frees up the play of a lot of those feelings.

T: That would explain why it's so

successful. It works for you while it works for the kids.

LEE: That's right. And people of my generation probably need to free up. The trouble is now there's so much emphasis on fun culture, on getting your kicks, that I start to worry whether my kind of playing in words couldn't easily get co-opted. Even the possibility makes me squirm. Does my stuff get read as if it were Saturday morning TV cartoons? Real play is different from just getting kicks; it's grave or tender just as often as it's rambunctious.

I've got one or two more kids' poetry manuscripts that I'm finishing up, then I think that will exhaust what I can do, in poetry at least. I'd be turning myself into a Dennis Lee factory. If I do any more children's writing I think it'll have more to do with sorting out how to be human when you're three years old or six years old.

T: Does this mean you'd become a moralizing writer? As opposed to working from the "play" angle?

LEE: I hope I'll never become a moralizing writer. Perhaps I'll write something for children that doesn't make a person think of "play" and "moral" as being mutually exclusive categories.

T: Have you ever worried about television role models usurping your own model as a parent?

LEE: I've already got a fine supply of inadequacy as a *person*. If I had to spend a lot of time contemplating my performance as a "role model," in competition with TV, I'd probably crack up.

From that point of view, the way I lead my life day-to-day doesn't make a whole lot of sense. When I'm not traipsing around the country making a spectacle of myself, I spend most of my time upstairs in the third storey wrestling with rhythms on a page. When I come down — and I mean from upstairs — I'm a weird mixture of high and low from all that. I make too-large demands on the people around me as a result. So actually I'm pretty dissatisfied with my way of being a parent. There may be less inept ways to manage than the ones I've found, but when you scribble and you have a scribbler's temperament, there don't seem to be many alternatives.

I've got this in-between feeling generally. There's a free-floating part of me that would like to pedal back in time or psychic space, and disconnect from all that shallow, secular, trendy downtown Toronto civilization. I'd like to stand back from my ways of making a living, making a life, and take a deep breath. If I miss the brass ring or whatever, well, tough luck on me. I'd be in that waiting space I spoke of in terms of when I write. A person could reach out for things which ring a lot truer.

T: It sounds like you never stop re-evaluating yourself.

LEE: Well right now I'm teetering on the edge. First I finish writing a couple of things, see, wind up my obsessions of the last decade; then I have a male menopause. I expect it's already marked down on some invisible calendar. It's likely set for a Thursday afternoon. . . I just hope they serve coffee.

Norman Levine

NORMAN LEVINE was born in Ottawa in 1923. He was raised in the city's Lower Town where his father was a fruit and vegetable peddler. At eighteen he joined the RCAF, flew the last few months of World War Two in England and then attended McGill University in Montreal. He went to live in St. Ives, Cornwall, England in 1949, and lived there until 1980. A cross-

Canada travel memoir, *Canada Made Me* (1958), gave birth to the uniquely subdued and direct autobiographical style for his subsequent fiction. His novel of Cornwall poverty, *From a Seaside Town* (1970), was followed by internationally acclaimed short story collections, *I Don't Want to Know Anyone Too Well* (1972), *Selected Short Stories* (1975), *Thin Ice* (1979), *Why Do You Live So Far Away* and a paperback retrospective, *Champagne Barn* (1984).

Norman Levine lives in Toronto. He was interviewed in 1985.

T: On several occasions you have mentioned your interest in painting. In what ways would you say painting and your conversations with painters have had an impact on your writing?

LEVINE: When I left Canada in the summer of 1949, I was fortunate to come to St. Ives, Cornwall. From around then until the early 1960s, St. Ives was the centre of painting activity in England. There were young painters around my age who were my friends, and some have become well known. There were older artists — Ben Nicholson and Barbara Hepworth — there as well. They made me want to write, because they would say, "Come to the studio. I've just finished a new picture. I'd like you to see it." And in return I wanted to write a poem or a story in order to have something to show them. It was this kind of atmosphere that made me work.

I also would see Ben Nicholson go around with a sketch pad and sketch the beached boats in the harbour. So I used to go out with a notebook and try to describe the various things I could see. It was this exercise that had a lot to do with the way the writing changed.

Then later, in 1959, I met Francis Bacon when he came down to St. Ives. He would come to the house for dinner, and we would talk. Later, when he went back to London, I would see him up there. And it was through conversations with him that my writing opened up and became more personal. I remember coming away one evening convinced that the height of sophistication was to be direct and simple.

With a book you have to be led in, but you see a painting right away. I realized that when you remember a short story, you don't remember the sentences; you remember images, you see pictures. A lot of my work comes across in images.

And I've always liked the physical world and what it stands for. This little park outside the window, for instance, has its existence whether there is a funeral going on or a wedding.

T: The clarity of your writing helps me to see the action of my own everyday life. Do you recognize that teaching element in your work?

LEVINE: No, I don't. Not as teaching, but I see what you mean. I like to think that what writers do is more what Ford Madox Ford wrote about Turgenev: "It was as if a remotely smiling face looked up from the page and told you things."

T: What did you learn from Chekhov?

LEVINE: That the plot wasn't that important, providing you could tell enough about a character. And since I don't use plot I have to use other ways of stitching it together. Often I sense a connection between different human situations — in different places, in different times.

T: Do you have favourite stories of your own?

LEVINE: I like "To Blissland," and I like this new story "Django, Karfunkelstein, & Roses" — usually I like the story I have just finished.

T: The story I particularly like is "Thin Ice."

LEVINE: I'll tell you something of how that came about. I was in England and picked up the *Times*. I read about a snowstorm in New England and eastern Canada. There were photographs as well. And as I read the newspaper and looked at the picture I began to remember Canadian winters. Here I was in England — with the first daffodils coming out — missing snow and ice.

At the same time, I remembered an incident that happened eight years before. In 1970 I was flying to Toronto from Ottawa and staying in one of the better hotels. I flew in with just a briefcase. My photograph was on the entertainment page of a Toronto paper — *From a Seaside Town* was just being published in Canada. It had not long before come out in England where they seemed to like it. There were long reviews, the BBC made a film, and from the treatment I was getting I got carried away and thought that, as a writer, I had put certain things behind me. Then the man behind the reception desk in the Toronto hotel said, "Is that all your luggage? If that is all your luggage you will have to pay in advance."

Reading the *Times* about the snowstorm, at the same time remembering this incident in a Toronto hotel, I felt, instinctively, that there was a connection between these two unconnected situations. So I began to write the story. And as I did, certain things began to suggest themselves.

T: You have said that several of your stories often start where you feel a connection between human situations that have, on the surface, very little in common. Why do you think this is?

LEVINE: I don't think I can give you a logical answer. Perhaps it's because in every writer there has to be a writing animal. And the writing animal is amoral, anarchistic, disloyal. And this writing animal is housed in a civilized human being — family, society, friends, country. And it is the tension between the writing animal and this civilized human being that gives the cutting edge to most writers.

T: How do you know when a story is finished?

LEVINE: When I can't do any more to it. And when I feel a distance between the story and myself.

T: Flying to Toronto, looking down at the fields and the towns, I thought of your experiences bombing Germany. There's an abstract, cold view you get from the sky. Have those times affected your writing perspective?

LEVINE: Well, I'm sure World War II has dated me for myself. I feel this has determined my attitude for life. The way we were conned into it. World War II was fought by people who were essentially civilians who put on uniforms. Because it was a very extreme situation, a lot of poets turned up. As soon as the war was over, they went back to being butchers and bakers and candlestick makers. But I was just old enough to get in on the tail end of it. Part of the reason I'm a writer is definitely the war. Even now, the first story I wrote after coming back to Canada is called "Because of the War," and "Something Happened Here" is set in present-day Dieppe. I think a lot of people of my generation are who they are because of the war.

T: In "I Like Chekhov," the character Chester feels he's more comfortable in the presence of women than men. "And women seem to realize this." I thought that passage might be an indirect way of saying that women are attracted to you.

LEVINE: I've had more letters from women than from men. I remember one letter from this lady saying that after reading one of my books, she felt she knew me better than she knew her husband after twenty years of marriage and six or seven kids. In my experience, women seem to go much more for the written word. Men go much more for the visual.

T: Yours seems to be an aesthetic of understatement, as for instance in "Something Happened Here." What do you expect from the reader?

LEVINE: I don't expect anything from the reader. But, as a reader, I prefer writers who understate than those who exaggerate. I like to have the volume turned down, so that small perceptions can be noticed.

T: Your early stories, about going up to London to try to earn some money to feed your family, aren't really exaggerations?

LEVINE: No, they are the fantasies I have made from what happened. I remember once going for a walk in the Sussex countryside. A police car stopped. They said, "Where do you live?" I said, "Just around here." They heard my accent. They thought I was on holiday. They said they were looking for men who couldn't support their wives and children. Who couldn't make their payments. Before they drove off they told me to have a nice holiday. I was writing *Canada Made Me* at the time. And what was even more ironic, all those early hard-up stories were being published regularly in *Vogue* and *Harper's Bazaar*.

T: In *Canada Made Me* you were attracted to "the place across the tracks, the poorer streets not far from the river. They represent failure . . ." Are you still like that?

LEVINE: Well, for many years, I've been working in different areas. Just recently I have written six new stories. And the main interest there is how memory works. But certainly in the past the seedy always attracted me, especially people who have this feeling of just passing through. The English, after the war, had that quality. To me, it's a human quality I rather like.

T: As Canadians, we've lately become especially proud of our short-story writers. Do you think that is justified from an international perspective?

LEVINE: I don't know about the international perspective. But some of the people I've met in Europe — academics and publishers — think that the contemporary Canadian short story is more interesting than the American or British.

T: What accounts for this flowering of the Canadian short story?

LEVINE: A lot of things have contributed, and some of them are interlocked. It has been encouraged by individual people, and in this game one or two people appearing at the right tie can make all the difference. Robert Weaver at the CBC, Michael Macklem at Oberon, John Metcalf and his anthologies, and annual *Best Canadian Stories*, Wayne Grady and his two Penguin books. But when it really comes down to it, it is because certain Canadian writers are writing, or have written, short stories.

T: Whom do you write for? Or don't you write for anybody?

LEVINE: Early on I realized that writing had become an obsession. When I'm writing, I write for myself. I try to make sense of things that have happened. But after it's done it's another matter. Since 1971 nearly all my stories have been written on commission for Robert Weaver of *Anthology*. And he is the first person outside the house to see a finished story.

T: How do you feel when you finish a story?

LEVINE: An immediate feeling of gratification mixed with relief at having finished it. Followed, in a day or so, by depression. I think this is because of the excitement there was in writing it, the mental alertness. Then the sudden end to this.

And part of the feeling of being down is also the growing distance between yourself and what you have written. Several weeks later I may read the manuscript. And I know how all the bits and pieces came to be where they are. But I also see how it is something separate. It has a life completely of its own. I know I did it. But it now has little to do with me.

Dorothy Livesay

DOROTHY LIVESAY was born in Winnipeg in 1909. Educated in Toronto and Paris, she moved to Vancouver and evolved a turbulent literary career as a "social realist." Winner of Governor General's Awards for *Day and Night* (1944) and *Poems for People* (1947), Livesay has expanded her work beyond its initial leftist, proletarian focus to produce some of her best work

such as *The Unquiet Bed* (1967), *Ice Age* (1975) and *The Woman I Am* (1977). In addition to her fictionalized reminiscences in *Beginnings: A Winnipeg Childhood* (1973), her memoirs include *Right Hand Left Hand* (1977).

Dorothy Livesay has lived in most parts of Canada. She currently resides in Victoria. She was interviewed in 1978.

T: In the thirties it must have been more difficult for a woman to take an activist role outside the family than it is now. Where do you think you got your strength for your non-conformity?

LIVESAY: Well, there have always been women rebels. But I don't think there have been very many women revolutionaries. For that I would think you have to be a militant since childhood, which I never could be. My father called himself a radical, a man who went "to the root of things." Being a newspaper man involved with sending a news service across the country, he'd never committed himself to the Liberals or the Conservatives. But he was interested in the development of the CCF. He had an open mind, until I went out on the picket lines!

T: Do you think it's more difficult to create social change nowadays because a class structure is not so obvious?

LIVESAY: Yes. What we'd hoped for was that the soldiers would come back from the Second World War and be ready to change society. Instead, they were very accepting of society. The working class that we used to think of has become very much a middle class, therefore they are afraid of change.

T: It seems to me that liberalism dominates our age but it's unprogressive because it's basically just individualism. How do you feel about social change for the eighties?

LIVESAY: Well, when you get to seventy, every decade seems to be swinging one way, then the other. *Plus ça change, plus c'est la même chose.* Certainly, though, there's been a great liberalization in the areas of sex. What we did surreptitiously as university students in the thirties, is now all completely in the open.

But as a whole, I would say North America is still very reactionary. In Europe there's a great deal of this splitting up, of wanting to be independent over there, amongst the Bretons, the Basques and what have you. It's happening in England with the Welsh and the Scottish. This is an age not of disintegration but of refraction, of splitting off and becoming culturally and linguistically aware of oneself. So I don't find it disturbing that this is happening in Canada too, even though others do. It may be that Québec can move much faster towards a socialist society than the rest of Canada.

T: When you were a student in Paris you wrote, "I don't see any way out but the death and burial of capitalism." Forty-seven years later, do you still believe that?

LIVESAY: It's taking much longer than we thought, but of course it is happening all over the world. Capitalism has taken on many practical socialist ideas.

T: You've always been a great believer in proletarian literature, or writing which is readily accessible to everybody. Do you think Canadian writers are adequately responding to their social obligations?

LIVESAY: No, not at all. We have no writers like Sartre or Simone de Beauvoir who believe that the writer in any country must be committed to seek better things for humanity. If he doesn't speak out then he's committed to reaction.

T: Certainly there must be some writers whom you read nowadays and admire, whom you could recommend to other people?

LIVESAY: I had high hopes for the grass roots poets in Canada like Milton Acorn, Al Purdy and Pat Lane. And Pat Lowther was certainly very much a committed poet before her murder. And Tom Wayman. It would seem to me that these poets and those that follow with them are speaking out, but there isn't anything like the commitment of the writers in the thirties. We were so stirred up by what was happening in Spain. The takeovers by Mussolini and Hitler created an anti-Franco situation in Canada which was very strong.

T: We have lots of capable words-lingers, but very few people are concerned with international matters.

LIVESAY: It's pitiful what some of the young writers are doing. They are completely ignoring what's happening in the world, which is the threat of nuclear war. But it isn't so with the youngest group. I've been in contact with students in Ottawa and Manitoba who are nineteen and twenty and they seem very concerned.

T: In the thirties, when you were writing for *New Frontier*, you were more consciously propagandist in your poems than you are now.

LIVESAY: Well, in those days you didn't have any mass media. You didn't have people participating so much in the level of, say, folk songs or jazz. Now the scene is changed. Beginning with the sixties, in Canada and perhaps around the world, the poet is now asked to come and speak to musical gatherings or pop weekends. There was never any of this in the thirties. Of course we tried to join in on picket lines and have mass chants, but it was somewhat schematic, or unreal. What's very good today is that poets are now part of popular art. I don't spurn popular art. Many songsters are very good poets.

T: In your poem, "Last Letter," you write: "I am certain now, in love, women are more committed." Do you think that opinion will ever change?

LIVESAY: It's going to be very tough. Young men are having an awful time adjusting to the idea that a woman is a person, completely free to do what she pleases. I have confessions from young men who tell me their problems with their girlfriends. I sympathize with them, but we're absolutely flooded with television and magazines which work against change. The consumer market for women's products is appalling! Girls must have more and more dresses for more and more occasions to attract men. How are you ever going to break that down?

T: Let's talk a little about your latest book of poetry. Is the title *Ice Age* intended to have personal and political implications?

LIVESAY: And human. I had been reading, as we all have, of the possible changes in our world climate. The ice age is moving down again. This is a symbol of what's happening to humanity psychologically and spiritually. And of course personally, as one is approaching seventy, one begins to sense that this will be the end. All I have said will turn to ice.

T: Your style as a poet has not fluctuated a great deal since you began writing. How consciously have you been concerned with manipulation of technique?

LIVESAY: I used to be very conscious of punctuation. All my early poetry was very carefully punctuated. But I think my style changed when I came back from Africa in '63. That was the year the Black Mountain thing descended on Vancouver. Earle Birney brought Robert Creeley and Robert Duncan and that whole crowd. I heard them that summer and met Phyllis Webb and all the *Tish* people. But I got bored with the way they were all talking the same way. Lionel Kearns would use a metronome finger as he read. But I did come around to thinking that capitals at the beginning of a line were unnecessary. So I started arranging my lines as much as I could according to the breath. George Bowering helped me quite a bit on that. But I'm conservative. I don't want to make it look far out, like bissett and these people.

T: Many poets nowadays write poetry which is meant to be read aloud. Do you keep that in mind when you write?

LIVESAY: If I'm alone, I'll go over a poem aloud. I'll pace it out. I'll find that a particular stress or syllable doesn't work there at all.

T: Did you undergo a problem of adjustment becoming a poet as performer?

LIVESAY: Well, I remember the Ford Foundation once invited Canadian poets to come from all over the country to Kingston to discuss the literary scene for a weekend. The government was concerned with setting up the Canada Council. This would be around '56. Between these long sessions with publishers on the state of publishing, we organized little poetry circles. Layton and Dudek were there, people of that sort. I was asked to read. I read a recent poem that hadn't been published called "Lament," about the death of my father. I was absolutely terrified. I believed in the poem before I read it, but while I was reading it, didn't believe in it at all. It didn't make much of an impression. Now it's probably the most anthologized of my poems, that and "Bartok." But it was definitely not an easy time to read aloud.

T: Did you get much support from the CBC?

LIVESAY: I don't know when I was first asked to read for the CBC. I had a longstanding fight with Bob Weaver, who was doing *Anthology*. He insisted that the poetry be read by an actress. I couldn't stand their women actresses. They read it all wrong. I didn't think my voice was that bad. Some of us had a ten-year fight with Weaver to allow the poet to read it his own way. They swore an actor could do it better. Part of it was they had to pay the actor, to help them survive. Now it's pretty well

the rule that a poet reads his own poems.

T: Most of the power of your poetry comes from your ability to make the personal reflect the universal. Do you ever consciously write poetry as a social function, starting with the universal deliberately?

LIVESAY: My earlier documentaries were full of immediate passion, like *Day and Night*. It just sprang out of my experience. But *Call My People Home* was planned. I had to present what happened to those people. So I did a lot of research beforehand. The same is true of an Indian play I wrote for the CBC called *Momatkom*. This was in the fifties, long before George Ryga's *The Ecstasy of Rita Joe*. I was dealing with these radical conflicts way back. In '45 I was writing a poem about Louis Riel. I had to get a Guggenheim grant for that because there were no Canadian grants. Well, I missed getting the grant and couldn't finish the poem. It's now called "The Prophet of the New World." Now suddenly there's nothing but Louis Riel poems, plays and operas!

T: Do you ever look back on things you wrote, perhaps, forty years ago, and want to change them?

LIVESAY: No, I've objected very much to W.H. Auden changing his poems about Spain. I think it's dreadful, sinful. Because that was the feeling at the moment and that's what made the poem. Earle Birney's done the same thing. He's revised and I think it's wicked.

T: Birney was a Trotskyite when you knew him, aside from his poetry.

LIVESAY: Yes. We were all against Hitler during the war. That's how I got to know Earle best. He brought Esther home from London and they had a son born about when my children were born. We met often on picnics and literary evenings. But I had known him even in his Trotskyite days. Earle at that time wasn't a poet at all, as far as I knew him. He was a Canadian interested in literature while he was becoming a Trotskyite.

Then Earle corresponded with me during the war, from Europe. We were always quite close. I dedicated the poem *West Coast* to him. He represented the poem's central figure, the intellectual, who didn't know what to do. So he finally went down to the shipyards to see what that was all about. Then he enlisted. We've had terrible schisms since.

T: Generally, do you have a low opinion of Canadian critics?

LIVESAY: They're myopic. They have no vision.

T: Has reading the criticism of your work ever been a learning experience for you?

LIVESAY: I don't think I've had any serious critical work done on me in the earlier years. The whole group that centred around Frye ignored me completely. You won't find any of them even looking at my books.

T: Is the Canadian writing scene more fragmented than ever?

LIVESAY: Well, I don't think we ever were fragmented because we were small enough to be a company, a community of writers. We all knew each other. Now it's just become more regional. You have communities in five regions but you don't have a unification for the country. That's significant for the future.

In a remark he made in the introduction of Emily Carr's first book, Ira Dilworth said Carr was absolutely rooted in her region, in the history of BC and Indian life. But because she was dedicated to that region she's an international genius. It's true of Hardy; it's true of Balzac. The more you really absorb a locale or community, the more international you become.

T: Are there poems of yours which you think will stand the test of time?

LIVESAY: Some poems have meaning now and some poems have meaning for always. A poem like "Bartok and the Geraniums" might have meaning for always. It's a male/female poem, but it's also about art and nature. Then there are poems about women's plight. And perhaps a poem which predicts the androgynous future, "On Looking into Henry Moore." I think he was androgynous. He was the humanity of man and woman, the complete thing, which I've been striving to express. I also think in the Canadian scene that my documentaries will have importance. *Day and Night* and *Call My People Home* are being put into anthologies quite frequently.

T: Has your writing been affected by your earlier work as a journalist?

LIVESAY: Yes, I think that helps. I hated newspaper work because you have to do such dirty things to people. My year of apprenticeship on the Winnipeg *Tribune* was painful. I had to compromise people to get my story. hated that. Then I worked for the *Star*. I sent articles about France and then after the war I did a series on post-war rehabilitation in England. I was freer then, but as a younger reporter you simply had to get a story out of people. I hated that.

T: I don't think there's any particular route one should follow to become a writer. However, would you recommend a career in journalism as opposed to the university route?

LIVESAY: Both things that I did, journalism and social work, have been significant. But I actually would have liked to have been an anthropologist. There are a number of anthropologists who are also poets and writers. That sort of area is far better than going into English. The last thing I'd tell people to do would be to go through as an English major. I took languages,

French and Italian, and that was far more broadening. But then I'd read all the English literature at home in my teens. I tell every single promising poet, "Don't go through and be an English major. It kills your poetry." That's my great message!

T: Yet you were in Vancouver teaching a course on woman writers. Which are your favourites?

LIVESAY: I've always tremendously admired Virginia Woolf, Katherine Mansfield and Edith Sitwell. Recently, Doris Lessing, Rebecca West, Simone de Beauvoir. I don't know American writers very well at all. I've had to close myself off from that. I'm doing so much Canadian reading.

Canadian women writers have been neglected. All the best and first Canadian women fiction writers have come from the west. The Canadian novel had its roots in the west, certainly not in Montreal or Ontario. But when Mordecai Richler came to give a talk in Alberta, he hadn't read anything by Frederick Philip Grove. He didn't know he existed. It's that kind of incredible insularity that I've been fighting against. Emily Carr's style was utterly unusual and she had a brilliant mind. And another BC writer, Ethel Wilson, also had a totally individual style. But all people think of back east is Marian Engel or Margaret Atwood. These weren't the first, and they're not the best. But I should mention that I have not read as much as I should have of French-Canadian women writers. Gabrielle Roy is absolutely a top novelist. And Anne Hebert.

T: But it seems like the Canadian theatre scene, as a whole, is coming along well?

LIVESAY: It's the healthiest. It's not looking at its navel. That's the worst thing about the poets in this country; they're writing from an ivory tower. Even the young ones. All that *Tish* group is ivory tower in my view.

T: Are there major projects on your mind that you're worried about not getting done?

LIVESAY: Well, I've done a lot of work on the first woman poet in Canada, who was a Confederation poet, Isabella Valancy Crawford. She was an Irish child brought to Canada in 1855 or 1858. She was a remarkably visionary poet. I discovered and edited an entirely new manuscript that had never been seen. There are now about five people writing theses on her.

The other writing I would like to do is some work on popular women writers like Pauline Johnson, Mazo de la Roche and Nellie McClung, who were neglected and spurned by the critics. There needs to be a whole critical book looking at popular writers in Canada. Their work laid the basis for more mature work like Margaret Laurence's. I don't think a mature novel can arise in a country unless there's been a lot of popular writing as a base.

T: Certainly one of the signs of maturity in a country's literature is when all books do not have to aspire to be *War and Peace*.

LIVESAY: Yes! What's wrong with the ballads of Robert Service? It's a genre. It's great fun. A lasting literature has to have a base from which to grow. She who went before Margaret Laurence was Nellie McClung.

T: And Dorothy Livesay. That must be a good feeling, to know you helped lay the foundation for what others are now writing.

LIVESAY: Yes, it is. But I've never felt that the poetry belonged to me. I am the vessel through which it comes. My tentacles are out recording. What's coming through has been for everybody.

Hugh MacLennan

HUGH MACLENNAN was born in Glace Bay, Nova Scotia in 1907. After a classical education he became the most significant member of what Margaret Laurence has referred to as the first generation of non-colonial Canadian writers. He has received the Governor General's Award five times. Oedipal struggles for power often generate psychological conflicts in his

novels which are *Barometer Rising* (1941), *Two Solitudes* (1945), *The Precipice* (1948), *Each Man's Son* (1951), *The Watch That Ends the Night* (1959), *Return of the Sphinx* (1967) and *Voices in Time* (1980). He has loved and tried to understand Canada for as long and as deeply as any major Canadian author.

Hugh MacLennan lives in Montreal, where he taught for many years at McGill University. He was interviewed in 1979.

T: There's a remark in *Return of the Sphinx*, "If you ever let them see inside your soul, they'll crucify you to save themselves from seeing what's inside their own." That explains why artists have been persecuted throughout history.

MacLENNAN: That's right. Often painters got the worst of it because we will go insane at a new vision if it destroys an old one. I remember once in Montreal somebody did a damn bad piece of sculpture out of wood on Sherbrooke Street in the early fifties and two guys came along with axes and chopped it to pieces. With two policeman watching, looking on. And even the Group of Seven was denounced in Montreal in 1927 for obscenity. For trees and rocks!

T: How much do you think you expose parts of your soul in your work?

MacLENNAN: Well, I don't write straight autobiography, but you know Flaubert's famous remark, "Madame Bovary, c'est moi." It's just a question of empathy.

Of the stuff I've written, the one that ripped out my guts the most was *Return of the Sphinx*. The epilogue of that I can't read very easily even now. I said more there than anything I've ever been able to say. I didn't realize it until the very end when I found myself writing, "One more step would have set us free but the Sphinx returned." And it has.

T: Yet that novel wasn't well received.

MacLENNAN: It was well received in the States. But every paper here panned it. I must say that hurt me. I'd never had that much hostility in this country.

T: I think *The Sphinx* is valuable because it argues that a man's morality is not necessarily determined by his political views. That's somewhat of an unfashionable opinion these days.

MacLENNAN: It certainly was in 1967. What happened was that *Return of the Sphinx* arrived in the bookstores less than a week after DeGaulle's famous speech in Montreal where he said, "Vive le Québec libre!" To my utter astonishment the book was regarded by Canadian reviewers as an insult to Canada in her centennial year! One of them wrote Edmund Wilson about it and he told me. An insult to Canada in her centennial year! I thought we'd grown up beyond that.

T: I think it was received that way because you were arguing that Canada's problems were essentially psychological, not political.

MacLENNAN: And of course that's nonsense. Politics, for God's sakes, is simply property. It begins in the nursery. That book wasn't about Canadian politics. I had a very universal subject there.

T: Have you been branded a reactionary for refusing to view social problems in strict economic terms?

MacLENNAN: Sure. But not originally. Originally I was branded a revolutionary, as obscene and so forth. Then I was branded a nationalist in the fifties when it was more fashionable to be an Angry Young Man. Then in the sixties people tried to reduce everything to politics. Now I'm simply not sexy enough.

T: Certainly the pace of some of your novels is leisurely compared to many novels today. Is that because you felt obliged to supply a sense of place when you wrote about Canada?

MacLENNAN: Yes, I had to. It was necessary then. I was panned by some highbrow critics for this but people have to know where they are. Drama depends upon the familiar. Otherwise it's just an accident. It's necessary to build the stage. That takes a lot of craftsmanship. They ruined *Two Solitudes* as a movie because they didn't understand that. The French and the English never met socially. That's the idea of *Two Solitudes*. But the scriptwriter directed it and he didn't understand the book. The reviewers absolutely massacred it and I couldn't disagree with them.

T: There's been an obvious progression in your work from understanding where Canada is coming from, with novels like *Two Solitudes*, to worrying about where we're going. Why do you object to being called a nationalist writer?

MacLENNAN: Because nationalist that you have with the Parti Québécois and nationalism in various European countries is a substitute for religion. I have no use for that.

T: But I think you are a nationalist writer because you've been so intimately concerned with the growth of Canada as a nation.

MacLENNAN: The growth of any nation starts with a family. Then it becomes a tribe. Then it becomes a confederation of tribes. Ultimately maybe a nation. It can't be done overnight. It's a matter of evolution. All I've been asking is for people to know what their potential is.

T: Would you agree that Canada's potential is particularly fascinating because we're coming of age at a time when mankind seems to be coming to a major crossroads?

MacLENNAN: Sure. Western civilization is dying. Civilization, as we know it, is in decline. As it happened with the Romans. That puts Canada in a unique position. An Irishman named Dennis Brogan, at some conference I was at in the early fifties, once said, "Poor Canada. It's the most successful country in the world. What a tragedy it should become successful in the middle of the twentieth century."

T: Few Canadians are going to appreciate that tragedy because few of us appreciate the extent of our success in the first place.

MacLENNAN: That's exactly right.

T: You wrote that if Sisyphus was a saint, he could serve as your patron. As a Canadian struggling to become a writer in the 1940s, what made the uphill struggle so steep?

MacLENNAN: Voltaire said that if he had a son who wanted to write, he'd strangle him out of the goodness of his heart. It was particularly hard in Canada because we had no publishers except Ryerson, which was owned by the Methodist Church. So you could forget about them. Then later, if you signed with a Canadian publisher you had to give them rights to the whole world. It was terrible. The war just made it worse. *Barometer Rising* was a Book Society choice in England but they didn't have enough paper for more than fifteen thousand copies.

T: And the money was poor. I understand that at age fifty you had only a thousand dollars, after thirty-five years of writing.

MacLENNAN: When I published *Barometer Rising* in New York, it got great reviews and drew a huge response. It sold twenty thousand in hardcover and a hundred thousand in paperback. But out of that I got less than seven hundred dollars. When *Two Solitudes* sold sixty-eight thousand hardback copies in Canada at three dollars each, I made forty-five hundred dollars.

T: Do you ever question how much international attention you might have received if you had been writing as a citizen of a more powerful country?

MacLENNAN: It would have been much greater. No question of that. The territorial imperative is mighty in literature. Because language is so powerful.

I remember I was in England with C.P. Snow and we were dining with some reviewers. One of them said, "Look, Charles, don't you think it's about time we started putting down these bloody South African writers?" I took offense and said, "You think you've got anybody in England as good as Alan Paton?" He said, "My dear chap, you can't be serious. He's a South African." It was all boudoir politics. So I told them Alan Paton could write the pants off any Englishman they had, with the possible exception of Evelyn Waugh.

That's why I didn't wish to be known as a Canadian writer. It's still a diminutive term, even after you've been translated into thirteen languages.

T: We often hear that Canadian writers felt obliged to set their stories in American or British locales. You never did that.

MacLENNAN: No, I didn't. But certainly anybody connected with movies had to. It still happens. For example, when Margaret Laurence's *A Jest of God* was sold to the movies, they set it in the States. Personally I've had some hilariously funny interviews with Hollywood people about this. They would set *Barometer Rising* somewhere other than Halifax. "Gotta be American. Boy meets girl in Paris, France. Okay. Boy meets girl in Winnipeg. Who cares?" That's a literal quotation.

T: What about the spectre of censorship back then? Was that ever a problem for you?

MacLENNAN: I never worried about it with my work. After all, it certainly didn't bother Tolstoy that he couldn't use four-letter words. What did bother me was when they tried to actually ban books. I got involved in two court cases, not for myself, defending books. The worst

time was when the Americans tried to ban Nobel Prize-winners in the fifties.

T: How much response did you get to your work in the forties compared to the sixties?

MacLENNAN: More. The Canadian reading public took to books very, very eagerly. A young writer had a much better chance to be read than now. In the first place, you weren't in competition with television. Secondly, you had a much better chance of being reviewed. Thirdly, hardbacks were cheaper. In 1959, *The Watch that Ends the Night* was 160,000 words and sold in New York for five dollars. Now people wait for paperbacks. The big contracts are in paperbacks. That's not been good.

T: How have the older writers like yourself and Morley Callaghan felt about seeing some of the garbage being passed off as literature these days?

MacLENNAN: There's always been garbage. The point is that garbage made money in other countries. It hasn't made money here.

T: *Each Man's Son, Two Solitudes* and *Barometer Rising* were all set before or during World War One. Was World War One the turning point for Canada as far as you're concerned?

MacLENNAN: It certainly was. Canada entered the war as a completely colonial nation, not a power at all. Then Canada found herself.

Canadians were the first to go under gas attack and hold the line. Then when Canadians broke the Hindenburg Line on the 8th of August, 1918, Ludendorf called it the black day of the German Army. "Wherever the Canadians were," he said, "we knew we were in trouble." And finally Canadians ended the war by capturing Mons. After that, the feeling of pride in this country was enormous.

But our casualties were appalling. We had one-quarter more killed in action than the Americans lost. That was sixty-nine thousand killed from a population of seven million. We lost so many of our best men that for twenty years Canada had no fundamental leadership. Do you know what the casualties were in the first battle of the Somme? On July 1, 1916, fifty thousand died in three hours. The next day they tried it again and lost seventy thousand. They kept on insanely charging barbed wire and machine guns. It was almost like committing suicide. The average life of a second lieutenant in the British Army those days was two weeks. That's why Churchill wrote that Anthony Eden was almost the only person of first-class ability to survive the First World War.

But the worst tragedy of World War One for Canada was that the Orange Society in Toronto deliberately jammed conscription down the throats of the French Canadians. This meant, with their huge families, a farmer might have had six or seven sons drafted. The French served in the First World War and had magnificent regiments. But they never forgave us for that. And we're still paying the price for it.

T: So the First World War not only gave Canada a sense of identity, it also served to split us apart.

MacLENNAN: Yes, it did. The French Canadians were perfectly willing to go along with both wars, providing they had a volunteer system for those who wanted to go to them.

Can anybody say there was any sense to it at all? The only thing worse than that war was the peace treaty. It guaranteed a second war.

T: *Barometer Rising* was very critical of the way Canada was used by the Allied Forces during World War One. Did you come under any fire for those opinions?

MacLENNAN: No, because three-quarters of the country agreed with it. I was writing a column for the *Toronto Star*, syndicated across the country, when Winston Churchill wrote his version of the Second World War in the sixties. God knows I admired him. But in the first four volumes of ninety thousand lines — I very carefully measured them — Canada got only fifty-three lines for her contribution. Of those, twenty-eight were in some letter to Mackenzie King about Newfoundland. Canada's contribution to that war was enormous! But the English couldn't have cared less. It was a great shame that Canada's two most stupendous efforts were made as part of the British Empire, not for Canada.

T: I loved that comment about Churchill in *The Sphinx*, the one made by the Russian ambassador.

MacLENNAN: The one where he says you people love to quote old Churchill, especially when he's rude? That's a reference to Churchill's remark about Atlee, of course. You remember? He said, "Mr. Atlee is a very modest man, with much to be modest about."

T: The explosion you describe in *Barometer Rising* happened when you were ten. Were you living right in Halifax at the time?

MacLENNAN: Yes. And I had had a sixth sense that something like that was going to happen. Kids are queer like that sometimes. I knew the Germans had these two enormous submarines, the *Braemen* and the *Deutschland*. The whole of Halifax was blacked out at night because it would have been possible for these submarines to have had aircraft with folding wings like they had in the Second World War. They could have simply surfaced off Halifax harbour and bombarded the place. It would have been worthwhile doing.

When the explosion hit, that's what I thought it was. All the windows came in. One step further I'd have had my head knocked off. There was silence. I did verification of temperatures and things like that to write *Barometer Rising* but there was nothing else I didn't know. I remembered everything about it.

T: Do you think that was a great psychological shock to you as a child?

MacLENNAN: Well, you did see some pretty horrible things. Then rumours were soon flying around that there would be another one. And there damn near was.

I remember a terribly cold day when a man came into the school, shouting at us to evacuate. He said there was going to be another explosion. We were dragged out on sleighs into the hills and told to get under cover. We nearly froze to death for three hours. When I got home my mother didn't know anything about it. But it turned out the guy was right. There was a ship called the *Picton* and it caught fire. The Halifax stevedores were handling these six-inch shells with heavy gloves but the shells were so hot they scalded their hands lowering them into nets in the water. Finally they towed her out. She didn't go up but if she did it would have wrecked the whole south end. Halifax nearly had three of those things.

T: There's often a psychological explosion in your books, with a youngster involved. Do you think there's any correlation?

MacLENNAN: I suppose there's something, but it's hard to know where these things come from.

T: What were your main literary influences?

MacLENNAN: I never read any novels at all, except *Treasure Island* and *Ivanhoe*, but at a young age I read all of Homer in the original. And a great deal of Greek literature. When I finally got to Greece, looking up the coast towards Athens, apart from the slight difference in ground cover, I could have been on some marvellous bay in Nova Scotia. What Homer was describing was exactly like the coast of Nova Scotia. It was the same kind of life. People going out to sea in small boats, people going off to war. Homer described what I knew better than any other writer.

T: Would you agree your work has been essentially about the frictions between generations?

MacLENNAN: I suppose you'd have to say that's true. This crossing over of generations...oh my God, I've seen some tragedies there. It's a bad thing.

T: Was there a strong generational clash between yourself and your father?

MacLENNAN: Not as bad as the sixties. But I would say there was. He was a stern Victorian, yet he was a highly emotional Highlander. So he was a difficult person, yes.

T: What are some of your memories of him?

MacLENNAN: Well, I remember my mother and sister and I were living in a single room on captain's allowance, which was only a few dollars a day, while he was overseas in the medical service. He was overage and he nearly killed himself with overwork after the Somme battles. Then he nearly lost an arm from an infection. He came back to be an invalid at home in 1916. What little money he had vanished with the war. We rented a house sight unseen in Halifax and it blew up as soon as we got in it, from gas in the walls. They were both in the hospital. Then my father got back to practising medicine again and was back in uniform.

He was a helluva good surgeon. He was the only person east of Montreal who could do a labyrinth operation, which is practically a brain operation. He'd gone to Vienna and learned how to do it. He died as a result of his last operation, when he was dragged on a sleigh in a winter blizzard into the fields somewhere near Windsor, Nova Scotia, to operate on a farm table. He came back and had a stroke the next day.

T: You've used the term "son hungry" in one of your novels. What about the other side of the cycle? Have you had children yourself?

MacLENNAN: I didn't because my first wife had rheumatic heart disease so it was impossible. But I'm very, very fond of children. For a time I missed having them terribly. That's really why I went back to McGill. To associate with young people. I couldn't do without them.

T: I think there's a lot of beauty in your work which comes out of that yearning.

MacLENNAN: That's nice to hear.

T: I'd even go so far as to say your conception of God is somehow linked to this idea of the perpetuation of the species.

MacLENNAN: Yes, I think it's a form of energy built into the evolutionary system. But you have to wait and work for it. What I said in *The Watch that Ends the Night* was true as far as it goes. Theology is pretty well hopeless. You should read Dr. Penfield's book *The Mystery of the Mind*. He was the greatest of all brain surgeons and the founder of the Neurological Institute. He developed

the science of neurology and was certainly the greatest Canadian of our time. He said to me twenty years ago, "I know I know a good deal about the brain, but I know nothing about the mind." So he called his book *The Mystery of the Mind*.

Penfield had not been a religious man when he was younger but his own work in science eventually drove him to where the poets and philosophers were centuries before.

We have learned more about humanity in the last twenty years than has been learned since people knew how to think. And we have our newspapers taking our federal elections seriously! We have student demonstrations! We have people who are complete materialists teaching psychology! They're back in the Stone Age.

T: So what does the future hold?

MacLENNAN: The Arabs have such fantastic money power they will soon have A-bombs. They can very easily get the plutonium. There's no problem in hiring the technicians. That's all such a terrifying prospect that it makes what's going on in Canada today utterly trivial. I'm not sure the world will survive it. It's very, very dicey.

T: And yourself?

MacLENNAN: I like to think that fifteen thousand years ago is only yesterday. And it is. The ice was a mile high on top of Toronto fifteen thousand years ago. That gives me a certain sense of being more at ease in this universe. With that thought behind me, I'm quite sure I'll be able to finish a new book.

T: I didn't think you were going to write another novel.

MacLENNAN: Neither did I.

George Melnyk

GEORGE MELNYK was born in Augsburg, Germany in 1946. He came to Canada with his Ukrainian parents in 1949 and settled in Winnipeg. In 1968 he left to attend graduate school in Chicago and Toronto. In 1972 he returned to Western Canada to launch *NeWest Review* in 1975. He subsequently founded NeWest Press. He lived in Edmonton from 1972 to 1985.

His books are *Of the Spirit: The Writings of Douglas Cardinal* (1977), *Radical Regionalism* (1981) and *The Search for Community: From Utopia to a Cooperative Society* (1985). He has recently left his position as Executive Director of the Alberta Foundation for the Literary Arts to prepare a new manuscript on worker-ownership in Canada.

George Melnyk lives in Calgary. He was interviewed in 1985.

T: *The Search for Community* is a hyper-analytical book. Do you ask yourself whether it's the most successful type of book to write in terms of creating ripples in society?

MELNYK: Sometimes I even hate to ask myself that question. . . But let me answer it this way. I don't consider it as a popular book. I don't consider myself a popular writer. And I don't intend to ever change to become a writer of popular books. Basically I'm a political writer. And I can't think of any political writers in Canada, people who write social criticism or political commentary, who are popular writers, except perhaps political biographers. And I think any person who's a left-wing writer in this country is not going to be popular. We don't live in a left-wing country!

T: In your book you mention that the co-operative movement in Canada has lost its missionary zeal. It strikes me that anybody who takes the care to write this book must ask himself: how best to be a missionary?

MELNYK: Yes. There is definitely within me, as you put it, a missionary sense. And so can you be a missionary by writing a book? I suppose if I were a popular writer I would say, "Look, this is going to change your life. This is going to make you happy for ever and ever." Which is sheer BS. It isn't true. Co-operatives are not some kind of nirvana. They're not a guru-charismatically-led kind of thing. It's people helping themselves. And it's not going to solve all of people's problems. I want to make it very clear when I write that when you create something and you work towards something like a worker co-op, it doesn't come easy. You can fall flat on your face.

So my book is not full of boosters. It's not full of hoopla. If one wants to build co-operative communities in Canada, which is what I want to do, it's a very sobering experience.

Especially when you look at the history of co-operatives. It is not fun and games. There's a lot of suffering and seriousness in something like that. Everything we do in life we pay a price for. You get something at one end, you lose something at the other.

T: How many people are there like you?

MELNYK: Well, my prediction when I talked to my publishers was that the book would sell two thousand copies in five years. There's twenty-seven million people living in this country, four-and-a-half million in the region that I'm from. But the kibbutz movement in Israel began with less than a dozen people. Worker co-ops in Mondragon, Spain, which are big model for me, started with five guys. So we aren't talking about mass movements. We're talking about a small number of very seriously committed people who feel that they can make this idea work and it makes sense to them. If someone's going to go through two hundred pages of text trying to understand the history of the co-operative movement, what it's all about, what are its problems and all the rest of it, then is still willing to talk about this utopian idea at the end of it, *then* they're serious people. And only serious people can handle something like this.

So I'm a serious writer and I'm not popular. So what am I going to do about it? It's not pop psychology!

T: And yet what's your estimate of the percentage of adult Canadians involved in some form of co-op? Forty-three percent?

MELNYK: Something like that.

T: That's a dynamic statistic.

MELNYK: I know. But I'm not going to yell that from the rooftops with my book. It's in there for people to find.

T: I discovered in your book that I happen to be a member of the largest credit union in the world. . .

MELNYK: Vancouver City Savings.

That's right. It used to be the biggest. But now the US Army one is larger. I didn't want to put that in the book!

T: So there's a failure of missionary zeal right there. For instance, whenever I leave the house to go to my credit union, I still say, "I'm going to the bank." There's a propaganda failure in that.

MELNYK: Well, it's not only that. It's also the society we're in. Our society doesn't want anybody to think too much about co-operation. They just want somebody who's a consumer, right? They wouldn't want to get you thinking that you're part of something important, because if you do, you might start asking questions and want to do something about it. So basically our society is anti-ideological and anti-philosophical.

T: Where did you get your impetus to become ideological and philosophical? North Winnipeg?

MELNYK: Well, I have a degree in history from the University of Chicago and a degree in philosophy from the University of Toronto. My books reflect that. But you're right. I think my experience of growing up in Winnipeg is really fundamental. I can't ever shake that. That's where my roots are. I'm part of what I jokingly call the "Ukrainian-Jewish Conspiracy." I'm not a rich kid who's gone and turned into a lefty. I come from a right-wing Ukrainian refugee family where the parents had to work hard to survive in Canada.

My father worked in the same factory for twenty-seven years. So I'm interested in factory issues and I write about worker co-ops. I mean, I worked in that factory, too, with my dad. Being Ukrainian, being ethnic, always put me in what I felt was an underdog position in the social hierarchy of society. I think what happened is that my unhappiness eventually became creative rather than negative.

T: And how did that occur?

MELNYK: Well, when I reached maturity, I found Manitoba politics to be extremely polarized between right and left. I thought that this polarization was counter-productive. I still do. I said this keeps people from thinking new ideas. Eventually the big issue for me was to be on the left but to think creatively rather than just mouth the old traditions. That resulted in my second book, *Radical Regionalism*, and then the social co-ops idea that resulted in *The Search for Community*. I'm always struggling to be original because I don't want to be tied down by this polarity. But of course in a sense I am tied down by that polarity because I'm reacting against it. That's partly where the creative impulse comes from.

T: Was there ever a time when you were less sober than you are now? More euphoric in your idealism?

MELNYK: No, I don't think so. But that doesn't necessarily mean I'm not hopeful. *Radical Regionalism* has optimism in it. I'm now talking about developing in Western Canada a world-class co-operative community to match what we have in Israel and Spain. That's optimism.

T: Do you ever look at yourself and say, "I'm exploring all these things with a lot of adventure intellectually, in books, but on a personal day-to-day level, how do these ideas and projects fit into my life?"

MELNYK: Sure I do. One way I do this is through the totem animals I have. These are self-adopted symbols to correspond with the phases of my life. In the NeWest phase, my totem animal was a wolf-buffalo. If you see the front page of any NeWest book you'll see the wolf-buffalo. That image comes from a poem I wrote in 1972 called "Confessions to an American Friend." It's a poem in which I describe myself as "a wolf-buffalo man." Eventually the artist Norman Yates in Edmonton, in 1977 or '78, drew me a wolf-buffalo which I used as the logo of NeWest Press. It's a buffalo with a wolf howling inside it. During the NeWest phase of my life, the cultural regionalism phase, that's what I was, that's how I saw myself. I wrote two books during that phase, *Of the Spirit: The Writing of Douglas Cardinal* and *Radical Regionalism*, both wolf-buffalo books.

I'm now in a new phase of my life, the co-op phase, and I intend to do two more books. My totem animal is a turtle. The Spanish for it is "tortuga." Turtles are not beautiful. They're incredibly slow. In fact my life is going so slow these days, I hate being a turtle... but I am a turtle. Social change is a very slow process. Slow and steady. The first turtle book was *The Search for Community* and I'm preparing a second one on worker ownership in Canada. There may even be a third turtle book.

T: What's beyond the turtle phase? Do you know?

MELNYK: Well, I've written a poem called "The Empty Quarter" that talks about how the turtle turns to a dragon. The next stage beyond co-operatives is the dragon phrase. Then there's a stage beyond that. My writing is linked to the totem animals because I can announce a new phase through the books, begin a phase with a book and end it with a book. That's how it all fits in.

T: It's interesting you choose these animal symbols...

MELNYK: Yes, it's always got to be an animal.

T: ...to express the stages you're in. It shows you're willing to incorporate instinctual elements even though you write these books out of a super-rationalist perspective.

MELNYK: Right.

T: So you have to balance your super-

rational self.

MELNYK: With something mystical and artistic.

T: The mystical element doesn't come through in *The Search for Community.*

MELNYK: No, it doesn't, but it is there in both the Cardinal book and *Radical Regionalism.* Although I don't express my personal mythology often, it's actually what keeps me moving; it helps me understand why I'm changing. I mean, instability is really hard for me to handle. Why I am doing this stuff on co-ops when I was doing NeWest before? The totem animals and the books explain the changes, the phases.

So I have this succession of totem animals. Maybe when I'm eighty I'll write about all this in an autobiography. But right now what has my being the turtle, being "tortuga" now, got to do with promoting co-ops? It tells me it will take a long time to get where I am going. I write a book every four years. The first one was in '77, the Cardinal book. Then in '81, the book on regionalism. This co-op book is '85. I've got the next one planned for '89. There will be another one four years later. I've got two books already planned for the dragon phase of my life. I'm already collecting material for them and the dragon phase it at least a decade or more away.

T: So what is the dragon going to do?

MELNYK: He's going to be involved in politics. The dragon breathes fire and destruction and all the rest of it. But every mythology has to come full circle. Mine will come back to the famous myth of St. George slaying the dragon. There is a circular path. The final stage is the mythology of where I got my name from, the phase in which there is no totem animal. I am free. I am dead!

T: You destroy the dragon and become St. George.

MELNYK: That's right. But what I can't understand is what does St. George mean? Is he a suicide symbol? Does he mean self-destruction, since I am also the dragon? St. George killing the dragon within? Or does it mean some kind of fame in the sense that sainthood would be fame? The symbol is there but I don't understand it because it's twenty or thirty years down the road of my life. I'm now the turtle and that's frustrating. It was much more fun being a wolf-buffalo. The turtle is just driving me nuts. Nothing is happening in my life! I didn't start out saying, "I'm going to write a turtle-like book." I just went and wrote the book I wanted to write. And it's turned out to call for a new kind of co-op that two years after the idea was launched has yet to appear.

I'm hoping that if the social co-op idea takes off, that in twenty-five years, when I'm an old man, there will be twenty-five or thirty thousand people involved. That would be success. That's one half of one percent of a population of six million. That figure is similar to the number of Hutterites that we have in Western Canada, twenty to thirty thousand, and that's their number after sixty years. They came here in 1920. If you reach that level, you can say you're successful. If you don't reach it, you can say you're a failure.

T: So as a modest Karl Marx, what's your relationship with your conservative father back home?

MELNYK: My father is disturbed by some of the things I do. But he's not totally opposed to them. My father is a right-wing person for two very good reasons. One, the communists killed his father and his sister. Second, he's a religious man. When you put those two things together, I understand my father's point of view. If I was him, I would think the same way! But my experiences have been different from his. What he feels is that I'm a misguided kind of left-wing individual. But we get along. He doesn't see me as a Marxist and he doesn't see me as a communist. And he's right, because I'm neither. He doesn't write me off as something totally antithetical to his values.

My father, in many ways, is an extremely interesting individual and I wish I could get to know him better. Underneath there are some incredible traumas that he and my mother have experienced, as refugees and as war survivors. It is from my mother that I get the creative side and from my father the institutional side. To her I attribute my writing; to him my administrative livelihood. In spite of the different ideologies in the family, our love for each other overcomes all that.

If you look at my book on co-ops, you'll find there's a big stress on the family. The family structure to me is fundamental. In a mass society, if you want to build a strong community of people, it's got to come out of a family structure. To me, the importance of the family, loyalty to the family, is the only thing that keeps one sane and full of these things like love and courage and caring. I also find my individuality within the family. I don't find it in mass society. The family is the door on community.

Ken Mitchell

KEN MITCHELL was born in Moose Jaw, Saskatchewan in 1940. The Renaissance Everyman of prairie literature, he edited *Horizon: Writings of the Canadian Prairies* (1977) but is probably best known for his numerous plays such as *Davin: The Politician* (1977), *Chautaqua Girl* (1982), *Gone the Burning Sun* (1985) and most notably *Cruel Tears* (1976), a very

successful adaptation of Othello as a musical about truckers. His seriously comic fiction includes two novels, *Wandering Rafferty* (1972) and *The Con Man* (1979), and his short stories in *Everybody Gets Something Here* (1977). A traveller to China and Tibet, he has also written poetry such as *Through the Nan Da Gate* (1986).

Ken Mitchell lives in Regina with his family. He was interviewed in 1980.

T: The characters in your plays don't seem to be concerned about the so-called search for identity. Do you think people who grow up on the prairies, where there's such strong ethnic presence, are less likely to be navel-gazers?

MITCHELL: Yes. The ethnic thing is part of it. But, as in Québec, there's a strong sense of regional involvement. There's where the strength of prairie writing has come from. I believe prairie people know their identity in the same way that Québécois people know their identity.

Also, there isn't a process of abstraction going on here, because everybody in the prairies is equally a newcomer. Even the native Cree were originally immigrants from the bush country of the east. When everybody's an immigrant, there's less development of hierarchical standards of privilege.

The Depression in the prairies was important, too. Everybody survived a large number of adverse factors together. Anyone who was weak — emotionally, physically or culturally — simply didn't survive. Those that couldn't hack it simply went elsewhere. That's why prairie people brag about the incredibly difficult conditions. It's a posture that's given them identity.

T: Maybe, as a result, you tend to look more outward in your work than inward. It seems writers in the west are less obsessed with tapping their actual experiences and emotions than writers in the east.

MITCHELL: I think that's generally true. Although I would characterize Canadian writing that way as opposed to American culture. We're less autobiographical, less internalized, less confessional.

Marginally, I do see a difference between east and west but I think it's because the west is more extreme. The further you get from the metropolitan centres — like the centre of the commu-nications industry, which is Toronto, where they tend to imitate British and American models much more — the less self-centred it becomes. I believe a natural writer or poet is really somebody who is only a voice for a people or region. Jack Hodgins is a good example. He almost has no identity at all. Obviously he's a very interesting and attractive and clever person. But he's being the voice of Vancouver Island.

T: Jack Hodgins is the perfect example because he's the most physically removed writer from Toronto and he's also the least overtly egocentric.

MITCHELL: I think in the metropolitan, cosmopolitan, cerebral centres people tend to be much too concerned with the rational process and self-analysis. If I give you any difficulty in this interview, it's probably because I have a tendency to resist self-analysis. I think, in part, it's unhealthy for a writer to do that.

T: What other conclusions have you drawn about the nature of prairie lit?

MITCHELL: I think that a great deal more literature has come from the prairie than people in Canada have yet to realize. History is slowly realizing that the art which originates from the prairies is stronger, on a per capita basis let's say, than art which originates elsewhere. There's no reason why this physically barren, thinly populated area should turn out any art at all. It goes against most theories of art, which say art comes from metropolitan centres.

That's why, if you look back at the Nellie McClungs and Ralph Connors, then to Frederick Philip Grove and Sinclair Ross, and then finally at the contemporary writers such as Margaret Laurence, you'll find they were almost all unrecognized when their work first appeared. Grove died in virtual neglect and was extremely bitter about his relationship with the Canadian public. Other writers were doing quite well from the urban centres. Yet it's history that makes the final judgment on the value of literature. It's the next generation that judges. Mazo de la Roche is probably not going to last and Frederick Philip Grove and Sinclair Ross probably will.

T: Which do you think has had a greater influence on prairie writers, landscape or history?

MITCHELL: You're trying to separate oranges and apples there, I think. Because I believe that landscape deeply affects history and politics.

The thing that makes the prairies a unique and strong source of art is that the landscape is one of extreme openness. There are no natural barriers immediately obvious to the eye. That has quite an unconscious influence. It's a very freaky experience for people to come here who are not accustomed to seeing that much sky and openness. Plus the climate is as extreme as the openness of the landscape.

The extremes of temperature and openness make you feel like you are the only thing around. But at the same time you are dwarfed by the enormity of it all. You see the universe around you all the time. You're not allowed to live in a little microcosm. When you can see the stars all the time you are constantly reminded of the insignificance of your being. So there's this kind of tension that develops. Extreme significance and extreme insignificance. You're the only erect thing in the landscape. I believe, in a subconscious way, this brings artists down to very fundamental observations of life. They are close to the roots of existence. Ultimately their work is going to mean more to people than the reproduction of social manners, which is where urban writing tends to be located. People in cities are often too obsessed

with the artifacts of pop culture rather than the basic realities of life. Consequently prairie art may not be popular, but it does last.

T: The effect of that openness is certainly reflected in your work. The protagonists in your novels seem to have an almost obsessive urge to travel. Is that something you felt growing up in the prairies, a need to explore all that openness?

MITCHELL: I guess so. I like to travel a lot. But I couldn't say for sure whether people generally like to travel in that part of the world.

After a while you tend to see the whole prairie as a kind of community. You may know the same number of people as someone who lives in a city, but the people you know are spread over a million square miles. My social life tends to exist in an inter-city way, not a neighbourhood way. But obviously that's a result of modern technology so it can't be interpreted as a reflection of how people have felt in the prairies historically.

T: In the short stories in *Everybody Gets Something Here* you use humour as an antidote to pain, but in the novels it seems travelling takes the place of humour.

MITCHELL: That's a really interesting idea. I'd never thought of that before. But it makes sense. Those are two ways of blunting the painfulness of reality.

T: And it seems there's been a progression in your work from dealing with how individuals "blunt" reality to treating alienation on a much broader scale. Do you think your writing might be becoming more overtly political?

MITCHELL: No. But I do believe that fundamentally I'm quite a political writer. Maybe more than most. I have a political sense of what I'm doing.

However there isn't much parliamentary politics or debate that happens in my work. Politics is much larger than the House of Commons. It's only when people realize that politics is a much deeper force than electing somebody and sending them off to Ottawa to engage in legalistic debate that only they can understand, that people will develop a sense of control of the political direction of their own country. Of Canadian unity.

T: How did you come to write *The Great Cultural Revolution*, a play about the Chinese Cultural Revolution?

MITCHELL: A friend who directed *Cruel Tears* showed me a play he'd come across called *Hai Jsi's Dismissal*. This is a play of great historical significance because it ignited the Great Proletarian Cultural Revolution in China. He had the idea of presenting it to North American audiences, but it was in traditional Peking Opera style. We eventually decided on a fictitious staging of this play in Peking in 1966, at the height of the Cultural Revolution.

One of the things my play is about is the dominant role or influence of culture in political movements. You can see that clearly in China. The Cultural Revolution was very important in deciding whether art was for the people or for the elite. So my play is not so much about China as about the relationship between art — specifically theatre — and politics. It's a question which should engage us here in Canada.

T: Is this play correlative to the cultural scene in Canada?

MITCHELL: Inevitably. There aren't direct references to the Canada Council or the Secretary of State. But we all know that the distinction between art and propaganda is sometimes difficult to define. I think it's a definition that's needed. So much of the art in Canada is clearly heavily influenced by government policies. It's time for artists to take a fairly critical look at their role in society.

T: Canadian theater is very healthy and active these days. do you think that's because so many of our playwrights are dealing with the problems of underdogs and we see ourselves as underdogs beside the US?

MITCHELL: Yes, that's true. There certainly isn't a tendency in Canadian theatre at the moment to write domestic drawing room comedies.

I think that part of the excitement of Canadian theatre is that it's almost approaching epic theatre. There's a strong sense of Canadian plays being oriented not to the miniature "room" metaphor that I believe most British and American plays concentrate on, but rather on the large-scale sweep of history and landscape. That's more consistent with our culture. And I believe, yes, that means there's probably a greater sympathy for Everyman.

T: Let's talk a little about your play *Booze*.

MITCHELL: Actually it's more of a show than a play.

T: Written by a non-drinker.

MITCHELL: Wait a minute. Let me nail this down right now. I've drunk heavily in my life. Like, I've been there. I've wallowed in the gutters with the lowest of the low! I've won drinking contests and all the rest of it. I'm not particularly ashamed of that, although I am ashamed of things that I did at the time. But I don't have a moral attitude towards the consumption of alcohol at all. I just try to restrict my own consumption of alcohol to the best champagne that I can find on opening nights of my plays.

T: But every time a Ken Mitchell character is offered a drink, you know he's going to fall flat on his face in the next scene or the next page. It's like when Lucy offers to hold the football for Charlie Brown.

MITCHELL: I didn't realize that. It's not a conscious thing.

T: I think it's consistent throughout your work.

MITCHELL: I'm sure there are exceptions. I'll have to try and find a couple of exceptions! However, I think that that's generally true. I use alcohol as a kind of metaphor for social poison. It's an escape from reality which is used quite consistently by exploiters to exploit the exploitable.

Drinking is a habit that has really become quite a destructive pattern of behaviour in our culture. *Booze* is designed to give that awareness to people, to show that alcohol as a drug has a much more pervasive and sinister influence on their lives than is generally believed.

T: If you're writing to communicate an idea, don't you think you might get more mileage by working in an electronic medium like film or television?

MITCHELL: Yes, that whole relationship between television and a writer needs a lot more examination. I don't think artists can afford to be so contemptuous of the medium as they have been. If you don't accept the challenge and try to use television in some realistic way, then the challenge might disappear for good. Technologically speaking, especially with the development of cable systems, television could conceivably be the greatest educational tool ever put in the hands of civilization. For artists to back away from that is an abrogation of responsibility.

You have to allow for the possibility that MacLuhan is right. That after four hundred years, the world of Gutenberg and movable type is becoming obsolete. That writers who can't learn to tell stories visually are as doomed as the dinosaur. Writing novels takes up a great deal of concen-

tration and energy. I'm not sure it's always worth it, because other media might be more productive.

T: Do you agree with the character in *The Con Man* who maintains the whole world is a con?

MITCHELL: He's a cynic.

T: And he's not Ken Mitchell.

MITCHELL: I don't think so.

T: I got the same message from that novel as we get from Brecht's *Three-Penny Opera*. Criminals are merely the people who get caught.

MITCHELL: And that accounts for the cynicism of that character in prison. It also accounts for the cynicism of someone like Richard Nixon. Politics is a con game and Nixon was as good a practitioner as any. He just got to believe it too much, until it destroyed him.

The worlds of advertising and professional sport are other facades for con games. These con games are designed to expropriate money from the pockets of working people and put that money in the pockets of the people who live on their backs.

T: But your con man doesn't deliberately con people. He just gets into situations where people want to con themselves.

MITCHELL: Exactly. That's very perceptive.

T: It's as if you're saying Canadians so desperately want to assuage their small town, inferiority-complexed lives that we fall victims to ourselves.

MITCHELL: That's the central dramatic point. I'm really pleased somebody is able to refine that because it's not stated. *The Con Man* is an innocent who is really exploited by other people's gullibility. No professional con man could operate in a world where people don't want to get everything for nothing. I've kind of reversed the formula and created a number of worlds where people desperately want something for nothing so badly that they'll create a con man to perform illusions for them. Basically he's a victim of everyone else's greed. He ends up spending his entire life in prison because a con man is needed everywhere!

T: The con man is innocent and suffers. But all the other characters who understand how the world works have to also suffer, because they become jaded and invulnerable. Isn't there any middle ground?

MITCHELL: Yes, there is. I personally believe there is a large middle ground that most of us occupy. All children occupy it, for example. We have to work harder at expanding that ground to make a better world. That's why I teach. I want to show there is space between the exploiter and the exploited for people to exist and grow.

T: Has it ever occurred to you that writing can be seen as another con game? Where you manipulate people's reactions to make readers think a certain way?

MITCHELL: It's not only occurred to me, it's a basic philosophical principle upon which I operate! People love fantasies. They like to be taken away from the brutal reality, if you want to call it, of their everyday life. So writing is the essence of con artistry. Writing a novel like *The Con Man* is a con game where you try to draw people in to perceive a reality they don't normally see. And to make them think that they're getting something for nothing. Or for only $8.95.

W. O. Mitchell

W.O. MITCHELL was born in 1914 in Weyburn, Saskatchewan, where he also spent his early years. He attended high school in St. Petersburg, Florida for health reasons. Illness and marriage interrupted his medical studies. He taught school in rural Alberta, moved to High River, Alberta in 1944 and became a full-time writer with his famous prairie novel, *Who Has Seen*

the Wind (1947), hailed as a Canadian classic of boyhood. He was fiction editor of *Maclean's* (1948–51) and later won the Stephen Leacock Medal for *Jake and the Kid* (1962), an amalgam of his popular CBC radio scripts. He is a much-produced playwright and an avid teacher. His other novels are *The Kite* (1962), *The Vanishing Point* (1973), *How I Spent My Summer Holidays* (1981), *Since Daisy Creek* (1984), and *Ladybug, Ladybug* (1988).

W.O. (William Ormond) Mitchell lives in Calgary. He was interviewed in 1984.

T: In *Since Daisy Creek* Dobbs, the protagonist, has been maimed by a bear while out grizzly hunting. What's your experience as a hunter with *Ursus horribilis*?

MITCHELL: About twenty-five years ago, a rancher friend of mine took me out, and he shot the grey horse, just like in the book. What you read up to the point of the attack is precisely what happened. The bear came along and went to work on that dead horse. She lifted that goddamn horse with the entrails. I was about twenty yards away. I had a notepad with me, and I was getting down smells, sights, tastes, sounds. I whispered to my friend, "What do I do if she...?" And he said, "Stuff your pencil up her ass!"

T: So you're not much of a big game hunter.

MITCHELL: I'm a shotgunner. Geese, upland game. Indeed, I had a very tough time with this, wondering how the hell does a man justify going out and knocking over something that he ain't gonna eat. I mean, I'm not all that comfortable with digging goose pits and going after upland game. It suddenly hit me: the guy who hangs trophies — and incidentally, *Trophies* was my working title for this novel — is simply saying "I'm important!" It's that crass and that simple.

T: That fits with Dobbs being a bastard.

MITCHELL: Yes. Structurally it all fell into place when I realized he wants to say to the world, "I'm important. Look at that grizzly hide!" He's also a writer but he's failing. He has the wrong attitude. You'll notice at the beginning he's saying he wants to be better than so-and-so. He's simplifying it into a competition — he wants another score, another trophy.

T: Since the actual attack by the bear is fictional, was there any other specific incident akin to it that helped trigger the book, that re-emphasized for you what Dobbs refers to as the "capsize quality of life"?

MITCHELL: Five years ago, one of my grandchildren was showing me a back somersault. I said, "Can you do a snap-up?" I used to be a diver and a tumbler, so I demonstrated a snap-up for him and broke two cervical vertebrae. I had neuro-surgery in Toronto. My arm has atrophied now as a result of the pinched nerve. That capsize quality of life is the most autobiographical thing.

T: Did the capsize quality of life also start *Who Has Seen the Wind* for you?

MITCHELL: Yes, I think the loss of my father when I was five was the genesis of *Who Has Seen the Wind*. Also, just being a prairie child, seeing a dead gopher or a lockjaw steer, and smelling the rot of death. I think that darkness comes very early to a prairie child, especially to one whose father died and whose mummy keeps reminding him of their long lost daddy.

T: *Since Daisy Creek* is about learning and teaching, a philosophical study of morality. But it's also about darkness, about corruption.

MITCHELL: I was very conscious of *Heart of Darkness* as I did it. I had come across the idea that corruption corrupts. It's a chain that must stop somewhere. Then my son Orm, who's a William Blake scholar, reminded me of *Heart of Darkness* and the "whited sepulchre" — the idea that sticking with a simplistic principle can result in the ultimate in corruption. Witness Jamestown, Reverend Ian Paisley, Ayatollah Khomeini, the Spanish Inquisition. I had a whole list of these bastards! I realized that the categorical moral imperative is truly cant.

T: And so you have that quotation at the outset of the book: "Act as if the maxim of thy will were to become by thy adopting it, a universal law of nature."

MITCHELL: That goes back to my philosophy professor at the University of Manitoba, Rupert Lodge, a great Platonist. Incidentally, Marshall McLuhan, who was just two years behind my class, was another Lodge boy. Lodge introduced me to philosophy. At first it was a challenge. I couldn't understand the sonofabitch all that well. But I thought it was great. I wanted to include that whole list of names — Reverend Paisley, Ayatollah Khomeini — with the Kant quotation on the frontispiece. Finally I said to Doug Gibson, who was then my publisher at Macmillan, "Am I trashing up the front of this book?" He said, "Not necessarily trashing it up, but being too didactic." So I didn't include the names.

T: Ultimately, Dobbs can only break the chain of corruption in the novel with an act of mercy. It's a very moving, unexpected, and almost religious climax. Do you mind the term religious being applied to your writing?

MITCHELL: I am an extremely religious man who is considered one of the first for people such as Ken Campbell to attack. They go after books like *Who Has Seen the Wind*; it's been challenged in New Brunswick, in Ontario, in the west. For the fundamentalists, Satan is a great deceiver. Mitchell's pretending, so he becomes their most dangerous kind of guy. I'm not at all dogmatically or ritualistically religious. I got cheesed off with Sunday school by the time I reached eleven or twelve. I could not accept the inadequate rituals. They were not graceful to me. But I think I'm an honourable man.

T: You've mentioned Professor Lodge. He's one of four "IOUs" listed in the front of *Since Daisy Creek*, beneath the dedication to your daughter Willa. Who are the other three teachers you feel indebted to?

MITCHELL: Mildred Mitchell was a much older cousin who taught me in kindergarten and grade one. I loved her dearly. Indeed, I recall at my father's funeral, in the bedroom afterwards, seeing Mildred, rushing in happy to see her, not aware what it was all about, and Mildred throwing her arms around me and crying. The next one, Emily Murray, taught me public speaking in high school in St. Petersburg, Florida. She used the word grace once in our English class. I was a suckhole. I went up to her and asked, "What do you mean by grace?" She said, "You're a springboard diver, aren't you? Well, that's what grace is. Doing something so that it looks easy even though it isn't." That's the best description of grace I've ever heard. She also taught me how to act — I was an actor before I was a writer — so she was really important to me. Then of course there's Professor F.M. Salter from the University of Alberta. He looked over my shoulder during the writing of *Who Has Seen the Wind*. What a beautiful teaching sonofabitch he was! Many of the quotations in this new book that I've attributed to the Dr. Lyon character are really from Salter.

T: Dr. Lyon says in the book that all fine fiction is regional, rooted in the illusion of specific place. Yet *Since Daisy Creek* is set mostly at an imaginary university.

MITCHELL: Let's not limit region to the natural geographic thing. That university could not exist in Montreal, Toronto, or Windsor, not even in Manitoba. It could in Wyoming or Idaho or Alberta. So substitute unique for "regional." It's very easy to think of Hardy and Mark Twain as being regional if one realizes that regionality can transcend time and geography. If a thing is done only for its regionality, then it's fourth-rate art.

T: Paradise Valley, where the grizzly

attack occurs, is the same Paradise Valley you used in *The Vanishing Point*. And that's based on Eden Valley in Alberta?

MITCHELL: Yes, and I used the same Stony Indian satellite band I've known for years. Indeed, I've used some of their names, like Carol Rollin'-in-the-Mud. She herself would never beat the shit out of a beer parlour as she does in the book, but I'm sure she'll forgive me. When I knew I was going to do the grizzly thing, I couldn't resist bringing back the character of Archie Nicotine from that earlier novel. Archie was a character that threatened to take over *The Vanishing Point*. He's an amalgam of an Indian I knew, my second son, and a Hungarian guy I've who moulded the boat you came across the lake in. That Hungarian and I would be working and he'd say, "Beel, Beel, ah, gypsy Beel. You sweet, kindly, gentle, generous Beel. The one trouble, you're focking stupid!" Then he would always end up saying, just like Archie, "And dat is de whole situation. Whole situation!"Three native Indian reviewers have praised Archie as being true to life.

T: As a writer, do you have a fear of becoming too civilized?

MITCHELL: Yes, because once you become the too civilized person, just on that primitive level of dramatic storytelling, you lose one of the important life qualities: surprise. The more careful and civilized the writer becomes, the more blueprinted the writing becomes, and then the more likely that the creative partner, the reader, is not going to be surprised. But I always feel uncomfortable talking about dramatic qualities. For instance, I tell my writers again and again, they'll never hear me using the word plot. It's a dirty, four-letter word. Plot suggests that blueprint sort

of thing. So I use every other euphemistic bloody term I can think of: narrative arc, structure . . .

T: In *Since Daisy Creek*, Dobbs, a creative writing professor, has a two-step approach he uses in teaching, the same two steps you also use in your workshops. Can you elaborate on what you call "Mitchell's Messy Approach"?

MITCHELL: The first step is finding and free-fall thinking. The finding is the most pleasant kind of self-indulgent thing. There are no strictures. You say yes to everything. This is the initial potential if one has stored and watched and listened and smelled and touched. The more one stores, the more there is to go back and find. If students can say yes, it comes out. They're away to the races; ten pages a day is nothing, sometimes twenty. But it's chaos. Then step two is the creative leap away from that. It's the toughest thing I've had to communicate. That's where the problems start. The person has to think of destinations, both thematic and story. Not just this follows this follows this but, as E.M. Forster says, this *causes* this *causes* this *causes* this. You tend to simplify and say, Jesus, it starts here and then this happens and this happens. You blueprint it. But that's when the writer gets into trouble. Then it turns out to be like the person who starts on a Monday of the month of April and says he's got to finish it in six months or nine months. And you end up with something that's thick, cheesy, one cell deep, contrived, carpentered, with no life resonance. The blueprint is always tentative, tentative, tentative. The trick is to keep open the sea caves, so new stuff is always surfacing as you write.

T: You've written that "the writer must tell the left side of the brain—the assessor, the critic—to bugger off." The more you teach and understand your own work, doesn't that get more difficult to do?

MITCHELL: This is one of the things I worried about. I talked with Wallace Stegner once about this when we were both at the University of Toronto. We walked through the ravines and we talked a lot. Wally is about five years older than I am, and I asked him, "As you get older, do you lose that fluky quality, that spontaneous given, that joyful surprise?" He said, "No, it's like any other creative act — you just don't do it quite so often!" But I've found the left part doesn't overtake things. I've found the right side is taking over a little bit more. Still, the big thing that concerns me is the gaps. The dangerous time is when one has finished the long haul of a novel, and then going off to Hawaii or somewhere. The gap gets wider and wider and wider. Then you think Jesus, it's been two whole months and I haven't come up with anything. And you know the next thing you say? The well has gone dry. And you don't stop to think, You stupid bastard, you haven't lowered the bucket in the well! That's the thing I have to keep reminding myself. That's what Wally and I talked about.

T: Are you sensitive to other people's criticism of your work?

MITCHELL: I would lie if I said I wasn't.

T: Is it useful to you?

MITCHELL: Not really, and again, I think it's an honest answer. If a writer has done all his work, a critic should not be able to tell a writer what he didn't know. If a writer is surprised by criticism, it's probably because he hasn't been able to step away and be objective enough.

T: George Woodcock suggested that sexuality as evil predominates over sexuality as good in *How I Spent My Summer Holidays*.

MITCHELL: He's right. That's what it is within the framework of that book. The guardians come into the sanctuary, the child cave, and leave a serpent — a viper — which later stings. But if someone imputes that I would only write of sex in that fashion, then he's wrong.

T: As in *Since Daisy Creek*, for instance, when Dobbs begins to feel a sense of recovery when he gets his first erection in the hospital.

MITCHELL: Right. Also, his wife has the loveliest tits in all of Spain. Incidentally, how did you like my explicit sex scene? Doug [Gibson] phoned me and said, "You know, Mitchell, you seem to have made a recent discovery." And I said, "What's that?" He said, "Sex!" But I'm a clean dirty old man compared to others nowadays.

T: Are you ever disturbed by your image, as you once put it, as "the folksy old foothills fart"?

MITCHELL: There's nothing that gets me more pissed off than that. I am often referred to as "the prairie humourist" or "the prairie regional writer." Those tags imply that the reason I write is to celebrate a goddamn region. I'm no more celebrating a goddamn region than fly! Some people were disappointed when *How I Spent My Summer Holidays* came out that it wasn't just like *Who Has Seen the Wind*. Especially Bill French. Well, we change. God almighty, how we change. Don't forget, I'm seventy. I grew up through the 1920s. When I was nineteen, on the bum in Europe, I was told you could get a room for five francs a night in Paris. I looked all over. I ended up in the Hotel du Nord. It was ten francs and I couldn't really afford it. It was a whorehouse and I didn't know about it! Now that's pretty bloody innocent. That's where I'm coming from. But like I said, we change.

T: In these two most recent novels you've been handling evil in a much more overt way. As you get older are you going deeper into the dark side of things in your personal life?

MITCHELL: Not really, no. But a former student of mine, who had had as many as three shock treatments a week, wrote me after seeing *Back to Beulah*, wondering how the hell I knew so much about those three schizophrenic ladies and the schizophrenic mind. He talked about the play with his therapist and the therapist told him I was probably a manic depressive. I thought, Oh Jesus, Jack, get yourself another analyst! Then as I thought about it, I realized in my childhood I would be blue often. And I would be high often. And that probably my swings were a little wider than normal. Then I thought again, Come on, everybody has those pendulum swings. I would suspect with any artist, whether it be an actor, director, or a painter, it would be the same. If the highs are high, probably the lows are low.

T: Have you ever been curious about psychoanalysis for yourself?

MITCHELL: In the first place, I started out in medicine. I was interested in psychology. That's how I got into philosophy. I had intended to be a psychiatrist. My tubercular arm kicked up when I was in Winnipeg at university. My mother hadn't told me. When I told my specialist I was in pre-med, he said, "You can't, son, you got TB. You won't be out of the woods with it until you're forty or more." Then, at forty-six, I hit what I think of as the rubber-ice period in human beings. A person thinks, I ain't got that many years left, what the hell? I had two bad years. I quit smoking, which was dreadful. It took me two years to do it. And my mother died. As Merna can tell you, I went through a very rough time. I knew I was not lovable. And I did not write one creative thing. I did documentaries, I did rewrites, but during those two years nothing really happened. At that time — and this is a long-winded answer to your question — Billy Mitchell should have sought professional help.

T: Dobbs in *Since Daisy Creek* uses fly-tying in the basement to "anaesthetize failure pain." Do you periodically suffer from "failure pain" as a writer?

MITCHELL: You should really talk to Merna a bit, Merna knows. I sometimes come home and she asks, "How did it go?" I say, "Oh shit, I'm a fake, I'm in the wrong business." I've made a point of asking the writers I know or I am fond of about this feeling: Ernest Buckler, Wallace Stegner, Alice Munro, Margaret Laurence. And I remember Alice's answer. I said, "Do you ever figure sometimes you're a goddamn phony, a fake, a pretender?" and Alice whispered to me, "Oh God, Bill, I look out the window a helluva lot!"

T: So self-doubt is normal.

MITCHELL: Yes. I have to tell this to all young writers because they're feeling it. I've said to them the most usual state of a writer is contradiction, dilemma, confusion. If you ever lose that, forget it. I can look at a novel now, and I know how long it took that writer to produce. I can tell when they don't have the steam to carry it through, when they're shooting from the hip, just pushing through. I can tell when they're not bombarding it with all their past and letting it give the energy. I can tell when it's too easy. I've told my writers there is no shoot-from-the-hip, lightning-stroke-of-genius approach. The end result is a product of accretion, of build-up, build-up, build-up. And I've told my daughter and my two sons, "Only amateurs are confident."

Farley Mowat

FARLEY MOWAT was born in Belleville, Ontario in 1921. He grew up in Saskatoon and attended university in Toronto. After serving in World War Two he spent two years in the Arctic and wrote *People of the Deer* (1952), blaming government officials and missionaries for the plight of the Ihalmiut Eskimos. His over thirty books about environmental and non-

urban concerns include the acclaimed *Never Cry Wolf* (1963), *Sibir: My Discovery of Siberia* (1970), *A Whale for the Killing* (1972), the monumental *Sea of Slaughter* (1984) and *Virunga: The Passion of Diane Fossey* (1987). After being refused entry to the US he wrote *My Discovery of America* (1985). He has also written fiction for children and memoirs about his war experiences. He is easily one the world's best known Canadian authors.

Farley Mowat lives in Port Hope, Ontario. He was interviewed in 1984.

T: Sealand of Victoria is getting another killer whale from Iceland. They've had six whales die there already. And the manager of Sealand was on the radio tonight saying there was absolutely no reason to be worried.

MOWAT: *He* has no reason to be worried. And *we* have no reason to be worried. But if I was that killer whale, that orca, I'd be worried stiff. I'd have written my will. You take a thirty-foot sea mammal and put it in a little enclosure and lock it up, one way or another it's going to die.

T: Meanwhile the Vancouver Aquarium is building another whale pool. Its Board of Directors represents captains of industry. Perhaps commercial-spirited people aren't the best people to be involved in managing wildlife.

MOWAT: Put "managing" in quotes, eh? It's exploiting. I have the same feeling about all zoos. I have no use for zoos. When I become world dictator my first job is to go around carefully opening all the cells of all the zoos in the world. I say carefully because most of the animals have been locked up for a few years and may be a bit...unreliable.

I think zoos are an abomination. And the rationales we use: zoos educate the public. Educate them to what? We educate them to thinking about putting animals—and we are one—in cages. The other rationale is preserving endangered species. That's bullshit. You can raise them alright in captivity but you have a very limited gene pool to draw on and they're totally without the indoctrination courses they need for learning how to live in the wild. We can raise whooping cranes. We can release them in Texas in an area that is highly protected. If they can make it from that outdoor zoo to the other outdoor zoo in the Arctic or sub-arctic then maybe you'll succeed in keeping one or two alive. But the idea that zoos serve a purpose for protecting endangered species, well, forget it.

The whole problem is the same as in *Sea of Slaughter*. It's commerce.

T: Were you aware of the extent of the destruction of wildlife on the Atlantic Coast before you started *Sea of Slaughter*?

MOWAT: I didn't have a clue. Three times during the course of putting the book together, I quit. I just had enough. I didn't want to hear anymore. I put my fingers in my ears. But that was one of the reasons for staying with the book. If I thought I had a pretty good grasp of how bad we'd been, how horrible and destructive and deadly we'd been, and *I* was wrong—so wrong—then Christ, it was incumbent on me, or somebody like me, to put the whole magnitude of the disaster on the record.

T: After reading the book my appreciation of someone like Paul Watson, someone who takes direct action on these issues, has risen considerably.

MOWAT: Me, too. I didn't have a high opinion of a lot of these people fifteen years ago. I was so unimpressed that I wouldn't extend a helping hand. I started out wanting to distance myself from them. It seemed to me that Greenpeace was sometimes irrational in their behaviour. They'd go after the Russians when the core of the whaling matter was the Japanese. The Russians have stated categorically, three times, that they would quit whaling as soon as the Japanese did. The target was the Japanese, pure and simple. It has been and always will be until it is stopped. And Greenpeace was putting the emphasis on the Russians. I thought this was cold warmanship.

Now I see the whole activist movement in a different light. I'm behind them a hundred percent.

Because I know what kind of results I got trying the cool approach. Going to the bigshots. Trying to work from within. Nothing. Evaluating what happened with these guys I have concluded there is only one way to go. And that is direct action.

T: Going outside the law . . .

MOWAT: It's never bothered me that much. We know for a start that the law is mostly framed to protect property. It's the people who have property who have a vested interest in the law. In that area I am perhaps quite rebellious and un-law-abiding.

T: In a rather sober, law-abiding country.

MOWAT: Yes. I prefer law of consensus, which is natural law. Tribal law. If someone is getting out of line, if someone is causing distress to the group they're living in, then the group will get them one way or another. That's consensus law and very changeable. Variable according to conditions. Our law is artificial like everything else. It's an arbitrary imposition of contrived ethics and morality. In place of natural ethics and natural morality.

T: You had strong feelings of misanthropy even prior to *Sea of Slaughter*. I would think collecting the information for that book would have put you right over the edge.

MOWAT: This is a peculiar thing. I dislike my own species less now that I've done the book.

T: Why's that?

MOWAT: Because I'm beginning to feel very sorry for homo sapiens instead. I think pity is entering into my evaluation of my own species. Before it was just rage. I don't think I've ever felt *hatred* for mankind because hatred implies malice. But I've felt every degree of rage. Now I look at us and see a very pitiable animal. We had every Christly break, every possibility going for us, and we opened that

Pandora's Box and decided we would become masters of our own destiny. Masters of our own world. We were clever enough to be able to do it. The kiss of death. I also feel sorry for us because not only are we a bad animal, but we're almost inevitably a doomed animal. Every species dies out. But our doom is here and now.

T: It's amazing, when you think about it, that there isn't more collective self-loathing from the human race.

MOWAT: We mask our evil deeds. This has always been the case. Every great writer has made a point of bringing that up. We have a marvelous displacement procedure. We convert the evil we do into some other form. Otherwise we couldn't live with it. Mind you I'm not talking about the earlier exploiters. Who can get furious at the Basque whalers? You can't. They really had no conception of what they were doing. There were doing an evil thing in the natural morality without any awareness of it. They were innocent actually.

T: Whereas with this book, we can hold *Sea of Slaughter* aloft and say, hey, look, we're not ignorant.

MOWAT: You've got it! This is the key to the book. This is the reason for the goddam book's existence. There is no other casebook like this. I don't want to sound like a braggart but I don't mind bragging when it comes to this. I see this book in the same context as *Silent Spring*. It's a book to be used for people in the conservation movement as a resource book. For an individual species, if we exterminate it or reduce it to the zero point, we can find a rationale for that. But you can't find a rationale to cover the reduction of the whole of animal creation the way we reduced it in the Atlantic region.

I didn't mention it in the book but we did a computer run-through of the data I collected for the book and the data collected through my researchers. The thing came up with an absolutely mind-boggling answer to the question of how much damage we've done. The answer was we have destroyed between eighty and ninety percent of the *biomass* for the large forms of life: mammals, fishes and birds. It's shattering.

T: The idea of biomass is an interesting concept. Apparently something like eighty percent of the biomass in the Amazon is now insects.

MOWAT: That's right. Insects are surviving. I quote from the secretary of the Smithsonian. There won't be anything left alive bigger than the proverbial breadbox.

T: How is it that after the two-hundredth mind-numbing statistic, you are still able to react emotionally?

MOWAT: I can tell you very simply why. I don't see much hope for us. I don't get much comfort looking at my own species and belonging to it. But I get increasing comfort knowing that, shit, we're only one form. One part of the entire Jesus-ly structure of life. And this is not a metaphysical or even an intellectual approach to the situation. It's real. I feed the seagulls because I happen to feel an empathy for those creatures. These days we have a domestic seagull that travels with us. We rescued the thing out of a ditch in Nova Scotia. His head and his neck were askew. He had something wrong with his lung. And his digestion was bad. He still can't fly and he limps. There's no way we can turn him loose. He lives with the dogs in the backyard. He's now decided he's a dog.

T: Your approach to nature and to wildfire seems far more Buddhist than Christian. . .when you talk about empathy.

MOWAT: Practically every formal or informal religion in the world beyond the Mediterranean group of religions —

beyond the Judaeo/Christian/Arabic group — *all* believe in that empathy. This misconception that man is somehow a distinct and absolute creation, that everything else is somehow subservient to him, grew up in a very small area. If I could rewrite religious history I would, without a quiver of regret, eliminate Judaeo/Christian/Arabic/Moslem religions from the fate of this planet.

T: That's basically all of western culture.

MOWAT: Well, those religions have alienated us. They've made us aliens.

T: I notice you use a phrase in the book, "the other beasts."

MOWAT: Or just "the others." I use the word beasts very seldom because it's a loaded word. But "the others" is good. There's a guy by the name of Best who has written a helluva good book that begins by talking about "the others." You suddenly realize who "the others" are.

T: There are so many "others" to be concerned about, you must have had some problems with the scope of *Sea of Slaughter*. For instance, you've tossed in information about the wolf kill in BC and whale killing in Antarctica.

MOWAT: I kept trying to hold myself to the geographic limits. Then finally I told myself why bother? If the story goes on, then we go with the story. Certainly the whales went on until I finished up in the Antarctic. Wolves, well, I must admit I was bit arbitrary on that one. But I was so Christly mad at that BC government! Everything they said to justify their wolf kill fitted the thesis of my book. Everything they did fitted the description of man, the great killer.

T: Your other books, like *Never Cry Wolf*, work as personal testimonies. But *Sea of Slaughter* works on a much more impersonal, political level. Is that why you're calling it your most important book?

MOWAT: There's such a mass of material. This book does not allow any instant rationality to excuse what we're doing. You know, I've been categorized over the years as writing subjective non-fiction. I've always said, half-jokingly, that I never let facts interfere with the truth. People say I should really win the Governor General's Award for fiction. But in this case I made myself subservient to the facts. I had no choice. This has to be as close to unquestionable as anything I can do. Nobody can be bloody perfect. But essentially the facts in this book are unassailable.

T: Yet you do allow some emotionalism to creep in.

MOWAT: I really felt around for a long time trying to find a tricky way of doing it without repetition. Finally I gave up. I realized that this was the essence of the book. Repetition. It was a machine gun firing, not a rifle.

T: It's the sort of book that could convert a passive environmentalist into an active one.

MOWAT: Jesus. That's the nicest thing I've heard yet. I'll drink to that. I had a lot of doubts about this book. My Canadian editor was determined I should do it but my American editor could see no way it could be done without telling the same story over and over again. After publication I thought, well, it's over. I've done my best. I hope it helps.

T: It's obviously going to create far more ripples than most novels. For that reason I'm becoming increasingly drawn towards non-fiction these days.

MOWAT: Heaven be praised. Heaven be praised. I have nothing whatsoever but good to say about storytellers, in fiction or non-fiction, but I have had a feeling for some years in this country that fiction is becoming more and more concentrated on people looking at their own entrails. Trying to read the omens in their own entrails. I'm sure this has a tremendously valuable and cathartic use for the authors, and in many cases it might be of great use to the reader, too. But it's a narrowing down. I think it is due to a loss of contact with the natural world. I really do. I think man as a species has turned inward so much that it's like an ingrown goddam hair.

As a result, he can only feel his own pain. He can only sense his own needs. If he wasn't turning inward, if he was turning outward, if he could sense what's around him, then he would feel more stable, more secure and less frightened. He'd be a better writer. The nineteenth-century writers, almost without exception, had a sense of nature. It permeated their work. You saw a man in perspective, in proportion with the world at large. But most modern fiction? You see the guts of a tormented individual or a bunch of individuals all looking inward.

T: From what I know of your upbringing, you had personal pain you could have written about. And *The Snow Walker* shows that you can write fiction well. So why didn't you go

MOWAT: The reason I never wrote much fiction, very simply, is my father. He was *determined* that I would be a novelist in the footsteps of Conrad and people like that. He'd tried and failed so he was determined, as all fathers are, that their sons will do what they couldn't do. My inability to write novels is probably due to nothing more complicated than that. Thank God for it now. Who needs another third-rate novelist? Or second-rate? Or even first-rate novelist? There's lots of 'em. But people who can write about the overall human condition in context with the condition of nature are scarce.

T: Did you father actually coach you to write novels? Like piano lessons?

MOWAT: Oh, no. Not like that. But

when I wrote my first book, *People of the Deer*, he made it clear to me that this was only a step in the progress of the writer. Eventually I would move on from semi-journalism, as he thought it, to the ultimate holy of holies, the novel. He had grown up in the great age of the novel. Galsworthy, Hardy, all these guys. He was a librarian who read extensively and intensively. He worshipped these people.

T: But you wanted to live in the world of today?

MOWAT: Sure. Times have changed. In the nineteenth century the novelist had a lot more to do than today. In those days they weren't limited to one little aspect of life, one little community. They roamed over the goddam human scene. We don't do that much anymore. Sylvia Fraser has tried in a sense, with her novel, *Berlin Solstice*, but it's not tried much in Canada. Maybe that's a natural procedure for a country that has a huge inferiority complex. Maybe we have to start by writing about our pimples.

T: I understand you're not in favour of creative writing courses.

MOWAT: They're for the birds. They scare me to death. If he or she goes through a creative writing course and survives, they are a survivor against almost unbelievable odds. The last thing that a writer needs is a creative writing course.

T: So what makes a writer?

MOWAT: I think writers are essentially good observers. People who have learned the trade of describing their observations. You're fifty percent a tradesman. The other side is the observer. The observer should not be a detached observer. He should be a highly emotional observer. And I don't think it's necessary to translate life into imitation of life. That's what fiction normally is. Do it straight. Why go through the in-between process?

What do we know except what we've seen, felt, drunk, heard and touched? What else do we know? People feel compelled to dress up life in novels and I think it's just the invidious influence of the literary establishment over the last hundred years or so that says you don't amount to anything unless you're writing in novel form. I think we've been forced into a mold.

T: That's a real outsider's viewpoint.

MOWAT: Sure it is. And I'm an outsider. We like to look at Dickens as a great exposer of human conditions in the nineteenth century but I doubt whether he had much effect. In retrospect, we see the difference between then and now and think he must have had an effect. Perhaps he did. But maybe he would have had more effect if he would have described Little Nell as a *real* person. Maybe that wasn't possible in his time. Maybe it would not be publishable. But it is now. You can tell the truth without pretending to disguise it, without sugar coating.

T: What about film. Maybe Dickens would have been a film director in this century?

MOWAT: There's something very ephemeral about film. It's balloons floating in the sky. When something is written down, we have the sense that it isn't going to go away.

T: This comes back to *Sea of Slaughter*. The importance of writing it down.

MOWAT: Yes. If I went across the country and told those stories from a podium they would have an immediate effect on the audience. But it would fade. But if it's in a book or engraved on a tablet, hieroglyphs on clay or whatever, it has a kind of *endurance* that no other medium has had.

T: Speaking of which, I understand you're increasingly involved in McClelland & Stewart.

MOWAT: I now own McClelland & Stewart, you know that, don't you?

This fall they went bankrupt for the nineteenth time. In the end they set up a company to buy out M&S. It ended up with me getting stuck buying a unit and a half of this thing. I own $75,000 worth of the goddam company. I had no choice. The critics wouldn't print the books! Not only would I lose my current book, but I would lose my backlist if the company went bankrupt.

Jack McClelland was very careful. Jack is such a beautiful son-of-a-bitch. He really is. I love him dearly. I guess he's my closest male friend. I understand him perfectly. He phoned me up at two or three in the morning. I'm down in Cape Breton. The phone rings. It never rings at night. It hardly ever rings at all. In the middle of the night it's ringing and I know it's Jack and I'm not going to answer it. And I lie there. And it rings and rings and rings. He knows I'm there and he's going to get me up. I finally get up. He says, "Farley, the whole thing is falling apart. If I don't have another fifty thousand tomorrow, it's gone." And I say, "Oh, no, Jack. Not again!"

Never mind. I don't mind pouring my money down that drain. It's a good drain. And besides, Claire will support me in my old age.

I think it's marvellous. Her first book, which is a small book, sold twenty-four thousand in hardcover. And in paperback it's doing even better. So I'm looking forward to retirement! I'm thinking of taking over from Bill French! I think somebody has to take over pretty soon. I think I will become the book page editor for the *Globe & Mail*.

T: I remember when Hugh MacLennan's *Voices in Time* came out. I feel some love for this guy as a father figure and I wanted to do some justice to the book. So of course my review gets cut in half to make room for a huge picture and story about a local punk rocker.

MOWAT: I'm delighted you should talk about Hugh that way. That was an incredible book. That Hugh MacLennan should have written a book like that! It's absolutely extraordinary. He's so goddam honest. And kind. I remember when I wrote my first book, *People of the Deer*, it was jumped on from all sides. I was called a liar in the House of Commons. The Hudson Bay company bought space in magazines and hired guys to prove I was a liar. They were going to finish me off in a hurry, eh? And then I got a *letter* from Hugh MacLennan. I treasure it to this day. He said, "Dear Farley Mowat. I don't know you well enough to call you by your first name as a person, but as a writer, I do. I think yours was a superb book, a beautiful book, an honest book and a human book. God bless you. Hugh MacLennan."

Right on! Sonofabitch, that guy can do no harm as far as I'm concerned. He was a biggie and I was a nobody. He didn't have to do that. But he knew I was getting it from all sides.

T: He understands the lonely voice. Crying in the wilderness.

MOWAT: Because he is one. Right. Always has been. We know our brothers when we see them, friend. And there aren't too many around.

Alice Munro

ALICE MUNRO was born in Wingham, Ontario in 1931. After two years at the University of Western Ontario, she married and moved to Vancouver and Victoria where she became the mother of three daughters and was eventually divorced. In 1972 she remarried and returned to live in Ontario.

Twice winner of the Governor

General's Award for fiction and a frequent contributor to the *New Yorker*, she has firmly established her reputation as one of Canada's leading writers with her impeccable style and exacting honesty. Her six books are *Dance of the Happy Shades* (1968), *Lives of Girls and Women* (1971), *Something I've Been Meaning to Tell You* (1974), *Who Do You Think You Are?* (1978), *The Moons of Jupiter* (1982) and *The Progress of Love* (1986). All have been well received and feature heroines who seek to gain some measure of control over their lives through understanding.

Alice Munro lives in Clinton, Ontario. She was interviewed in 1978.

T: Your writing is like the perfect literary equivalent of a documentary movie.

MUNRO: That is the way I see it. That's the way I want it to be.

T: So it's especially alarming when *Lives of Girls and Women* gets removed from a reading list in an Ontario high school. Essentially all they're objecting to is the truth.

MUNRO: This has been happening in Huron County, where I live. They wanted *The Diviners, Of Mice and Men* and *Catcher in the Rye* taken off, too. They succeeded in getting *The Diviners* taken off. It doesn't particularly bother me about my book because my book is going to be around in the bookstores. But the impulse behind what they are doing bothers me a great deal. There is such a total lack of appreciation of what literature is about! They feel literature is there to teach some great moral lesson. They always see literature as an influence, not as an opener of live. The lessons they want taught are those of fundamentalist Christianity and if literature doesn't do this, it's a harmful influence.

They talk about protecting their children from these books. The whole concept of protecting eighteen-year-old children from sexuality is pretty scary and pretty sad. Nobody's being forced to read these books anyway. The news stories never mention that these books are only options. So they're not just protecting their own children. What they're doing is removing the books from other people's children.

T: Removing your books seems especially absurd because there's so little preaching for any particular morality or politics.

MUNRO: None at all. I couldn't write that way if I tried. I back off my party line, even those with which I have a great deal of sympathy, once it gets hardened and insisted upon. I say to myself that's not true all the time. That's why I couldn't write a straight women's lib book to expose injustices. Everything's so much more complicated than that.

T: Which brings us to why you write. Atwood's theory on Del Jordan in *Girls and Women* is that she writes as an act of redemption. How much do you think your own writing is a compensation for loss of the past?

MUNRO: Redemption is a pretty strong word. Mu writing has become a way of dealing with life, hanging onto it by re-creation. That's important. But it's also a way of getting on top of experience. We all have life rushing in on us. A writer pretends, by writing about it, to have control Of course a writer actually has no more control than anybody else.

T: Do you think you've chosen the short story form because that requires the most discipline and you come from a very restrictive background?

MUNRO: That's interesting. Nobody has suggested that before. I've never known why I've chosen the short story form. I guess in a short story you impose discipline rather soon. Things don't get away from you. Perhaps I'm afraid of other forms where things just flow out. I have a friend who writes novels. She never touches what she's written on the day she's written it. She could consider it fake to go aback and rework the material. It has to be how the work flows out of her. Something about that makes me very uneasy. I could never do it.

T: You're suspicious of spontaneity?

MUNRO: I suppose so. I'm not afraid spontaneity would betray me because I've done some fairly self-exposing things. But I'm afraid it would be repetitious and boring if I wrote that way. It's as if I must take great care over everything. Instead of splashing the colours of and trusting they will all come together, I have to know the design.

T: Do ideas ever evolve into something too big for a short story?

MUNRO: Yes

T: I thought the title story of *Something I've Been Meaning to Tell You* was a good example of that. It didn't work because you were dealing with the lifetimes of four different characters.

MUNRO: You know I really wanted to write a novel of that story. Then it just sort of boiled down like maple syrup. All I had left was that story. For me it would have been daring to stretch that material out into a full novel. I wouldn't be sure of it. I wouldn't be sure it had the strength. So I don't take that chance.

T: Do you write your stories primarily for magazines now, or for eventual inclusion in a book?

MUNRO: Writing for magazines is a very sideline thing. It's what enables me to survive financially, but it isn't important to me artistically. Right now I'm working on some stories and I might not be able to sell any of them. This has happened to very established writers. Markets are always changing. They say to beginning writers—study the market. That's no use at all. The only thing you can do is write what you want.

T: You once said that the emotional realism of your work is solidly autobiographical. Is that how your stories get started? When something triggers you back to an emotional experience?

MUNRO: Yes. Some incident that might have happened to me or to somebody else. It doesn't matter which. As long as it's getting *at* some kind of emotional core that I want to investigate.

T: Do ever worry that goldmine of your past will dry up?

MUNRO: I never know. I never know. I thought I had used it all up before I started this book. Now I'm

writing out of a different period. I'm very interested in my young adulthood.

T: Has there been a lot of correlation between your writing and raising your daughters?

MUNRO: Tremendously. When I was writing *Lives of Girls and Women*, some of the things in there came from things my daughters did when they were ten or eleven. It's a really crazy age. they used to go to the park and hang down from their knees and scare people, pretending to be monkeys. I saw this wild, ferocious thing in them which gets dampened for most girls with puberty. Now my two older girls are twenty-five and twenty-one and they're making me remember new things. Though they live lives so different from any life possible to me, there's still similarities.

T: Do you feel a great weight has been lifted now your kids are older?

MUNRO: Yes. I'm definitely freer. But not to be looking after somebody is a strange feeling. All my life I've been doing it. Now I feel enormous guilt that I'm not responsible for anybody.

T: Maybe guilt is the great Canadian theme. Marian Engel wrote Canada is "a country that cannot be modern without guilt." And Margaret Laurence said she came from "people who feel guilty at the drop of a hat, for whom virtue only arises from work." Since intellectual work is not regarded by many people as real work, did you face any guilt about wanting to write?

MUNRO: Oh, yes. But it wasn't guilt so much as embarrassment. I was doing something I couldn't explain or justify. Then after a while I got used to being in that position. That's maybe the reason I don't want to go on living in Huron County. I notice when I move out and go to Toronto, I feel like an ordinary person.

T: Do you know where you got your ambition to write?

MUNRO: It was the only thing I ever wanted to do. I just kept on trying. I guess what happens when you're young has a great deal to do with it. Isolation, feelings of power that don't get out in a normal way, and maybe coping with unusual situations . . . most writers seem to have backgrounds like that.

T: When the kids play I Spy in your stories, they have a hard time finding colours. Was your upbringing really that bleak?

MUNRO: Fairly. I was a small child in the Depression. What happens at the school in the book you're referring to is true. Nothing is invented.

T: So you really did take a temperance pledge in the seventh grade?

MUNRO: Yes, I did.

T: Sounds pretty bleak to me!

MUNRO: I thought my life was interesting! There was always a great sense of adventure, mainly because there were so many fights. Life was fairly dangerous. I lived in an area like West Hanratty in *Who Do You Think You Are?*. We lived outside the whole social structure because we didn't live in the town and we didn't live in the country. We lived in this kind of little ghetto where all the bootleggers and prostitutes and hangers-on lived. Those were the people I knew. It was a community of outcasts. I had that feeling about myself.

When I was about twelve, my mother got Parkinson's disease. It's an incurable, slowly deteriorating illness which probably gave me a great sense of fatality. Of things not going well. But I wouldn't say I was unhappy. I didn't belong to any nice middle class so I got to know more types of kids. It didn't seem bleak to me at the time. It seemed full of interest.

T: As Del Jordan says, "For what I wanted was every last thing, every layer of speech and thought, stroke of

light on bark or walls, every small, pothole, pain-cracked illusion . . ."

MUNRO: That's the getting-everything-down compulsion.

T: Yet your work never reads like it's therapy writing.

MUNRO: No, I don't write just out of problems. I wrote even before I had problems!

T: I understand you've married again. And that it's quite successful.

MUNRO: It's a very happy relationship. I haven't really dealt much with happy relationships. Writers don't. They tell you about their tragedies. Happiness is a very hard thing to write about. You deal with it more often as a bubble that's about to burst.

T: You have a quote about Rose in *Who Do You Think You Are?*, "She thought how love removes the world." With your writing you're trying to get in touch with the world as much as possible, so does this mean that love and writing are adversaries?

MUNRO: Wordsworth said, "Poetry is emotion recollected in tranquillity." You can follow from this that a constant state of emotion would be hostile to the writing state

T: If you're a writer, that could have some pretty heavy implications.

MUNRO: Very heavy. If you're a writer, probably there's something in you that makes you value your self, your own objectivity, so much that you can't stand to be under the sway of another person. But then some people might say that writing is an escape, too. I think we all make choices about whether we want to spend our lives in emotional states.

T: That's interesting My wife's comment on *Who Do You Think You Are?* was that your character Rose is never allowed to get anything. She's always unfulfilled. Maybe she's just wary of emotion.

MUNRO: She gets something. She

gets herself. She doesn't get the obvious things, the things she thinks she wants. Like in "Mischief," which is about middle-aged infidelity, Rose really doesn't want that love affair. What she does get is a way out of her marriage. She gets a knowledge of herself.

T: But only after a male decides the outcome of the relationship.

MUNRO: I see that as true in relations between men and women. Men seem to have more initiative to decide whether things happen or don't happen. In this specific area women have had a lack of power, although it's slowly changing.

T: When you write, "outrageous writers may bounce from one blessing to another nowadays, bewildered, as permissively raised children are said to be, by excess of approval," I get the feeling you could just as easily substitute the word male for outrageous.

MUNRO: I think it's still possible for men in public to be outrageous in ways that it's not possible for women to be. It still seems to be true that no matter

what a man does, there are women who will be in love with him. It's not true the other way round. I think achievement and ability are positively attractive qualities in men that will overcome all kinds of behaviour and looks, but I don't think the same is true for women.

A falling-down-drunk poet may have great power because he has talent. But I don't think men are attracted to women for these reasons. If they are attracted to talent, it has to be combined with the traditionally attractive female qualities. If a woman comes on shouting and drinking and carrying on, she won't be forgiven.

T: Whenever I ask writers about growing older, they not only answer the question, they *respond* to the question. I suspect you're enjoying getting older, too.

MUNRO: Yes. Yes. I think it's great. You just stop worrying about a lot of things you used to worry about. You get things in perspective. Since I turned forty I've been happier than ever before. I feel so much freer.

Susan Musgrave

SUSAN MUSGRAVE was born in California of Canadian parents in 1951. She grew up in Victoria. In her earlier work she is not unlike the foreign correspondent on the evening news who reassures us that the rest of the world is indeed in chaos. Subjective poems as precious and desperate as notes in bottles have brought notoriety in Canada and abroad. Her books of

poetry include *Songs of the Sea-Witch* (1970), *Entrance of the Celebrant* (1972), *Grave Dirt and Selected Strawberries* (1973), *Gull-band* (1974, children), *The Impstone* (1976), *Becky Swann's Book* (1977), *Selected Strawberries and Other Poems* (1977), *Kiskatinaw Songs* (1978, with Sean Virgo) and *A Man to Marry, A Man to Bury* (1979). *The Charcoal Burners* (1980) was her first novel, a dream-like vision of rituals in a primeval society. It was followed by a comedy of manners, *The Dancing Chicken* (1987).

Susan Musgrave lives in Victoria. She was interviewed in 1980.

T: What are the types of poems that get the most response from people?

MUSGRAVE: The love poems. I met a woman recently who had carried around one of my love poems for six months.

T: Yet you can still question writing as a profession for yourself.

MUSGRAVE: Well, it's hard for me to get any vicarious enjoyment out of what I've written. Once I've written it, that's it. It's just there to be found for someone else. It doesn't have much to do with me any more. My problem, being the creator, is that if a poem is really strong, it doesn't need me any more. It's like giving birth constantly, and constantly weaning.

That's not to say I'm only some sort of medium. But I don't feel I can take the credit very long for something that I have written. People quote great lines of poetry without even knowing who the poet was. That's how poetry works.

T: Does that mean you would write to create those special lines as much as special poems?

MUSGRAVE: I think so. It's *the* line. Individual lines stick in my head. Every poem usually has a couple of lines in it that are better than the rest.

Once, around New Year's, I wrote a poem about looking back at what had happened in the last ten years. Ten years before, I had been in hospital on New Year's Eve. "My father rocked in his chair, unable to share his last breath with anyone. That was years ago when we didn't think he would live much longer. He still drives down the highway to see me." When I showed the poem to a friend, what stuck out for her was the line about my father driving down the highway to see me. For me, that is the whole poem. But I can't figure out why. That is what is so great and so tricky about poetry. To get that to happen. You can't really try. It just has to fall into place.

T: When you publish a book, do you wonder what people are going to say about it because you're wondering yourself about it?

MUSGRAVE: Oh yes, I never really know. I put a book together but I don't have much idea what I'm attempting it to be. One of my problems has always been this approach. If it works, then it's great. If it doesn't work, it's not so great.

T: But art requires form. My E.M. Forster guide to novel writing says so, so it must be true.

MUSGRAVE: Yes. I'm sure that's right. I can see there's a lot more for me to learn about prose than poetry. These days I'm thinking more and more in terms of prose. Even the poems I'm writing are becoming more narrative. I want to be accessible, at least to myself. I figure if I am accessible to myself, then I will be accessible to other people. I admire writers who are accessible.

T: Would you agree much of your poetry functions basically on the level of dream?

MUSGRAVE: Yes. A lot of poems come right out of dreams. Lately I've been especially interested in how being in love with someone is very much like being on a dream level. It attacks the same areas of my head as a poem. It's a kind of vague hit of something, of adrenalin, of psychic energy. I just don't know what it is. But it's all connected. In my work I use dreams and being in love the same way. I get the same kind of inspiration from it. It's quite unconscious.

T: The talent of your poetry then is trusting your instincts to such a pure extent that whatever you write cannot be dishonest.

MUSGRAVE: A lot of my early poems I don't even understand any more. I get quite embarrassed when people come up to me and ask what's this poem all about. I just haven't a clue. In fact, I end up thinking that they're badly written and I obviously missed the point. I trusted the vision, the spirit and the mood and all those things, but I missed what I was really trying to communicate.

T: Maybe you didn't know enough about how to properly shape a poem.

MUSGRAVE: Yes. Eliot, when he was older, said he didn't understand *The Wasteland* any more. He thought it was a case of having had too much to say and the not the understanding of how to say it. I think that really applies to me when I was nineteen or twenty. I had an amazing amount in me to write about but I wasn't ever sure really how to do it.

T: Nevertheless, the level of maturity of your first book is really quite exceptional. If you hadn't gone through that exceptional experience of spending time in a psychiatric ward, would that maturity have come so quickly?

MUSGRAVE: I don't know. I feel that I was more mature then than I am now. I had some sort of wisdom but I couldn't cope with it very well. Obviously—because I kept going mad all the time. Which may have meant I was very wise but I wasn't quite sure how to handle that!

T: Do you get hostile reactions from people because of your witch persona?

MUSGRAVE: Oh, I think so. yes. People try to make it hokey. They try to make it nonsense. More blood and darkness. More preoccupation with morbidity and death. They try to attach words to it that lessen the impact of what I'm trying to talk about. They don't tackle the essential ideas of, I suppose, spirituality.

T: Because we have so little training for that.

MUSGRAVE: Yes. Even people who respond positively cannot articulate why they like my poems. It's like the pioneer mentality, all hard work,

make money and get ourselves set. We don't want anybody saying there's more to it than just that. Maybe you should just sit and look at the mountains for a day. People can't be told that. It upsets what they've come here to do. So people walk out of a bill bissett poetry reading shaking their heads.

T: Yes. There ought to be a book analyzing Canadian literature from a spiritual poverty angle.

MUSGRAVE: *Canadian Literature: A Christian Interpretation*.

The theory I'm developing now is that the writer should be slightly afraid of what he's writing about. When the writer is in too much control, that excess will get communicated. For instance, I think Atwood was too much in control in *Life Before Man*. I actually liked the book. It was extremely well written. But people couldn't like the characters because of her control over them. Whereas in *Surfacing*, I felt the author was afraid. Perhaps a really successful book will have both elements. It will have fear and control.

T: You're talking about fishing into the subconscious.

MUSGRAVE: Yes. Writing can be likened to fishing. Except I hate fishing. Things never surface for me. I've never once caught a fish that came to the top. The rod bends double. Something's down there that never comes up. I think how can people go out there and idly catch fish? As if they're not doing some mystical thing? People always think I'm crazy, but that's how I feel. You hook the darkness.

T: A novel gives you another world to go into.

MUSGRAVE: Yes. Where *The Charcoal Burners* fails is that I didn't come to grips with my fear. The fear overcame me in the end. I didn't have enough control. I was so anxious to get it over with because I was so frightened. It could have been a novel of nine hundred pages. But I was too terrified. Next time I'd like to get more balance between control and fear.

T: Maybe if you learn more control in your writing, you'll eventually learn more control over your life. You won't get possessed by people and things.

MUSGRAVE: Yes. When I'm writing, I'm very calm and happy. I don't need a quarter as much from the world as when I'm not writing. When I feel those outside attractions happening, I'm not nearly as strong.

T: When you feel that state of being possessed coming on, are you frightened? Or are you expectant? Or do you merely find it intriguing?

MUSGRAVE: A bit of all those things. I get incredibly energetic and ecstatic. That usually is accompanied by a total loss of appetite. And I don't sleep very much. There's some sort of overload going on. It's usually a person I feel I'm possessed by, but it's very hard to tell somebody, "I am possessed by something in you that you may or may not recognize or see or know."

T: So that attraction can be highly impersonal.

MUSGRAVE: Yes. Of course a lot of people are confused by that. Not many people are going to be interested in return. I mean, if somebody does that to me, I don't think I'm going to be impressed! Matt Cohen, who has known me for a long time, says I don't fall in love with personalities, I fall in love with what is invisible.

T: That fits, because your poetry is trying to come in contact with what is unrealized, too.

MUSGRAVE: But maybe I'm just projecting onto someone else something that is mine. I attach it to someone else in order to lose it. If I project it hard enough, it can become real. Then when I see that, actually, that special quality in someone else

isn't really there, that I've invented it, it's very disappointing. The magic wears off.

I'm at the stage of wondering what it is I'm doing, what it is I need, why do I keep doing this to people? I was reading something by Jung about poets; he said when poets aren't writing, they regress. They become children. They become criminals. That describes a lot of my behaviour pretty well.

T: Certainly our image of a poet is someone who is outside society in some way. The falling-down-drunk poet is outside society because society expects self-control. Maybe poets are people who are willing to relinquish control more easily.

MUSGRAVE: I don't think it's a case of willingness, though.

T: That shows you how *I* look at behaviour.

MUSGRAVE: Yes, I don't believe in words like willingness. I don't believe, to use your analogy, that people set out to get drunk. I believe that drunkenness happens by accident. Suddenly there you are, drunk. There are men I know who will say, "Let's go out and get drunk tonight." I don't know how to do that. I don't set out to behave any certain way. Behaviour creeps up and takes over.

T: You get psychologically drunk by accident.

MUSGRAVE: Yes. I don't *like* giving up control. My reaction to finding myself in a position of having given up control is usually an extreme one. That reaction causes huge difficulties in my life, and the lives of people around me. I don't like things to be utterly mysterious to me. Yet at the same time, I suspect there are whole areas of our lives that should remain mysterious. There's a line in Fowles' *Daniel Martin* where he is talking about his wife and he says that his wife didn't appeal to the unconscious in him enough to make the relationship work.

T: That's a heavy one.

MUSGRAVE: Right. You can't live with someone day after day and have that happen. It has to be a mysterious process. "You can't catch the glory on a hook and hold onto it."

T: That has rather depressing implications.

MUSGRAVE: It does. I always want to know, I want to own, I want to keep. Yet there's that line, "Every time a thing is owned, every time a thing is possessed, every time a thing is loved, it vanishes." Knowing that, I still want to do those things. I still want to own and possess and control. That's killing something but it's also a way of getting on top of something and not being dragged down. Not becoming its victim.

T: Is this why you collect talismans? To get power on your side and have control?

MUSGRAVE: I don't know. I've always had huge collections of things. I found a dried-out lizard on Pender Island just the other day. For years I've been collecting these objects, but lately I'm beginning to see that I should trust them more. I'm believing again in power objects.

T: Why do you think people collect things?

MUSGRAVE: To build a little net around themselves. To make external something that is internal. Collected objects reassure people that there is something tangible about life. What's odd about me is that I collect things that are pieces of bodies that once had life, bones and dried-out things. The reassurance there is that it's all ephemeral.

T: If you don't have a body, you can't be hurt. You might simply be seeking the sanctity of spirituality. Have you ever been religious? Or does that word mean anything to you?

MUSGRAVE: I suppose I am religious. Yes, it does. I went through a phase of being a born-again Christian. I was converted through Bob Dylan! People got incredibly upset. They thought I was a write-off. They thought I was going to start handing them pamphlets. They didn't understand what it means to be born-again. When the light shines on you, it shines on you. It can also stop shining on you.

I used to think of religious people as weak people. I thought it was a weakness to believe in anything. But it doesn't mean you're a fanatic to be religious. For instance, Catholicism makes sense to me. One day maybe I'll become a born-again Catholic for a while. It's a very powerful force. I don't believe there are answers. I don't believe that Christ is the answer. But I believe in all gods. How can I believe in the power of a bone or a lizard skin without believing in Christ?

T: When you were a teenager, did you have any career ambitions to be a writer?

MUSGRAVE: No.

T: Did you have any ambitions at all?

MUSGRAVE: There are two things I've always wanted to be. A ventriloquist and a tap dancer. I remember Shirley Temple did some great tap dancing in a film I saw once.

T: Aha. Now this interview is finally getting somewhere.

MUSGRAVE: Yes, I want to die in my ruby red tap shoes! Also I remember I once wanted to be a spy.

T: This is all highly significant. Now tell me, what is common to all these professions?

MUSGRAVE: They're all disguises, I guess.

T: So being a poet allows you to do all three things at once.

MUSGRAVE: Yes. Projecting the voice, performing, spying. I never thought of that. Here I am, everything I ever wanted to be. I've made it.

Al Purdy

AL PURDY was born at Wooler, Ontario in 1918. He grew up in Trenton, Ontario, rode the freights to the West Coast, and took mainly working class jobs as he evolved his poetry of engaging frankness, sardonic humour and reflective depth. Some of his many poetry books are *Poems for All the Annettes* (1962), *Cariboo Horses* (1965), for which he received

the Governor General's Award, *A Handful of Earth* (1977), an anthology *Being Alive* (1978) and *The Stone Bird* (1981). He has travelled extensively.

Al Purdy lives in Ameliasburg, Ontario. He was interviewed in 1978.

T: What was your family upbringing like?

PURDY: We were lower middle class, I guess you'd call it. My father was a farmer who died of cancer when I was two. My mother moved to town and devoted her life to going to church and bringing me up. I suppose I reacted against religion. But I remember when I rode the freight trains west for the first time, when I was sixteen or seventeen, I got lost in the woods and couldn't get out. So I prayed. I wasn't going to take any chances, no chances at all.

T: If a person reacts that way when he's very young, they say he'll react that way again when he's old.

PURDY: Christ, I'll never make it! I haven't prayed since that time. I doubt if I ever will again. I'm not religious in any formal sense, not in any God sense.

T: Do you think riding the freights appealed to you because it put you in touch with your survival juices?

PURDY: Well, let me give you the story about the first trip I took. I was hitchhiking north of Sault Ste. Marie when suddenly the Trans-Canada Highway didn't go any further. So I had to catch a train. I waited till after midnight. I got onto a flatcar that had had coal on it. It was raining and so I huddled there, all self-equipped with two tubes of shaving cream and an extra pair of shoes and a waterproof jacket.

We went all night into a town called Hawk Junction. I was desperate from the rain. I got out my big hunting knife and tried to get into one of the boxcars. I ripped the seal off one of the cars and tried to open the door but I couldn't do it. So I went back and huddled miserably on the flatcar. I didn't know I was at a divisional point.

A cop came along and said, "You can get two years for this." He locked me up in a caboose with bars on the windows. There was a padlock on the outside of the door, which opened inward. Then he came along a couple of hours later and took me home to have lunch with his family. They gave me a *Ladies' Home Journal* to read.

I began to get alarmed. What will my mother think? Two years in jail. The window of the caboose was broken where other people had tried to get out and couldn't do it. But I noticed, as I said, that the door opened inward. There was a padlock and a hasp on the outside. I put my feet up on the upper part of the sill and got my fingers in the hasp. I pulled the screws out of the padlock on the outside.

I started to walk back to Sault Ste. Marie, which was a hundred and sixty-five miles. Then I got panicky. They'll follow me. I'm a desperate criminal. I broke a seal. So I thought I'd walk a little way in the woods so they won't see me. But I got in too far. I couldn't get out. I was there for two bloody days. It rained. That was the last time I prayed, as I said.

T: What were your ambitions as a kid?

PURDY: To stay alive. To get along with other kids. Growing up in a small town, the only son of a very religious woman, I was always alone. Until I got into the Air Force at the age of twenty or so, I didn't get along with anybody.

I became a great reader. I read all the crappy things that kids read. I remember there was a series of paperback books back then called the Frank Merriwell series. When I was about thirteen, a neighbour moved away and gave me two hundred copies of Frank Merriwell. This guy Frank Merriwell went to Yale University and he won at everything he did — naturally he was an American — and anyway, he went through many vicissitudes. I pretended I was ill and went to bed. My mother fed me ice cream and I read all two hundred books. I stayed in bed for two months. Then I went back to school and passed into the next form.

T: Were you good in school?

PURDY: Not really. I even failed one year so I could play football. One year I got ninety percent or something and the next year I got forty. Don't ask me why. I started writing when I was about thirteen. I thought it was great when in fact it was crap. But you need that ego to write. Always.

T: You sound like you were probably pretty harem-scarem in those days.

PURDY: No, I wasn't harem-scarem at all. I was pretty conventional. Also I was always very discontented. A miserable little kid. I started, out of sheer desperation, to ride the freight trains. There's a quality of desperation about riding the freights. In my own mind, I was sort of a desperate kid. At a certain age you're always uncertain how other people will take you. I was desperately unhappy trying to adjust to the world. Finally I didn't give a damn.

T: Was the RCAF the next step in your life, after the freight trains?

PURDY: I was doing odd jobs around Trenton. What you did was you picked apples or you worked for Bata shoes. You quit one and then the other. I got into the Air Force for a job. I was there six years. I took a course and became a corporal, then an acting sergeant. Then I was demoted from acting sergeant to corporal and all the way down.

T: You got demoted "to the point where I finally saluted civilians." Why?

PURDY: By this time I was...going out with girls. I'd been too scared to go out with them up to the age I got into the Air Force. Once, when I was corporal of the guard, I drove the patrol car over to Belleville to see this girl after midnight. I got caught at it. I was acting sergeant at Picton where I had a big crew of Americans waiting to

get into training. What I did was appoint a whole bunch of acting noncoms so that I would have plenty of freedom. I went out on the town again.

Actually I was enjoying myself for the first time in my life. I hated the town of Trenton and I was finally out of it.

T: You've described your first book of poetry, *The Enchanted Echo*, as crap. Did you pay for its publication?

PURDY: Sure. Clarke and Stuart in Vancouver printed it for me. I cost me two hundred dollars to do about five hundred copies. About one hundred and fifty of them got out so I guess about half of those have been destroyed. I went back there ten years ago and they'd thrown them all out. Or they'd burned them. I'd been afraid to go back because I didn't think I could pay storage charges.

T: Around this time you got married. Your wife plays a pretty integral part in your poetry, yet we never get a clear picture of what kind of person she is...

PURDY: Oh, she's good material. She fixes small television sets and bends iron bars. I picked her up in the streets of Belleville, way back when. Her name's Eurithe because I think her parents were scared by the *Odyssey* or *Iliad* or something. It's a Greek name. I don't know why they picked such an oddball name because they're pretty straight people.

T: Have you ever tried writing a novel?

PURDY: Yes, I got sixteen thousand words once but it was terrible. I used to write plays, too. Ryerson Press accepted a book and the first play I wrote was produced, so my wife and I moved to Montreal so I could reap the rewards for my genius. She went to work to support me, as any well-behaved wife should. It turned out I had to write a dozen plays before I could get one accepted by the hard-boiled CBC producers. She decided if I could get away with not working, she could too. She quit her job, though I advised her against it.

That's when we built the house, which would be in ah . . . oh hell, '57 or something like that.

T: Were those the good ol' days or the bad ol' days?

PURDY: Oh, the bad old days. We were so broke! We spent all our money buying a pile of used lumber and putting a down payment on this lot. It was very bad for a while. You know how insecure your ego is when you have no money and you're jobless. There's nothing more terrible than walking the streets looking for a job. I'd been so sick of working for somebody else. Things were so bad we ate rabbits that neighbours had run over and gave to us because they knew we were broke.

I was picking up unemployment insurance for quite a while. When I built the house, I was still getting it in Montreal. I didn't dare move the unemployment insurance to Belleville because they'd give me a job. I used to drive to Montreal every two weeks to pick up the unemployment insurance. I'd drive like hell. Finally I had to get a job. So I decided to hitch-hike to Montreal. It was twenty below zero. I always pick a day like that. I got seventy miles and I couldn't make it any further. I had no gloves and I was freezing to death. Finally I got so disgusted I hitch-hiked back again. Things like that always happen. Born loser.

T: Isn't it possible to perpetuate that "born loser" image yourself?

PURDY: Oh, sure. It's your own attitude. Now I don't figure I'm going to lose hardly anything. But I used to always have that in the back of my mind, that I was going to lose or be defeated.

T: Is a talent for writing something you're born with?

PURDY: I had no talent whatsoever. If you look back at that first book, it's crap. It's a craft and I changed myself. Mind you, there are qualities of the mind which you have to have. I don't know what they are.

Still you look at some precocious little bastard like W.H. Auden — who was one of the closest to genius in this century — and you wonder. My God, there's some beautiful lines, beautiful poems.

T: How did you come to meet Irving Layton and Milton Acorn?

PURDY: I'd been corresponding with Layton because I'd found a couple of his books and liked them. After I got out of working at a mattress factory, I decided to go to Europe. I went to Layton's place in Montreal and slept on his floor before we caught our boat. I met Dudek through him. I can remember being at this drunken party in Montreal and lying on the floor with Layton, arm-wrestling. Dudek was hovering above us, supercilious and long-nosed, saying, "And these are sensitive poets!"

Milton Acorn had come from Prince Edward Island to sell his carpenter tools. He'd visited Layton. I was writing plays and Layton told Acorn to come around and see me and I'd tell him something about writing plays. I couldn't tell him anything. I couldn't even write them myself.

T: What made you head off to the Cariboo when you got your first Canada Council Fellowship in 1960?

PURDY: I was looking for an excuse to do anything. I only got a thousand bucks so I decided to write a verse play. I'd been stationed at Woodcock during the war, which is about a 150 miles from Prince Rupert. Totem poles, Indians and the whole works. We were building an airstrip.

T: So did you intuitively think the

Cariboo would stimulate you? Likewise for your trip to Baffin Island?

PURDY: I thought I was so damn lucky to be able to go up there to Baffin Island. I'm the only writer on the whole damned island! The feeling that nobody'd ever written about it before!

T: Now you've published twenty-five books, fourteen in the seventies alone. Do you consider yourself prolific?

PURDY: I'm not prolific like Layton. I'll publish a small book and there'll maybe be three or four poems which I think are worth including in *Being Alive*. It's a frightening thing to look backward and see that the earlier books have more poems in the collection than the later ones.

T: How closely did you work with Dennis Lee in editing *Being Alive*?

PURDY: He's a friend of mine. There are about fifteen poems which have been changed a bit because he'd look at a poem and say, "I don't quite understand this" or "I think this could be a little bit better." Picking the poems was a mutual thing. The idea was to be able to read through the sections and be able to go on to a new section easily. The divisions are not so clear cut as in *Selected Poems*.

It's by far the best book I've ever brought out. It amounts to a "collected" but it feels like a gravestone at the end of a road. There's a feeling of where the hell do I go from here? I certainly write less as I grow older. I'm writing very good poems at infrequent intervals. Like "Lament" and "A Handful of Earth."

T: Do you ever force yourself to write?

PURDY: Occasionally. I think a prose writer forces it out like toothpaste, but I prefer not to. Sometimes you've got a thought and you want to explore it. I dunno. The title poem of *The Cariboo Horses* was written in about half an hour. Another poem, "Postscript," took seven years.

T: Ten years ago you said people who develop a special way of writing, like b.p. Nichol or the Tish-Black Mountain people, were going down a dead end. Yet they're still travelling after a decade.

PURDY: It's still a dead end. They don't have any variety. The Black Mountain people talk in a certain manner in which they make under-emphasis a virtue. It's dull writing. It's far duller than conversation. I can't understand how people can write it except kids can write it and think, I too can be a poet. They can ignore a thousand years of writing poems, not read what's come before. There's so much to read, so much to enjoy. That's the reason to read poetry, to enjoy it.

T: Do you have any thoughts on the general characteristics of Canadian literature?

PURDY: The most prominent characteristic of Canadian literature is that it's the only literature about which the interviewer would ask what the characteristics are.

T: I think your best poems are those that cover the eerie meeting place between past and present, such as "Method for Calling Up Ghosts," "Remains of an Indian Village," "Roblin's Mills 1 and 2," "Lament for the Dorsets." Do you believe you have a soul?

PURDY: Well, Voltaire had some thoughts on that. He tried weighing himself before and after death. I don't think he came up with anything. I don't think I do have a soul. But there are areas in our nature that we don't know about. It's possible that we may find something that we haven't found before and we may use that word that's already invented and call it a soul. We use that word because it's the only word we have. You can feel this, of course, this so-called transmigration of souls. I thought it was a fascinating concept to imagine everybody living to leave lines behind on the street where they've been in "Method for Calling Up Ghosts." What it means is you're walking across the paths of the dead at all times. Every time you cross the St. Lawrence River you're crossing Champlain's path.

T: You think a lot about death?

PURDY: Quite a bit.

T: You were born in 1918. Has feminism affected your life at all?

PURDY: Every time I read my poem "Homemade Beer" it affects me. The audience thinks, "male chauvinist." It's a bawdy, exaggerated poem. Then I can read "The Horseman of Agawa" and it's exactly the opposite. People think you want to be one thing. You're not one thing. You're everything. Of course women have been second-class citizens for years. To gain a position of near equality, which they certainly haven't done yet, they've got to exaggerate. I exaggerate, too. Those remarks about my wife were facetious, of course, but I'm trying to imply with exaggerations that she's a tremendously capable woman

T: In "The Sculptors" you enjoy the imperfections of the broken Eskimo carvings and in "Depression in Namu, BC" you write, "beauty bores me without the slight ache of ugliness." There seems to be a streak in your that feels affinity with imperfection, that wants things to be blemished.

PURDY: Don't you ever want to splash muddy water into a sunset? A sunset is so marvellous, how are you going to paint it? How are you going to talk about it? So there is a quality of wishing to muddy up perfection, I agree.

T: You end many of your poems with a dash, as if the poem is not really completed.

PURDY: Yes, a lot of poems are in process, as if things happen after you stop looking at it. A poem is a continual revision, even if you've written it down without changing a single word. I like the thought of revision. When I copy a poem, I often change it. When I've written a poem in longhand, as I always do, I'll type, then I'll scribble it all up with changes.

T: What is there in you that needs to commemorate your existence thorough poetry?

PURDY: You have to back to when you started to write. I think most young poets begin to write through sheer ego. Look at me, no hands, Mom. There's always going to be the element of ego, because we can't escape our egos. We don't necessarily want to. But there has to be a time when we can sit down and write and try to say a thing and the ego isn't so important. When you are just trying to tell the truth, you're not trying to write immortal lines that will go reverberating down the centuries. You're saying what you feel and think and what is important to you.

T: Are you at all optimistic about our future?

PURDY: I'm pessimistic about everything the older I get. We're going to wade through garbage. We're going to split up. The Americans are going to take everything, even though they don't need to, of course, because they have it already. The world is going to explode and we'll all be dead. Life is awful.

Jane Rule

JANE RULE was born in Plainfield, New Jersey in 1931. She came to Canada in the late 1950s to teach at the University of British Columbia. She encourages change by creating characters who struggle, increasingly as a group, to step beyond the limitations of social conventions to seek love born of strength, not weakness. *Desert of the Heart* (1964), a first

novel about two women who fall in love in Reno, Nevada, became a film called *Desert Hearts*. Other fiction includes *The Young in One Another's Arms* (1977), *Contract with the World* (1980), *Inland Passage* (1985) and *Memory Board* (1987). Non-fiction works include *Lesbian Images* (1975) and *A Hot-Eyed Moderate* (1985).

Jane Rule lives on Galiano Island, BC. She was interviewed in 1978.

T: Do you consider yourself an American writer or a Canadian writer?

RULE: Well, simply a writer in English is always best. Some of my work is set in England because I lived there for a while. Then I went back to the States and found it very alien. When I came to to Vancouver and found a beautiful place to be, I simply elected the city. I came on a beautiful August day, twenty-some years ago, so that it was still a little charming city. I didn't even think of it as Canada. I mean I knew it was Canada, but I was that kind of American. It was north of Seattle and it was a place called Vancouver. Now I've spent just about half my life in Canada — all my adult life — so, since I didn't really have roots in any specific place in the States, my commitment to a nation is really much clearer as a Canadian.

T: Have you resented being pigeon-holed as a "lesbian" novelist?

RULE: I reacted to it at first, but I don't much any more. If there was a usefulness in resenting it, then I would. But I also know that it's politically important to other people. I'm a responsible person, so it seems to me I have to put up with it.

T: Do you put much faith in politics to solve social problems?

RULE: Well, it seems to me politics is housekeeping. I don't look to politics as a place to change anything. We get the politics we deserve. Politics really are to clean up the house. You have to do it every week. I don't find it interesting, just as I don't find sweeping the floor every week interesting. I do it. I vote.

I prefer to work wherever there's a possibility of changing things. I work with lesbians, I work with gay men, I work with the women's movement. I really believe through the counter-movements in society change can be made. We're living witnesses of it. The last ten years have shocked even the most optimistic of us.

T: Are you consciously evangelical for your own politics when you write?

RULE: No, I don't suppose so. In fact, the thing that is peculiar for me about reaction to my books is that I've had an awful lot of reviewers take me to task for not being political, for having no other great interest than writing some kind of gentle soap opera. *Desert of the Heart* got a very bad review in Québec because I got all the social analysis correctly, I understood everything that was wrong, then I bloody well accepted it instead of blowing the place up!

Of course I do get reviewers who say that I'm a revolutionary, that I really ought to be called to confess my revolutionary zeal, which is hidden under a slick surface. But I don't feel politics lurk in my books or dominate them.

T: Actually it's often not politics people find threatening. It's ideas. People read "only the good can be guilty" in *Desert of the Heart* and it shakes them.

RULE: Sure. That's why I expected to get absolutely fried with that book. But what I didn't expect was to hear from all the readers who were in anguish. I was shocked by the number of people who were needy for that book.

T: Coming from a different generation, I'd almost say I don't understand what the fuss could be about.

RULE: Absolutely. I think it would be very hard for anyone to imagine what it was like in the fifties. I think about the only valid criticism I got when *Desert of the Heart* was released was that there's no hostility surrounding Evelyn and Ann. The landlady is consoling. There isn't any climate of hostility. But I chose that consciously. So many people in those days were trying to get sympathy for homosexuals by showing how mean everyone was to them. I didn't want to get into propaganda. I wanted them to say what they really would say and feel what they really would feel. I didn't want to drag in a lot of social pressure to overshadow that.

T: I think many readers would agree today with Virginia Woolf's description of *The Well of Loneliness* as a "meritorious, dull book." Do you think *Desert of the Heart* will ever replace it as *the* lesbian novel?

RULE: I don't suppose so, alas. Radcliffe Hall wrote *The Well of Loneliness* as a piece of propaganda and therefore included all kinds of theory and minor characters. It's also a tragic story and I think that as long as people are willing to be broad-minded, *The Well of Loneliness* is an ideal book. Because the people suffer and get punished. *Desert of the Heart* has already taken the place of *The Well of Loneliness* for lesbians, but for the range of society, no. Because Evelyn and Ann apparently get it together. It's not tragic.

T: After having written *Lesbian Images*, where do you stand on the question of rationalizing the origins of lesbianism?

RULE: I think there is only one origin: that you love another woman. The person you love is the motivation.

As physical creatures, we react to sexual stimulus. So it's probably true that we are capable of responding sexually to either sex. Of course the predisposition for reproduction is heterosexual so the majority of people move in that direction. But there are lots of people who are so frightened of sexual feelings that they don't feel anything for either sex.

T: Would you agree with Havelock Ellis that sexual inversion tends to occur in individuals who are above average in intellect and character?

RULE: No. That was one of those

defensive statements that you'll find coming out of any minority that feels threatened. You know, that Shakespeare was bisexual. And Plato. To get your act together and claim everybody under the sun is good, strong, brave and true.

T: Where do you suppose you got your strength for living a life of non-conformity? From your family?

RULE: Partly, yes. But partly also by not finding it easy to conform. A lot of people find strength because they have to have it, not because they go around courting it.

For instance, I didn't grow up in one place. Therefore I never experienced a lot of intimate social pressure. It didn't really matter to me much what people thought because I knew I'd be gone in a year. I could really base my choices on what I wanted to do. My parents were also very supportive and taught us all to be non-conformists, even though they're conformists themselves. They conform because they can.

T: Which brings us to Jane Rule on morality. "Morality is a test of our conformity rather than our integrity."

RULE: Yes, I do think morality is simply part of the quality of life, sometimes a very bad part and sometimes a very good part.

T: One of your characters says, "What you lose is what you survive with." Does that statement come out of your life?

RULE: No, it comes from observing more than experiencing. Some of the people I know who have carried the heaviest burdens are people who figured how to let those things work for them. So I wanted to create a character who had that kind of guts. As long as you're alive, what you lose becomes part of your understanding.

T: With that what-you-lose-is-what-you-get angle, was *The Young in One Another's Arms* meant as a definitive novel of the sixties?

RULE: No. The experiences that come from me for that book go back to the end of the Second World War. In that respect, it's really too bad when something like draft-dodging gets to be associated only with the sixties. I'm always startled when a reviewer says, "Oh well this is about the sixties, no point, dead issue." I think fiction isn't about those issues. Those issues are part of the climate of fiction. The notion that a book should be "new" is new since television.

I remember I sent a short-short to *Redbook*. A short-short is only about a thousand words long. I wrote it at the time of the Cuban Crisis and sent it off. They accepted the story two months later but they said they needed me to invent a different world crisis because the Cuban Crisis was dated. Crazy, just crazy.

T: But *The Young in One Another's Arms* is essentially about people trying to set up an economic and emotional commune. So it is a reflection of the sixties.

RULE: Sure. But the word is politically loaded for me. At that time I was listening to an awful lot of young people out at UBC who were so earnest about living in a commune you knew it wouldn't last. Everybody had to have exactly the same amount of space. I remember saying to one girl, "What happens if I'm a writer and my friend Tak Tanabe is a painter? I could work in a closet and he couldn't." She said, "Oh well, those are only hobbies." And every Tuesday night you have a criticism period. That whole era is what "commune" got stamped with.

T: Were you personally affected by all that sixties idealism floating around?

RULE: No. But it certainly affected the young people I knew at the time. I was very busy being a teacher and trying to find time to write. We always had draft dodgers with us, or people who couldn't cope with the university,

but I was too involved with the commitment I had made to writing. Consequently I've never been one to think of solutions for my own life coming from things I do with other people.

T: Yet you're writing these books where you're almost prescribing communalism, or at least the notion that a communal way of life is a very real and worthwhile alternative.

RULE: Well, I know it is. It can be done. But art is a job that has to be done alone. *Contract with the World* is about artists and what it is like to be committed to that kind of job. The kinds of good friends I have are people who are perfectly willing to have me say I'll see them in six months, and live right next door. A number of people do that with me, too. But you don't do that and live in a commune.

T: How do you feel about the anti-academic sentiment of the sixties and seventies?

RULE: I am "anti" a lot that's going on, at the big universities particularly. But I'm an academician. I really care about the academy. When I feel critical, it isn't that I'm being anti-intellectual. I'm saying this is one of the important places and you better clean up your act. I feel very strongly that they haven't been emphasizing teaching and that's death to learning.

T: Is it important for you to keep in touch with other writers?

RULE: Not as a thing in itself. But it's very important for me to keep in touch with people who happen to be my friends and are writers. Certainly in Canada we're very fortunate in that the government helps us keep in touch. We all go to Ottawa once a year on the government. I need to see Marie-Claire Blais once a year. And Peggy Atwood. And Margaret Laurence.

T: With the setting of *Desert of the Heart*, you gave equal time to how relationships work and how society works. But as your books become more technical, it appears social analysis is becoming less emphasized.

RULE: That's probably true. Essentially what I've been trying to teach myself over these last few novels is how to deal with a group of people. Technically that is more difficult than doing the structural things, as in *Desert*. *Desert* is the most structured of anything that I've ever done. From natural to social to individual. The characters were provided with certain intellectual chores that they had to get through in that book, never mind make love to each other and all those other things.

The Vancouver setting for *The Young* was nowhere near as important. And in *Against the Season*, the setting was even less important again. I was mostly interested in people living in a no-place, a place that was dying. Also in that book I wanted to try to write that conventional kind of English novel. It has an omniscient narrator, which I hadn't done before. That's conventional. But it wasn't conventional for me. It was far out to sit there and let the quips come and have them be my own.

T: That's something I really enjoy about your books—the humour. Your characters' talk is very modern, like people I know. They're always using humour to break social ground, as a reaching out.

RULE: Well, I have a feeling that the kind of dialogue I write is very West Coast. I get an awful lot of flak from eastern editors saying this is absolutely unbelievable dialogue. Their claim is that the only people who are witty are people who use lots of references to books and other intellectual paraphernalia. There's a kind of snobbery in the east, and also a slowness. People are not kindly offhand. There's not the kind of teasing that has nothing to do with anybody needing to be defensive.

A sort of joking attentiveness that goes on in a more relaxed world.

T: I think another strength of your writing is the repeated appreciation for the aged. What accounts for all the elderly characters in your books?

RULE: I spend a lot of time with people a good deal older than I am. I always have. I grew up with grandparents and was very close to them. On Galiano Island, most of the population is over sixty-five. Elisabeth Hopkins, the painter, is eighty-six and is, I suppose, our closest friend. So older people are very much a part of the world I live in.

T: Living on an island is another recurring motif. Do you get special comfort or stimulation from being here on Galiano?

RULE: No, I suppose I think of this mostly as "away." One of the characters in my new book says, "If there was a town called Away I would drive to it." Galiano is for me a bit of a fortress. I was beginning to be bugged in town, I couldn't lead my own life. Coming over here, I can spend my time as I want to. When I go to an event here, it's as treasurer of the Galiano Club. I take the quarters. Nobody pays much attention.

T: One last highly pertinent question. Do you really drink Coca-Cola for breakfast?

RULE: Yes, I do. Except they don't sell Coca-Cola on the island. I had to switch to Pepsi. The guy who owns the store over here had a fight with the Coca-Cola people and he won't buy it. I said, "Vic, I am nearly fifty years old. This is a lifetime addiction. You didn't tell me when I moved onto this island that you were going to have a fight with the Coca-Cola company."

T: So Jane Rule took the Pepsi challenge.

RULE: I did. And I can't tell the difference.

Andreas Schroeder

ANDREAS SCHROEDER was born in Hoheneggelsen, Germany in 1946. He emigrated with his parents in 1951. He developed a keen interest in surrealism at UBC, founded *The Journal of Contemporary Literature in Translation* (1968–80), contributed a literary column to the Vancouver *Province* (1968–73), chaired the Writers Union of Canada (1976–77) and is

chiefly responsible for the institution of Public Lending Rights in Canada. For possession of hashish he was incarcerated for eight months and subsequently wrote his superb non-fiction memoir, *Shaking It Rough* (1976). Earlier experimental fiction has been eclipsed by an incredible documentary-style novel, *Dustship Glory* (1986), based on the true story of a dirt-poor Finnish-Canadian farmer in Saskatchewan named Tom Sukanen who endured seven years of toil and poverty to build an ocean-bound, dustbowl freighter fifteen miles from the nearest river.

Andreas Schroeder lives in Mission, BC. He was interviewed in 1986.

T: Did it ever strike you in the course of writing *Dustship Glory* that building a ship in the middle of the prairie is somehow analogous to trying to finish a novel?

SCHROEDER: I didn't consider it at the time. But there are certainly many similarities. Sitting at a desk for years and years hammering away at pieces of paper that no one may ever want. Trying desperately to keep the original idea in focus. Fending off people who keep trying to apply mere logic to the problem. For whom it's all just a lunatic exercise.

T: The big difference is that Tom Sukanen went about his lunatic exercise in public view.

SCHROEDER: Right. And I can relate to that from another angle, too. I find writing so hard, so painstaking, that whenever I lose traction, whenever I can't hear myself anymore, I grab a hammer and nails and go out and build something. Something indisputably *there*. Because at least with building something physical, you don't have to doubt your vision. One of the things that draws me to a man like Tom, which is to say a man with a grand vision, is that he was a builder. Now I live in a crazy house with a tower and cathedral arches all over the place. There's hardly a right angle anywhere. Getting the vision of what we wanted to build took Sharon and me a number of years of just fantasizing until we had it straight. After that it was just the hassle of trying to get from here to there, to get it done. I was prepared to spend twenty-six hours a day at it, because I could *see* it so clearly. I couldn't understand why the helpers I hired were only interested in putting in eight. The project was huge but it was also such a treat. Just knowing that, no matter how challenging the undertaking, there's a solution for every problem you might run up against. In many ways it's even

immaterial whether you stumble a whole lot in the process, or even if the damn thing caves in once or twice. Whereas with writing, I have never felt I had the privilege of a vision so clear and sharp. You can only hope you end up with more or less what you had in mind, though you never do. It can't possibly be exactly what you fantasized it to be. There's always going to be a rueful sense that it's not exactly what you intended, it's not quite the same.

T: So obviously you used the experience of building your own house to understand Tom Sukanen.

SCHROEDER: That's got to be true. I certainly understood that for Tom Sukanen the reasons for building his ship and his visions of what he was going to do with it were far more important than the trivial horseshit of cold-rolling half-inch steel, however unbelievable people have found that in retrospect. His tragedy was that he miscalculated on the timing. That's about the only thing he couldn't manufacture himself: enough time. With enough time, he could have launched that ship, I'm convinced of it. He could have pulled it off.

T: If only the people in the community had got their John Deere tractors together and hauled the bloody thing . . .

SCHROEDER: Yes, that's one of the things that became clear as I did the research. There are still a few men sitting around looking just little guilty about that.

T: Everybody was smaller than Tom Sukanen's vision and now they have to realize it in retrospect.

SCHROEDER: That's right. So now they've either got to shit on him even more, to protect themselves, or they've got to admit that. To their credit, there are some, a few at least, who faced up to it. Some of the men, but very few of the women. Not that I blame them, the women I mean. Tom treated them pretty badly.

T: Would you agree there's a male/female antipathy in this story that goes beyond personalities? Because traditionally it's only men who behave as visionaries?

SCHROEDER: I was troubled by that fact. Because, fundamentally, I've always believed that's a crock. But maybe it's also got something to do with those times — the dustbowl, the scratching to survive, and the fact that women often manage to come up with the most level-headed approach when push really comes to shove.

T: Did you ever try to write a straight biography of Tom Sukanen?

SCHROEDER: No, no. What I saw in this story was a lot bigger than that. And that required the freedom to invent where the record or people's recollections failed the story. And that happened a lot. It's astonishing, really, how full of holes someone's story can turn out to be when you change focus from wide-angle to close-up. Probably up to seventy-five percent of the book needed to be "invented" in some way. Which sounds like a lot, I'm sure, but what's important is exactly where that seventy-five percent is located. And in this book it's represented by a blizzard of mostly little things, conjunctions, bridges, a lot of fine-line detail. The main ingredients of the story, or most of them anyway, remain what is conventionally known as fact.

I discovered that a lot of what people told me was invention anyway, though they were convinced it wasn't. And by the time I got through with all my research I felt I knew the old bugger better than anybody that was left around anyway, even his relatives, who'd never bothered to get very close to him. And from that, I just started putting him back together. When pieces were missing, I filled them in. I

was allowed, I think, to step into that place because people who claimed to have known him had, in effect, abrogated the position. They hadn't ever made the effort to really appreciate the possibilities of this man and his story. All their lives they'd watched him through the wrong end of the telescope. And I was damned if I wasn't going to turn that telescope around.

T: Because you were thinking big? Creating a myth for someone like me who lives two thousand miles away?

SCHROEDER: Right. Exactly.

T: Whereas the people around Macrorie, Saskatchewan are going to read *Dustship Glory* and be very angry. They're not thinking of the ship in terms of the Taj Mahal or the Pyramids... They'll say, "This guy Schroeder's a liar!"

SCHROEDER: They'll probably say that because they think having been neighbours gives them the right to consider their inventions more accurate than mine.

T: Even though it clearly says that this is a novel on the cover. That it's fiction.

SCHROEDER: Yes. I mean, I guess I could get into a full-blown debate on the question of historical truth here, point out that historians like Fernand Braudel have consistently kicked the stuffing out of the notion in book after book, proving that most of what has passed for historical truth has merely been the convenient invention of the prevalent aristocracy and so on and so on, but I'll tell you: I frankly don't much give a damn which side wins. To me, the issue centres on the *purpose* of setting down history, and a novelist's is clearly different from a historian's. A historian, I suppose, wants to make a simple case of who did what to whom, what caused what, without any ulterior moral purpose. Where a novelist, so long as he's not trying merely to entertain, always has a much larger hidden agenda. He's always looking for the archetypal experience, the moral parable, for the events or incidents in which the most telling wisdom is demonstrated. I mean sure, some are more conscious of this than others, but we all do it. I mean, there's a damn good reason why the myths of Sisyphus or Icarus, in whatever form we come across them, are as applicable today as they ever were. It's because their authors managed to find or invent experiences that sum up our hopes and frustrations so adroitly, people throughout the ages kept sitting up in astonishment and saying, "Goddamn, that's me, that's exactly what I'm struggling with, dead on, man." And who in his right mind cares whether Icarus wore blue pants or green pants or any pants at all? Or whether he really wore wax-and-feathers wings. Let him have strapped on fusion-thrust rockets from General Dynamics for all I care. That's a total red herring; the wisdom in the myth isn't dependent on that. By the same token, what I tried to do in *Dustship Glory* was to serve the mythic resonance of Sukanen's story, to make sure that those elements which make it ageless got the necessary backlighting. I wasn't interested in any lesser reasons for writing that story — which is what I always suspect people of who quibble over the colour of Icarus's pants.

T: Rudy Wiebe took much the same approach in writing *The Temptations of Big Bear*. He's also a German-Canadian Mennonite. Are there any more connections?

SCHROEDER: Actually, Rudy and I have had a strange relationship. For some time we approached each other, it seems to me, like wary wolves, trying to figure out our territory. He was always in a much better position for that than I, obviously. But there was

one thing I seemed to have that Rudy didn't, and which, I suspect, interested him in me. I think I seemed to him back then something of a loose moral cannon on deck, divested of all the standard Mennonite taboos and restraints, and he wanted to see what happened when a defunct Mennonite jumped off the deep end into the steaming waters of moral depravity. I think I must have ultimately disappointed him though, because I remember him saying once, when I was describing my commonlaw but pretty conventional relationship with a certain young woman, "Aw gee, you sound just like the rest of us."

Speaking of *Big Bear*, by the way, I'm also getting a lot more intrigued by the notion of digging into Canadian history for my central characters. We do seem to have a downright gratifying rogues' gallery of them. Amor de Cosmos. Brother Free-John. General "Puff" Brackendale. Canadian eccentrics seem to have a certain patina . . .

T: And *Dustship Glory* is a deeply Canadian story.

SCHROEDER: Yes, it is that. If you tried to write it for American history, if you wanted to custom-design it for the States, you'd have to look at it quite differently. Not to mention making it a lot "noisier." But I'm convinced that Americans could really benefit by seeing the world from a Canadian perspective now and then. Calm them down a little.

I'm fundamentally content with the Canadian perspective on the world, but there is a distressing Canadian tendency to want to, well, the German word is *ernüchtern*, which means to neutralize, to deflate, to trivialize with sobering detail. The tendency to say, 'Yeah, that sounds pretty wonderful, but really, didn't this guy also beat his wife and cheat on his income tax? So he couldn't really have been all that great, could he?" It's going to take some time and a lot more books like Hodgins' *Invention of the World* before we stop being so self-deprecating about our heroes. It's not Greek gods we're inventing here, after all. We may be celebrating vision, but it's a *grounded* vision after all.

T: When you just said, "It's not Greek gods," it just flipped into my mind, "Okay, then it's Canadian gods." Why is that immediately laughable? "Canadian gods."

SCHROEDER: I know what you mean. But it shouldn't be, and maybe some day it won't. However there's a distinction I'd like to make about this now that you've brought it up, and it's this. The problem with Greek gods is that they have no really believable human roots—that is, all those silly human attributes they exhibit always felt to me tacked on like those sticker eyes on Cabbage Patch dolls. Quite mechanical. Not the slightest room for empathy there. They feel like a bad novelist's inventions. I can't take them seriously; I've always had trouble believing that the Greeks really did. For me, there are only two believable kinds of gods: one that has an existence totally outside all human invention or experience, some inexplicable, unpredictable, invincible Outside Power—and since I can't see any convincing evidence for that so far, I don't believe we've yet encountered such a god—or there should be gods who are actually just idealized people, once-real people whose magnificent vision or wisdom or performance—good or evil—warranted putting their images on pedestals, their thoughts and histories into "bibles," either as warnings or encouragements. Their power, in other words, would reside in the strength of their examples, their ideas or visions—not the colour of their pants. And however high we felt the

need to elevate them, they would still continue to convince people of the possibility of emulation because they'd once, after all, been human and started off with roughly the same flaws and virtues as everybody else. Now for my money, *that's* the only kind of humanly invented god that makes any sense—a god you can pray to, but also, in some sense, run into at the supermarket any day of the week. Like Jesus, for example—just ignore all that nonsense about his pedigree and you've got yourself a perfectly workable god.

T: This idea must come directly from your Mennonite background.

SCHROEDER: Well, you're right in the sense that that's precisely where the rupture originated. We were constantly being told to feel all this reverence and adulation for a god who had so obviously been invented by men looking for a handy way to control and push around humankind, all protestations to the contrary, that I just couldn't buy it. It was just too obvious. Now if this god had truly stood for anything genuinely worthy, it might have been different, but as far as I could see, he merely stood for raw, unadulterated power. The combination of suspiciously human motives and a handily vengeful god trivialized conventional religion utterly for me. That god who was presented to me as a goddamn monument, someone to look up to and revere, had never done anything to earn any of my deepest feelings. In fact, if you want to get really specific about it, the god in the Old Testament is a prick. He's the most unjust, spleenful, Jealous, capricious, unfair son-of-a-bitch that ever had the nerve to masquerade as a "just god" anywhere.

T: So it would make as much sense to worship Tom Sukanen.

SCHROEDER: That's about it. But at least I can relate to what this man was prepared to sacrifice his life for. I can admire the breadth and splendid craziness of his vision, and all the desperation that went into it. *That* I can relate to. And I'm prepared to carry that a step farther, to elevate it to a height where it operates as myth. Whereas I'm not prepared to put the sum total of my admirations, translated into four or five years of sweat at a desk, into contributing toward the mortgage payments on a lot of religious real estate belonging to an enormous patriarchal religious bureaucracy. I mean, sure, the needs of community are always served to a degree whenever two or three are gathered together in His name, but that can be accomplished with a lot less overhead, thank you very much. All puns intended.

T: And this has resulted in a schism with your father.

SCHROEDER: My father lives in an increasingly different world. For one thing, he doesn't read English, which means he doesn't read my books. But more to the point, he speaks a completely different spiritual language. From my perspective, it's religious jargon, which means the world to him but very little to me. I wouldn't be surprised if I sound the same to him a lot of the time. It's hard to tell; he doesn't open up much to me. So I guess there's a schism. There's certainly a language problem. And a very fundamental difference of opinion about what's important. One thing I guess I know for sure, and it's sad but unalterable: I'm not the son he had in mind when he made me.

T: It makes sense you turned to surrealism at UBC. As a rebellion of language.

SCHROEDER: Well, surrealism had a purpose at the time. It had to break up a whole Victorian mindset, my own included. And it did that. It did that

very effectively. But there is a reason why it faded as fast as it did, all over the world; there was always something missing, something slightly empty about it. It was a half-truth blown up to full-truth proportions. And on the negative side, it fostered a climate at the Creative Writing Department in those days which said, in effect: "We'll be as experimental and obtuse and impenetrable as we like, and if readers can't stick with it, then screw them." I had to work my way through that. Mind you, some part of me does see the world that way, so it was good to work through it, but I got stuck in it too long. I became a disciple. It cost me almost as much to get out of the voice I wrote in in those days as it took me to acquire it. Now I don't have to invent theatres that blow up at the end of the last act any more. And I don't have to try to invent people like Tom Sukanen either, because I eventually discovered that you can find them almost ready made and much more compelling if you simply drive down Highway 2 south of Moose Jaw, or live on West Seventh Avenue in Vancouver — that's where the main character of the novel I'm working on now used to live. It's really quite wonderful. Nobody believed me when I set my stories into Magritte-like landscapes with great rolling balls clear back to the horizon, but since I've found those exact landscapes hay-ball for hay-ball thirty-five miles northwest of Wood Mountain, Saskatchewan, they've had no choice. And I can continue to indulge my predilection for the bizarre under a new flag of convenience. It's like that wonderful line in a Paulette Jiles poem: "Texas is not my fault." Well, Tom Sukanen is not my fault either. And that leaves my hands free to plunge into him up to my eyeballs.

Josef Skvorecky

JOSEF SKVORECKY (pronounced Shor-etzky) was born in Nachod, Bohemia, Czechoslovakia in 1924. He entered medical school in Prague but eventually received his PhD in philosophy in 1951. A co-writer of the Milos Forman film *Closely Watched Trains*, he was central to the post-war Czechoslovak cultural renaissance and later wrote a non-fiction book on Czech

cinema, *All the Bright Young Men and Women* (1972). After the Soviet invasion of Czechoslovakia he immigrated to Canada with his writer/actress wife Zdena Salivarova and became an English professor in Toronto. His major works in English are *The Cowards* (1970), *The Mournful Demeanor of Lieutenant Boruvka* (1974), novellas *The Bass Saxophone* and *Emoke* (1977), a collection of short stories, *The Swell Season* (1982), *The Engineer of Human Souls* (1983) — for which he received the Governor General's Award for fiction — and *Dvorak in Love* (1986). *Sins for Father Knox* (1988) is a newly translated collection of ten tongue-in-cheek detective stories. Both comic and tragic, his books often feature an autobiographical character named Daniel Smiricky who serves Skvorecky as an East European everyman.

Josef Skvorecky lives in Toronto. He was interviewed in 1983.

T: Are you comfortable with Graham Greene's assessment that you have always been a writer-in-exile? Even before coming to Canada?

SKVORECKY: Yes, in the sense that every good writer in a totalitarian state is really an exiled writer. It's internal exile. If you are a really good writer in a totalitarian dictatorship you have just two choices. Either you don't strive for publication at all and you just write samizdat literature for the desk drawer, you make copies and you lend them to friends, and you are in danger because it is not permitted to disseminate literature that does not go through the censorship office. Or you can become your own censor. That is auto-censorship, self-censorship. And you remain in exile. Your real feelings and your full potential remain unused. You cautiously write things so the censors will pass them.

T: Why did the censors allow your first novel, *The Cowards*, in 1958? And then the novel was banned afterwards?

SKVORECKY: My first novel was really banned in 1956, before publication. It was called *The End of the Nylon Age*. It described one night at a big dance given by the American Institute in Prague one year after the Communist takeover. It was the last event that this institute ever organized before it was dismantled and people were arrested. In those years the publishing houses had an agreement with the censors that those manuscripts which were politically safe were shown to the censors in page proofs, after having been set in type. But if they had a manuscript about which they were not certain, they'd send it to the censors as a manuscript. That's what happened to my first novel. It never made it to the printers.

The Cowards was published in 1958 before Christmas. It was in the bookstores for about a month. Then the Party led an attack on it and the police confiscated copies. I was fired from my job at a magazine. The President himself spoke about me at a gathering of Communist functionaries. He condemned the novel although I'm sure he never read it. I was preparing to go to jail.

T: But why?

SKVORECKY: The whole affair had a very political background. The Stalinists in the Communist Party were advocating stricter surveillance and policing and the more liberal, less dogmatic Marxists were advocating a loosening up. The Stalinists needed a good example of where things would lead if they loosened up, if they let things be published which were not exactly kosher. That's why the novel was passed by the censors. It was passed with the purpose of demonstrating where permissiveness leads. It was passed with the purpose of being banned later.

So there was a big splash for two weeks. There was a purge of the publishing houses because of the book. They also used it as a pretext for purging the media. But they were not strong enough. In the next few years the Stalinists lost power and the more liberal faction won. *The Cowards* was re-published five years later. It became a *cause célèbre*, an extremely popular novel. Literary critics used to refer to it as the beginning of the end of socialist realism in Czechoslovakia. After that came the Czech new wave in the cinema and a flowering of Czech culture in the sixties which was, unfortunately, very brief.

T: What were the circumstances of your coming to live in Toronto in 1969?

SKVORECKY: After the Russians came in August '68, the Dubcek leadership remained in office for about eight months after the invasion. They were just shifting papers while the real decisions were made elsewhere. But they still had certain powers and one of them was issuing passports. They warned some of the people who had been involved in the reform movement that they could no longer guarantee our safety.

I had been through so many political upheavals I was not a political innocent. I saw that there was no future for me as a writer. The Party would not repeat the same mistake twice. They would not permit any unorthodox writing. I hadn't been thinking of leaving the country. For a writer who writes in a minor language to come to a country where a different language is spoken, that's a very difficult situation. But I was in the underground in the fifties and I knew I was too old for that again. So I simply left.

T: Tell me about 68 Publishers.

SKVORECKY: That was an idea of my wife. When we came to Canada, she didn't speak English. Her other languages were French and Russian. So she felt very isolated in Toronto. Very frustrated and homesick. Then I was approached by a man from New York, the chairman of a Czech scholarly society, who offered to publish one of my novels. My wife thought, why should you give it to them? Why not publish it ourselves? In this country we can open a publishing house, pay twenty dollars somewhere for registration and that's all.

So we started that publishing house. It's called 68 Publishers to commemorate the year 1968. We published a novel of mine called *The Tank Corps* which is a satire on the army. That is a guarantee of interest among Czech readers because everybody likes to read something funny about the army. We sold about seven thousand copies. We re-invested the profit into the publishing house. After the first ten years we'd published about 130 titles.

T: All in Czech?

SKVORECKY: All in Czech. There are only something like sixty thousand Czechs in Canada so it's a mail order business. We send out catalogues all over the western world. The majority of the readers live in North America, West Germany and Australia but we have some readers in very unlikely places, in Nepal, in the Pacific Islands. The idea is simply to help save good manuscripts that otherwise would be in danger of disappearing. We publish only manuscripts that have never been published and that have been written either by writers in exile or writers who live in Czechoslovakia but can't publish there for political reasons.

T: Had you been born and raised in Canada, do you think would have been a writer?

SKVORECKY: Yes, I think I would have been a writer anyway. You have this talent or whatever it is and you cannot avoid it. But I do think it is much more difficult to become a really influential and great writer in a society like Canada. For the past half century or more, since the Great Depression, no really terrible, shocking, radical thing has happened here. Whereas if you grew up in Europe, you simply lived through so many terrible upheavals and changes and dangers that it's hard to write an uninteresting book.

T: Perhaps there's a connection to be made here to something you say in one of your books about hate being more perceptive than love.

SKVORECKY: Yes. I don't think writers discover new things but they have the gift of formulating feelings and ideas that most people feel but never formulate. That's the role of the writer. If he happens to live in a country where there is much oppression, and therefore much hatred, he formulates feelings of hatred which everybody feels. That can make him popular. It would be difficult to become popular that way in Canada.

T: There's a line in *Emoke*, "There is no such thing as a superman, but it has always seemed to me there is such a thing as a subman." Do you see less "submen" in a place like Canada, in a democratic state?

SKVORECKY: No. It's just that in a totalitarian dictatorship these submen, the lunatic fringe, the bad people, get a much better chance to influence society. Every society has a certain percentage of pathological or semi-pathological people. Every society has its percentage of freaks.

T: How do submen gain control of a society?

SKVORECKY: Well, I, of course, have my Czech experience. The advent of Communism in Czechoslovakia had been prepared by leftist intellectuals who, because they lost their faith in democracy, saw that perhaps dictatorship of the proletariat is a better solution. They prepared the way. Dictatorship came and for some time these intellectuals were in the leading roles. But then they discovered things developing differently than they expected and they became dissenting Communists. Eventually they are executed and hanged and exiled. So I think the dangerous thing is uncritical acceptance of non-democratic ideas.

T: The obvious question arises: how does a democracy protect itself against anti-democratic elements?

SKVORECKY: The opinion is divided. Some people believe that it's not undemocratic to ban parties which openly advocate an overthrow of democracy. There is something logical to that.

I simply believe that democracy, with all its faults and imperfections, at least is a safeguard that we shall have no concentration camps, no legal frame-ups like the trials in Russia, and that to me is the important thing: legal safety and freedom of the mind. That you can conduct such an interview and I can tell you what is on my mind and we don't have to be afraid that tomorrow we will both be locked up. That's a great thing. If you lose this thing, you can never know what might happen.

T: When you wrote *The Bass Saxophone* in three days, did you have any idea it would become your best known work?

SKVORECKY: No, that's only the case in the west. This is a society where there are so many people who love jazz. Jazz is a very important component of North American culture. But among Czech readers other books are much better known. For instance, *The Engineer of Human Souls*. And *Emoke* is much more popular in Czechoslovakia than *The Bass Saxophone* because it's a love story and it's sad.

T: What were the circumstances that prompted *The Bass Saxophone*?

SKVORECKY: Well, in the sixties, when the power of the Stalinist establishment was broken and Kafka was rehabilitated, suddenly everybody wanted to be very modern, very experimental, very existential, absurdist, non-objective, non-realistic and so on. There was a deluge of experimental writing, most of which is dead now. The literary critics, in most cases the very same ones who in the late fifties were socialist realists, suddenly developed interests in Beckett, in Kafka. They started saying of course I was an important writer historically, I had written this historically important novel, but I was a very traditional writer. I continued to be very popular. People bought my books. But I never experimented. As if literature had to offer new things! We are not fashion designers. We are not fashion writers. Every season need not have a new fashion. We are concerned with life, and that never changes.

But I was in a sort of mental crisis. I tried to emulate the example of William Faulkner, who never read his critics because he knew that a critic can undermine your self-confidence and that may be very dangerous. Hemingway was killed by the critics. He lost his self-confidence and he never really produced anything good after a certain point. But I wanted to be recognized by the critics as more than just historically important. You do not want to become an object of history while you are still alive. So I wrote this novella, *The Bass Saxophone*.

T: As a sax player, did the story actually happen to you? Or was it invented?

SKVORECKY: The basic situation happened. Not to me but to a friend of mine, who was also a saxophone player, a baritone saxophone player. He was invited by a German band to play. It was not nearly as colourful as I made it in the story, of course, but this was a German band in my native town that performed for the German community. Their saxophone player got sick. My friend wanted to blow. So he grabbed at this opportunity to try out his skill.

T: And you grabbed at the opportunity to experiment. All those improvised solos in the writing make it an adventuresome book.

SKVORECKY: Yes, I think that's the book where I tried to achieve what I had always wanted to achieve, mainly to express music through words.

T: "If you haven't got too much talent and aren't equipped with absolute pitch, playing is always a pleasure." Are you describing yourself there?

SKVORECKY: Well, yes, I played on a very minor level. I never played well. I think I was rather awful as a

saxophonist. But I enjoyed it. It was in a student band. We just played the regular dance music of the day, swing music. Eventually I had to quit. I had problems in my breathing so I couldn't blow. Also I had not much opportunity in Prague. I became a writer and I moved in writers' circles. By that time swing was practically over and I knew I would never be able to play "bop" and things like that because it was too difficult. So I drifted out of it. When I realized I could never make it professionally as a musician, I started writing seriously.

T: The character in *The Bass Saxophone* speaks of life as being "a migration of failure."

SKVORECKY: Yes. That probably reflects on my state of mind in those days. On the one hand I was loved by the masses and on other hand the critics said, alright, he's good but he's passé. So there are elements of this state of mind that show in the story.

T: I was grateful for *The Swell Season* because it put me back in touch with my own adolescent feelings. When you also harkened back to your youth to write that book, did those stories wake you up again as an adult?

SKVORECKY: Well, yes, first of all I simply wanted to recreate those days. Many writers like to remember their young days because that's the period of life when your sensitivity is at its best. Things are new to you so everything comes fresh. That's why everybody remembers the first girl he loved. As you get older you develop a sort of crust. You may still fall in love at forty but it's not the same thing. That feeling of freshness, of novelty, of intensity, is reserved for the teens. So for me those stories were simply a joy to write. But also I technically wanted to write well-built stories, with a twist in the tale. I wanted to prove to myself that I could write a well-built, traditional, well-constructed, well-thought-out story with some surprise at the end.

T. As I get older I have some mixed feelings about the morality of the predatory chase. After all, the systematic seduction of a woman can be looked upon as an oppressive business. That book was striking to me because it reaffirmed the "goodness" of that youthful, male, predatory sexual instinct.

SKVORECKY: That's the primal urge and I think it's very healthy. Without it there would be no people. It's the human expression of a law of nature. The men are the aggressive part but the girls are not so innocent. Most of these so-called chases are really very welcome. It's clearly a game. These girls who refuse to have anything to do with Danny still encourage him. They don't close the doors right away. In the first story Irena invites him to her room, then tells him that they will discuss literature. Why? Why should she invite him into her private room to discuss literature? The males are the so-called active element and the girls are the so-called passive element but in many cases the passivity is really active. So it's both ways. I don't view this as anything moral or immoral. Danny just loves the girls and he has this urge to get one and he's unable to. It's simply normal. It's nature.

Audrey Thomas

AUDREY THOMAS was born in Binghamton, New York in 1935. She moved to BC after her marriage in 1958, received her MA from UBC in 1963 and accompanied her husband to Ghana (1964–66). Upon returning to Vancouver she published her first short story collection, *Ten Green Bottles* (1967), followed by *Ladies & Escorts* (1977), *Real Mothers* (1981), *Two in*

the Bush and Other Stories (1981) and *Goodbye Harold, Good Luck* (1986). Her mostly autobiographical novels and novellas are *Mrs. Blood* (1970), *Munchmeyer* (1971), *Prospero on the Island* (1971), *Songs My Mother Taught Me* (1973), *Blown Figures* (1974), *Latakia* (1979) and *Intertidal Life* (1984) for which she earned the first Ethel Wilson BC Book Prize.

She lives on Galiano Island, where she has maintained a cabin since 1969. She was interviewed in 1986.

T: You once said the challenge of people's lives is to organize one's pain. Are you getting your pain more organized as you grow older?

THOMAS: I've got my *craft* more organized, man! Mind you, I hope I don't avoid painful situations. I hope that I will never avoid painful situations.

T: What about what Eleanor Wachtel says in *Room Of One's Own* about the women in your books becoming saner and stronger?

THOMAS: Stronger, yes. But I hope they don't become saner.

T: Surely the more you become "craftsman-like," the more sanity creeps in. As you develop more objectivity.

THOMAS: Well, you know there's a lovely phrase in one of Malcolm Lowry's letters that I often relate to myself. It's raining and everything is wrong. He's really despondent. Maybe it's after his cabin has burned down. He says, "But cheerfulness is always creeping in." I've always loved that line. I feel that's really the story of my life. I'm basically quite a cheerful person. I'm hardly a depressive at all. People are usually very surprised when they meet me. Somebody once told me at a conference, "I never realized that you were funny."

T: Something I like about your work is what you call "quick language," and in order to have "quick language" you can hardly be a depressive.

THOMAS: Yes. And I'm getting less and less of a depressive as I get older. As I realize more and more that everybody's screwy. I'm not alone!

T: Speaking of not being alone— you've described Faulkner's fiction as "meticulous and outrageous at the same time." It struck me that's entirely appropriate for your writing, too.

THOMAS: Well, on that score I think I've learned a lot from the Australian novelist Patrick

White. He'll actually stop sentences in the middle, things like that. Tricks of emphasis. I didn't know prose writers could do that until I started reading White. I thought poets were the only ones who were allowed to be as meticulous as that.

T: At the same time there's an uninhibited, willing-to-be-unconventional quality to your prose that is quite overt.

THOMAS: Well, the novel is essentially a middle-class form. I know I'm not unique in saying that. The novel has a tradition of received morality behind it. And if you no longer believe in that—or if you believe there isn't any such collective morality in the society in which you live—then the novel is about breaking down all that. And the minute your novel is about breaking down, it's not a novel anymore. It's a book. I write books.

T: Looking at those "books," George Bowering has decided there is a huge difference between your short stories and your novels.

THOMAS: And that interested me. He thought I was more experimental in my novels. But he hadn't read *Goodbye Harold, Good Luck*. There are some very experimental stories in there.

T: For example, "The Man with Clam Eyes." It reminded me a little bit of Leonard Cohen. Just the way you were loading up the language and purposely not explaining things.

THOMAS: You know who that story reminds me of? Browning. I grew up on Browning and the idea of the dramatic monologue.

T: Where did that title come from? "The Man with Clam Eyes"?

THOMAS: I sometimes read manuscripts for the Canada Council. In one of them there was this typo. It said this man had "clam eyes." I was tired and I just thought, Jesus, what a strange image! It took me about an hour to realize it must have been a typo. Then David McFadden told me he has a poem that has a line "calm as a clam." The whole dramatic monologue got started from that.

T: When you first lived in Scotland at age twenty-six, you said "the ghosts talk." Given the changes, could you still get in tune with that romanticism in Scotland?

THOMAS: Oh, I think so. Especially in Orkney. I think the largest deposits of uranium in Britain are under the ground in Orkney. And yet they have this mythical landscape. It looks a lot like Saltspring Island. Very soft, rolling greenery. Meanwhile there's uranium underneath. It was interesting to see the romanticism and the reality together. They had big signs saying Keep Our Island Uranium Free. There's an uneasy truce with the government for the time being. Because it's so easy to feel the mysticism of that place, there's a lot of anger that they might think of mining the uranium. I happened to be there just after the cloud was passing from the Chernobyl nuclear plant disaster. The radiation levels were high. I was very aware of everything at stake there.

T: Chernobyl could turn out to be the best thing that ever happened to the twentieth century.

THOMAS: I know what you mean. I don't believe in God. But there was God's warning to us all.

T: Yes. Everybody on earth was touched by that accident. It was wonderful because for the first time it all went from theoretical to practical overnight. We have to stop having such blind faith in technology.

THOMAS: There is no god in the machine. It's madness. It's as though we have this terrible desire to kill ourselves. A death wish. I wanted to start a Lysistrata society. Have you ever seen that play? The women refuse to sleep with the men until they stop

waging war. That play is one of the great moral comedies. I'd like all the women of the world to become Lysistrata members. And they would not sleep with the men until disarmament takes place. We could put on the play everywhere. All across Canada on a particular day. Using the nuclear issue. Except you'd have too many women feeling it was unnatural.

T: You'd have to make it a Lysistrata Day. That way you'd get supportive publicity for it at first. All the male-dominated media wouldn't feel it was a real threat. They'd be willing to play it up. It would be good for ratings.

THOMAS: I'm really tempted to do it. It's the women who've got to stop this. We've got to prove to the men that they're the losers.

T: You've always participated in the Writers Union. You must welcome its new swing towards more political activism.

THOMAS: I do. I left the United States for political reasons. And for years I've been writing letters for Amnesty International. And I belong to PEN. So what am I doing sitting on my ass in Canada doing nothing politically? That's how the Writers Union can be important. I would never run for government because then I wouldn't write. I'm that selfish. I think intelligent women should run for politics and I think it's awful that more of us don't, but I'm not a good enough organizer. I've been on the executive of the Writers Union but I would never be the chairman. I'm not good at organization. I was good as a second vice-chairman, writing letters to Trudeau, sending telegrams, that sort of thing.

T: I know you're sensitive to the criticism that as a feminist you are not fully and overtly a feminist writer.

THOMAS: Yes.

T: But I feel that if you stop in a story to analyse language, as you do, that can be as progressive as anything on a more didactic scale.

THOMAS: I agree. When I point out the word other in mother, to me that's a political statement. Because mothers sometimes lose that sense that they are another person. Or the word harm in pharmacy. Because I think there are far too many drugs passed over the counter. Or the word over in lover. I certainly think there should be people who make direct political statements about inequities —

T: They're called politicians.

THOMAS: Or polemicists. Or else non-fiction writers. But it's just not my way of doing it. In a story, if I have a child turning a grapefruit around because she's terribly confused about saying which parent she's going to spend the next Christmas with, that's an image that I hope will stay in people's minds for when they're considering splitting up.

T: Since you've brought that up, the story of yours that had the most resonance for me was the one about the boy in Greece...

THOMAS: Oh, do you like that? That's one of my favourite stories.

T: I like it because it shows how children are instinctually sensitive and understanding of the adult sexual climate. They're affected by it. And that's such a huge area to be writing about.

THOMAS: The original impetus for that story came when my daughter Claire and I saw an incident on a Greek beach. A little boy found this octopus. He was very excited about it. He kept shouting, "I'm the one who found it. I'm the one who found it." Meanwhile there was this real jerk who used to strut around the beach in his Panama hat and his tiny bikini briefs. And he was very hairy. And he took the octopus away from the boy. And he started playing very sexual games with it which the boy didn't

understand. The boy was a little afraid of the octopus but he was certainly afraid of this man. And that's how the story started. Claire said, at the age of fifteen, "Hmmm, there's a story in that."

T: The boy's shyness about sexuality is quite convincing.

THOMAS: He's jealous of the blind man in the story because a blind man can look towards a woman with bare breasts and not feel embarrassed. I'd like to make a film out of that. There's too many films about young girls going into puberty. And not enough about young boys.

I've always been interested in boys, maybe because I don't have any. Boys are shy and modest, I think. Much more than girls. And they have reason to be. Because their bodies really betray them. So I made Edward, the boy in the story, around eleven or twelve. He's precocious and yet he literally doesn't know where to look. I thought this could make a good film if you keep it from the focus of Edward, who is always turning his head.

T: You mentioned to Eleanor Wachtel that you thought women have a lot of advantages over men...

THOMAS: Well, they can fake an orgasm for one thing. It was about ten years ago that that occurred to me. That that puts men at a terrible disadvantage. I think women have more control over their bodies in some ways. That story about Edward was the hardest story to write. It took me two years. But I really love that story.

T: I thought it was the most complex. Whereas some of the other stories strike me as being simply slices of life, reproduced.

THOMAS: Vitamin-enriched slices of life.

T: Well, putting it that way, I was intrigued to see how you rewrote your story "May Day" and "enriched" it with a second version called

"Mothering Sunday." But both versions about those two women in a restaurant made me think it was you and Alice Munro getting together...

THOMAS: That's very interesting. Alice and I do often have lunch together. And I do often write stories to her. Because we have the same kind of perverse sense of humour.

T: And you both have three daughters.

THOMAS: Yes. Two older, one younger.

T: And you both left husbands who fathered the daughters.

THOMAS: I didn't leave my husband. He left me. There is a difference. I'm the person who hangs on to the very end of things.

T: Well, anyway, I see Alice Munro as being very eastern, and you as being very western.

THOMAS: Even though I come from the east.

T: Yes. But the reason you came out to the west...

THOMAS: ...because I couldn't stand the east! That's true!

T: Whereas Alice Munro came out west for a while, and had to move back to the east.

THOMAS: It's interesting you've thought of this. I often write stories and I think, "Oh, Alice would like this story." I also think this is funny. Maybe she was there in that story in my head?

T: Now that you're an established writer, can you expect your money situation to change?

THOMAS: There's no such thing as an established writer until you've been put on a pedestal and you're dead.

THOMAS: Very few writers make that kind of money that puts them above the poverty line. That's why most of them teach. If you decide that your first commitment is to your family and your writing, if you're a single parent and you also write, and you

think that that's two full-time jobs right there, it's very, very hard. I really don't make money off my writing. But I know how to live minimally and I don't mind. I quite like it. It's a challenge. No, that's not true. Actually I don't like it. But it's a challenge.

T: What was the first story you ever sold?

THOMAS: It was about the seven-hundredth story I'd ever written. The *Atlantic* bought it. We were living in Africa at the time. They asked where they should send the cheque. It was a lot of money then. Five hundred dollars in 1965. I felt rather embarrassed to be discussing money so I wrote and said if we must speak about a sordid subject like money, don't send it to Ghana or we'll never get it. Put it in our Canadian bank account. I got a letter back almost immediately from Edward Weeks, the editor, saying, 'Get something straight right at the beginning. There's nothing sordid about money except the lack of it."

T: That's a good letter to keep.

THOMAS: I kept it for years. Then I moved and I lost it. I've always spent too much of my time adding up columns of figures. I never know what my income is from one month to the next. And I'm not one of those writers who is drawn to teaching.

T: I would think teaching would be a drain on creative energy.

THOMAS: It's exhausting.

T: It's exhausting, that is, if you do it with heart.

THOMAS: And if you're not going to do it with any heart, you just become cynical.

T: Despite the struggles, you sound as if you're very glad that you went ahead and had your children at a relatively young age.

THOMAS: Yes! We didn't debate it. I think it's harder for women now. Our kids are almost grown up and we're still relatively young. It's a wonderful feeling. I feel like my daughters are three of my very best friends. We all get on really well. I can be who I am rather than the mother.

T: Although you can still play the mother role when it's required...

THOMAS: You're not playing. You are it. They still call me Mum. I'm not crazy about children calling me by my first name. My children. Occasionally they call me Audrey. But I am their mother after all.

T: You're out of synch.

THOMAS: I was walking down the street with a couple of guys from the *New Edinburgh Review.* One said something like, "Do you feel like an alien in Edinburgh?" And I said, "All my life I've felt like I'm not in the right town." I feel comfortable being an alien. I feel comfortable on Galiano.

But in terms of society, I've never felt right. I've usually been out of synch.

T: How do you mean?

THOMAS: My mother kept giving me Tony home permanents because she wanted me to have curly hair. Curly hair was "in." Then it became straight hair. My hair was wavy. It won't straighten. When I was a teenager, Marilyn Monroe boobs were in. And I was really skinny, if you can believe it. Then when people were really skinny, I was nursing my children. I had children when I was a graduate student. Now everybody's having children it seems. I was never in fashion. But that sort of thing no longer bothers me.

T: Well, I think it's quite fashionable to be the author of eleven worthwhile books.

THOMAS: So do I.

Michel Tremblay

MICHEL TREMBLAY was born in Montreal in 1942. He is Quebec's and possibly Canada's foremost playwright. His early plays such as *Forever Yours, Marie-Lou* (1971), *Les Belles-Soeurs* (1972), *Hosanna* (1973) and *Bonjour la, Bonjour* (1974) helped ignite the rebirth of indigenous Quebecois culture. While he continues to write for theatre, Tremblay has also turned to

novels about the neighborhood in which he was raised, commencing with *The Fat Woman Next Door is Pregnant* (1978/translated 1981). His work is readily available in English and his plays are produced around the world.

Michel Tremblay lives in Montreal. He was interviewed in 1979.

T: Will there always be a strong link between the power of any government in Québec and the presence of the Catholic Church?

TREMBLAY: Probably. But it's very strange what I feel about the Catholic religion. In a way they helped to keep the French language in Québec. But they screwed up everything else. I always say the Catholic religion is horrible but they kept us French. Women and priests kept us French.

T: Can you differentiate between the reactions of francophone audiences and anglophone audiences?

TREMBLAY: They're just the same. It's very gratifying to know that the basic things I want to say come across. All that is lost in English is the folklore and the *joual.* I always say I hope Chekhov is better in Russian, but it's not a reason not to produce him in English and French. An author that would be better in translation would be an author with big problems.

T: Maybe your plays translate well because most of your characters communicate best with anger, which is pretty universal.

TREMBLAY: Yes, but not in my novel, *La Grosse Femme.* That's a big difference for me between novels and plays. Theatre is only people talking. But in the novel I am the narrator. When the characters talk they can be as mad as they are if they're on stage. But in between there is me talking about them and I can show I love them.

T: Is that the main reason you're moving into novels? Because you want to be more compassionate with your characters?

TREMBLAY: Yes. The reason I wrote *La Grosse Femme* was basically to tell the public that I love these characters. I have been much accused the past eleven years of hating them. I love them very much. So I wrote a novel to tell people that I love them.

Perhaps that's why it's so successful.

T: It was given a first printing in Québec of forty thousand copies. Is there a temptation to alter your work as you become more and more aware of its potential audience?

TREMBLAY: No, I don't think so. Since I know years in advance what I want to write, that cannot be changed. I'm very stubborn and cold-headed in that area. Nobody can change what I want. Even before *La Grosse Femme* was published I knew two other novels were coming. Even if the reviews for *La Grosse Femme* had been very bad or even if people had not read it, I would still write those books. Because I need them.

T: Why?

TREMBLAY: Well, what happened was that I realized, after having written *Damnée Manon, Sacrée Sandra,* that I didn't have anything else to say. It was very clear. That was the end of something. So when I finished I said, "Oh my god, here I am thirty-three or thirty-four years old and I don't have anything else to say." So I went on TV and I said, "Hey, people, wait for me. I want to try something else. Please do wait for me."

T: Was that "end of something" in *Damnée Manon, Sacrée Sandra* when the two characters tell the public that they were invented by a small child named Michel?

TREMBLAY: Yes, that's on a public level. I tried to say to people in *Damnée Manon,* please, after eleven years you thought that what I said was the truth but look, I'm just a mere child trying to say things. What I say is not *the* version of *the* reality. It's my own vision. It's art, it's theatre, it's not the real thing. You pay your ticket to see actors earning their living saying lines written by a boy named Michel.

I never wanted anybody to think I was telling the truth. I was telling some kind of truth. When I come to the theatre and I see actors trying to tell me that they are real characters, I don't like it. That's why, when I write plays, you never forget it's a show.

T: But there is truth in your work. There's always the emphasis that people must "take action" against their repression.

TREMBLAY: Sure. When you go home from the theatre you don't just go to sleep and snore. You think about what you saw. Hopefully what you saw will make you do something about what is happening in real society. That's what theatre is about. Theatre is there not only to entertain. We are there to change the world. I'm telling people this is what society looks like now. If you want it that way, that's okay with me. But don't you think you should do something to change something somewhere?

When I sit every morning at my table I don't say hey, this morning I'm going to write a masterpiece. People used to think like that. Now the notion of a masterpiece in Québec is vanishing. We think, let's be useful.

T: Is that one of the reasons you wrote *Damnée Manon, Sacrée Sandra*? Because once your notoriety becomes so great, people start looking at your work in terms of masterpieces and not in terms of its usefulness?

TREMBLAY: Not as masterpieces but as the truth. I just wanted to help people realize that theatre is only theatre.

When we do a show in Montreal with my director, André Brassard, there is always something at the beginning of the play which says it's only a play. For instance, at the beginning of *Bonjour la, Bonjour* the last time we did it, the eight actors came on stage and Serge said, "Lights, please." Nobody in the house forgot that. Some people were asking why we did that. But it was for people to say,

oh yeah, they're actors. That's very Brechtian and very useful.

T: Yet you purposely don't give any explicit directions in terms of production for your plays.

TREMBLAY: None at all. I decided a few years ago that I would write for intelligent directors. Because I'm not a very visual man. I hear my characters very much. That's why it's so musical. I don't see them at all. That's why I don't like stage directions. I would direct my own plays if I put stage directions. Like I think Eugene O'Neill is one of the greatest geniuses in theatre in the twentieth century, but I hate reading him. There are more stage directions than actual dialogue.

T: Carmen in *Forever Yours, Marie-Lou* says, "I'd rather be a whore on la rue St. Laurent than an old maid playing with candles." Why don't you ever give your characters a chance to live on middle ground?

TREMBLAY: Because it's theatre. Life can't be grey on stage. It's got to be black or white. There's no middle ground in the theatre because theatre is there to announce, to say things. The basic problems are always all black or all white.

For instance, in the second act of *St. Carmen of the Main* there is a girl who is a western singer and she wants to talk to the people about themselves instead of only yodelling. Her manager wants her to continue yodelling. That scene is very black and white.

T: Some people might argue that black and white isn't real. That a mixture gives balance.

TREMBLAY: If you mix black and white together you get grey. Grey is horrible. Black and white gives life. If you wear something white or black with another colour, the white or black will give life to the rest of you. If you wear grey, it will kill everything. I hate grey!

T: That would account for your going

from early surrealism in your teens to the point where the political allegory in *La Grosse Femme* is very direct.

TREMBLAY: Yes...I wrote that experimental book, *Stories for Late Night Drinkers*, when I was seventeen years old. I was still believing that anything that was Québécois was vulgar and ugly. I was raised like every young Québécois thinking that you couldn't talk about Montreal or Québec City in a song or book. So when I began writing I never dreamed of talking about myself.

Then one day the flash struck me that I was born to write about my country. I was twenty-three years old.

T: Tell me about that day.

TREMBLAY: One afternoon I was with André Brassard. We used to go to the movies every afternoon because he didn't work and I was working at nights. There were quite a few Québécois movies at that time and there was something in them that I didn't like. I didn't know why. Then one afternoon, schlack!, we were sitting side by side looking at a film and it struck me. I realized only the characters on that film talked that language. Nobody else in the world talked like that. It was not Québécois. It was not French. It was some kind of in-between, romanticized Québécois.

I said to André, I think I'm going to try to write a sketch in which two old maids will come back from a funeral parlour. I would just write like people talk. Nobody did that. Three days later I had fifteen characters. Two months later *Les Belles-Soeurs* was written.

T: Does your best work usually come so spontaneously?

TREMBLAY: I'm not spontaneous at all. I'm not the kind of writer who jumps on napkins, writing notes. I keep everything in my head for months, sometimes even years. I have fits with my characters. I make love with them. I yell with them. They yell at me for years. It's the best part. I don't like sitting at my table writing that much. It's my trade and I like it, but the process before is much more invigorating. For instance, it took me four years before I wrote a single word of *St. Carmen of the Main*. Then it took me two weeks to write.

T: So the actual writing is almost secondary.

TREMBLAY: Yes. I could write dialogue forever. Because I'm good at it. know I'm good at it. I could write for TV and be paid five thousand dollars to write half an hour. But I don't like TV. It would be very easy to get out of politics and to sit on my big ass and just make money. But I refused $210,000 to write twenty-one half hours at ten thousand dollars each. I wanted to write my new play and my new novel.

I don't want to make a hero out of myself. It's just a choice of liberty over money.

T: As you personally gain more freedom, isn't there a danger that you may lose touch with your subject matter?

TREMBLAY: I did in a way. And since I'm very honest, I'm writing now a play about the bourgeoisie in Québec. Because I lost contact with the working class completely. I know perfectly everything about the forties, the fifties and the sixties, but I don't know anything about the working class in the seventies. I'm not abandoning them. I'm living other things.

I'm living now in Outrement. I have a big house and somehow people understand that you live somewhere else. I make a lot of money. It's great. So I would be a son-of-a-bitch if I bought a house in eastern Montreal and disguised myself as a poor man. I have the honesty of saying I'm rich. I bought a big house. I'm very happy in that house. It's just plain honesty.

T: As Leopold says, "There's nothing in the world worse than a steady job." Does a person have to be a masochist in order to work at a nine-to-five job for forty years?

TREMBLAY: Probably. It's horrible to think that people will do the same gestures two thousand times every day for forty years. And then go and watch TV at night like the women in *Les Belles-Soeurs*.

But then we're four billion people on earth. Someone has to work, I know that. I was a linotypist myself. In my head, Leopold was always a linotypist but I didn't say it in the play. Because I was a linotypist for three-and-a-half years of my life. And they were the worst. I know what it is to have a steady job.

T: Which is probably why you're so strongly against people who live conventional lives. You resent being held back in that position.

TREMBLAY: It's a question of sensibility. No, not sensibility...ah...

T: Temperament?

TREMBLAY: Yes, temperament. Probably some linotypists just can't understand how somebody can sit at a table and just write.

T: Reading your plays chronologically, I thought a tenderness surfaced in *Bonjour la, Bonjour* that was missing in your earlier plays.

TREMBLAY: Yes, *Bonjour* was the first one in which tenderness came. Because of the love between Serge and Nicole and because of the father.

T: I wondered if that play was a result of experiences you might have had handling the social stigma of being gay?

TREMBLAY: Yes, it was the first time I was talking about myself. That relationship between Serge and his father is exactly like my relationship with my father. He was deaf too. And I was raised by women. I felt I needed to go to my father and say I love you.

But I couldn't do that. North American society kept me from doing that.

T: What was your father's reaction to that play?

TREMBLAY: He was still deaf! He came on opening night and he didn't hear anything! My two brothers who were there just cried their guts out.

My father read the play after. He never talked to me about it but somehow I felt the message came across. He was seventy years old, okay, but why couldn't I just do it? I could never do it. I could never, never do it.

It's very strange, North America. There are basic needs which you don't have the right to fulfill.

T: Did you also want to tell your father you were gay?

TREMBLAY: I told him in my plays. He saw *La Duchesse le Langeais* and *Hosanna*. But I couldn't talk with him. That came from him because he raised me. That came from his part of society.

T: Did you grow up with as much sexual guilt as your characters?

TREMBLAY: Like anybody in the fifties and sixties in a way, I lived a double life of ten years, maybe. Because I knew I was gay when I was thirteen. I began doing things then. When I found a way to express myself I went all the way. I eventually said it's much simpler to tell people what you are and how you are and how nice it is instead of how monstrous it is.

As I was trying to help people get out of shit in *Les Belles-Soeurs* I was trying to help myself, too. Instead of leading a double life and going out with girls and never sleeping with them and having them suffer, I decided why don't I let people know? It's so simple.

T: I'd be interested to hear your opinion of the movie *Outrageous* which purported to depict the Toronto gay club scene.

TREMBLAY: It was outrageous,

funny, and not one bit intelligent.

T: Too much titillating voyeurism for liberals?

TREMBLAY: Well, people say that about me, too. Gay people say that about *Hosanna*. Gay critics, I mean. There was not one single gay reviewer who wrote a good review of *Hosanna*. They all loved *Outrageous* but they say *Hosanna* was a farce. But *Hosanna* was not about homosexuality. *Hosanna* was not at all about the life of a drag queen with his lover.

T: It's about self-acceptance.

TREMBLAY: Yes, it's a psychological strip-tease.

T: Maybe those gay critics weren't judging on the quality of art so much as the extent to which the art can help them be accepted more readily by the rest of society.

TREMBLAY: That's it. Because I love my marginality. I don't want gays to be accepted by society at all. It doesn't interest me. I don't want to be a straight couple with another man. I resign that. But this is what gay people are fighting for. I can understand that if somebody works in a bank and wants to lead a nice simple life with his lover. But not for me. I want to be a marginal. I love being a marginal.

T: So gays are sacrificing gayness for conventionality.

TREMBLAY: And it's very sad. It will kill whatever is alive in being gay. I don't care about going on the street hand in hand with my lover. I would do it anyway.

T: In a book called *Gay Sunshine Interviews* most of the major gay American writers who were interviewed mentioned how they were finally establishing permanent relationships after age forty.

TREMBLAY: That's because they're afraid they're not beautiful any more. That whole macho thing is so horrible. Society is just making soldiers out of gay people now. They're all becoming men with big moustaches. They are being drafted by society. And in a few years they'll be in Vietnam or somewhere killing poor Viet Cong.

T: They're being drafted by society because society realizes there's a great deal of money to be made from gay people.

TREMBLAY: Sure. They buy things. They are rich and they don't have families. They are very useful to the moneymakers.

It's horrible. When you go to a gay bar, everybody's dressed the same. The same moustache. The same hair. The same shirt. My god, it's soldiers again. The disco music is very military, too. I freak out. I haven't been in a gay bar for years because I just fell like unplugging everything. I want to tell them, "Go to the army if that's what you want. You'll be with men and you'll be very happy. And you'll have real guns."

Peter Trower

PETER TROWER was born at St. Leonard's-on-Sea, England, in 1930. He immigrated to British Columbia at age ten, following the death of his test-pilot father in a plane crash. His mother married a West Coast pulp mill superintendent who drowned soon after. Trower quit school to work in logging camps for over two decades. Poetry collections like *Moving*

Through the Mystery (1969), *Between the Sky and the Splinters* (1974) and *The Alders and Others* (1969) express his admiration and resentment at the magisterial power of nature. *Ragged Horizons* (1978) is a Trower anthology. In recent years he has turned increasingly to prose memoirs and non-fiction.

Peter Trower lives and writes full time in Gibsons, BC. He was interviewed in 1978.

T: When did somebody start taking notice of your poetry?

TROWER: I met Al Purdy in 1972. We cut up in the Marble Arch Hotel one time. We were drunk and playing pool. Purdy can't play pool worth a damn. And I don't even try any more. So the balls were flying off the table. It had nothing to do with literature. We were just drunk in a bar.

T: You more or less had to drop out of school to go and work. Do you think your life would have been different if there had been more money around and you could have gone to a university?

TROWER: Yes, like if World War Two hadn't happened I might have gone to Oxford or something. All my family have followed tremendously traditional paths. But the way things went down I ended up in this weird maverick situation.

T: Do you think you could have been an academic?

TROWER: No, I think I would have blown it sooner or later. I would have been an angry young man or something. I would have been involved in some haywire trip. I couldn't have stuck that stuffy nonsense. I enjoy maverick situations. It's like all the best writers in the world have been mavericks. Like Purdy. Or even Earle Birney, falling out a bloody tree at seventy-two years old . . .

T: Have there been special people for you in the way of influences?

TROWER: I used to read a lot and never paid much attention to style. I read Ray Bradbury. Early Bradbury fantasy stories were full of poetic imagery. Bradbury's a lousy poet but he writes good prose. It's peculiar. His book of poetry is absolutely rotten. But he was grinding stuff out for cheap pulp magazines using poetic imagery. So I began to become aware of science fiction. I had wall-to-wall science fiction stories. I read every science fiction magazine there was and I never read anything else. Then one day I woke up and the real world was still there.

T: It seems to me that some of that sci-fi has rubbed off into your poetry in that you have this mystical sense of the powers of the forest. It's not quite science fiction but you're very aware that there's another world there.

TROWER: It's what the Indians already know.

T: Exactly. Like at the close of "The Animals" you say "As the day dwindled/ the season took aim on us/ and the animals knew." Then again there's another bit in "Booby Trap" where you're falling a tree and it just misses killing you. You say, "around us the woods hiss disappointment."

TROWER: I've heard some strange stuff happening with guys falling trees. There's a story I haven't written about yet. I came to this camp and a guy had been killed just a couple of weeks before. He got pinned between the butt of a tree and the stump. He was a very tidy guy. As he was dying, because he was already cut in half, he took out all his ID and put it all out on the edge of the tree that killed him. When they finally found this guy all bust open, there was no blood on any of his ID.

T: Do you usually write from an incident like that or does it come from a phrase that sparks you?

TROWER: I write totally from real life. I don't build words from words. Like there's a poem in *Ragged Horizons* about a little girl dying of cancer. That comes right out of a heavy-duty real experience. It was unbelievably heavy. For years I couldn't even write about it. But I thought, dammit, I better write about it . . . The first poem I ever wrote that was any good was "Grease for the Wheels of Winter." I was just trying to describe leaving the camps. It was a heavy thing because they'd been my life. It was always where I ran away to when nothing went right. The danger incidence was starting to close in on me. It was like I better quit this before I get killed.

T: Do you ever take your poems and songs to the camps and read to working-class guys?

TROWER: I haven't done it yet. I've often wondered about that. The young dudes might like it, but some of those old guys might think I was some kind of smartass. I made this film a few years ago called *Between the Sky and the Splinters* when we went into a logging camp called Jackson Bay. I had to act in this film. All my life I've been waking in bunkhouses, putting on cork boots. This time I woke in the morning, and instead of being a logger I was an actor. It was weird. The guys in the camp started looking at me like I was some phoney-baloney. I'd come back to play the part of myself when I was young in a logging camp where they were doing it for real. I went through some funny head changes.

T: You mentioned earlier that you're going to move uptown now. what do you mean by that?

TROWER: I mean, man, I'm going to maybe quit being broke. But I ain't going to change my way of living. I don't like staying in fancy hotels with a bunch of smartass TV people. I'll stay around here, or the Marble Arch or the Cecil.

T: Where did the title *Ragged Horizons* come from?

TROWER: It's just a title. I thought certain mountains I've seen look like they've ripped through the sky. And also I thought of being raggedy-assed in the street. It's a double trip. But if I think about all that it means I can't explain it. I don't know, many times I thought I would never make it. Like that suicide poem about the Marble Arch is a true poem. There ain't

nothing in that book that's BS. There's no place in that book where I can't drag out some old dude from the past to verify it. That's what scares them back east. Mostly back there it's games-playing.

T: In "Kisses in the Whiskey" you wish you "could be that ignorant again/ embark on some old sopho-moric fling/ far too callow to understand/ that life is other than a Friday thing." Does that bother you, that you feel like you've gone beyond your youth?

TROWER: Not really. I can look back at myself walking down the street when I was nineteen and I was stupid. Very naïve. But I ain't even finished growing up yet. Anybody who thinks they have is really dead. Everybody's just a kid growing old.

T: What was it like when you were young in Vancouver?

TROWER: It was heavy. Maybe it's just as bad now but it's not organized. There were actual kid gangs. You could get in trouble just by walking into the Marble Arch Hotel at the wrong time. In those days it was more structured. There was a book called *The Amboy Dukes* and everybody was copying that. Big rumbles with gangs from the next district. It was heavy, even though it was all bogus.

T: Were you a real part of that scene?

TROWER: I was always an observer, sort of neutral. In those days I couldn't talk to anyone. It was a redneck era. I used to go to bars, man, and sit down at a table but all people could talk about was hockey games and work. Boring stuff, I'd get so bored, man, I'd just OD on beer and slide under the table.

T: Are you ambitious for yourself?

TROWER: I want the books to sell. I put everything I got behind them. I can still write from the gut. I hope I don't get soft and start writing from the mind. I went through that once but it all came out crap. I have to use experience. I've read a hundred books of poetry by people who purport to know what's going on in the universe. It's just a bunch of fakery. I'm just fed up with academic trips by people who think they know what's going on. Nobody knows what's going on.

If you said I had a fierce drive for success, it would be true. I've wanted to make it but I kept getting kicked in the face.

T: Does a poem happen for you in an hour or in a couple of days?

TROWER: It can take twenty years. That poem "Atlantic Crossing" took twenty years. I couldn't get it across because a lot of what I write about is melodramatic in the material itself.

T: So that's one of the key things about your poetry then —

TROWER: Right. The hardest thing is to get the balance between melodrama and reality. If you go over the edge with melodrama, as I frequently have, you end up with Robert Service. Someone once told me I was a cross between Dylan Thomas, Robert Service and William Burroughs. I don't know.

T: Which of your poems do you think will outlive the other ones?

TROWER: "Grease for the Wheels of Winter." Maybe "The Last Spar-Tree." I guess they'll stand because nobody else has said those things.

T: The one that struck me was "The Animals."

TROWER: That's the one Purdy liked. Purdy and I were sitting in the Arch and he said, Jesus. Like I blew his mind or something. A lot of poets write to be heavy or intellectual. I write directly for communication. I'm trying to communicate to the world. I've read so much that's pure BS. People who purport to know more than other people are liars and fakers. Look what happened to Ezra Pound. He died in his own intellectual garbage. T.S. Eliot died of dry-rot. The answers aren't in going to university for a million years and getting endless doctorates and never facing the world. Going to UBC I feel like I'm entering another country. You go into the faculty lounge and it's a weird place, man. These people work on a different wavelength than me. I don't understand their trip. They've never been out and scuffled. They've never had the crap kicked out of them. They don't know anything about the real world... And you can quote me on that. I got the boondog universe.

W.D. Valgardson

W.D. VALGARDSON was born in Winnipeg in 1939. He passed most of his childhood in Gimli, Manitoba, a hardy fishing community that emphasized his Icelandic-Canadian roots. He received his MFA in creative writing from the University of Iowa in 1969 and currently teaches at the University of Victoria. A poet and scriptwriter, Valgardson is best known for his

bestselling fiction collections, *Bloodflowers* (1973), *God is Not a Fish Inspector* (1975) and *Red Dust* (1978). His first novel, *Gentle Sinners* (1980), earned the Books in Canada First Novel Award and became a successful film. More complex than his dramatic short stories, Valgardson's novel is about a country boy learning to interpret the danger signs for surviving town corruption and adulthood.

W.D. (William Dempsey) Valgardson lives in Victoria. He was interviewed in 1981.

T: The schoolteacher in your story "Beyond Normal Requirements" says, "Tragedy is all around us. We must get to know it so we can guard ourselves against it." Is that a fair explanation of why you write?

VALGARDSON: Yes. I would say that really sums it up. I think there is a real danger in not looking at things. Mostly yourself. For instance, I believe in the rather Jungian statement that North Americans will never deal in a successful way with the Russians until they deal with the Russians within themselves.

T: So has Bill Valgardson dealt with the Russian within himself?

VALGARDSON: I've spent a long, long time confronting what a Jungian would call my shadow. I've recorded hundreds and hundreds and hundreds of dreams. I've accepted the fact that I'm capable of any crime.

T: Goethe once said exactly the same thing.

VALGARDSON: Yes, it's particularly important for writers. I tell my students that there are two journeys that every writer must take. The first journey is into the lives of others. But the second journey is the most terrifying. It is the journey into the self. I think what happens with a lot of people is that they turn away. They suddenly become aware of their motivations and they realize some of the things they are capable of. They don't understand that just because they're capable of something, they don't have to do it.

T: *Gentle Sinners* began with a dream you had, a dream that became the final scene in the book. How did you know enough to trust that dream?

VALGARDSON: It was just the intensity with which it came. You see, I believe in sitting down and writing out of emotion. I don't know where I'm going. For me writing is like an Eskimo carving. The form is in the stone. The trick is for me to find the form. And so it's a case of exploration. I write to discover what I think. I don't think and then write. If you think and then write, you often get propaganda.

For instance, I think one of the worst things any writer can do is impose symbols. That's a dreadful thing, to nail them on. It should be like driftwood. You don't nail the knots on. The water washes and erodes and what's left are these hard knobs. That is the way that symbols should be. They should rise out of the material naturally. Then you go back over your material and see what you've got. Then you heighten it. You see connections. Because one's genius is often in spots. It's not necessarily coherent all the way through. So you try to make it coherent. It's like painting. You add touches.

T: Your characters aren't analytical and you are. Do you feel that people who lack that analytical sense are more prone to tragedy?

VALGARDSON: ...I think that people who lack that analytical sense are often drawn into tragedy like people who are drawn into a vortex. Like a helpless swimmer in a whirlpool who is only cast out by luck. But there's a danger on the other side and that is to be like Hamlet. To be so analytical that one no longer can act. I think that always what one is doing is searching for balance.

T: Is that how you've changed over the years? You've become more balanced?

VALGARDSON: Good god, how have I changed? That would take years to answer! I think maybe I've become more perceptive. And I think I've become much more accepting of other people. I can be pretty intolerant. You see, I was brought up Missouri Lutheran. I cannot say, with any sense of honesty, that the Christianity I was brought up with in any way made me into a better person.

T: Many of your stories seem to strip people of the frills of life. The characters are put into situations where they must make a difficult choice. Usually it's a choice of animal survival, of practicality.

VALGARDSON: Given the environment, yes. Where I grew up was for a long time a kind of Appalachia of Canada. People were very, very poor. And also the emotional choices people had were incredibly restricted. When Icelanders moved to Ontario from Iceland, in one year every child under the age of four died. There was nothing to be done. The helplessness and the rage got trapped inside a group of people for whom stoicism was the ultimate virtue.

The poverty, the foreignness, the displacement from an ocean environment, a sense of loss of identity, an idealization of the past — all those things went towards creating a society in which there weren't very many choices. So people were living, in a sense, at a pretty primitive level.

T: So what was it like to grow up in Gimli, Manitoba?

VALGARDSON: My father was a commercial fisherman who also had a barbershop. My mother was a housewife. She was seventeen when I was born, my father was twenty-two. My mother's parents were Irish from Ireland. Everybody thinks of me as being Icelandic, but that's only part of the picture.

It was smalltown country living in the 1940s and 1950s. Rural Canada in those days seemed to me an incredibly good time and I had the kind of parents who were always taking us on picnics in the summer. Gimli is a beautiful place in the summer. A kid could spend the evenings playing tin-can cricket or going fishing at the dock. I got my first rifle when I was twelve. It was one of the high points of my life. I had my own snare line. I loved it. It was a wonderful life. And in the winter we spent an awful lot of time skating on the lake or skating at the rink.

T: Why did you need to become a writer?

VALGARDSON: Well, I grew up in an environment in which an awful lot of emphasis was placed on physical strength and being big. People made livings as farmers and fishermen and they required tremendous physical stamina. I'm all of five-seven, five-eight. I'm slightly built, light. And with poor eyesight. In prairie towns, the way to succeed and have power and be admired is to be good at hockey and football and be able to fight. I obviously don't fit those categories.

I was a dreamer and a reader. At some stage I obviously learned that you can fight with words. You can lay people wide open with words! You might have to learn to run like hell after you've said what you said . . . but I think there's a lot of people who become lawyers for that reason. And politicians. And writers.

T: So there's an element of revenge in success.

VALGARDSON: Yes. Now I love winning contests. I'm very, very aware of the fact that when I do win something, who I'm winning for isn't Bill Valgardson, Associate Professor. I'm winning for the guy who always got chosen last for the baseball team. When you're in school and you're the best pitcher in the grade seven class, what is so wonderful about it is that one is admired. That's the wonderful thing about being an adult and being fortunate enough to be a writer or a painter or whatever. Most people go into jobs and nobody ever knows what you do. You file stuff or something. This other kind of job means you still continue to be admired.

T: What were your ambitions as a

kid? Were you always interested in being a writer?

VALGARDSON: Not really. I don't particularly remember having great aspirations. When I was sixteen I got a job in a warehouse in Winnipeg, unloading boxcars. I did that for five summers. It never occurred to me to go to university.

In those days people didn't just go to university. It was for the doctor's son or the dentist's son. I was busy working at the warehouse when a bunch of these city kids, who were much more sophisticated than me, came in with their grades one day. Everybody was showing everybody else their grades. They were all going to university. I looked and I thought, "Jeez, my grades are higher than anybody's here." It was a real shocker.

T: So it was off to United College.

VALGARDSON: No. I went to the University of Manitoba the first year and that was a disaster. It was a bloody disaster. It was the wrong place for me. I didn't know that most country kids went off to United College because it was smaller. I was plunged from a small country school where we didn't have a real library into this huge university with classes of two hundred people. I'm sure it was a perfectly good university. It just wasn't the right place for me. The next year I went to United College and that was much better.

T: Were you writing stories by this time?

VALGARDSON: In third year I joined the Creative Writing Club and began to write poetry. I wrote a tremendous amount of poems. Finally somewhere I actually did write a short story and it got published in an Icelandic-Canadian magazine. I also got married in my third year. It was a real scandal in those days to get married so young. I went off teaching high school on a permit. By that time I was really writing a lot, evenings and weekends, while I was teaching high school.

Teaching high school was wonderful at first because I got a chance to learn all the things I'd missed when I was a student. I mean, I didn't know any grammar, didn't know any punctuation. But I had to teach it. So you have to learn. Gerunds and participles and commas. I've talked to a lot of teachers and heard the same thing. At first they learn more than the students.

T: You said "wonderful at first."

VALGARDSON: Yes. After I got my teaching certificate I went and taught art full time at the Transcona Collegiate. That was baptism by fire. The low man on any totem is the art teacher. I didn't know that. I went from there up north to Snow Lake to teach. That was a very good year. Except that the only people paid the same amount of money as the teachers were the garbagemen. And the miners earned double the money that the teachers and the garbagemen were making. The prices in the town were controlled by the two stores. Everything was so expensive. By that time we had two kids. I ended up with a severe case of scurvy by the end of the year. We didn't know what it was. Because we were feeding the kids and we were skipping things for ourselves... You couldn't get fresh milk. Fruit juice was so expensive you just gave it to the kids.

When I went to Snow Lake it was the end of the world, up in the bush. I was still writing. I managed to get a story in *Alphabet* with James Reaney. The name James Reaney didn't mean anything to me at the time. And *Fiddlehead* took a story. I very wisely realized my deficiencies. I wrote away to the University of North Dakota for correspondence courses. I took those courses for the next couple of years. Things like grammar, composition and feature article writing. They were wonderful courses.

T: How did you end up studying writing in the States?

VALGARDSON: Are you into romantic stories? I'll give you a couple of romantic stories.

When I went to teach in Pinowa, two very important things happened. I was in the library one day and I came across a book by an author I'd never heard of before named Al Purdy. It was *Cariboo Horses*. Every writer I've talked to has had this kind of experience where they have suddenly been given permission to be Canadian. And Al Purdy did that for me with *Cariboo Horses*. For the first time I realized I didn't have to be T.S. Eliot or Ernest Hemingway. I didn't have to be an Englishman or an American. It was okay to write like a Canadian with Canadian content. As a Canadian, what I had to say and what I had to talk about were important. It was like a logjam bursting. At university we had only studied English and American literature, so there was a whole denial of who you were. I had been trying to write "The Wasteland" for years. Suddenly I was writing a dozen poems a day.

The next thing that happened was that I was ordering books for the school library when I came across a book on how to write by Paul Engel. I'd never heard of him or the University of Iowa but it said he was the director of the Creative Writing program there. Hell, a Creative Writing program! I'd never heard of such a thing in Canada. That was like Underwater Basketweaving.

I had all these poems. And in the meantime I had sold every lesson from the correspondence course in feature article writing. So I had this coalescing of success. That was tremendous adrenalin. So I bundled up all these poems to send them to Paul Engel. But

I was so bashful that when I went down to the mail I didn't mail them. I went through this three times. Finally one day I went down there, closed my eyes at the mail slot and shoved it in. Nothing happened. A month went by. Two months went by. I thought, "Famous people like that get all kinds of people writing. Who is going to reply to a Canadian living on an island in a forest reserve?" One day this envelope came. I'd got a whole bunch of crap in the mail that day, advertisements and stuff, and this looked like an advertisement. I threw the whole goddam thing in the garbage. As I was going out the door I thought, "Jesus, I shouldn't do that." I walked back, looked through it more carefully. I opened it. It wasn't from Paul Engel. It was a letter from George Starbuck, the Yale poet. In typical American fashion they said they really liked the poetry, we've accepted you for graduate work, we've obtained a half-time teaching position even though you haven't asked for it, but we figured you're married so you're probably going to need it, when are you arriving?

That to me is typically American. That's what I love about the Americans. That whole enthusiastic quality that if you want to do it, do it. As opposed to the Canadian defeatist attitude that has certainly existed in the past on the academic level. You'd never get Canadians getting a strange letter and responding like that. I mean, they enrolled me, they got me a job and said when are you coming?

T: So in Iowa you learned your craft. What about style? Do you see where yours comes from?

VALGARDSON: No, I don't think so. I have all these pet theories but I think that if you learn from other writers you never have to worry about becoming a copy of them. I think everybody goes through romances with other writers. You love Hemingway, you love Updike. But ultimately, time is like water. It erodes. What I learned from Updike was to really love the complex sentence. What I learned from Hemingway was to love the simple sentence. What I learned from both of them was to love an eye for detail and yet both of them use totally different details. From Jane Austen I learned to love a complexity of structure from what appears to be an easily told tale. And from Hardy, a love of description.

T: I see similarities between the world view of Hardy and your own.

VALGARDSON: Except I don't believe in fate as a determiner the way he does.

T: There's a poem of Hardy's to the effect "if only there was a God to blame all this on."

VALGARDSON: Well, I don't know that particular poem but let me give you mine. "If God is a white-haired and bearded old man, when I get to the gates of heaven or hell I'm going looking for him with a six-shooter." Maybe in the end one does not assign blame for all the suffering in the world. But if there is an old man with a white beard, I'm going looking for him.

I think my mother said recently she has now gone to my step-grandmother's fourteen times to get together before going to the church for a funeral. In one summer when I was six the baby in the family died, my grandfather died and my great-grandfather died. Two of my great-uncles were drowned on a boating trip for a picnic. Eight years ago my brother, who was first mate on a boat on the Mackenzie River, was working on a forklift and went over the side of

the barge and was trapped inside, couldn't get out. Left a wife and two little children.

T: When you were confronted with death as a boy, did you have resources to help you deal with that?

VALGARDSON: No.

T: So is there a connection there to the earlier quote about the need to recognize tragedy?

VALGARDSON: Sure. It hasn't been until very recently that you have academics studying death and the needs of the survivors and what needs to be done to help people cope. Even well-intentioned people wanting to help often weren't helpful. Even today, it's amazing. You have a death and people say, "Oh, we don't want the kids to go to a funeral. It'll be too upsetting for them." Not realizing what they're really saying is that it will be too upsetting for them to have the kids there. The adults put their needs ahead of the kids' needs to participate in the grieving.

There are tremendous failures in North American society in coping with a lot of the elements of life that other societies have dealt with with ritual. The use of the wake or the use of public mourning. As opposed to a kind of dismissal in our society of all ritual. Ritual exists for a reason. It didn't just happen. It happened because of people's needs. We've dismissed ritual but we haven't replaced it with anything. I guess in *Gentle Sinners* I said something along the lines of, "it's not whether one will have gods but which ones one worships." Often if we're too quick to dismiss the rituals of the past, we leave a kind of vaccuum into which the behaviours that we substitute are not really adequate emotionally.

Guy Vanderhaege

GUY VANDERHAEGHE was born in 1951 in Esterhazy, Saskatchewan. He majored in history at the University of Saskatchewan and worked as a teacher, archivist and researcher before the publication of *Man Descending* (1982), a collection of short stories that earned the Governor General's Award. A slovenly character in the volume's last two stories, Ed,

narrates Vanderhaeghe's first novel, *My Present Age* (1984), about his forlorn search for a wife who no longer tolerates him.

Guy Vanderhaeghe lives in Saskatoon. He was interviewed in 1984.

T: When you wrote your first two "Ed" short stories for *Man Descending*, did you have an inkling you would use that same character to go into a novel?

VANDERHAEGHE: No, I didn't. What had happened was that I thought I might write a series of short stories about him. Then I began to write a third story that showed me that if I continued along that vein I would merely turn him into the fool at court, entirely flippant, frivolous. And I thought that in all such people there is a much darker side. I needed a novel to explore that.

T: I expect some people have reacted adversely to Ed in *My Present Age*. As if the author is merely bringing more negativity into the world.

VANDERHAEGHE: Right. Exactly. There are some people who really dislike him. And in a sense I can understand that. I knew there was a risk in writing about a guy like that. People say, "Well, what does this teach us? What can we learn from this?" I can't answer those kinds of questions.

T: You answered once when you said the will to endure with imagination is a redemptive thing in itself.

VANDERHAEGHE: Yes. But if someone isn't on that wavelength, you can't persuade them that that in itself is sufficient. I had an interviewer once who said, "I'm no literary critic but I want to take you to task. Why are you writing a book about this obnoxious jerk?" I sort of stumbled through my answer.

T: "Look. I'm no critic of someone who is no literary critic..."

VANDERHAEGHE: Right. I think I said, "Properly read, this is a kind of cautionary tale." Of course she picked up on the word *properly* and said, "Oh, I guess I can't read a book properly." I gave up after that. I think there are people who don't want to acknowledge that there is any Ed in them. I also think one of the things

that can be upsetting about the story is the implication that there's no such thing as abiding success. This may not be fair, but this particular person had come from Toronto, she was moving up on the CBC ladder, and she probably had that feeling that at some time in her career she would reach a level where she would be invulnerable, where she would be a success and everything would be okay. At one point in the interview I said that failure intrigued me more than success, and she was really offended by that. So here's this guy Ed going around with the obvious intelligence to *make something* of life and yet he's the epitome of un-success. Some readers probably find that irksome.

T: You should have quoted the lines, "There's a certain amount of pleasure that comes from seeing somebody who is obviously intelligent fail. It's reassuring. It emphasizes the importance of character over brains."

VANDERHAEGHE: I suppose I should have.

T: Was it difficult stretching out from the short story? To maintain a sense of flow?

VANDERHAEGHE: I think that's probably one of the things that a person who's been writing short stories has the most difficulty with. Pacing a first novel. I tended to sort of throw myself into it. But the real technical problem was, in fact, to change the perspective in the book as Ed begins to disintegrate, to show his disintegration. In a way, the feel of the book was supposed to be almost schizophrenic. A realistic novel that I wanted to take on hallucinogenic qualities. The first third of the book I wanted him just carrying on, as it were, then suddenly have the book become darker.

T: I'm interested in why you as a writer have veered towards examining the darker side. Obviously you must have thought about this in terms of your family influences and experiences... First of all, what are the origins of Vanderhaeghe?

VANDERHAEGHE: Belgian. But I'm actually more Irish than Belgian. My mother is Irish and my father's mother was Irish. So if you want to go at it ethnically, though the name is Vanderhaeghe, I'm more Irish than I am Belgian.

T: Your numerous references to Kierkegaard made me wonder if Vanderhaeghe might be Danish. But an Irish temperament makes sense. The Irish are given to...

VANDERHAEGHE: Blackness!

T: What about isolation as a writer? As someone sitting on the west coast I tend to think, "Saskatoon. Isolation." And yet I know the Saskatchewan Writers Guild is one of the most active in the country.

VANDERHAEGHE: This whole question of isolation is interesting. I believe you can live almost anywhere as a writer and not be isolated because you can always get your hands on books. The intellectual communion that I have does not necessarily have to be personal. It can go on through books. And I can get a book from anywhere in the world in Saskatoon. And there's an advantage to living in Saskatoon in that it isolates you from all those extracurricular things like literary feuding, literary social life, all those things that sometimes attach themselves to writing and sometimes deflect from writing. Think of Faulkner sitting in Oxford, Mississippi and writing some of the great novels of the twentieth century in this little backwoods city that only had a little rinky-dink university. In one sense he was isolated but not isolated in any important way.

T: The relationship between a writer and the person the writer lives with is always important. Your wife's an artist. Is that a significant help to you?

VANDERHAEGHE: Yes. She's a painter. She's the one person who sees my manuscripts. I never send a manuscript-in-progress to an editor. And at the same time I'm one of the few people who comments on her paintings. So it is a very symbiotic relationship. It's based, I think, at least in my mind, on being as honest as possible. Sometimes I'll go down and look at a painting and I know she really wants me to like it. And I'll say, "I'm really sorry, this is going to cause difficulties perhaps for the next few days, but I think this." It's the same thing with the writing. She'll know that I really want her to like something and she'll go thumbs down.

T: Philosophically you've formed this notion of "man descending" after age thirty or so...

VANDERHAEGHE: Yes, I feel that very profoundly.

T: Did that theory or feeling liberate you at all? In terms of becoming a serious writer?

VANDERHAEGHE: I think there were a whole series of circumstances that suddenly made me more serious, that turned me around and made me want to write. Physical illness. Personal life. And not exactly at thirty. At about twenty-six.

T: Your own illness?

VANDERHAEGHE: Yes. I became a diabetic when I was twenty-six. Because I held off treatment, thinking there couldn't be anything the matter with me, by the time I went into the hospital I was practically blind. I couldn't recognize my wife's face across the room. That altered my life significantly. Just in terms of day-to-day living. I sort of said, well, you know, if I'm going to do what I want to do I better start doing it now. That, I suppose, was the spur to do what I wanted to do.

But I had been germinating, as it

were, for a number of years, half-heartedly writing. Writing in fits and starts, doing a lot of reading, pursuing philosophical interests. In fact, I feel I was sort of examining everything that I had believed up until about age twenty-three or twenty-four. I had what I would have thought of as body of beliefs and then I began questioning it. Out of that I've come to believe in freedom, much more strongly than I ever believed in it in the past.

T: And not just political freedom.

VANDERHAEGHE: Not just political freedom. Personal freedom. Freedom to think and choose.

T: So *My Present Age* could be seen as a radical expression of that. Making this extreme character and then letting him loose, letting him out.

VANDERHAEGHE: Yes, but only because if I turned into anything, I suppose I turned into a moderate skeptic. I think what's most innate in my nature is a kind of measured skepticism, a kind of belief in the moderation in all things. I think moderation is there in the approach I've taken to a man like Ed, who's immoderate. I mean, most people reflexively say forget it, who wants to even look at this sort of thing. But it seems to me that these people are like icebergs. They're useful because they're indications of things that are going on underneath.

In a very profound way, that's what Kierkegaard was. This little fanatic, Danish hunchback who, in fact, signaled an entire revolution in European thinking. He made his appearance and shortly after him came Dostoevsky, came Nietzsche, came the philosophers of the irrational. But he was the first. He was personally grotesque, a man that people made fun of in the streets.

T: "I, like Kierkegaard, don't mix at parties, have terrible love affairs."

VANDERHAEGHE: That's Ed being flippant. In some ways, Ed is almost the reverse of Kierkegaard. Fat. Aggressive. Kierkegaard, like Ed, employed wit whenever he possibly could but he was a true wit, a philosophical wit. Ed is not. Ed is a social wit.

T: It's interesting you also admire Samuel Johnson, another extraordinary wit and another iceberg figure.

VANDERHAEGHE: Johnson is the iceberg of eighteenth-century England. Kierkegaard is the iceberg of Europe.

T: An iceberg situated in the middle of the Canadian prairies would be an interesting self-concept...

In "Going to Russia" you wrote, "Some other kind of will in me turns away in misery and distaste from all of culture, from all that is being said and done around me." That story is about the importance of writing, believing in the subtleties of writing and the power of ideas, almost in opposition to society.

VANDERHAEGHE: Yes, I believe very strongly in print. Arguments in print can be examined again and again and again. You can live with them for years. Whereas television and radio and cinema primarily leave impressions. They persuade us by impressions rather than by analysis and logic. I often feel like I'm in a way like one of those highly specialized, nineteenth-century industrial workers who were destroyed by technological innovation. It seems to me that writers now are one of those dying species overwhelmed by technology. Television, records, video and film are the important means of mass communication now. It's not the book. But obviously I believe in the book.

T: The main problem I found with *My Present Age* was that the story kept unraveling backwards so much. It sometimes got weighted down by backward motion.

VANDERHAEGHE: I suppose the only thing I could say in defense of that is that the forward motion makes no sense without the backward motion. That goes back to what the historian Donald Creighton said about history being a combination of character and circumstance. The importance that Ed's wife has in his life is predicated on the past. You have to show that. There's also the problem that the novel has to stand on its own for anyone who may not have read the two short stories.

T: The book took off for me in terms of scenes. When Ed haggled over a parking space. Or when he went down into the basement with his father-in-law to shoot air pistols. Or at the end when he goes to Victoria's hotel room, he knocks on the door and she calls out another man's name.

VANDERHAEGHE: This is what happens with a book. In talking about this book, everybody hits on something different. The things you have mentioned have never been mentioned before. Everybody reads a book differently. I used to think a person wrote a book, the book was finished and everybody read it in the same way. But now I realize consensus about a book is only arrived at far, far into the future.

tephen Vizinczey

STEPHEN VIZINCZEY was born in Hungary in 1933. After the defeat of the Hungarian Revolution he went to Italy and subsequently arrived in Canada at age twenty-four, knowing about fifty words of English. After some initial years of destitution and despair he self-published *In Praise of Older Women: The Amorous Recollections of Andras Vajda* (1965). He

made a fortune and spent most of it in lawsuits against those he thought had cheated or slandered him. A temperamental perfectionist, he waited almost two decades before publishing his highly successful ironic allegory, *An Innocent Millionaire* (1983). An early collection of essays, *The Rules of Chaos*, was followed by a moralistic survey, *Truth and Lies in Literature* (1986). His next book is a fictional study of a man who confronts the Mafia in Sicily.

Stephen Vizinczey lives in Toronto, London and Italy. He was interviewed in 1983.

T: You must be gaining a clear sense by now of what it is you're writing about, what it is you have to give to people.

VIZINCZEY: It sounds awfully simple if you put it in a sentence, but basically I think it's how to be decent. It's hard to be decent. I'm very fascinated by that. Or let's put it this way, I'm interested in the struggle between good and evil.

Nowadays there is all this talk about the complexity of the modern condition, about how you've got to realize there are grey areas. Well, it hit me how phony that was when I watched on television Ziegler, the man who was Nixon's press agent. He's the guy who was lying for sixteen months or whatever, from the beginning of Watergate. I was fascinated by what he was going to say. Would he say, "I'm sorry I lied to you?" No. He said, "I appreciate that we had our differences. And I realize that things are more complex than I thought." I hate people who say that. I don't believe that moral questions are really all that complicated or complex.

T: Perhaps being raised in Europe, where there's a stronger memory of Nazism and Stalinism, you have a stronger sense that good and evil exist.

VIZINCZEY: They killed my father. There's nothing grey about that!

T: The reverse of this is that once a person faces up to the reality of evil, it means a person must also face up to the reality of good, and of trying to be good.

VIZINCZEY: You're right. That's very important. But it's the same in Europe now as it is in North America. Everybody flees from responsibility like crazy. Nobody wants to be considered responsible for anything in the world, correct? What it means really is, "I can do whatever is advantageous to me." And if it's not very nice, well, "things are complex."

T: You must have thought about the significance of your father being murdered, even though you were only two at the time. Do you accept that that event has shaped you?

VIZINCZEY: I think that was very significant. My father's murder was very central to my growing up. Probably in more ways than I fully realize. My father was murdered, stabbed in the back. He was sitting at his desk, facing the window. He was stabbed by a Nazi he had never seen before. The Nazi sent to kill him had never seen my father before. It was a terrorist killing. There was somebody else in the room when it happened. My father turned to him and said, "Why am I bleeding?" He was stabbed in the back twice but the knife was so sharp, apparently he hardly felt it. The blood came onto his hand as he was writing. So he turned around and said, "What is this blood? Where is this blood coming from?" And as he turned, the guy cut his main artery with the same knife.

To this day I always like to sit, and I certainly cannot write, unless my back is against the wall.

T: It's interesting that your central character in *An Innocent Millionaire* is also killed by an assassin. "This is the mystery of our age: people get killed but there are no murderers."

VIZINCZEY: Yes. I feel just as strongly about the chapter in which Mark's father, the actor who has many friends in the media, goes around and asks the media for help, but nobody will talk to him. They explain to him that it's just not a story. Because they really don't want a story from the victim. You might see something there with my father's death. I never identify with the guy who is committing the evil. I identify with the victims. I think that's what makes my book original. I may be wrong, but I don't know of any other modern novel right now, a crime story like *An Innocent Millionaire*, in which the victim is the hero.

Usually you read about the crook nowadays, how cleverly they set up the crime. The criminals are beautiful people and the police are morons. They wouldn't show you somebody on the screen being decent for two minutes without him saying, "Ah, it's not that I'm decent or anything. I'm just looking out for number one." Think of Humphrey Bogart. In every Humphrey Bogart film they always say, "Oh, you're a good guy." And he says, "No, no, no. I just want to get my money."

T: You're basically saying that people who are virtuous are seldom portrayed as being intelligent.

VIZINCZEY: And that's not true! I know *fantastic* guys who are virtuous! I've spent a lot of time in Palermo and I know a lot of judges. Brilliant guys. I tell you, you talk to a judge in New York or Toronto, they're usually stuffy. But these guys are on the front line. Every week one of them is murdered. All their career is service. You sometimes have Chief Magistrates at twenty-six. Nobody else would take the job! The kind of men who do this are really brave and intelligent, obviously superior people.

And the reason they're so virtuous is because they understand something which all these stupid crooks don't understand. That unless there is some kind of human solidarity, society is going to fall apart. I mean, is it stupid to care that your children will be able to drink the water? Is it sophisticated to think, "We'll pour this dioxin into the river and save a hundred thousand bucks and if my child dies of cancer at age ten, so what"?

T: I love the line in your book where you talk about a corporation not bothering to answer a letter of enquiry. "No doubt eliminating

politeness from society is a cost-effective way of hastening the day when people will bite each other in the street."

VIZINCZEY: Yes. That's a good example. You can say it's sophisticated and smart, it's good business, not to answer letters which don't lead to good business. It saves secretarial time. But to my mind it's not sophisticated enough. It is not only not decent, but it's stupid. It's stupid to be indecent. You see, what you're doing to people in that situation, especially to people who are in trouble, you're delivering a psychic blow. I know because I have been in the situation where I have needed to get a goddamn letter.

Suffering distances people and damages them. When you deliver psychic damage, you're destroying the human community. I have suffered from that. I am not going to start biting people in the street, but I understand the temptation this gave me towards indifference and callousness. You can make people more callous by ignoring them like that. As Bernard Shaw used to say about poverty, you have to fight against it not because it's bad for the poor but because it's bad for the rich.

T: *An Innocent Millionaire* opens with Mark's little diary entry. He feels it's not worth telling his story because nobody would care.

VIZINCZEY: Because there's no human community.

T: But on the other hand, you contradict him.

VIZINCZEY: Yes. That's the book. I say people do care. Because if nobody cared, we're finished! I do believe there are millions and millions of decent and intelligent and brave people in the world who can respond to Mark's story and want to hear it. It won't be as big a bestseller as Harold Robbins or Judith Krantz. It won't be as big a bestseller as the lies. But I certainly believe there are at least twenty million decent, intelligent, literate people in North America and that's not such a low number out of 250 million. So there is hope.

T: Along those lines, how does a country like Canada fit in?

VIZINCZEY: It fits in with the most appalling modesty and self-effacement. When I came to Canada I was surprised to see how little impact intellectuals had on public life. Yet Canada has as many bright people as any country. More. Because you have very bright people coming here from all over the world. So the percentage of bright people is fantastically high. So what is the difference? What is the difference between life here in Canada and the life in Italy? Or anywhere in Europe? And I realized the difference is only in this: that a bright Canadian thinks of himself as a spook. I mean, as an oddball. He reads and he thinks he's unusual. And he's wrong. He's just lonely. He's very keenly aware that most people like baseball or hockey. And so he's very shy, and a bit ashamed. Because who the hell likes to be in the minority, correct?

I realized that Canada didn't have an intellectual/political magazine. That's why I did this magazine called *Exchange*. I thought the main purpose of such a magazine in Canada would be to let all these guys know they're not alone. It went from nothing to fifteen thousand copies. It was in *Exchange* that you could first read about Separatists, what they were thinking. That was in '61. I had a short story that was banned in Quebec translated. I had a nuclear issue. And a humanist issue. The main idea behind *Exchange* was that you ought not to feel inferior and guilty just because you don't care for hockey. In the media as a general rule, Presley gets front page treatment while Bach is buried in a small

paragraph somewhere. And that's not right. But if you say so, they say you're arrogant. I guess you could say that *Exchange* tried to be an arrogantly intellectual magazine. But please don't confuse this with the pretentious conceited nonsense which is associated with high culture. By intellectual I mean a thinking person.

T: You also took the extraordinary step of self-publishing your first novel, *In Praise of Older Women*. Why did you do that?

VIZINCZEY: Because I couldn't help feeling the uncertainty and the fear publishers have about the book of an unpublished author. I found it insulting, humiliating. Several publishers rejected the manuscript. An agent wrote to me from London that she couldn't possibly risk her reputation by submitting it to publishers. There were publishers which were willing to publish it, but without much enthusiasm. Jack McClelland, who is actually one of the best publishers I have ever come across, offered me a small advance on the strength of the first few chapters, but it seemed that no one thought as highly of the novel as I did, so in the end I decided to publish it myself. The lot of the writer is worse today than ever before. To begin with, publishers publish almost anything—but only from the right people. If you belong to the right media circles, you can get the most appalling garbage published. In the whole history of literature there weren't as many good novels written as are published every year, just in North America. By the same token I know of several good novels which don't get published simply because the author is unknown, and publishers just don't know how to sell unknowns. Selling even famous writers is hell, there are so many of them, so many TV hosts write books, not to mention all the demented actresses—so who the hell can bother about the book of an unknown, even if it is a masterpiece? It's worse today than at the time I decided to publish *In Praise* myself, but it was the predicament of the unknown novelist which drove me to it.

T: As far as I know, *In Praise of Older Women* is still the best-selling serious novel ever written in this country. Did you expect it to be so successful?

VIZINCZEY: I expected it to be far more successful. Its time is still to come. *In Praise of Older Women* will be published for the first time this year in Italy, Spain, Brazil and Yugoslavia. New translations are being published in Swedish and German. It has sold around three million copies in twenty-odd years, and I think it still hasn't reached most of the kind of unhypocritical, unpretentious and intelligent readers for whom it was written. In Canada it will always remain a more or less underground book, in spite of its fame. It isn't on university reading lists, which means that most booksellers don't stock it. If I had to live on the money my books earn for me in Canada, I would starve.

T: I notice most of the reviews of *An Innocent Millionaire* are remarking on the time spread between your two novels. As if it's almost bizarre.

VIZINCZEY: But I don't feel I am unusual. I think what I did was perfectly natural and ordinary and the only sensible thing to do! Their wonderment has to do with not understanding what is involved in writing.

T: For one thing, a more prolific writer can run the risk of writing the same book he wrote the year before. As somebody once joked, "I love Mordecai Richler's book. I buy it each time he writes it."

VIZINCZEY: Yes. I couldn't have written a different book if I published another novel in two years' time. It would have been another version of *In Praise of Older Women*. Everybody was sure I was going to write that. But why hurry? As a critic I see most books would be much better if the author had spent another year on them.

On the other hand, I don't think I've changed basically as a writer. I haven't changed my style. My attitude to writing is the same. I will continue to be a realist writer, an ironic writer. And I live much the same. I live a totally private life. I'm not going into an office. I love people. I always have to be with people. I'm not a loner. But I don't live a social life. I don't go to literary parties. I'm not a part of the literary scene anywhere.

T: You spend much of your time in London and Italy. Do you expect to also keep your ties with Canada?

VIZINCZEY: My ties to Canada are personal. I have my best friends there, I have children, grandchildren there, I love Toronto, I'm happy with the critical reception of my work in the press, I'm happy with the readers I have—but as I had already mentioned, my books are not in the shops. I never got the kind of institutional backing—like the Governor General's Award, the academic backing—which would have enabled me to make a living in Canada. My book of essays and reviews, *Truth & Lies in Literature*, which was very generously and appreciatively reviewed in Canadian papers and which is being translated—as few collections of reviews and essays are—into Swedish, German, Italian, Spanish—it was well received even in the States—still, it sold only some four hundred copies in Canada. You might say I have ties to some four hundred people in Canada. But to end on an upbeat note—it could be worse!

Rudy Wiebe

RUDY WIEBE was born near Fairholme, Saskatchewan in 1934. He attended universities in Alberta, West Germany, Manitoba and Iowa, and edited a Mennonite newspaper. He is best known for his historically-based fictions which have emphasized communalism, self-discipline and spirituality. *The Temptations of Big Bear* (1973) recounts how the spiritual link

with the land was broken with the coming of the white man to the prairies. It earned a Governor General's Award. *The Scorched-Wood People* (1977) is about the Metis and Louis Riel struggling for independence. His other novels are *Peace Shall Destroy Many* (1962), *First and Vital Candle* (1966), *The Blue Mountains of China* (1970), *The Mad Trapper* (1980) and *My Lovely Enemy* (1983). He was chairman of the Writers Union of Canada from 1986 to 1987.

Rudy Wiebe teaches English and lives in Edmonton. He was interviewed in 1979.

T: Your work emphasizes how closely spirituality and tough-mindedness must be linked in order for us to develop any sort of useful moral code. Most people these days don't seem willing to even consider qualities like self-denial and self-discipline, let alone try them.

WIEBE: You're right. "Indulgent" is the key word today. If we like something, we do it. That's why the whole tradition of Russian spirituality has appealed to me. If you really want to search what your soul is, you go and live on an island. You cut down the demands of the outer world to find out the demands of the inner world.

T: The prairies is probably an ideal place for that process of self-evaluation. Would that be why the Canadian novel seems to have its roots in the prairies?

WIEBE: Possibly. Certainly it's true the prairies have inspired a good number of our major novelists, far out of proportion to the number of people who have lived there. The first generation was Frederick Philip Grove and Sinclair Ross and W.O. Mitchell. They stuck more or less to the pioneer end of things, especially Grove. Now we're trying to go beyond that era in both directions. We're trying to look at what came before the pioneer and what has come after.

T: Would you say prairie writing, in general, is less imitative than writing in eastern Canada?

WIEBE: Yes. Because the landscape of the prairies is much more alien to the landscape of England than the landscape of Ontario. You can see a parallel to this in Australia. They're still grappling to come to grips with an alien landscape because they had less varied immigration. But you can't build a little England in a land of marsupials. We learned that in the prairies because we had more varied immigration than Ontario.

T: Are you implying Eastern European immigrants were better settlers on the prairies than British people?

WIEBE: Sure. My parents were Russian Mennonite farmers, living in very much the same latitude as Canada. In fact, the Mennonites who came to Canada in 1870 from the steppes of the Ukraine were really the first people to settle Western Canada on the prairie. Up to that point, the Scots and the French had only settled along the river valleys, using the river lots system. They stayed close to the rivers, using them as their means of transportation. But the Mennonites in 1874 literally settled on the prairie.

They built sod houses. Now who's going to live in a sod house? A Russian peasant will, if it's necessary. Nobody thought they could make a go of it. But they brought wheat from the Ukraine. It wasn't supposed to be exported so they sewed it into the children's dolls. That's how our grain industry started.

T: So you grew up thinking of yourself as a Mennonite first and a Canadian second?

WIEBE: I had to. I lived in a Mennonite community, a settlement of two or three hundred people. Before age six I spoke no English at all. We spoke Low German. My parents hadn't had a penny to get to Canada so the CPR gave them a loan and brought them all the way to Alberta. My father finally paid the CPR back fourteen years later.

All the stories my parents told us during the long winter nights were about Russia. The revolution and all that. So yes, my world was very, very Mennonite in those early years.

T: Did you ever feel a need to break away from the fundamentalism of your upbringing?

WIEBE: Well, I grew up relatively free. I was the youngest child in our family by quite a few years. And my parents were quite old people. My father was forty-five when I was born. So when we moved from northern Saskatchewan to southern Alberta when I was about twelve, I was relatively free to explore. I sensed there was something wrong with the heavy fundamentalist preaching fairly early on. When I was older I realized it was the narrow, legalistic system into which it forces you. It made of spirituality a kind of syllogism: All men have sinned . . . God has to reach into man's life to change life . . . so all you have to do to change your life is accept conversion. There's nothing spiritual about it. Christianity becomes logic. You're levered into a philosophical position by an emotional demand. These kinds of things always angered me. I knew there had to be more to the demands of a truly good life than that logical syllogism.

But I was lucky. I went to a Mennonite high school that had a lovely community spirit to it. So my Christian values were affirmed when I was young. I don't think I ever tried to smoke at all as a kid — that was a great concern of parents in those days — and we never had the hassle of adolescents growing up and pairing off and boys and girls getting into trouble. That kind of jazz was never a problem. Nobody ever thought of things like going out on a single date because there were so few kids in that school. It was a community.

T: I suppose you already recognize all the similarities between your beliefs and Tolstoy's.

WIEBE: He's becoming more and more of an influence. In fact, I usually read *War and Peace* every three or four years. Tolstoy sees where his country is coming from and knows where it's going. Also he was an outspoken moralist. But it's more than that. He was a Christian moralist who saw in the life of Christ and the doctrines of the Bible the highest ideals that man has achieved so far. Especially in the field of pacifism. Tolstoy brought pacifism to world attention at a time when it was very low on the scales during the Imperialist world of the late nineteenth century. To be a pacifist then was to be a ninny. But he showed the world that pacifism was not some abstract human condition. It can be rooted in action, as best exemplified by Christ.

T: Do you think your books might be better appreciated at a future date when Christianity is not so unfashionable?

WIEBE: Actually, I've already gained a lot of ground in the seventies. People have become so tired of that emptiness which came with liberal attitudes. People are tired of that pseudo-scientific liberalism that assumes all is provable. Scientists no longer talk like that. Only outdated liberals talk like that.

So it goes in cycles. Some writers try to anticipate what's going to be popular two years form now. I just say the heck with that. To me the point is that there are eternal human values that must be spoken for. Sometimes the concept of pacifism in my books is popular; sometimes it's not. In the early sixties, at the time of the Cuban missile crisis, being a pacifist was just giving in. Then at the end of the Vietnam war, pacifism became one of the most powerful forces in North America. When that happened, *Peace Shall Destroy Many* started getting popular again.

T: In the event of a Third World War, how would our society treat pacifists?

WIEBE: I don't see the Canadian public responding to pacifists much differently than in the Second World War. A few people believe there's no such thing as a just war. But a lot of people who became pacifists during Vietnam still figure the Second World War was a pretty good war as far as wars go. We had to handle a tyrant. Besides, things were pretty tough economically so let's go off and have an adventure. It's that kind of stupid male world that wars exemplify. The Second World War was basically men's games. Very deadly, but for that reason, all the more enjoyable.

Maybe the women's movement can help us now. Maybe we have a lot clearer understanding because women are fitting into more things. But women are very aggressive, too. If they don't now have the killing ways that men have, maybe they just haven't learned them yet. It's like the Nellie McClung campaign for temperance. She thought temperance would immediately solve a lot of problems if women got the vote. She never imagined that women like to drink, too. Maybe that's the way it is with war.

T: *The Scorched-Wood People* is not just the story of Louis Riel and Gabriel Dumont. It's the story of the Métis people. Do you think the novel may be getting misread as just another book about Riel?

WIEBE: Right. It's the story of a people, a people who have almost disappeared because they no longer live to express a communal will. The Métis are scattered now. For a long time they have shown very little commonality of purpose.

T: It's also happened to the Doukhobors.

WIEBE: Yes. The world has broken down their whole sense of community. History has broken them down. Riel saw this coming. In his prayers he prayed that his people would not lose sight of what they were and what they could be together. Not just as individuals.

T: In that book, Riel is a man of spirit and Dumont is a man of action. In *First and Vital Candle* there's a similar division where Josh is the man of spirit and Abe is the man of action. Is that a dichotomy you feel in yourself?

WIEBE: No, it's probably more a fiction device. It's a way of handling the complexities of human nature. It's given to me in history with Riel and Dumont and I use it for what it's worth. I tried to show that the man of action can be dominated by the man of the spirit. In his biography, *Dumont*, George Woodcock couldn't seem to grasp how such a free-spirited guerrilla leader could be dominated by Riel. Woodcock is a pacifist but — like most people — he doesn't like to believe in the power of the *Christian* spirit.

T: Some people will argue that if Riel had followed some of Dumont's instincts instead of his own, things might have been better for the Métis.

WIEBE: Things would have been momentarily different. Dumont could have covered the prairies in blood. But there was no way he could have won the war.

Big Bear understood this better than anybody, better than Riel. You can't fight the white man with his own weapons. Guns are white man's weapons. You've got to fight him with other powers.

T: *The Temptations of Big Bear* is your best known novel. Is it also your best?

WIEBE: Actually a lot of critics whose opinions I value think that *Scorched-Wood People* is a better book than *Big Bear*. I would like to think so. I would like to think that not only my skill as a novelist but also my comprehension of human beings is increasing. Also the form of *Scorched-Wood People* was most satisfying to me in contrast to the multi-voiced *Big Bear*. It's the voice of the Métis people that writes the book. The attempt to capture that voice was very satisfying to me.

T: But Big Bear is your most powerful character. How did you discover him?

WIEBE: I discovered him while I was at university. I read William Blaisdale Cameron's *Blood Red the Sun*, which discusses the Frog Lake massacre and the part that Big Bear played there. I discovered in Big Bear the ideal character for what I wanted to write. A great native man who had understood what had happened to his people, hadn't liked it, and had tried to change the course of history.

When I discovered Big Bear had actually lived where I had lived during the first part of my life, it was a perfect gift. It's like Bach saying every tune is a gift from God. His character was certainly a gift from God for me.

T: Since you're not a believer in total rationality, how much do you structure your novels beforehand?

WIEBE: I usually have a pretty clear idea where the novel's going. The first novel I ever wrote, I wrote the last chapter first. Then I started at the beginning and wrote towards it. I've never written a novel in that method again but I am quite careful.

T: Since you're an avowed moralist, do you ever despair about the limitations of literature, about how few people you're influencing?

WIEBE: It's a limited audience, sure. I once wrote a script out of one of my weakest short stories for CBC television, and between two and three million people watched it. And that's not even a big television audience. But I don't think it's necessarily the job of an artist to reach as many people as possible. The job of an artist is to make a genuine article. Like a potter who makes a pot. It exists. It carries on.

A novelist is scattering seed, I guess. In the good earth it grows. And in the long run, it will make a bit of difference.

T: Since you've led a life of relative self-denial — I mean in terms of restricting yourself to certain beliefs — do you think your fiction writing might be an especially important outlet for you because when you indulge your imagination it can sometimes be an almost ecstatic release?

WIEBE: Oh, it is. It is.

T: The power of that release comes through in your writing. Like a way of getting high almost.

WIEBE: Yes, if the writing is going well, the writing just carries you along. I've been told I didn't write parts of *Big Bear* at all, Big Bear wrote it through me. At its best, you're quite right, that can be a kind of ecstasy. But I easily get those contact highs from other people, too. So I can go to the beer parlour, like Robert Kroetsch says, and drink nothing but Tang and come out higher than anybody there.

T: Kroetsch thinks realism may be becoming counterproductive to art. Do you think of your subjective realism as a dislocation of perception?

WIEBE: I'll leave it to the analysts to decide what kind of realism I have. But Kroetsch obviously is not a realist. *What the Crow Said*, for example, takes tall stories to an incredible end. In its own way it's more imaginative than *Beautiful Losers*. But I still have faith in the straight story. Ordinary human experiences. There's still something to be said for that kind of storytelling.

T: The awkwardness of your syntax can be quite disturbing to some readers. Do you purposely want your readers to put extra effort into your books because the more effort they put in, the more they can take away from it?

WIEBE: That's part of it. You say it well and clearly. When I read the first chapter of *Peace Shall Destroy Many* and the first chapter of *The Scorched-Wood People*, I'm very aware that neither of them is very easy reading.

But in both instances, I'm trying to keep people from reading the sort of novel where you know it all the first time. I want to keep you on edge, feeling you're not getting it all. I want you to feel this so strongly that you read it again when you're finished.

T: So flawlessness can be a flaw.

WIEBE: In a way, yes.

T: Do you ever encounter resentment that a Canadian writer is experimenting with language to such a degree? As if it's okay for James Joyce but not for some guy from Alberta?

WIEBE: I get it all the time. Professors of English who are friends of mine tell me *The Blue Mountains of China* is too hard to read. I say, what? You've been reading Joyce and Faulkner all your life. Don't tell me that. We think language has to always be logical and explanatory. It isn't necessarily. Language is often parabolic. If you want to understand a Mozart concerto, you play it over again.

T: I didn't like *The Blue Mountains of China* as much either, but not because of the language. You took it for granted that your reader would be sympathetic to all your characters long before the reader got a chance to learn who each character was. Whereas your preceding novel was totally the opposite. Do you consciously try different approaches for each book?

WIEBE: Sure. You read all five and all five are different. *Peace Shall Destroy Many* is an omniscient novel. *First and Vital Candle* is a limited exploration of an individual. *The Blue Mountains of China* is almost stream-of-consciousness. I think once you've done a certain novel, it's such a long job that you don't want to do another book the same way. Besides, each book demands a different form. If you're going to have a novel about a people who are scattered all over the continents of the world throughout an

entire century, like *Blue Mountains of China*, you can't write a third-person, central-intelligence novel. I could have done that. I could have concentrated on two or three people. But I didn't think that would capture the genius and particular historical insight of the Mennonites between 1880 and 1970.

T: Could you explain the importance of naming in fiction. I know that's an idea Doris Lessing has about her work, too, but it's a difficult notion to get hold of.

WIEBE: Naming is the origin of language. Language is the way man handles his world. My child is sitting in the train with me and sees hills in the distance and he says, "What's that?" I say "hills." He says, "What are they though?" I say, "The Sweet Grass Hills." That satisfies him. You've had that experience too, I'm sure. Kids have an incredible curiosity about language. Once they catch on to what language is all about, they want to know more and more. They want names. That to me is the genius of language. It's how man dominates his environment. Man's greatest invention to me is not getting to the moon; it's the invention of language. And naming is the beginning of language.

To me, this is the genius of Jesus. He expressed his world view by telling stories. A person who wants to express a different world view than has been expressed before does not come around talking about philosophic principles. That's a back-assed way of doing it. You should begin with the stories and then deduce the principles. That's the way Aristotle arrived at his great criticism. He looked at all the extant literature of the time and he deduced certain principles from it. That is the way all great minds work, I think. Not the other way around.

The power of Jesus over the power of St. Paul is exactly that. Jesus tells the stories and you work them out for yourself. St. Paul comes along with the principles and gets everybody mad. Even though Jesus and St. Paul were basically talking about the same things.

T: Do you despair about the spiritual morass North American society is in?

WIEBE: It's pretty terrible. The standard ideals are such terrible models of behaviour.

T: It seems there's a pervasive hopelessness these days that people use as an excuse to embrace selfishness.

WIEBE: I'm sure you're exactly right there. It avoids being involved with any second or third human being. But there are always young people who will reject selfish values. They realize dreams about being dropped off in front of theatres from Rolls Royces are essentially no good.

T: Margaret Laurence believed optimism was unrealistic, but that a good writer has to be someone with hope. Is hope at the basis of why you write?

WIEBE: Certainly that's one thing. I think man is good. He longs for good things. Often our basic humanity gets perverted but man has been made by a good creator. So I'm basically hopeful in many ways.

T: Wouldn't a historian say ours is simply another society in a state of decadent decline? That the tide can never be turned?

WIEBE: Maybe. But you can always keep seeing societies in states of decline. Look at the kind of society from which my parents came in Russia in 1917. They were literally starving, socially and religiously abused and harassed. Yet people kept on loving. People kept on having children. People kept affirming life. When I look at those times and I look at my own, I can't believe how fortunate we are. People say they wouldn't bring a child into today's world. They're crazy. They know nothing about the world. They know nothing about history.

Eric Wilson

ERIC WILSON was born in Ottawa in 1940. As a teacher in BC he began to write for reluctant readers with *Murder on the Canadian* (1976). His subsequent books about a brother and sister team of young sleuths from Winnipeg, Tom and Liz Austen, have well-researched settings in provinces across the country. While incorporating social issues such as the destruc-

tion of forests, disabled children, Minimata disease and terrorism, Wilson's suspenseful, easy-to-read books and his popular appearances in schools have attracted ten thousand readers to the Eric Wilson Mystery Club. Translated internationally, his fourteen books over a twelve-year period include *The Lost Treasure of Casa Loma* (1980), *Vampires of Ottawa* (1984), *The Unmasking of 'Ksan* (1986), *The Green Gables Detectives* (1987) and *Code Red at the Supermall* (1988).

Eric Wilson lives in Victoria. He was interviewed in 1980.

T: They're now calling you "Canada's best-selling writer of fiction for young adults." When did that title emerge?

WILSON: I don't know. I'm not going around advertising myself as such. But the books are doing really well. That phrase is Collins', my publishers', decision.

T: Is Collins responsible for the Eric Wilson Fan Club?

WILSON: Well, they sponsored it but it was really my idea. I found that when I was visiting schools, kids asked, well, when's your next book going to be? Kids don't generally browse in bookstores. There was no way for these kids to find out what specifically my next book would be. So I suggested to Collins that we have some kind of club. I also suggested that we unite the kids by having them write reviews of other mysteries by other authors. Then it slowly expanded. Now the kids are creating the contests. The newsletter comes out a couple of times a year. Essentially it's a way for kids to know what happening with my books.

T: With the success you've had both in Canada and internationally, do you still see yourself writing for the reluctant reader?

WILSON: I do, yes. But what has happened is that my books have become very popular with what you call bookworms as well. The nice thing about that is that kids in a gifted class will have copies of my books and also kids who have a lot of trouble in school have them too. So not only is there no stigma attached to my books, the great bonus is that the gifted kids are also reading them. The kid who is having trouble with his reading can feel good about himself.

T: And that social usefulness aspect seems to inspire you as much as any artistic resolve. You get to see it working. You could just sit at home and write but you don't do that.

WILSON: Right. Last school year I think I talked to fifteen thousand kids in school groups from BC to Ontario and Quebec. That certainly creates the adrenalin. I'm also finding by going into schools that teachers and librarians are using my books not only with reluctant readers but also with social studies classes. A lot of teachers are telling me that because my books are specifically about an area and they have historical information, they're good ways to teach a unit, say, on northern British Columbia.

T: I can certainly see that with *The Unmasking of Ksan*.

WILSON: Yes. That's got lots of research in it.

T: How long did you spend in Hazelton for it?

WILSON: I spent about two months up there in the summer of 1985. I usually spend about two months in each location. I went to a death feast. That was the first thing I went to . . .

T: I was going to ask you about that. The detail in that story about attending a death feast where there was an electronic basketball clock on the wall struck me as something that wouldn't have been invented.

WILSON: No, none of that was invented. What happened was there was a teacher in the Kispiox school who used my books with his students. He had written to join the mystery club. I kept his name aside and when I got up there I phoned him. He said, well, I'd love to meet you but this evening I can't because I've been invited to a death feast of the wolf clan. As you can imagine, my ears perked up and I asked to be taken along. He set it up with the chief of the tribe. That was the very first thing that I attended. We were there from about seven p.m. till about two or three in the morning. The things I said in the story about the fact that it's considered disrespectful to leave your place are true. And about the food, where they keep filling your bowl.

T: When you go into these research periods, do you have half a story in your mind? Or no story at all?

WILSON: Each one is a little bit different. When I went up to Ksan, I'd been there about ten years before. So I went specifically because I knew about Ksan and I knew about the museum. It was a logical thing to do a story about a mask being stolen from the museum.

But each book is different. *Spirit in the Rainforest* is set around Ucluelet. The starting point for that was the controversy around the logging of Meares Island. I feel really strongly about the destruction that's been done in British Columbia by the logging companies. Obviously logging is a very important industry, but I think the government has allowed these companies to get away with terrible stuff. There was all this arguing about whether or not they'd log Meares Island. People were talking about occupying the island in protest. That really was the starting point for that book.

One of the characters is a woman who's involved in Greenpeace. She says, "You kids can help." Tom says, well, children don't have any influence. She says, "But it's your country, too." I'm trying to say that to kids. Become involved. Some of these kids who are reading my books are going to be voting pretty soon.

T: I did a biography on Hubert Evans, who wrote a great deal of juvenile fiction. His wife was a Quaker who kept reminding him that you can still change a person's mind about things in their teens.

WILSON: I really think that's very true. I feel very fortunate that my career has evolved in such a way that I am writing for kids who are willing to listen. They're old enough and mature enough to listen. I don't expect them to accept it all, by any means, but it's nice to know that I can speak through my books to them and perhaps affect their lives.

T: Another important aspect of your stories is that the central characters all have self-doubt. Perhaps reluctant readers can particularly relate to characters who sometimes have low self-esteem.

WILSON: I think that's true of all kids. It may be true of all people. Even a lot of kids who are gifted can be kids who feel like wimps or nerds. I think this goes right across the board. This is a good example of how I feel very fortunate that I'm in a position to be able to write. When I was a teenager I felt like the world's worst nerd. I had trouble dating and all that sort of stuff. I know kids are always going to go through that. Feeling unattractive. That's why I had the guy in the Ksan story tell the boy not to worry. Join the high school band or go skiing. It's standard advice. You and I know that. But when I was fifteen I didn't know that. It never occurred to me. I really feel that if I can put that into a book, it's going to affect some kids. That's the power of the printed word.

T: Like yourself, I grew up on the Hardy Boys. It was probably my main book-reading experience.

WILSON: I think it still is for a lot of kids. I've gone into schools and asked, "Has anyone here read books about the Hardy Boys?" I would say ninety-eight percent or better put their hands up. It's fascinating. Because those things were started in the twenties or something like that. And they're popular with girls and boys.

T: Have you looked at the Hardy Boys analytically? To see what makes them popular?

WILSON: No. But when I started writing my own series I remembered what it was about the Hardy Boys that appealed to me when I was a kid.

T: And what were they?

WILSON: Well, the technical things like getting off to a quick start. The fact that each chapter ends with a hook. That's very important when you're writing for reluctant readers. "Look out!" Frank cried. Also the fact that the story is contemporary. I get a lot of response from kids indicating they appreciate the fact that my stories are about kids of today, urban kids. At the time, the Hardy Boys were supposed to be taking place in a modern, urban setting. Also I think the series concept is important.

T: I notice you've toned down the violence since your first book, *Murder on the Canadian*.

WILSON: That was conscious. *Murder on the Canadian* had some bad feedback because of that. Because the woman had actually been murdered. When I wrote it, I thought the fact that she was murdered off-stage made it palatable. But people objected.

T: Who?

WILSON: Reviewers who were librarians. It wasn't widespread but there were some influential ones. A person doesn't have to die to make a good story, but as *Murder on the Canadian* was based upon a classic, sort of Agatha Christie-style convention, it hadn't occurred to me that there would be any adverse response to that.

T: But ultimately it's the reaction of the kids that matters in the long run.

WILSON: Yes. The very first book I wrote, *Fat Boy Speeding*, I read it to the kids in the class I had in White Rock. They were grade eight reluctant readers. I said a friend of mine had written this book. Their response was really strong. Since then I have done that with new books. I test them and I also get other teachers to try them out.

T: What do you learn from that?

WILSON: They tend to criticize small details. For instance, I learned early on not to use too much slang. Because slang dates very quickly. Also you can make mistakes with slang. I'd read a story and get kids to write down who they thought the villain was, three-quarters of the way through. If eighty percent of the class had figured out the villain from the same clue, then I could take out or modify that clue.

T: That's invaluable.

WILSON: Yes. I try to start with vague clues and make them stronger and stronger. That's something the kids like. They get more excited as they go. The kids also say that it's really exciting that these stories are Canadian. Even at the age of ten or eleven or twelve, the kids are dismayed by the fact that they're reading primarily American stories.

I was doing an autograph session in Victoria once. A woman came in who was a librarian. She said when my first book came out, they couldn't get the kids to read anything Canadian. But she said now it's the other way round.

T: Well a sense of place is hugely important. Dennis Lee says that's one of the main reasons why *Alligator Pie* is so successful.

WILSON: It's important to me, too. I remember reading the Hardy Boys at age ten, and they went to Vancouver. It was described as a "sleepy little fishing village." The fact that that author hadn't bothered to find out anything about Vancouver really annoyed me. That's one thing I'm doing with these books, very definitely. I'm investing the time and the money to go to a locale and researching it properly. When I went to Toronto, for instance, I tried to see it through a twelve-year-old's eyes.

T: How do you see through twelve-year-old eyes? Is there a switch back there?

WILSON: No, I think it's because I

teach and maintain contact with young people. I don't consciously change my way of thinking. I'm aware of what kids like because I'm constantly in touch with them. Also, they say that a lot of people who write for children can remember their own childhoods vividly and I can remember my childhood very vividly. When I wrote the first Tom Austen book, I more or less modeled Tom on myself. In fact, I remember when I was twelve and living in Winnipeg I used to go downtown on Saturday afternoons and pick out suspicious-looking strangers and follow them around, in the hopes that a crime would be committed and I could solve the crime and be a hero.

T: The fact that your father worked for the RCMP must also be significant.

WILSON: Definitely. He'd sometimes talk about cases but he was involved in a lot of secret work that he couldn't talk about. He worked in an undercover capacity in Vancouver, combating the opium traffic.

T: Did you wonder about what he was up to?

WILSON: I thought about it a lot. And I questioned him about it.

T: Did you want to write when you were a kid?

WILSON: I guess I must have. My mother kept a story I wrote when I was nine. It was about a boy who goes around solving crimes. That story ends, "And so Jack was a great hero!" with a great big exclamation mark. The first time I got a chance to write in public was at age fourteen when I was writing reports for the local paper in Kitimat and getting paid for it. I don't know if I ever thought to myself, "I want to be a writer," but writing was always an interest.

T: Did you ever want to be a policeman?

WILSON: Yes. But I don't fit into that sort of institution. I was twice rejected from the school patrol. I was also rejected from Cubs. I can't remember why. I'm not a good person at taking orders, I suppose. But it appealed to me, the idea of being in the police like my father. For *Vancouver Nightmare* I was taken around to the police cells by a friend of mine who was in the police. It really fascinates me.

T: You've done eleven books now. Do the books get easier to write?

WILSON: I think so. You don't repeat your mistakes. For example, before I went to Toronto for *The Lost Treasure of Casa Loma*, I did an elaborate outline. The starting point was the Toronto Library, room 221-B, where they have all kinds of books about Sherlock Holmes. I thought it might be interesting to use Sherlock Holmes. I read the entire canon of Sherlock Holmes. It took months. I worked up this whole plot. It was far too elaborate. My editor said I had forgotten my audience. For someone to appreciate my story, they would have to know the stories of Sherlock Holmes extremely well. I junked the whole thing. Now I'll do preliminary reading, but I've learned not to do elaborate plotting.

Also I now know the type of things that will work in print. The Kensington Market in Toronto, for example. A boy carries red snappers by. You can't go into paragraphs of description but you can suggest what is happening with a few images. You learn to mentally sift rather than take lots of notes.

Photographs

Edna Alford by Reg Sylvester, courtesy Oolichan Books; Margaret Atwood by Lynda Koolish; George Bowering courtesy Talonbooks; bill bissett by Rose-Marie Tremblay; Sandra Birdsell courtesy Sandra Birdsell; Leonard Cohen and Al Purdy by David Boswell; Marian Engel by Paula Jardine; Brian Fawcett by Thomas Hayes courtesy Talonbooks; D.M. Fraser courtesy Bob Mercer; Mavis Gallant by Frank Grant; Robert Harlow and Peter Trower by Diane DeMille; Edith Iglauer and Alan Twigg by Oraf; Myrna Kostash by D. Clark; Robert Kroetsch by Dennis Cooley; Ken Mitchell by Rick Greer; Farley Mowat by John de Visser; Susan Musgrave by Bev Davis; William Valgardson by Old Masters Portrait Studio; Eric Wilson by Brenda Silsbee; the remainder by Alan Twigg.

Alan Twigg

ALAN TWIGG is the publisher and editor of *BC BookWorld*, a quarterly newspaper. He is also a contributing editor of *Quill & Quire*, Canadian books columnist for the Vancouver *Province*, books columnist for *Vancouver* magazine, a contributor of profiles to the *Toronto Star* and the Writers Union of Canada representative on the board of

directors of the Canadian Centre for Studies in Publishing.

His previous books are *For Openers: Conversations with 24 Canadian Writers, Hubert Evans: the First Ninety-Three Years, Vancouver and Its Writers* and *Vander Zalm: from Immigrant to Premier*. He lives in Vancouver with his wife Tara and their two sons.